# Webster's Notebook Thesaurus

Created in Cooperation with the Editors of
Merriam-Webster

FEDERAL
STREET
PRESS

A Division of Merriam-Webster, Incorporated
Springfield, Massachusetts

# Preface

This thesaurus is a conveniently concise guide for the understanding and selection of synonyms and antonyms. It is intended to serve as a quick reference for those who want a compact and handy thesaurus.

This thesaurus shares many details of presentation with more comprehensive works, yet unlike many thesauruses, it provides at each **main entry** a concise statement of the **meaning** shared by the listed synonyms (indicated by a ♦ symbol), and it includes an entry at its own alphabetical place for every synonym that appears at a main entry. Additionally, many entries for which there are words with directly opposite meaning show these **antonyms** to give the user additional pertinent assistance.

For those entries that are not main entries, the first word in the synonym list is in SMALL CAPITALS to indicate that this word is the main entry for the list and that at this entry you will find the shared meaning element for the list.

Words spelled the same but having different meanings are **homographs** and are given separate entries and identified with an italic part-of-speech label, as at **fair** *adj* and **fair** *n* for the adjective *fair*

and the noun *fair*. Headwords that are synonyms and alphabetically close to each other are sometimes listed together, as **finicky, finicking, finical.** Multiple meanings (senses) of an entry word are distinguished by bold numerals.

Headwords ordinarily conform to normal dictionary practice: nouns are styled as singulars, verbs as infinitives. Special situations, such as plural usage, are signaled by the use of boldface, as at the entry **wage, wages** or at sense 2 of **game,** where the plural **games** is shown as the form synonymous with *athletics*.

Parentheses enclose a particle or particles usually associated with a word. They may accompany a headword, as **rely** (on *or* upon), or a word in a list, as *fail (in)* in the antonym list at **fulfill** and *fall short (of)* at another antonym list in the same entry. Parentheses also enclose material indicating a typical or, occasionally, a sole object of reference, as in the meaning core at **money** or the antonym list at **gaudy,** where the antonym *quiet* carries the parenthetical note (*in taste or style*).

A semicolon separates subgroups of words which differ in their relation to the headword.

This edition published by
Federal Street Press
A Division of Merriam-Webster, Incorporated
P.O. Box 281
Springfield, MA 01102

Federal Street Press books are available for bulk purchase for sales promotion
and premium use. For details write to the Sales Department,
Federal Street Press, P.O. Box 281, Springfield, MA 01102

ISBN    978-1-59695-057-3

Printed in Canada in 2021

6th printing    Marquis, Toronto, ON    7/2021

# English and the Thesaurus

## A Brief Look at the English Language

The English language is peculiarly rich in synonyms, which is not surprising considering its history. Over its history of more than a thousand years the language of England has woven together strands of the Celtic language, of earlier Roman words and later church Latin, and then of the Germanic tongues of the early invaders from the European continent.

Because English has so many words derived from Latin and from Greek by way of Latin, the casual observer might guess that English would be—like French, Spanish, and Italian—a Romance language derived from the Latin spoken by the ancient Romans. But although the Romans made a few visits to Britain in the first century A.D., long before the English were there (before there even was an England), English is not a Romance language. English is actually a member of the Germanic group, and thus a sister of such modern languages as Swedish, Dutch, and German.

We often speak of English as having its beginnings with the conquest and settlement of a large part of the island of Britain by Germanic tribes from the European continent in the fifth century, although the earliest written documents of the language belong to the seventh century. Of course these Germanic peoples did not suddenly begin to speak a new language the moment they arrived in England. They spoke the closely related Germanic languages of their continental homelands. And it was from these languages that the English language developed. In fact, the words *English* and *England* are derived from the name of one of these early Germanic peoples, the Angles.

From its beginnings English has been gradually changing and evolving, as language tends to do. To get a sense of how far evolution has taken us from the early tongue, we need only glance at a sample of Old English. Here is the beginning of the Lord's Prayer:

Fæder ūre, þu þe eart on heofonum: si þin nama gehālgod.
Tōbecume þin rīce. Geweorþe þin willa on eorþan swāswā on heofonum.

There is a certain continuity between the vocabularies of Old English and Modern English. Of the thousand most common Modern English words, four-fifths are of Old English origin. Think of such words as *asleep* and *awake* or *alive* and *dead*, words relating to the body, *blood, flesh, arm, leg, bone, tooth*—even words for the daily activities of farming, *acre, barn, plow, till*, or for after the harvest, *drink, eat, meal*.

Of the foreign languages affecting the Old English vocabulary, the most influential was Latin. Church terms especially, like *priest, vicar*, and *mass*, were borrowed from Latin, the language of the church. But words belonging to aspects of life other than the strictly religious, like *cap, inch, kiln, school*, and *noon*, also entered Old English from Latin. The Scandinavians, too, influenced the language of England during the Old English period. From the eighth century on, Vikings from Scandinavia raided and eventually settled in England, especially in the north and the east. In a few instances the influence of a Scandinavian word gave an English word a new meaning. Thus our *dream*, which meant "joy" in Old English, probably took on the now familiar sense "a series of thoughts, images, or emotions occurring during sleep" because its Scandinavian relative *draumr* had that meaning. A considerable number of common words, like *cross, fellow, ball*, and *raise*, also became naturalized as a result of the Viking incursions over the years. The initial consonants *sk-* often reveal the Scandinavian ancestry of words like *sky, skin*, and *skirt*, the last of which has persisted side by side with its native English relative *shirt*.

Additional foreign influence on English came about principally as a result of the Norman Conquest of 1066, which brought England under the rule of French speakers. The English language, though it did not die, was for a long time of only secondary importance in political, social, and cultural matters. French became the language of the upper classes in England. The lower classes continued to speak English, but many French words were borrowed into English. To this circumstance we owe, for example, a number of distinctions between the words used for animals in the pasture and the words for those animals prepared to be eaten. Living animals were under the care of English-speaking peasants; cooked, the animals were served to the French-speaking nobility. *Swine* in the sty became *pork* at the table, *cow* and *calf* became *beef* and *veal*. This Anglo-French also had an influence on the words used in the courts, such as *indict, jury*, and *verdict*.

English eventually reestablished itself as the major language of England, but the language did not lose its habit of borrowing. English still derives much of its learned vocabulary from Latin and Greek. We have also borrowed words from nearly all of the languages in Europe. From Modern French we have such words as *bikini, cliché*, and *discotheque;* from Dutch, *easel, gin*, and *yacht;* from German, *delicatessen, pretzel*, and *swindler;* from Swedish, *ombudsman* and *smorgasbord*. From Italian we have taken *carnival, fiasco*, and *pizza*, as well as many terms from music (including *piano*).

From the period of the Renaissance voyages of discovery through the days when the sun never set upon the British Empire and up to the present, a steady stream of new words has flowed into the language to match the new objects and experiences English speakers have encountered all over the globe. English has drawn words from India (*bandanna*), China (*gung ho*), and Japan (*tycoon*). Arabic has been a prolific source of words over the centuries, giving us *hazard, lute, magazine*, and a host of words beginning with the letter *a*, from *algebra* to *azimuth*.

## How Meaning Has Developed

Whether borrowed or created, a word generally begins its life in English with one meaning. Yet no living language is static, and in time words develop new meanings and lose old ones. A word used in a specific sense may be extended, or generalized, to cover a host of similar senses. Our word *virtue* is derived from the Latin *virtus*, which originally meant "manliness." But we apply the term to any excellent quality possessed by man, woman, or beast; even inanimate objects have their *virtues*. In Latin, *decimare* meant "to select and kill a tenth part of" and described the Roman way of dealing with mutinous troops. Its English descendant, *decimate*, now simply means "to destroy a large part of."

The development of meaning can easily be followed in this example. Today when we think of the word *fast* we probably think of the sense involving great speed. But the word's oldest meaning is quite different: "firmly placed" or "immovable," as in "tent pegs set fast in the ground" and "a fast and impassable barrier." It is easy to see how this sense developed expanded uses, such as "a door that is stuck fast and won't open." We see something of this sense in the expression "fast asleep."

In time, users added senses, some of which are common today, from being "unable to leave something, as one's bed" to being "stable and unchangeable," which we find in such uses as "hard and fast rules" or "clothes that are colorfast." Then came the sense of being "steadfast" or "firmly or totally loyal," as in "they were fast friends."

The sense that is most common today, "quick, speedy," came later. It probably developed from an obsolete sense of the adverb meaning "near at hand," which may have led to another meaning "soon." From this obsolete sense of "soon" it is just a short step, in terms of language development, to the sense meaning "quick."

In addition to what could be thought of as a horizontal dimension of change—the extension or contraction of meaning—words also may rise and fall along a vertical scale of value. Perfectly unobjectionable words are sometimes used disparagingly or sarcastically. If we say, "You're a fine one to talk," we are using *fine* in a sense quite different from its usual meaning. If a word is used often enough in negative contexts, the negative coloring may eventually become an integral part of the meaning of the word. A *villain* was once a peasant. His social standing was not high, perhaps, but he was certainly not necessarily a scoundrel. *Scavenger* originally designated the collector of a particular kind of tax in late medieval England. *Puny* meant no more than "younger" when it first passed from French into English and its spelling was transformed. Only later did it acquire the derogatory meaning more familiar to us now.

The opposite process seems to take place somewhat less frequently, but change of meaning to a more positive sense does occasionally occur. In the fourteenth century *nice,* for example, meant "foolish." Its present meaning, of course, is quite different, and the attitude it conveys seems to have undergone a complete reversal from contempt to approval.

## What Qualifies as a Synonym?

It is not surprising that with so much to work with, users of English have long been interested in synonyms as an element both in accuracy and in elegance in their expression. Synonyms relieve monotony and enhance expressiveness.

Earlier writers were clear on the meaning of *synonym.* They viewed synonyms as words meaning the same thing. Unfortunately, during the last century or so this simple, clear-cut meaning has become blurred. To many publishers of thesauruses the term has come to mean little more than words that are somewhat similar in meaning. But this loose definition is unsuitable for many people, since it deprives them of the guidance needed for finding the precise word in a particular context.

This thesaurus takes a different approach to describing the nature of a synonym. Groups of synonyms are organized around a segment of meaning that two or more words have in common. In order to create these groups, one has to analyze each word carefully, ignoring nonessential aspects such as connotations and implications and try to isolate the basic meaning, which we call an *elementary meaning.*

When we look at the synonymous relationship of words in terms of elementary meanings, the process of choosing synonyms is simpler and more exact. For example, it is easy to see that no term more restricted in definition than another word can be its synonym. For example, *station wagon* and *minivan* cannot be synonyms of *automobile,* nor can *biceps* be a synonym of *muscle.* Even though a very definite relationship exists between the members, *station wagon* and *minivan* are types of automobile and *biceps* is a type of muscle. So these words are narrower in their range

of application. On the other hand, a word more broadly defined than another word in the dictionary may be considered a synonym of the other word so long as the two words share one or more elementary meanings. In order to pin down the area of shared meaning for you, each main entry in this work contains after its synonym list a *meaning core* that states the elementary meaning shared by all the words in that particular synonym group.

## What Is an Antonym?

Like the word *synonym, antonym* has been used by some writers with a great deal of vagueness and often applied loosely to words that show no real oppositeness when compared one to another. As in the case of synonyms, the relation needs to be seen as one between segments of meaning that can be isolated, rather than between words or dictionary senses of words. As is the case with synonyms, antonyms need to have one or more elementary meanings precisely opposite to or negating the same area of meaning of another word. This definition excludes from consideration as antonyms several classes of words that are sometimes treated as antonyms but that actually contain words that neither directly oppose nor directly negate the words with which they are said to be antonymous.

For example, some terms have such a relationship to each other that one can scarcely be used without suggesting the other (as *husband* and *wife, father* and *son, buyer* and *seller*), yet there is no real opposition or real negation between such pairs. These are merely *relative terms*—their relation is reciprocal or correlative rather than antonymous.

Complementary terms in a similar way are usually paired and have a reciprocal relationship to the point that one seems incomplete without the other (as in such pairs as *question* and *answer, seek* and *find*). This relation that involves no negation is better seen as sequential than antonymous.

And contrastive terms differ sharply from their "opposites" only in some parts of their meaning. They neither oppose nor negate fully, since they are significantly different in range of meaning and applicability, in emphasis, and in the suggestions they convey. An example is *destitute* (a strong word carrying suggestions of misery and distress), which is contrastive rather than antonymous with respect to *rich* (a rather neutral and matter-of-fact term), while *poor* (another neutral and matter-of-fact term) is the appropriate antonym of *rich.* Basically, contrastive words are only opposed incidentally; they do not meet head-on.

What then is considered an antonym? True antonyms can be classified in three ways:

*Opposites without intermediates:* What is *perfect* can be in no way *imperfect;* you cannot at the same time *accept* and *reject* or *agree* and *disagree.*

*Opposites with intermediates:* Such words make up the extremes in a range of difference and are so completely opposed that the language allows no wider difference. Thus, a scale of excellence might include *superiority, adequacy, mediocrity,* and *inferiority,* but only *superiority* and *inferiority* are so totally opposed that each exactly negates what its opposite affirms.

*Reverse opposites:* These are words that are opposed in such a way that each means the undoing or nullification of what the other affirms. Such reverse opposites exactly oppose and fully negate the special features of their opposites. Thus, *disprove* so perfectly opposes and so clearly negates the implications of *prove* that it fits the concept of antonym, as does *unkind* with respect to *kind.*

In this book, antonyms, when they fit one of these criteria, are listed after the synonym to which they apply.

# A

**abaft** ♦ toward or at the stern (of a vessel) *Syn* aft, astern *Ant* afore

**abandon** *vb* 1 ♦ to quit absolutely *Syn* desert, forsake *Ant* reclaim 2 *Syn* RELINQUISH, surrender, yield, resign, leave *Ant* cherish (*hopes, opinions*); restrain (*oneself*)

**abandon** *n Syn* UNCONSTRAINT, spontaneity *Ant* self-restraint

**abandoned** ♦ utterly depraved *Syn* reprobate, profligate, dissolute *Ant* redeemed, regenerate

**abase** ♦ to lower in one's own estimation or in that of others *Syn* demean, debase, degrade, humble, humiliate *Ant* exalt; extol (*especially oneself*)

**abash** *Syn* EMBARRASS, discomfit, disconcert, faze, rattle *Ant* embolden; reassure

**abate** 1 *Syn* ABOLISH, extinguish, annihilate *Ant* perpetuate 2 *Syn* DECREASE, reduce, diminish, lessen *Ant* augment; accelerate (*pace, speed*); intensify (*hopes, fears, a fever*) 3 ♦ to die down in force or intensity *Syn* subside, wane, ebb *Ant* rise; revive

**abatement** *Syn* DEDUCTION, rebate, discount *Ant* addition

**abbey** *Syn* CLOISTER, convent, nunnery, monastery, priory

**abbreviate** *Syn* SHORTEN, abridge, curtail *Ant* elongate, lengthen

**abdicate** ♦ to give up formally or definitely a position of trust, honor, or glory *Syn* renounce, resign *Ant* assume; usurp

**abdomen** ♦ the part of the body between the chest and the pelvis *Syn* belly, stomach, paunch, gut

**abduct** ♦ to carry off (a person) surreptitiously for an illegal purpose *Syn* kidnap

**aberrant** *Syn* ABNORMAL, atypical *Ant* true (*to a type*)

**aberration** 1 *Syn* DEVIATION, deflection *Ant* conformity; regularity 2 ♦ mental disorder *Syn* derangement, alienation *Ant* soundness (*of mind*)

**abet** *Syn* INCITE, foment, instigate *Ant* deter (*with a personal subject*)

**abettor** *Syn* CONFEDERATE, accessory, accomplice, conspirator

**abeyant** *Syn* LATENT, dormant, quiescent, potential *Ant* operative; active; revived

**abhor** *Syn* HATE, abominate, loathe, detest *Ant* admire

**abhorrence** ♦ a feeling of extreme disgust or dislike *Syn* detestation, loathing, abomination, hatred, hate *Ant* admiration; enjoyment

**abhorrent** 1 *Syn* HATEFUL, abominable, detestable, odious *Ant* admirable; enjoyable 2 *Syn* REPUGNANT, repellent, obnoxious, distasteful, invidious *Ant* congenial

**abide** 1 *Syn* STAY, wait, remain, tarry, linger *Ant* depart 2 *Syn* CONTINUE, endure, last, persist *Ant* pass 3 *Syn* BEAR, endure, suffer, tolerate, stand, brook

**ability** ♦ physical, mental, or legal power to perform *Syn* capacity, capability *Ant* inability, incapacity

**abject** *Syn* MEAN, ignoble, sordid *Ant* exalted (*in rank, state, condition, mood, behavior*); imperious (*in manner, speech, attitude*)

**abjure** ♦ to abandon irrevocably and, usu., with solemnity or publicity *Syn* renounce, forswear, recant, retract *Ant* pledge (*allegiance, a vow*); elect (*a way of life, a means to an end, an end*)

**able** ♦ having marked power or fitness for work *Syn* capable, competent, qualified *Ant* inept; unable

**abnegate** *Syn* FORGO, sacrifice, eschew, forbear *Ant* indulge (in)

**abnegation** *Syn* RENUNCIATION, self-abnegation, self-denial *Ant* indulgence, self-indulgence

**abnormal** ♦ deviating markedly from the rule or standard of its kind *Syn* atypical, aberrant *Ant* normal

**abode** *Syn* HABITATION, dwelling, residence, domicile, home, house

**abolish** ♦ to make nonexistent *Syn* annihilate, extinguish, abate *Ant* establish

**abominable** *Syn* HATEFUL, detestable, odious, abhorrent *Ant* laudable; enjoyable, delightful

**abominate** *Syn* HATE, loathe, detest, abhor *Ant* esteem; enjoy

**abomination** 1 *Syn* ABHORRENCE, detestation, loathing, hatred, hate *Ant* esteem; enjoyment 2 ♦ a person or thing from which one shrinks with intense dislike *Syn* anathema, bugbear, bête noire *Ant* joy

**aboriginal** *Syn* NATIVE, indigenous, autochthonous

**abortive** *Syn* FUTILE, fruitless, vain, bootless *Ant* consummated

**abound** *Syn* TEEM, overflow, swarm *Ant* fail, fall short

**about** ♦ in reference to *Syn* concerning, regarding, respecting

**above** ♦ at a higher level *Syn* over *Ant* below

**aboveboard** *Syn* STRAIGHTFORWARD, forthright *Ant* underhand, underhanded

**abracadabra** *Syn* GIBBERISH, hocus-pocus, mummery

**abrade** ♦ to affect a surface by rubbing, scraping, or wearing away *Syn* excoriate, chafe, fret, gall

**abridge** *Syn* SHORTEN, curtail, abbreviate, retrench *Ant* expand; extend

**abridgment** ♦ a condensation of a larger work *Syn* abstract, epitome, brief, synopsis, conspectus *Ant* expansion

**abrogate** 1 *Syn* ANNUL, vacate, quash, void *Ant* institute (*by enacting, decreeing*) 2 *Syn* NULLIFY, annul, negate, invalidate *Ant* establish, fix (*a right, a character, a quality, a custom*)

**abrupt** 1 *Syn* STEEP, precipitous, sheer *Ant* sloping 2 *Syn* PRECIPITATE, sudden, headlong, impetuous, hasty *Ant* deliberate, leisurely

**abscess** ♦ a localized swollen area of infection containing pus *Syn* boil, furuncle, carbuncle, pimple, pustule

**abscond** *Syn* ESCAPE, decamp, flee, fly *Ant* give (*oneself*) up

**absence** *Syn* LACK, want, dearth, defect, privation *Ant* presence

**absent** *Syn* ABSTRACTED, preoccupied, absentminded, distraught *Ant* attentive

**absentminded** *Syn* ABSTRACTED, absent, preoccupied, distraught *Ant* wide-awake

**absolute** 1 *Syn* PURE, simple, sheer *Ant* mixed, qualified 2 ♦ exercising power or authority without external restraint *Syn* autocratic, arbitrary, despotic, tyrannical, tyrannous *Ant* restrained; limited 3 *Syn* ULTIMATE, categorical *Ant* conditioned

**absolution** *Syn* PARDON, amnesty *Ant* condemnation

**absolve** *Syn* EXCULPATE, exonerate, acquit, vindicate *Ant* hold (*to a promise, an obligation*); charge (*with a sin, the blame, the responsibility*)

**absorb** 1 ♦ to take (something) in so as to become imbued with it or to make it a part of one's being *Syn* imbibe, assimilate *Ant* exude, give out 2 *Syn* MONOPOLIZE, engross, consume *Ant* dissipate (*time, attention, energies*)

**absorbed** *Syn* INTENT, engrossed, rapt *Ant* distracted

**absorbing** *Syn* INTERESTING, engrossing, intriguing *Ant* irksome

**abstain** *Syn* REFRAIN, forbear *Ant* indulge

**abstemiousness** *Syn* TEMPERANCE, abstinence, sobriety, continence *Ant* gluttony

**abstinence** *Syn* TEMPERANCE, continence, abstemiousness, sobriety *Ant* self-indulgence

**abstract** *adj* ♦ having conceptual rather than concrete existence *Syn* ideal, transcendent, transcendental *Ant* concrete

**abstract** *n Syn* ABRIDGMENT, brief, synopsis, epitome, conspectus *Ant* amplification

**abstract** *vb Syn* DETACH, disengage *Ant* insert, introduce

**abstracted** ♦ inattentive to what presently claims or demands consideration *Syn* preoccupied, absent, absentminded, distraught *Ant* alert

**abstruse** *Syn* RECONDITE, occult, esoteric *Ant* obvious, plain

**absurd** *Syn* FOOLISH, silly, preposterous *Ant* rational, sensible

**abundant** *Syn* PLENTIFUL, copious, ample, plenteous *Ant* scarce

**abuse** *vb* ♦ to use or treat a person or thing improperly or wrongfully *Syn* misuse, mistreat, maltreat, ill-treat, outrage *Ant* respect, honor

**abuse** *n* ♦ vehemently expressed condemnation or disapproval *Syn* vituperation, invective, obloquy, scurrility, billingsgate *Ant* adulation

**abusive** ♦ coarse, insulting, and contemptuous in character or utterance *Syn* opprobrious, vituperative, contumelious, scurrilous *Ant* complementary; respectful

**abutment** *Syn* BUTTRESS, pier

**abutting** *Syn* ADJACENT, contiguous, adjoining, tangent, conterminous, juxtaposed

**abysm** *Syn* GULF, chasm, abyss

**abysmal** *Syn* DEEP, profound

**abyss** *Syn* GULF, chasm, abysm

**academic** 1 *Syn* PEDANTIC, scholastic, bookish 2 *Syn* THEORETICAL, speculative

**accede** *Syn* ASSENT, acquiesce, consent, agree, subscribe *Ant* demur

**accelerate** *Syn* SPEED, quicken, hurry, hasten, precipitate *Ant* decelerate; retard

**accent** 1 *Syn* EMPHASIS, stress, accentuation 2 *Syn* INFLECTION, intonation

**accentuation** *Syn* EMPHASIS, accent, stress *Ant* inaccentuation

**accept** *Syn* RECEIVE, admit, take *Ant* reject

**acceptance** ♦ the act or fact of accepting or the state of being accepted *Syn* acceptation

**acceptation** 1 *Syn* MEANING, sense, signification, significance, import 2 *Syn* ACCEPTANCE

**access** 1 *Syn* ENTRANCE, ingress, entrée, entry *Ant* outlet 2 *Syn* FIT, accession, attack, paroxysm, spasm, convulsion

**accession** 1 *Syn* ADDITION, accretion, increment *Ant* discard 2 *Syn* FIT, access, attack, paroxysm, spasm, convulsion

**accessory** *n* 1 *Syn* APPENDAGE, appurtenance, adjunct 2 *Syn* CONFEDERATE, accomplice, abettor, conspirator *Ant* principal

**accessory** *adj Syn* AUXILIARY, contributory, subsidiary, adjuvant, ancillary, subservient *Ant* constituent, integral; principal (*in law*)

**accident** 1 *Syn* QUALITY, character, attribute, property *Ant* substance (*in philosophy*) 2 *Syn* CHANCE, hazard, luck, fortune, hap *Ant* design, intent 3 ♦ chance or a chance event bringing injury or loss *Syn* casualty, mishap

**accidental** ♦ not amenable to planning or prediction *Syn* casual, fortuitous, contingent, incidental *Ant* planned; essential

**acclaim** *vb Syn* PRAISE, extol, laud, eulogize *Ant* vituperate

**acclaim** *n Syn* APPLAUSE, acclamation, plaudits *Ant* vituperation

**acclamation** *Syn* APPLAUSE, acclaim, plaudits

**acclimate** *Syn* HARDEN, acclimatize, season

**acclimatize** *Syn* HARDEN, acclimate, season

**accommodate** 1 *Syn* ADAPT, adjust, conform, reconcile *Ant* constrain 2 *Syn* OBLIGE, favor *Ant* incommode 3 *Syn* CONTAIN, hold

**accompaniment** ♦ something attendant upon or

found in association with another thing. **Syn** concomitant

**accompany** ♦ to go or be together with **Syn** attend, conduct, escort, convoy, chaperone

**accomplice** **Syn** CONFEDERATE, accessory, abettor, conspirator

**accomplish** **Syn** PERFORM, achieve, effect, fulfill, discharge, execute **Ant** undo

**accomplished** **Syn** CONSUMMATE, finished

**accomplishment** **Syn** ACQUIREMENT, attainment, acquisition

**accord** *vb* **1 Syn** AGREE, harmonize, correspond, tally, conform, square, jibe **Ant** conflict **2 Syn** GRANT, vouchsafe, concede, award **Ant** withhold

**accord** *n* **1 Syn** HARMONY, concord, consonance **Ant** dissension, strife; antagonism **2 Syn** AGREEMENT, understanding

**accordingly** **Syn** THEREFORE, so, consequently, hence, then

**accost** **Syn** ADDRESS, greet, hail, salute

**account** *n* **1 Syn** USE, service, advantage, profit, avail **2** ♦ a statement of actual events or conditions or of purported occurrences or conditions **Syn** report, chronicle, version, story

**account** *vb* **1 Syn** CONSIDER, deem, regard, reckon **2 Syn** EXPLAIN, justify, rationalize

**accountable** **Syn** RESPONSIBLE, answerable, amenable, liable

**accouter** **Syn** FURNISH, equip, arm, outfit, appoint

**accredit** **1 Syn** APPROVE, certify, endorse, sanction **2 Syn** AUTHORIZE, commission, license **3 Syn** ASCRIBE, credit, charge, assign, attribute, impute

**accretion** **Syn** ADDITION, increment, accession

**accumulate** ♦ to bring together so as to make a store or great quantity **Syn** amass, hoard **Ant** dissipate

**accumulative** **Syn** CUMULATIVE, summative, additive

**accurate** **Syn** CORRECT, exact, precise, nice, right **Ant** inaccurate

**accursed** **Syn** EXECRABLE, damnable, cursed **Ant** blessed

**accuse** ♦ to declare a person guilty of a fault or offense **Syn** charge, incriminate, indict, impeach, arraign **Ant** exculpate

**accustom** **Syn** HABITUATE, addict, inure **Ant** disaccustom

**accustomed** **Syn** USUAL, wonted, customary, habitual **Ant** unaccustomed

**acerbity** **Syn** ACRIMONY, asperity **Ant** mellowness

**ache** **Syn** PAIN, pang, throe, twinge, stitch

**achieve** **1 Syn** PERFORM, accomplish, effect, fulfill, execute, discharge **Ant** fail **2 Syn** REACH, attain, gain, compass **Ant** miss (*getting or attaining*)

**achievement** **Syn** FEAT, exploit **Ant** failure

**achromatic** **Syn** COLORLESS, uncolored **Ant** chromatic

**acid** **Syn** SOUR, acidulous, tart, dry **Ant** bland; sweet; alkaline

**acidulous** **Syn** SOUR, acid, tart, dry **Ant** saccharine

**acknowledge** **1** ♦ to disclose something against one's will or inclination **Syn** admit, own, avow, confess **Ant** deny **2** ♦ to take cognizance of in some way, usually in a way dictated by custom or convention and implying acceptance or assent **Syn** recognize **Ant** ignore

**acme** **Syn** SUMMIT, apex, zenith, culmination, climax, peak, apogee, pinnacle, meridian

**acoustic, acoustical** **Syn** AUDITORY

**acquaint** **Syn** INFORM, apprise, advise, notify

**acquaintance** **Syn** FRIEND, intimate, confidant

**acquiesce** **Syn** ASSENT, consent, agree, accede, subscribe **Ant** object

**acquiescence** **Syn** compliance, resignation **Ant** rebelliousness, rebellion

**acquiescent** **Syn** COMPLIANT, resigned **Ant** rebellious

**acquire** **Syn** GET, obtain, gain, win, secure, procure **Ant** forfeit

**acquirement** ♦ a power or skill that is the fruit of exertion or effort **Syn** acquisition, attainment, accomplishment

**acquisition** **Syn** ACQUIREMENT, attainment, accomplishment

**acquisitive** **Syn** COVETOUS, grasping, avaricious, greedy **Ant** sacrificing, abnegating

**acquit** **1 Syn** EXCULPATE, absolve, exonerate, vindicate **Ant** convict **2 Syn** BEHAVE, quit, conduct, demean, deport, comport

**acrid** **1 Syn** BITTER **Ant** savory **2 Syn** CAUSTIC, mordant, scathing **Ant** benign, kindly

**acrimonious** **Syn** ANGRY, irate, indignant, wrathful, wroth, mad **Ant** irenic, peaceable

**acrimony** ♦ temper or language marked by irritation or some degree of anger or resentment **Syn** acerbity, asperity **Ant** suavity

**across** ♦ so as to intersect the length of something **Syn** crosswise, crossways, athwart

**act** *n* **Syn** ACTION, deed

**act** *vb* **1** ♦ to perform esp. in an indicated way **Syn** behave, work, operate, function, react **2** ♦ to assume the appearance or role of another person or character **Syn** play, impersonate

**acting** **Syn** TEMPORARY, ad interim, provisional

**action** **1** ♦ something done or effected **Syn** act, deed **2 Syn** SUIT, cause, case, lawsuit **3 Syn** BATTLE, engagement

**activate** **Syn** VITALIZE, energize **Ant** arrest

**active** ♦ at work or in effective action **Syn** operative, dynamic, live **Ant** inactive

**actor** ♦ one who, for the entertainment or edification of an audience, takes part in an exhibition simulating happenings in real life **Syn** player, performer, mummer, mime, mimic, thespian, impersonator, trouper

**actual** **Syn** REAL, true **Ant** ideal; imaginary

**actuality** **Syn** EXISTENCE, being **Ant** potentiality, possibility

**actualize** **Syn** REALIZE, embody, incarnate, externalize, objectify, materialize, hypostatize, reify

**actuate** **1 Syn** MOVE, drive, impel **2 Syn** ACTIVATE, motivate **Ant** deter

**acumen** **Syn** DISCERNMENT, penetration, insight, perception, discrimination **Ant** obtuseness

**acute** **1 Syn** SHARP, keen **Ant** obtuse **2** ♦ of uncertain outcome **Syn** critical, crucial

**adage** **Syn** SAYING, saw, proverb, maxim, motto, epigram, aphorism, apothegm

**adamant, adamantine** **Syn** INFLEXIBLE, obdurate, inexorable **Ant** yielding

**adapt** **1** ♦ to bring into correspondence **Syn** adjust, accommodate, conform, reconcile **Ant** unfit **2 Syn** EDIT, rewrite, revise, redact, compile

**adaptable** **Syn** PLASTIC, pliant, ductile, pliable, malleable **Ant** inadaptable, unadaptable

**add** **1** ♦ to find or represent the amount reached by putting together arithmetically a series of numbers or quantities **Syn** sum, total, tot, cast, figure, foot **2** ♦ to bring in or join on something more so as to form a larger or more inclusive whole **Syn** append, annex, subjoin, superadd **Ant** subtract, deduct

**addendum** **Syn** APPENDIX, supplement

**addict** *vb* **Syn** HABITUATE, accustom, inure **Ant** wean

**addict** *n* ♦ a person who by habit and strong inclination indulges in something or the pursuit of something **Syn** votary, devotee, habitué

**addition** ♦ a thing that serves to increase another in size, amount, or content **Syn** accretion, increment, accession

**additive** **Syn** CUMULATIVE, summative, accumulative

**addle** **Syn** CONFUSE, muddle, fuddle, befuddle **Ant** refresh (*mentally*)

**address** *vb* **1 Syn** DIRECT, devote, apply **2** ♦ to speak to or, less often, to write or make a sign to a person in recognition or in order to obtain recognition **Syn** accost, greet, salute, hail

**address** *n* **1 Syn** TACT, savoir faire, poise **Ant** maladroitness, gaucherie **2 Syn** SPEECH, oration, harangue, lecture, talk, sermon, homily

**adduce** ♦ to bring forward by way of explanation, proof, illustration, or demonstration **Syn** advance, allege, cite

**adept** *n* **Syn** EXPERT, wizard, artiste, artist, virtuoso **Ant** bungler

**adept** *adj* **Syn** PROFICIENT, skilled, skillful, expert, masterly **Ant** inadept, inept; bungling

**adequate** **Syn** SUFFICIENT, enough, competent

**adhere** **Syn** STICK, cohere, cling, cleave

**adherence** ♦ a physical adhering **Syn** adhesion **Ant** inadherence, nonadherence

**adherent** **Syn** FOLLOWER, disciple, partisan, satellite, henchman, sectary **Ant** renegade

**adhesion** **Syn** ADHERENCE **Ant** nonadhesion, inadhesion

**ad interim** **Syn** TEMPORARY, provisional, acting **Ant** permanent

**adjacent** ♦ in close proximity **Syn** adjoining, contiguous, abutting, tangent, conterminous, juxtaposed **Ant** nonadjacent

**adjoining** **Syn** ADJACENT, contiguous, abutting, tangent, conterminous, juxtaposed **Ant** detached, disjoined

**adjudge** **Syn** JUDGE, adjudicate, arbitrate

**adjudicate** **Syn** JUDGE, adjudge, arbitrate

**adjunct** **Syn** APPENDAGE, appurtenance, accessory

**adjure** **Syn** BEG, entreat, beseech, implore, importune, supplicate

**adjust** **1** ♦ to set right or to rights **Syn** regulate, fix **Ant** derange **2 Syn** ADAPT, accommodate, conform, reconcile

**adjuvant** **Syn** AUXILIARY, contributory, ancillary, accessory, subsidiary, subservient **Ant** counteractive

**administer** ♦ to act on the behalf of another in or as if in the capacity of a steward **Syn** dispense

**admiration** **1 Syn** WONDER, wonderment, amazement **2 Syn** REGARD, esteem, respect **Ant** abhorrence

**admire** **Syn** REGARD, esteem, respect **Ant** abhor

**admission** **Syn** ADMITTANCE

**admit** **1 Syn** RECEIVE, accept, take **Ant** eject, expel **2 Syn** ACKNOWLEDGE, own, confess, avow **Ant** gainsay; disdain **3 Syn** ENTER, introduce **Ant** exclude

**admittance** ♦ permitted entrance **Syn** admission

**admixture** **1 Syn** MIXTURE, composite, blend, compound, amalgam **2** ♦ an added ingredient that destroys the purity or genuineness of a substance **Syn** alloy, adulterant

**admonish** **Syn** REPROVE, chide, reproach, rebuke, reprimand **Ant** commend

**ado** **Syn** STIR, fuss, pother, flurry, bustle

**adolescence** **Syn** YOUTH, puberty, pubescence **Ant** senescence

**adopt** ♦ to make one's own what in some fashion one owes to another **Syn** embrace, espouse **Ant** repudiate; discard

**adoration** **Syn** REVERENCE, worship, veneration **Ant** blasphemy

**adore** **1 Syn** REVERE, worship, venerate, reverence **Ant** blaspheme **2** ♦ to love or admire excessively **Syn** worship, idolize **Ant** detest

**adorn** ♦ to add something unessential in order to enhance the appearance **Syn** decorate, ornament, embellish, deck, bedeck, garnish **Ant** disfigure

**adroit** **1 Syn** DEXTEROUS, deft, handy **Ant** maladroit **2 Syn** CLEVER, cunning, ingenious **Ant** stolid

**adulation** **Syn** COMPLIMENT, flattery **Ant** abuse

**adult** **Syn** MATURE, grown-up, matured, ripe, mellow **Ant** juvenile; puerile

**adulterant** **Syn** ADMIXTURE, alloy

**adulterate** ♦ to alter fraudulently esp. for profit **Syn** sophisticate, load, weight, doctor **Ant** refine

**adumbrate** **Syn** SUGGEST, shadow

**adumbration** **Syn** SHADE, shadow, umbra, penumbra, umbrage **Ant** revelation

**advance** *vb* **1** ♦ to move or put ahead **Syn** promote, forward, further **Ant** retard; check **2** ♦ to move forward in space, in time, or in approach to a material or ideal objective **Syn** progress **Ant** recede **3 Syn** ADDUCE, allege, cite

**advance** *n* **1** ♦ movement forward in space, in time, or in approach to a material or ideal objective *Syn* progress *Ant* recession, retrogression **2** *Syn* OVERTURE, approach, tender, bid

**advanced 1** *Syn* PREMATURE, forward, precocious, untimely *Ant* backward **2** *Syn* LIBERAL, radical, progressive *Ant* conservative

**advancement** ♦ the act of raising a person in grade, rank, or dignity, or the honor that comes to one who is so raised *Syn* preferment, promotion, elevation *Ant* degradation; reduction (*in rank or status*)

**advantage 1** ♦ a factor or set of factors in a competition or rivalry giving one person or side a position of superiority over the other *Syn* handicap, allowance, odds, edge *Ant* disadvantage; handicap **2** *Syn* USE, service, account, profit, avail *Ant* detriment

**advantageous** *Syn* BENEFICIAL, profitable *Ant* disadvantageous

**advent** *Syn* ARRIVAL *Ant* leaving, passing

**adventure** ♦ an undertaking, an exploit, or an experience involving hazards and requiring boldness *Syn* enterprise, quest

**adventurous** ♦ courting danger or exposing oneself to danger in a greater degree than is required for courage *Syn* venturesome, daring, daredevil, rash, reckless, foolhardy *Ant* unadventurous; cautious

**adversary** *Syn* OPPONENT, antagonist *Ant* ally

**adverse** ♦ so opposed as to cause interference, often harmful or fatal interference *Syn* antagonistic, counter, counteractive *Ant* propitious

**adversity** *Syn* MISFORTUNE, mischance, mishap *Ant* prosperity

**advert** *Syn* REFER, allude

**advertise** *Syn* DECLARE, publish, announce, proclaim, broadcast, promulgate

**advertisement** *Syn* DECLARATION, publication, announcement, broadcasting, proclamation, promulgation

**advice 1** ♦ a recommendation as to a decision or a course of conduct *Syn* counsel **2** *Syn* NEWS, intelligence, tidings

**advisable** *Syn* EXPEDIENT, politic *Ant* inadvisable

**advise 1** ♦ to make a recommendation as to a decision or a course of conduct *Syn* counsel **2** *Syn* CONFER, consult, commune, parley, treat, negotiate **3** *Syn* INFORM, notify, apprise, acquaint

**advised** *Syn* DELIBERATE, considered, premeditated, designed, studied

**advocate** *n Syn* LAWYER, counselor, barrister, counsel, attorney, solicitor

**advocate** *vb Syn* SUPPORT, uphold, champion, back *Ant* impugn

**aeon** *Syn* PERIOD, age, era, epoch

**aerial** *Syn* AIRY, ethereal

**aesthete** ♦ a person conspicuous for his enjoyment and appreciation of the beautiful, the exquisite, or the choice *Syn* dilettante, connoisseur

**affable** *Syn* GRACIOUS, cordial, genial, sociable *Ant* reserved

**affair 1** ♦ something done or dealt with *Syn* business, concern, matter, thing **2** *Syn* AMOUR, intrigue, liaison

**affect** *Syn* ASSUME, simulate, pretend, feign, counterfeit, sham

**affect** ♦ to produce or to have an effect upon a person or upon a thing capable of a reaction *Syn* influence, touch, impress, strike, sway

**affectation** *Syn* POSE, air, mannerism *Ant* artlessness

**affecting** *Syn* MOVING, touching, pathetic, poignant, impressive

**affection 1** *Syn* FEELING, emotion, passion, sentiment *Ant* antipathy **2** *Syn* ATTACHMENT, love *Ant* coldness **3** *Syn* DISEASE, disorder, condition, ailment, malady, complaint, distemper, syndrome

**affectionate** *Syn* LOVING, devoted, fond, doting *Ant* cold; undemonstrative

**affiliated** *Syn* RELATED, allied, kindred, cognate *Ant* unaffiliated

**affinity 1** *Syn* ATTRACTION, sympathy **2** *Syn* LIKENESS, resemblance, similarity, similitude, analogy

**affirm** *Syn* ASSERT, profess, aver, avow, protest, avouch, declare, warrant, predicate *Ant* deny

**affix** *Syn* FASTEN, attach, fix *Ant* detach

**afflatus** *Syn* INSPIRATION, fury, frenzy

**afflict** ♦ to inflict upon a person something which he finds hard to endure *Syn* try, torment, torture, rack *Ant* comfort

**affliction** *Syn* TRIAL, visitation, tribulation, cross *Ant* solace, consolation

**affluent** *Syn* RICH, wealthy, opulent *Ant* impecunious; straitened

**afford** *Syn* GIVE, confer, bestow, present, donate *Ant* deny (*something one wants*)

**affray** *n Syn* CONTEST, fray, fight, combat, conflict

**affray** *vb Syn* FRIGHTEN, fright, affright, scare, alarm, terrify, terrorize, startle

**affright** *Syn* FRIGHTEN, fright, affray, scare, alarm, terrify, terrorize, startle *Ant* nerve, embolden

**affront** *vb Syn* OFFEND, outrage, insult *Ant* gratify (*by an attention*)

**affront** *n* ♦ a speech or an action having for its intention or effect the dishonoring of something or someone *Syn* insult, indignity *Ant* gratification

**afraid** *Syn* FEARFUL, apprehensive *Ant* unafraid; sanguine

**aft** *Syn* ABAFT, astern *Ant* fore

**after** *prep, adj, adv* ♦ following upon, esp. in place or in time *Syn* behind *Ant* before

**after** *adj Syn* POSTERIOR, hinder, hind, rear, back

**aftereffect, aftermath** *Syn* EFFECT, result, consequence, upshot, sequel, issue, outcome, event

**age** *n* **1** ♦ the period in one's life when one is old in years and declining in body or mind or both *Syn* senility, senescence, dotage *Ant* youth **2** *Syn* PERIOD, era, epoch, aeon

**age** *vb Syn* MATURE, ripen, develop

**aged** ♦ far advanced in years *Syn* old, elderly, superannuated *Ant* youthful

**agency** *Syn* MEAN, agent, instrumentality, instrument, medium, vehicle, channel, organ

**agenda** *Syn* PROGRAM, schedule, timetable

**agent 1** *Syn* MEAN, instrument, agency, instrumentality, medium, vehicle, organ, channel *Ant* patient **2** ♦ one who performs the duties of or transacts business for another *Syn* factor, attorney, deputy, proxy *Ant* principal

**agglomerate, agglomeration** *Syn* AGGREGATE, conglomerate, conglomeration, aggregation

**aggrandize** *Syn* EXALT, magnify *Ant* belittle

**aggravate 1** *Syn* INTENSIFY, heighten, enhance *Ant* alleviate **2** *Syn* IRRITATE, exasperate, provoke, rile, peeve, nettle *Ant* appease

**aggregate 1** *Syn* SUM, total, whole, number, amount, quantity *Ant* individual; particular **2** ♦ a mass formed by parts or particles that are not merged into each other *Syn* aggregation, conglomerate, conglomeration, agglomerate, agglomeration *Ant* constituent

**aggregation** *Syn* AGGREGATE, conglomerate, conglomeration, agglomerate, agglomeration

**aggression** *Syn* ATTACK, offense, offensive *Ant* resistance

**aggressive 1** *Syn* attacking, offensive *Ant* resisting; repelling **2** ♦ conspicuously or obtrusively active or energetic *Syn* militant, assertive, self-assertive, pushing, pushy

**aggrieve** *Syn* WRONG, oppress, persecute *Ant* rejoice

**agile** ♦ acting or moving with quickness and alacrity *Syn* nimble, brisk, spry *Ant* torpid

**agitate 1** *Syn* SHAKE, rock, convulse *Ant* quiet, lull, still **2** *Syn* DISCOMPOSE, perturb, upset, fluster, flurry, disturb, disquiet *Ant* calm, tranquilize **3** *Syn* DISCUSS, argue, dispute, debate

**agitation** *Syn* COMMOTION, tumult, turmoil, turbulence, confusion, convulsion, upheaval *Ant* tranquillity

**agnostic** *Syn* ATHEIST, deist, freethinker, unbeliever, infidel

**agog** *Syn* EAGER, keen, anxious, avid, athirst *Ant* aloof

**agonize** *Syn* WRITHE, squirm

**agonizing** *Syn* EXCRUCIATING, racking

**agony** *Syn* DISTRESS, suffering, passion, misery, dolor

**agrarian** *Syn* agricultural

**agree 1** *Syn* ASSENT, accede, consent, acquiesce, subscribe *Ant* protest (*against*); differ (*with*) **2** ♦ to come into or to be in harmony regarding a matter of opinion or a policy *Syn* concur, coincide *Ant* differ; disagree **3** ♦ to exist or go together without conflict or incongruity *Syn* square, conform, accord, harmonize, correspond, tally, jibe *Ant* differ (*from*)

**agreeable** *Syn* PLEASANT, grateful, pleasing, gratifying, welcome *Ant* disagreeable

**agreement** ♦ a reconciliation of differences as to what should be done or not done *Syn* accord, understanding

**agriculture** ♦ the science or the business of raising useful plants and animals *Syn* farming, husbandry

**ahead** *Syn* BEFORE, forward *Ant* behind

**aid** *vb Syn* HELP, assist *Ant* injure

**aid** *n* **1** *Syn* help, assistance *Ant* impediment **2** *Syn* ASSISTANT, helper, coadjutor, aide, aide-de-camp

**aide** *Syn* ASSISTANT, aide-de-camp, coadjutor, helper, aid

**aide-de-camp** *Syn* ASSISTANT, aide, aid

**ail** *Syn* TROUBLE, distress

**ailment** *Syn* DISEASE, disorder, condition, affection, malady, complaint, distemper, syndrome

**aim** *vb* **1** *Syn* DIRECT, point, level, train, lay **2** ♦ to have as a controlling desire something beyond one's present power of attainment *Syn* aspire, pant

**aim** *n Syn* INTENTION, end, goal, objective, purpose, object, intent, design

**air** *n* **1** *Syn* POSE, affectation, mannerism **2** *Syn* MELODY, air, tune

**air** *vb Syn* EXPRESS, ventilate, vent, utter, voice, broach

**airport** ♦ a place where airplanes take off and land *Syn* airdrome, airfield, airstrip, landing strip, flying field, landing field

**airy** ♦ as light and insubstantial as air *Syn* aerial, ethereal *Ant* substantial

**aisle** *Syn* PASSAGE, passageway, ambulatory, corridor, gallery, hall, hallway, cloister, arcade

**akin** *Syn* LIKE, alike, similar, analogous, comparable, parallel, uniform, identical *Ant* alien

**alacrity** *Syn* CELERITY, legerity *Ant* languor

**alarm** *n* ♦ a signal that serves as a call to action or to be on guard esp. in a time of imminent danger *Syn* tocsin, alert **2** *Syn* FEAR, fright, panic, terror, horror, dismay, dread, consternation, trepidation *Ant* assurance; composure

**alarm** *vb Syn* FRIGHTEN, fright, scare, startle, terrify, affright, terrorize, affray *Ant* assure; relieve

**albeit** *Syn* THOUGH, although

**alchemy** *Syn* MAGIC, thaumaturgy, wizardry, sorcery, witchery, witchcraft

**alcoholic** *Syn* DRUNKARD, inebriate, dipsomaniac, sot, soak, toper, tosspot, tippler

**alert** *adj* **1** *Syn* WATCHFUL, wide-awake, vigilant **2** *Syn* INTELLIGENT, clever, smart, bright, quick-witted, brilliant, knowing

**alert** *n Syn* ALARM, tocsin

**alias** *Syn* PSEUDONYM, nom de guerre, incognito, nom de plume, pen name

**alibi** *Syn* APOLOGY, excuse, pretext, plea, apologia

**alien** *adj Syn* EXTRINSIC, foreign, extraneous *Ant* akin; assimilable

**alien** *n Syn* STRANGER, foreigner, outlander, outsider, immigrant, émigré *Ant* citizen

**alienate 1** *Syn* TRANSFER, convey, deed **2** *Syn* ESTRANGE, disaffect, wean *Ant* unite; reunite

**alienation 1** *Syn* ABERRATION, derangement **2** *Syn* SOLITUDE, isolation, seclusion

**alight 1** *Syn* DESCEND, dismount **2** ♦ to come to rest after or as if after a flight, a descent, or a fall *Syn* light, land, perch, roost

**align** *Syn* LINE, line up, range, array

**alike** *Syn* LIKE, similar, analogous, comparable, akin, parallel, uniform, identical *Ant* different

**aliment** *Syn* FOOD, pabulum, nutriment, nourishment, sustenance, pap

**alive** 1 *Syn* LIVING, animated, animate, vital *Ant* dead, defunct 2 *Syn* AWARE, awake, sensible, cognizant, conscious *Ant* blind (*to*); anesthetic (*to*)

**alkaline** ♦ being a compound that reacts with an acid to form a salt *Syn* basic

**all** 1 *Syn* WHOLE, entire, total, gross 2 ♦ including the entire membership of a group with no exceptions *Syn* every, each *Ant* none

**all-round** *Syn* VERSATILE, many-sided

**allay** *Syn* RELIEVE, alleviate, lighten, assuage, mitigate *Ant* intensify

**allege** *Syn* ADDUCE, cite, advance *Ant* contravene; (*in law*) traverse

**allegiance** *Syn* FIDELITY, fealty, loyalty, devotion, piety *Ant* treachery; treason

**allegory** 1 ♦ a concrete representation in art of something that is abstract or for some other reason not directly representable *Syn* symbolism 2 ♦ a literary form that typically tells a story for the sake of presenting a truth or of enforcing a moral *Syn* parable, myth, fable

**alleviate** *Syn* RELIEVE, lighten, assuage, mitigate, allay *Ant* aggravate

**alliance** ♦ a chiefly political combination for a common object *Syn* league, coalition, fusion, confederacy, confederation, federation

**allied** *Syn* RELATED, cognate, kindred, affiliated *Ant* unallied

**allocate** *Syn* ALLOT, assign, apportion

**allot** ♦ to give as one's share, portion, role, or place *Syn* assign, apportion, allocate

**allow** 1 *Syn* LET, permit, suffer, leave *Ant* inhibit 2 *Syn* GRANT, concede *Ant* disallow

**allowance** 1 *Syn* RATION, dole, pittance 2 ♦ a change made by way of compromise or adjustment *Syn* concession 3 *Syn* ADVANTAGE, handicap, odds, edge

**alloy** *Syn* ADMIXTURE, adulterant

**allude** *Syn* REFER, advert

**allure** *Syn* ATTRACT, captivate, charm, fascinate, enchant, bewitch *Ant* repel

**alluring** *Syn* ATTRACTIVE, charming, fascinating, bewitching, enchanting, captivating *Ant* repulsive

**ally** *Syn* PARTNER, colleague, copartner, confederate *Ant* adversary

**almost** *Syn* NEARLY, approximately, well-nigh

**alms** *Syn* DONATION, benefaction, contribution

**alone** *adj* 1 ♦ isolated from others *Syn* solitary, lonely, lonesome, lone, lorn, forlorn, desolate *Ant* accompanied 2 *Syn* ONLY

**alone** *adv Syn* ONLY

**aloof** *Syn* INDIFFERENT, detached, uninterested, disinterested, unconcerned, incurious *Ant* familiar, close

**alp** *Syn* MOUNTAIN, peak, mount

**also** *Syn* too, likewise, besides, moreover, furthermore

**alter** 1 *Syn* CHANGE, vary, modify *Ant* fix 2 *Syn* STERILIZE, castrate, spay, emasculate, mutilate, geld

**alteration** *Syn* CHANGE, variation, modification *Ant* fixation; fixity

**altercate** *vb Syn* QUARREL, wrangle, squabble, bicker, spat, tiff *Ant* concur

**altercation** *Syn* QUARREL, wrangle, squabble, bickering, spat, tiff *Ant* concurrence; accord

**alternate** *adj Syn* INTERMITTENT, recurrent, periodic *Ant* consecutive

**alternate** *vb Syn* ROTATE

**alternate** *n Syn* SUBSTITUTE, supply, understudy, double, stand-in, pinch hitter, locum tenens

**alternation** *Syn* CHANGE, vicissitude, mutation, permutation

**alternative** *Syn* CHOICE, option, preference, selection, election

**although** *Syn* THOUGH, albeit

**altitude** *Syn* HEIGHT, elevation

**altruistic** *Syn* CHARITABLE, benevolent, humanitarian, philanthropic, eleemosynary *Ant* egoistic

**amalgam** *Syn* MIXTURE, admixture, compound, blend, composite

**amalgamate** *Syn* MIX, blend, commingle, merge, coalesce, fuse, mingle

**amalgamation** *Syn* CONSOLIDATION, merger

**amass** *Syn* ACCUMULATE, hoard *Ant* distribute

**amateur** ♦ a person who follows a pursuit without attaining proficiency or a professional status *Syn* dilettante, dabbler, tyro *Ant* professional; expert

**amative** *Syn* EROTIC, amorous, amatory

**amatory** *Syn* EROTIC, aphrodisiac, amative, amorous

**amaze** *Syn* SURPRISE, astound, flabbergast, astonish

**amazement** *Syn* WONDER, wonderment, admiration

**amazon** *Syn* VIRAGO, termagant

**ambassador** ♦ a diplomatic agent serving his or her sovereign or government in a foreign country *Syn* legate, nuncio, minister, envoy, internuncio, chargé d'affaires

**ambiguity** ♦ expression or, more often, an expression capable of more than one interpretation *Syn* equivocation, tergiversation, double entendre *Ant* lucidity; explicitness

**ambiguous** *Syn* OBSCURE, equivocal, cryptic, enigmatic, vague, dark *Ant* explicit

**ambition** ♦ strong desire for advancement *Syn* aspiration, pretension

**ambitious** 1 ♦ extremely desirous of something that will give one power, fame, success, or riches *Syn* emulous *Ant* unambitious 2 ♦ straining or exceeding the capacity of their authors or executants *Syn* pretentious, utopian *Ant* modest

**amble** *Syn* SAUNTER, stroll

**ambulant** *Syn* ITINERANT, ambulatory, peripatetic, nomadic, vagrant *Ant* bedridden

**ambulatory** *adj Syn* ITINERANT, ambulant, peripatetic, nomadic, vagrant

**ambulatory** *n Syn* PASSAGE, passageway, aisle, gallery, cloister, arcade, hall, hallway, corridor

**ambuscade** *Syn* AMBUSH

**ambush** *vb Syn* SURPRISE, waylay

**ambush** *n* ♦ a device to entrap an enemy by lying in wait under cover for an opportune moment to make a surprise attack *Syn* ambuscade

**ameliorate** *Syn* IMPROVE, better, help *Ant* worsen; deteriorate

**amenable** 1 *Syn* RESPONSIBLE, answerable, liable, accountable *Ant* independent (*of*); autonomous 2 *Syn* OBEDIENT, tractable, docile, biddable *Ant* recalcitrant, refractory

**amend** *Syn* CORRECT, reform, rectify, revise, emend, remedy, redress *Ant* debase; impair

**amends** *Syn* REPARATION, redress, indemnity, restitution

**amenity** 1 ♦ something that gives refined or exquisite pleasure or is exceedingly pleasing to the mind or senses *Syn* luxury *Ant* rigor 2 *Syn* COURTESY, attention, gallantry *Ant* acerbity, asperity; rudeness

**amerce** *Syn* PENALIZE, fine, mulct

**amercement** *Syn* FINE

**amiable** ♦ having or manifesting the desire or disposition to please *Syn* good-natured, obliging, complaisant *Ant* unamiable; surly

**amicable** ♦ marked by or exhibiting goodwill or absence of antagonism *Syn* neighborly, friendly *Ant* antagonistic

**amiss** ♦ otherwise than intended *Syn* astray *Ant* aright, right

**amity** *Syn* FRIENDSHIP, comity, goodwill *Ant* enmity

**amnesty** *Syn* PARDON, absolution

**among** *Syn* BETWEEN

**amorous** *Syn* EROTIC, amative, amatory *Ant* frigid

**amount** *Syn* SUM, total, quantity, number, aggregate, whole

**amour** ♦ an instance of illicit sexual relationship *Syn* liaison, intrigue, affair

**amour propre** *Syn* CONCEIT, self-esteem, self-love, egoism, egotism

**ample** 1 *Syn* SPACIOUS, capacious, commodious *Ant* meager; circumscribed 2 *Syn* PLENTIFUL, abundant, plenteous, copious *Ant* scant, meager

**amplify** *Syn* EXPAND, swell, distend, dilate, inflate *Ant* abridge, condense

**amplitude** *Syn* EXPANSE, spread, stretch *Ant* straitness; limitation

**amulet** *Syn* FETISH, charm, talisman

**amuse** ♦ to cause or enable one to pass one's time in pleasant or agreeable activity *Syn* divert, entertain, recreate *Ant* bore

**amusement** ♦ an agreeable activity or its effect *Syn* diversion, entertainment, recreation *Ant* boredom

**anagogic** *Syn* MYSTICAL, mystic, cabalistic

**analgesic** *Syn* ANODYNE, anesthetic *Ant* irritant

**analogous** *Syn* LIKE, alike, similar, comparable, akin, parallel, uniform, identical

**analogue** *Syn* PARALLEL, counterpart, correlate

**analogy** 1 *Syn* LIKENESS, similitude, resemblance, similarity, affinity 2 ♦ a comparison between things essentially or generically different but strikingly alike in one or more pertinent aspects *Syn* simile, metaphor

**analysis** ♦ separation of a whole into its fundamental elements or constituent parts *Syn* resolution, dissection, breakdown *Ant* synthesis

**analytical** *Syn* LOGICAL, subtle *Ant* creative, inventive, constructive

**analyze** ♦ to divide a complex whole or unit into its component parts or constituent elements *Syn* resolve, dissect, break down *Ant* compose, compound; construct

**anarchy** ♦ absence, suspension, breakdown, or widespread defiance of government, law, and order *Syn* chaos, lawlessness *Ant* order; discipline

**anathema** 1 *Syn* ABOMINATION, bête noire, bugbear 2 *Syn* CURSE, malediction, imprecation

**anathematize** *Syn* EXECRATE, curse, damn, objurgate

**anatomy** *Syn* STRUCTURE, skeleton, framework

**ancestor** ♦ a person from whom one is descended *Syn* progenitor, forefather, forebear *Ant* descendant

**ancestry** ♦ one's progenitors or their character or quality as a whole *Syn* lineage, pedigree *Ant* descendants; posterity

**anchor** *Syn* SECURE, rivet

**anchorite** *Syn* RECLUSE, hermit, eremite, cenobite

**ancient** *Syn* OLD, venerable, antediluvian, antique, antiquated, archaic, obsolete *Ant* modern

**ancillary** *Syn* AUXILIARY, contributory, subsidiary, adjuvant, subservient, accessory

**androgynous** *Syn* BISEXUAL, hermaphroditic, hermaphrodite, epicene

**anecdote** *Syn* STORY, tale, yarn, narrative

**anemic** *Syn* PALE, bloodless *Ant* fullblooded; florid

**anesthetic** *adj Syn* INSENSIBLE, insensitive, impassible *Ant* alive

**anesthetic** *n Syn* ANODYNE, analgesic *Ant* stimulant

**angel** *Syn* SPONSOR, backer, patron, surety, guarantor

**anger** *n* ♦ emotional excitement induced by intense displeasure *Syn* ire, rage, fury, indignation, wrath *Ant* pleasure, gratification; forbearance

**anger** *vb* ♦ to make angry *Syn* incense, enrage, infuriate, madden *Ant* please, gratify; pacify

**angle** 1 *Syn* POINT OF VIEW, viewpoint, standpoint, slant 2 *Syn* PHASE, aspect, facet, side

**angry** ♦ feeling or showing strong displeasure or bad temper *Syn* irate, indignant, wrathful, wroth, acrimonious, mad

**anguish** *Syn* SORROW, woe, heartache, heartbreak, grief, regret *Ant* relief

**angular** *Syn* LEAN, gaunt, rawboned, lank, lanky, spare, scrawny, skinny *Ant* rotund

**animadversion** ♦ a remark or statement that is an adverse criticism *Syn* stricture, aspersion, reflection *Ant* commendation

**animadvert** *Syn* REMARK, comment, commentate

**animal** *Syn* CARNAL, fleshly, sensual *Ant* rational

**animalism** *Syn* ANIMALITY

**animality** ♦ the animal aspect or quality of human beings or human nature *Syn* animalism

**animate** *adj Syn* LIVING, alive, animated, vital *Ant* inanimate

**animate** *vb* 1 *Syn* QUICKEN, vivify, enliven 2 *Syn* INFORM, inspire, fire *Ant* inhibit

**animated** 1 *Syn* LIVING, alive, animate, vital *Ant* inert 2 *Syn* LIVELY, vivacious, sprightly, gay *Ant* depressed, dejected

**animosity** *Syn* ENMITY, animus, rancor, hostility, antipathy, antagonism *Ant* goodwill

**animus** *Syn* ENMITY, animosity, rancor, hostility, antipathy, antagonism *Ant* favor

**annals** *Syn* HISTORY, chronicle

**annex** *vb Syn* ADD, append, subjoin, superadd

**annex** *n* ♦ an addition to a main (and, often, the original) building *Syn* extension, wing, ell

**annihilate** *Syn* ABOLISH, extinguish, abate

**annotate** ♦ to add or append comment *Syn* gloss

**annotation** ♦ added or appended comment intended to be helpful in interpreting a passage or text *Syn* gloss

**announce** *Syn* DECLARE, publish, proclaim, promulgate, advertise, broadcast

**announcement** *Syn* DECLARATION, publication, proclamation, promulgation, advertisement, broadcasting

**annoy** 1 ♦ to disturb and nervously upset a person *Syn* vex, irk, bother *Ant* soothe 2 *Syn* WORRY, pester, plague, tantalize, tease, harass, harry

**annul** 1 *Syn* NULLIFY, negate, invalidate, abrogate 2 ♦ to deprive of legal validity, force, or authority *Syn* abrogate, void, vacate, quash

**anodyne** 1 ♦ something used to relieve or prevent pain *Syn* analgesic, anesthetic 2 ♦ something used to dull or deaden one's senses or one's sensibility *Syn* opiate, narcotic, nepenthe *Ant* stimulant; irritant

**anoint** *Syn* OIL, cream, grease, lubricate

**anomalous** *Syn* IRREGULAR, unnatural

**anomaly** *Syn* PARADOX, antinomy

**answer** *n* ♦ something spoken or written by way of return to a question or demand *Syn* reply, response, rejoinder, retort

**answer** *vb* 1 ♦ to say, write, or do something in response *Syn* respond, reply, rejoin, retort 2 *Syn* SATISFY, meet, fulfill

**answerable** *Syn* RESPONSIBLE, accountable, amenable, liable

**antagonism** *Syn* ENMITY, antipathy, hostility, animosity, rancor, animus *Ant* accord; comity

**antagonist** *Syn* OPPONENT, adversary *Ant* supporter

**antagonistic** *Syn* ADVERSE, counteractive, counter *Ant* favoring, favorable

**antagonize** *Syn* RESIST, withstand, contest, oppose, fight, combat, conflict *Ant* conciliate

**ante** *Syn* BET, stake, pot, wager

**antecedent** *n Syn* CAUSE, determinant, reason, occasion *Ant* consequence

**antecedent** *adj Syn* PRECEDING, precedent, foregoing, previous, prior, former, anterior *Ant* subsequent; consequent

**antediluvian** *Syn* OLD, ancient, antiquated, obsolete, antique, venerable, archaic

**anterior** *Syn* PRECEDING, precedent, previous, prior, foregoing, antecedent, former *Ant* posterior

**anthropoid** ♦ resembling man *Syn* anthropomorphic, anthropomorphous

**anthropomorphic, anthropomorphous** *Syn* ANTHROPOID

**antic** *n Syn* PRANK, monkeyshine, caper, dido

**antic** *adj Syn* FANTASTIC, grotesque, bizarre

**anticipate** 1 *Syn* PREVENT, forestall *Ant* consummate 2 *Syn* FORESEE, apprehend, foreknow, divine

**anticipation** *Syn* PROSPECT, foretaste, outlook *Ant* retrospect

**antidote** *Syn* CORRECTIVE, check, control

**antinomy** *Syn* PARADOX, anomaly

**antipathetic** ♦ arousing marked aversion or dislike *Syn* unsympathetic *Ant* congenial

**antipathy** 1 *Syn* ENMITY, antagonism, hostility, animosity, rancor, animus *Ant* taste (*for*); affection (*for*) 2 ♦ the state of mind created by what is antipathetic *Syn* aversion

**antipodal, antipodean** *Syn* OPPOSITE, antithetical, contrary, contradictory, antonymous

**antipode** *Syn* OPPOSITE, antithesis, contrary, opposite, contradictory, antonym

**antiquated** *Syn* OLD, archaic, obsolete, antediluvian, antique, ancient, venerable *Ant* modernistic; modish

**antique** *Syn* OLD, ancient, venerable, antiquated, antediluvian, obsolete, archaic *Ant* modern; current

**antisocial** *Syn* UNSOCIAL, asocial, nonsocial *Ant* social

**antithesis** 1 *Syn* COMPARISON, contrast, parallel, collation 2 *Syn* OPPOSITE, antipode, contradictory, contrary, antonym

**antithetical** *Syn* OPPOSITE, contrary, contradictory, antonymous, antipodal, antipodean

**antonym** *Syn* OPPOSITE, contradictory, contrary, antithesis, antipode

**antonymous** *Syn* OPPOSITE, contradictory, contrary, antithetical, antipodal, antipodean

**anxiety** *Syn* CARE, worry, concern, solicitude *Ant* security

**anxious** 1 *Syn* WORRIED, concerned, solicitous *Ant* composed 2 *Syn* EAGER, keen, agog, avid *Ant* loath

**apartment** *Syn* ROOM, chamber

**apathetic** *Syn* IMPASSIVE, phlegmatic, stolid, stoic *Ant* alert; aghast

**apathy** *Syn* IMPASSIVITY, impassiveness, phlegm, stolidity, stoicism *Ant* zeal; enthusiasm

**ape** *Syn* COPY, imitate, mimic, mock

**aperçu** *Syn* COMPENDIUM, sketch, précis, survey, digest, pandect, syllabus

**aperitif** *Syn* APPETIZER

**aperture** ♦ an opening allowing passage through or in and out *Syn* interstice, orifice

**apex** *Syn* SUMMIT, peak, culmination, pinnacle, climax, acme, meridian, zenith, apogee

**aphorism** *Syn* SAYING, apothegm, epigram, saw, maxim, adage, proverb, motto

**aphrodisiac** *Syn* EROTIC, amatory, amorous *Ant* anaphrodisiac

**apiece** *Syn* EACH, severally, individually, respectively

**aplomb** *Syn* CONFIDENCE, assurance, self-assurance, self-possession, self-confidence *Ant* shyness

**apocalypse** *Syn* REVELATION, vision, prophecy

**apocryphal** *Syn* FICTITIOUS, mythical, legendary, fabulous

**apogee** *Syn* SUMMIT, climax, peak, culmination, apex, acme, meridian, zenith, pinnacle *Ant* perigee

**apologia** *Syn* APOLOGY, excuse, plea, alibi, pretext

**apology** ♦ the reason or reasons offered in explanation or defense of something (as an act, a policy, or a view) *Syn* apologia, excuse, plea, pretext, alibi

**apostasy** *Syn* DEFECTION, desertion

**apostate** *Syn* RENEGADE, turncoat, recreant, backslider

**apothecary** *Syn* DRUGGIST, pharmacist, chemist

**apothegm** *Syn* SAYING, aphorism, epigram, saw, maxim, adage, proverb, motto

**apotheosis** *Syn* PARAGON, nonpareil, nonesuch

**appall** *Syn* DISMAY, horrify, daunt *Ant* nerve, embolden

**appalling** *Syn* FEARFUL, dreadful, terrible, horrible, frightful, shocking, awful, terrific, horrific *Ant* reassuring

**appanage** *Syn* RIGHT, prerogative, privilege, perquisite, birthright

**apparatus** 1 *Syn* EQUIPMENT, gear, tackle, outfit, paraphernalia, machinery, matériel 2 *Syn* MACHINE, mechanism, machinery, engine, motor

**apparel** *vb Syn* CLOTHE, attire, dress, array, robe *Ant* divest

**apparel** *n Syn* CLOTHES, clothing, dress, attire, raiment

**apparent** 1 *Syn* EVIDENT, manifest, patent, distinct, obvious, palpable, plain, clear *Ant* unintelligible 2 ♦ not actually being what appearance indicates *Syn* illusory, seeming, ostensible *Ant* real

**apparition** ♦ a visible but immaterial appearance of a person or thing, esp. a likeness of a dead person or of a person or thing that is not physically present *Syn* phantasm, phantom, wraith, ghost, spirit, specter, shade, revenant

**appeal** *n Syn* PRAYER, plea, petition, suit

**appeal** *vb Syn* PRAY, plead, sue, petition

**appear** 1 ♦ to come out into view *Syn* loom, emerge *Ant* disappear; vanish 2 *Syn* SEEM, look

**appearance** ♦ the outward show presented by a person or thing *Syn* look, aspect, semblance

**appease** *Syn* PACIFY, placate, mollify, propitiate, conciliate *Ant* exasperate, aggravate

**appellation** *Syn* NAME, title, designation, denomination, style

**append** *Syn* ADD, subjoin, annex, superadd

**appendage** ♦ something regarded as additional and at the same time as subsidiary to another object *Syn* appurtenance, accessory, adjunct

**appendix** ♦ additional matter subjoined to a book *Syn* addendum, supplement

**apperception** *Syn* RECOGNITION, assimilation, identification

**appertain** *Syn* BEAR, pertain, belong, relate, apply

**appetite** *Syn* DESIRE, lust, passion, urge

**appetizer** *Syn* hors d'oeuvre, aperitif

**appetizing** *Syn* PALATABLE, relishing, tasty, toothsome, flavorsome, savory, sapid *Ant* nauseating

**applaud** 1 ♦ to demonstrate one's feeling, esp. one's approbation or joy, audibly and enthusiastically *Syn* cheer, root *Ant* hiss; boo 2 *Syn* COMMEND, compliment, recommend *Ant* disparage; criticize

**applause** ♦ public expression of approbation *Syn* acclamation, acclaim, plaudits *Ant* hisses; boos

**appliance** *Syn* IMPLEMENT, tool, instrument, utensil

**applicable** *Syn* RELEVANT, pertinent, apposite, apropos, germane, material *Ant* inapplicable

**applicant** *Syn* CANDIDATE, aspirant

**application** *Syn* ATTENTION, concentration, study *Ant* indolence

**appliqué** *Syn* OVERLAY, superpose, superimpose

**apply** 1 *Syn* USE, employ, utilize, avail 2 *Syn* DIRECT, devote, address 3 *Syn* RESORT, go, turn, refer 4 *Syn* BEAR, relate, pertain, appertain

**appoint** 1 *Syn* DESIGNATE, name, nominate, elect 2 *Syn* FURNISH, equip, accouter, outfit, arm

**appointment** *Syn* ENGAGEMENT, rendezvous, tryst, assignation, date

**apportion** 1 *Syn* ALLOT, allocate, assign 2 ♦ to divide something carefully and distribute it among a number *Syn* portion, parcel, ration, prorate

**apposite** *Syn* RELEVANT, pertinent, germane, apropos, applicable, material *Ant* inapposite, inapt

**appraise** *Syn* ESTIMATE, value, evaluate, assay, rate, assess

**appreciable** *Syn* PERCEPTIBLE, sensible, ponderable, palpable, tangible *Ant* inappreciable

**appreciate** 1 *Syn* UNDERSTAND, comprehend *Ant* depreciate 2 ♦ to hold in high estimation *Syn* value, prize, treasure, cherish *Ant* despise

**apprehend** 1 *Syn* ARREST, detain, attach 2 ♦ to lay hold of something with the mind so as to know it *Syn* comprehend 3 *Syn* FORESEE, divine, anticipate, foreknow

**apprehension** 1 *Syn* ARREST, detention, attachment 2 ♦ something that is known *Syn* comprehension 3 ♦ fear (or an instance of it) that something is going wrong or will go wrong *Syn* foreboding, misgiving, presentiment *Ant* confidence

**apprehensive** *Syn* FEARFUL, afraid *Ant* confident

**apprentice** *Syn* NOVICE, novitiate, probationer, postulant, neophyte

**apprise** *Syn* INFORM, advise, notify, acquaint

**approach** *vb* 1♦ to come or draw close (to) *Syn* near, approximate 2 *Syn* MATCH, touch, equal, rival

**approach** *n Syn* OVERTURE, advance, tender, bid *Ant* repulse

**approbation** ♦ warmly commending acceptance or agreement *Syn* approval *Ant* disapprobation

**appropriate** *vb Syn* ARROGATE, preempt, confiscate, usurp

**appropriate** *adj Syn* FIT, fitting, proper, suitable, apt, meet, happy, felicitous *Ant* inappropriate

**appropriation** ♦ money or property given or set apart by an authorized body for a predetermined use by others *Syn* grant, subvention, subsidy

**approval** *Syn* APPROBATION *Ant* disapproval

**approve** ♦ to have or to express a favorable opinion of *Syn* endorse, sanction, accredit, certify *Ant* disapprove

**approximate** *Syn* APPROACH, near

**approximately** *Syn* NEARLY, almost, well-nigh *Ant* precisely, exactly

**appurtenance** *Syn* APPENDAGE, accessory, adjunct

**apropos** *Syn* RELEVANT, apposite, pertinent, germane, applicable, material *Ant* unapropos

**apt** 1 *Syn* FIT, happy, felicitous, appropriate, fitting, suitable, meet, proper *Ant* inapt, inept 2 *Syn* likely, liable 3 *Syn* QUICK, prompt, ready

**aptitude** *Syn* GIFT, bent, turn, talent, faculty, knack, genius *Ant* inaptitude

**aqueduct** *Syn* CHANNEL, canal, conduit, duct

**arbiter** *Syn* JUDGE, arbitrator, umpire, referee

**arbitrary** *Syn* ABSOLUTE, autocratic, despotic, tyrannical, tyrannous *Ant* legitimate

**arbitrate** *Syn* JUDGE, adjudicate, adjudge

**arbitrator** *Syn* JUDGE, referee, arbiter, umpire

**arc** *Syn* CURVE, arch, bow

**arcade** *Syn* PASSAGE, gallery, cloister, ambulatory, passageway, corridor, hall, hallway, aisle

**arcane** *Syn* MYSTERIOUS, inscrutable

**arch** *n Syn* CURVE, bow, arc

**arch** *adj Syn* SAUCY, pert

**archaic** *Syn* OLD, obsolete, antiquated, antique, ancient, antediluvian, venerable *Ant* up-to-date

**architect** *Syn* ARTIST, artificer, artisan

**archive** *Syn* DOCUMENT, record, monument

**arctic** *Syn* COLD, frigid, freezing, frosty, icy, gelid, glacial, chilly, cool *Ant* torrid

**ardent** *Syn* IMPASSIONED, passionate, fervid, perfervid, fervent *Ant* cool

**ardor** *Syn* PASSION, fervor, enthusiasm, zeal *Ant* coolness; indifference

**arduous** *Syn* HARD, difficult *Ant* light, facile

**area** 1♦ a distinguishable extent of surface esp. of the earth's surface *Syn* tract, region, zone, belt 2 *Syn* SIZE, extent, dimensions, magnitude, volume

**argot** *Syn* DIALECT, cant, jargon, slang, lingo, vernacular, patois

**argue** 1 *Syn* DISCUSS, debate, dispute, agitate 2 *Syn* INDICATE, bespeak, prove, attest, betoken

**argument** 1 *Syn* REASON, proof, ground 2♦ a vigorous and often heated discussion of a moot question *Syn* dispute, controversy 3 *Syn* SUBJECT, theme, matter, subject matter, topic, text, motive, motif, leitmotiv

**argumentation** ♦ the act or art of argument or an exercise of one's powers of argument *Syn* disputation, debate, forensic, dialectic

**arid** *Syn* DRY *Ant* moist; verdant

**arise** 1 *Syn* RISE, ascend, mount, soar, levitate, surge, tower, rocket *Ant* recline; slump 2 *Syn* SPRING, rise, originate, derive, flow, issue, emanate, proceed, stem

**aristocracy** 1 *Syn* OLIGARCHY, plutocracy 2♦ a body of persons who constitute a socially superior caste *Syn* nobility, gentry, county, elite, society *Ant* people, proletariat

**aristocrat** *Syn* GENTLEMAN, patrician *Ant* commoner

**arm** *Syn* FURNISH, accouter, outfit, equip, appoint *Ant* disarm

**armistice** *Syn* TRUCE, cease-fire, peace

**army** *Syn* MULTITUDE, host, legion

**aroma** *Syn* SMELL, odor, scent *Ant* stink, stench

**aromatic** *Syn* ODOROUS, balmy, redolent, fragrant *Ant* acrid (*of odors*)

**arouse** *Syn* STIR, rouse, awaken, waken, rally *Ant* quiet, calm

**arraign** *Syn* ACCUSE, charge, impeach, indict, incriminate

**arrange** 1 *Syn* ORDER, marshal, organize, systematize, methodize *Ant* derange, disarrange 2 *Syn* NEGOTIATE, concert

**arrant** *Syn* OUTRIGHT, out-and-out, unmitigated

**array** *vb* 1 *Syn* LINE, line up, range, align *Ant* disarray 2 *Syn* CLOTHE, apparel, attire, robe, dress

**array** *n Syn* DISPLAY, parade, pomp

**arrear** *Syn* DEBT, indebtedness, debit, obligation, liability

**arrest** *vb* 1♦ to stop in midcourse *Syn* check, interrupt *Ant* activate; quicken 2♦ to seize and hold under restraint or in custody by authority of the law *Syn* apprehend, attach, detain

**arrest** *n* ♦ seizing and holding under restraint or in custody by authority of the law *Syn* apprehension, detention, attachment

**arresting** *Syn* NOTICEABLE, striking, remarkable, outstanding, salient, signal, prominent, conspicuous

**arrival** ♦ the reaching of a destination *Syn* advent *Ant* departure

**arrive** *Syn* COME *Ant* depart

**arrogant** *Syn* PROUD, haughty, lordly, insolent, overbearing, supercilious, disdainful *Ant* meek; unassuming

**arrogate** ♦ to seize or take over in a high-handed manner *Syn* usurp, preempt, appropriate, confiscate *Ant* renounce; yield

**art** 1♦ the faculty of performing or executing expertly what is planned or devised *Syn* skill, cunning, artifice, craft 2 *Syn* TRADE, craft, handicraft, profession

**artery** *Syn* WAY, route, course, passage, pass

**artful** *Syn* SLY, wily, guileful, crafty, cunning, tricky, foxy, insidious *Ant* artless

**article** 1 *Syn* PARAGRAPH, clause, plank, count, verse 2 *Syn* THING, object 3 *Syn* ESSAY, paper, theme, composition

**articled** *Syn* BOUND, indentured, bond

**articulate** *adj* 1 *Syn* VOCAL, oral *Ant* inarticulate, dumb 2 *Syn* VOCAL, fluent, eloquent, voluble, glib *Ant* inarticulate, dumb

**articulate** *vb* 1 *Syn* INTEGRATE, concatenate 2♦ to form speech sounds *Syn* pronounce, enunciate

**articulation** 1 *Syn* INTEGRATION, concatenation 2 *Syn* JOINT, suture

**artifact** *Syn* WORK, product, production, opus

**artifice** 1 *Syn* ART, cunning, craft, skill 2 *Syn* TRICK, ruse, wile, stratagem, maneuver, gambit, ploy, feint

**artificer** *Syn* ARTIST, artisan, architect

**artificial** ♦ not brought into being by nature but by human art or effort or by some process of manufacture *Syn* factitious, synthetic, ersatz *Ant* natural

**artisan** 1 *Syn* ARTIST, artificer, architect 2 *Syn* WORKER, mechanic, workman, workingman, operative, craftsman, handicraftsman, hand, laborer, roustabout

**artist** 1♦ one who makes something beautiful or useful or both *Syn* artificer, artisan, architect 2 *Syn* EXPERT, artiste, virtuoso, adept, wizard

**artiste** *Syn* EXPERT, artist, virtuoso, adept, wizard

**artless** *Syn* NATURAL, simple, ingenuous, naïve, unsophisticated, unaffected *Ant* artful; affected

**as** *Syn* BECAUSE, since, for, inasmuch as

**ascend** 1 *Syn* RISE, arise, mount, soar, tower, rocket, levitate, surge *Ant* descend 2♦ to move upward to or toward a summit *Syn* mount, climb, scale *Ant* descend

**ascendancy** *Syn* SUPREMACY

**ascension** ♦ the act of moving upward or the movement upward *Syn* ascent

**ascent** *Syn* ASCENSION

**ascertain** *Syn* DISCOVER, determine, unearth, learn

**ascetic** *Syn* SEVERE, austere, stern *Ant* luxurious, voluptuous, sensuous

**ascribe** ♦ to lay something (creditable, discreditable, or neutral) to the account of a person or thing *Syn* attribute, impute, assign, refer, credit, accredit, charge

**ash** ♦ the remains of combustible material after it has been destroyed by fire *Syn* cinders, clinkers, embers

**ashamed** ♦ acutely or manifestly conscious of embarrassment and humiliation *Syn* mortified, chagrined *Ant* proud

**ashen** *Syn* PALE, ashy, livid, pallid, wan

**ashy** *Syn* PALE, ashen, livid, pallid, wan

**asinine** *Syn* SIMPLE, fatuous, silly, foolish *Ant* sensible, judicious

**ask** 1♦ to address a person in an attempt to elicit information *Syn* question, interrogate, query, inquire, catechize, quiz, examine 2♦ to seek to obtain by making one's wants or desires known *Syn* request, solicit

**askance** *Syn* AWRY, askew *Ant* straightforwardly, directly

**askew** *Syn* AWRY, askance *Ant* straight

**asocial** *Syn* UNSOCIAL, antisocial, nonsocial *Ant* social

**aspect** 1 *Syn* APPEARANCE, look, semblance 2 *Syn* PHASE, side, facet, angle

**asperity** *Syn* ACRIMONY, acerbity *Ant* amenity

**asperse** *Syn* MALIGN, vilify, traduce, calumniate, slander, defame, libel

**aspersion** *Syn* ANIMADVERSION, reflection, stricture

**asphyxiate** *Syn* SUFFOCATE, stifle, smother, choke, strangle, throttle

**aspirant** *Syn* CANDIDATE, applicant, nominee

**aspiration** *Syn* AMBITION, pretension

**aspire** *Syn* AIM, pant

**assail** *Syn* ATTACK, bombard, assault, storm

**assassin** ♦ one who can be hired to murder *Syn* cutthroat, gunman, bravo

**assassinate** *Syn* KILL, murder, slay, dispatch, execute

**assault** *n Syn* ATTACK, onslaught, onset

**assault** *vb Syn* ATTACK, storm, bombard, assail

**assay** *Syn* ESTIMATE, assess, evaluate, appraise, value, rate

**assemblage** *Syn* GATHERING, assembly, collection, congregation

**assemble** *Syn* GATHER, congregate, collect *Ant* disperse

**assembly** *Syn* GATHERING, assemblage, congregation, collection

**assent** ♦ concurrence with what someone else has stated or proposed *Syn* consent, accede, acquiesce, agree, subscribe *Ant* dissent

**assert** 1♦ to state positively usu. either in anticipation of denial or objection or in the face of it *Syn* declare, profess, affirm, aver, protest, avouch, avow, predicate, warrant *Ant* deny; controvert 2 *Syn* MAINTAIN, vindicate, justify, defend

**assertive** *Syn* AGGRESSIVE, self-assertive, pushing, pushy, militant *Ant* retiring; acquiescent

**assess** *Syn* ESTIMATE, assay, appraise, value, evaluate, rate

**asset** 1 **assets** *pl Syn* POSSESSIONS, resources, means, effects, belongings *Ant* liabilities 2 *Syn* CREDIT *Ant* handicap

**assiduous** *Syn* BUSY, sedulous, diligent, industrious *Ant* desultory

**assign** 1 *Syn* ALLOT, allocate, apportion 2 *Syn* ASCRIBE, refer, attribute, impute, credit, accredit, charge 3 *Syn* PRESCRIBE, define

**assignation** *Syn* ENGAGEMENT, rendezvous, tryst, date, appointment

**assignment** *Syn* TASK, duty, job, stint, chore

**assimilate** 1 *Syn* IDENTIFY, incorporate, embody 2 *Syn* ABSORB, imbibe

**assimilation** *Syn* RECOGNITION, apperception, identification

**assist** *Syn* HELP, aid *Ant* hamper; impede

**assistance** *Syn* HELP, aid *Ant* impediment; obstruction

**assistant** ♦ a person who takes over part of the duties of another, esp. in a subordinate capacity *Syn* helper, coadjutor, aid, aide, aide-de-camp

**associate** *vb Syn* JOIN, connect, relate, link, conjoin, combine, unite

**associate** *n* ♦ a person frequently found in the company of another *Syn* companion, comrade, crony

**association** ♦ a body of persons who unite in the pursuit of a common aim or object *Syn* society, club, order

**assort** ♦ to arrange in systematic order or according to some definite method of arrangement or distribution *Syn* sort, classify, pigeonhole

**assorted** *Syn* MISCELLANEOUS, heterogeneous, motley, promiscuous *Ant* jumbled

**assuage** *Syn* RELIEVE, alleviate, mitigate, lighten, allay *Ant* exacerbate; intensify

**assume** 1 ♦ to put on a false or deceptive appearance *Syn* affect, pretend, simulate, feign, counterfeit, sham 2 *Syn* PRESUPPOSE, postulate, presume, premise, posit

**assumption** ♦ something that is taken for granted or advanced as fact *Syn* presupposition, postulate, posit, presumption, premise

**assurance** 1 *Syn* CERTAINTY, certitude, conviction *Ant* mistrust; dubiousness 2 *Syn* CONFIDENCE, self-assurance, self-confidence, self-possession, aplomb *Ant* diffidence; alarm

**assure** *Syn* ENSURE, insure, secure *Ant* alarm

**assured** *Syn* CONFIDENT, sanguine, sure, presumptuous *Ant* abashed; timorous

**astern** *Syn* ABAFT, aft *Ant* ahead

**astonish** *Syn* SURPRISE, astound, amaze, flabbergast

**astound** *Syn* SURPRISE, astonish, amaze, flabbergast

**astral** *Syn* STARRY, stellar, sidereal

**astray** *Syn* AMISS

**astute** *Syn* SHREWD, perspicacious, sagacious *Ant* gullible

**asylum** *Syn* SHELTER, refuge, retreat, sanctuary, cover

**atavism** *Syn* REVERSION, throwback

**atavistic** *Syn* REVERSIONARY

**atheist** ♦ a person who rejects some or all of the essential doctrines of religion and particularly the existence of God *Syn* agnostic, deist, freethinker, unbeliever, infidel *Ant* theist

**athirst** *Syn* EAGER, avid, keen, anxious, agog

**athletic** *Syn* MUSCULAR, husky, sinewy, brawny, burly

**athletics** ♦ physical activities engaged in for exercise or play *Syn* sports, games

**athwart** *Syn* ACROSS, crosswise, crossways

**atmosphere** ♦ an intangible and usually unanalyzable quality or aggregate of qualities which gives something an individual and distinctly recognizable character *Syn* feeling, feel, aura

**atom** *Syn* PARTICLE, bit, mite, smidgen, jot, tittle, iota, whit

**atone** *Syn* EXPIATE

**atonement** *Syn* EXPIATION

**atrabilious** *Syn* MELANCHOLIC, hypochondriac, melancholy *Ant* blithe

**atrocious** *Syn* OUTRAGEOUS, heinous, monstrous *Ant* humane; noble, moral

**attach** 1 *Syn* ARREST, apprehend, detain 2 *Syn* FASTEN, affix, fix *Ant* detach

**attachment** 1 *Syn* ARREST, apprehension, detention 2 ♦ the feeling which animates a person who is genuinely fond of someone or something *Syn* affection, love *Ant* aversion

**attack** *vb* ♦ to make an onslaught upon *Syn* assail, assault, bombard, storm

**attack** *n* 1 ♦ an attempt made on another or on others to injure, destroy, or defame *Syn* assault,

onslaught, onset 2 ♦ action in a struggle for supremacy which must be met with defense or by means of defenses *Syn* aggression, offense, offensive 3 *Syn* FIT, access, accession, paroxysm, spasm, convulsion

**attacking** ♦ initiating hostile action in a struggle for supremacy *Syn* aggressive, offensive

**attain** *Syn* REACH, compass, gain, achieve

**attainment** *Syn* ACQUIREMENT, accomplishment, acquisition

**attaint** *Syn* CONTAMINATE, taint, pollute, defile

**attempt** *vb* ♦ to make an effort to do something that may or may not be successful *Syn* try, endeavor, essay, strive, struggle *Ant* succeed

**attempt** *n* ♦ an effort made to do or accomplish something *Syn* endeavor, essay, try, striving, struggle

**attend** 1 *Syn* TEND, mind, watch 2 *Syn* ACCOMPANY, escort, chaperone, convoy

**attention** 1 ♦ the direct focusing of the mind esp. on something to be learned, worked out, or dealt with *Syn* study, concentration, application *Ant* inattention 2 *Syn* COURTESY, gallantry, amenity

**attentive** *Syn* THOUGHTFUL, considerate *Ant* inattentive; neglectful

**attenuate** *Syn* THIN, rarefy, dilute, extenuate *Ant* enlarge; dilate; enrich

**attest** 1 *Syn* CERTIFY, witness, vouch 2 *Syn* INDICATE, argue, prove, bespeak, betoken *Ant* belie

**attire** *vb Syn* CLOTHE, apparel, array, dress, robe *Ant* divest

**attire** *n Syn* CLOTHES, clothing, apparel, raiment, dress

**attitude** 1 *Syn* POSTURE, pose 2 *Syn* POSITION, stand

**attorney** 1 *Syn* AGENT, deputy, proxy, factor 2 *Syn* LAWYER, solicitor, counselor, barrister, counsel, advocate

**attract** ♦ to draw another by exerting an irresistible or compelling influence *Syn* allure, charm, fascinate, bewitch, enchant, captivate *Ant* repel

**attraction** ♦ the relationship between persons or things that are involuntarily or naturally drawn together *Syn* affinity, sympathy

**attractive** ♦ drawing another by exerting a compelling influence *Syn* alluring, charming, fascinating, bewitching, enchanting, captivating *Ant* repellent; forbidding

**attribute** *n* 1 *Syn* QUALITY, property, character, accident 2 *Syn* SYMBOL, emblem, type

**attribute** *vb Syn* ASCRIBE, impute, assign, credit, accredit, refer, charge

**attrition** *Syn* PENITENCE, contrition, repentance, remorse, compunction

**attune** *Syn* HARMONIZE, tune

**atypical** *Syn* ABNORMAL, aberrant *Ant* typical; representative

**audacious** *Syn* BRAVE, courageous, unafraid, fearless, intrepid, valiant, valorous, dauntless, undaunted, doughty, bold *Ant* circumspect

**audacity** *Syn* TEMERITY, hardihood, effrontery, nerve, cheek, gall *Ant* circumspection

**audience** 1 *Syn* HEARING, audition 2 *Syn* FOLLOWING, public, clientele

**audit** *n Syn* SCRUTINY, examination, inspection, scrutiny, scanning

**audit** *vb Syn* SCRUTINIZE, examine, inspect, scan

**audition** *Syn* HEARING, audience

**auditory** ♦ of or relating to the hearing of sounds *Syn* acoustic, acoustical

**augment** *Syn* INCREASE, enlarge, multiply *Ant* abate

**augur** *Syn* FORETELL, prognosticate, presage, portend, forebode, prophesy, forecast, predict

**augury** *Syn* FORETOKEN, omen, portent, presage, prognostic

**august** *Syn* GRAND, majestic, imposing, stately, noble, grandiose, magnificent *Ant* unimpressive; unimposing

**aura** *Syn* ATMOSPHERE, feeling, feel

**aureate** *Syn* RHETORICAL, euphuistic, flowery, grandiloquent, magniloquent, bombastic *Ant* austere (*in style*)

**auspicious** *Syn* FAVORABLE, propitious, benign *Ant* inauspicious; ill-omened

**austere** *Syn* SEVERE, stern, ascetic *Ant* luscious (*of fruits*); warm, ardent (*of persons, feelings*); exuberant (*of style, quality*)

**autarchic** *Syn* FREE, autarkic, autonomous, independent, sovereign

**autarchy** *Syn* FREEDOM, autarky, autonomy, independence, sovereignty

**autarkic** *Syn* FREE, autarchic, autonomous, independent, sovereign

**autarky** *Syn* FREEDOM, autarchy, autonomy, independence, sovereignty

**authentic** ♦ being exactly as appears or is claimed *Syn* genuine, veritable, bona fide *Ant* spurious

**authenticate** *Syn* CONFIRM, validate, verify, substantiate, corroborate *Ant* impugn

**author** *Syn* MAKER, creator

**authoritarian** *Syn* DICTATORIAL, dogmatic, magisterial, doctrinaire, oracular *Ant* liberal, libertarian; anarchistic, anarchic

**authority** 1 *Syn* POWER, jurisdiction, command, control, dominion, sway 2 *Syn* INFLUENCE, weight, credit, prestige

**authorize** ♦ to invest with power or the right to act *Syn* commission, accredit, license

**autobiography** *Syn* BIOGRAPHY, memoir, life, confessions

**autochthonous** *Syn* NATIVE, indigenous, aboriginal, endemic *Ant* naturalized

**autocratic** *Syn* ABSOLUTE, arbitrary, despotic, tyrannical, tyrannous

**automatic** *Syn* SPONTANEOUS, mechanical, instinctive, impulsive

**autonomous** *Syn* FREE, independent, sovereign, autarchic, autarkic

**autonomy** *Syn* FREEDOM, independence, sovereignty, autarchy, autarky

**auxiliary** ♦ supplying aid or support *Syn* subsidiary, accessory, contributory, subservient, ancillary, adjuvant

**avail** *vb* 1 *Syn* BENEFIT, profit 2 *Syn* USE, utilize, employ, apply

**avail** *n Syn* USE, service, account, advantage, profit

**avarice** *Syn* CUPIDITY, greed, rapacity *Ant* prodigality

**avaricious** *Syn* COVETOUS, acquisitive, grasping, greedy *Ant* generous

**avenge** ♦ to inflict punishment by way of repayment for *Syn* revenge

**aver** *Syn* ASSERT, declare, avouch, avow, profess, affirm, protest *Ant* deny

**average** *n* ♦ something (as a number, quantity, or condition) that represents a middle point between extremes *Syn* mean, median, norm, par *Ant* maximum; minimum

**average** *adj Syn* MEDIUM, middling, indifferent, fair, moderate, mediocre, second-rate *Ant* exceptional; extraordinary

**averse** *Syn* DISINCLINED, indisposed, loath, reluctant, hesitant *Ant* avid (*of or for*); athirst (*for*)

**aversion** 1 *Syn* DISLIKE, distaste, disfavor *Ant* predilection 2 *Syn* ANTIPATHY *Ant* attachment, predilection

**avert** 1 *Syn* TURN, deflect, sheer, divert 2 *Syn* PREVENT, ward, obviate, preclude

**avid** *Syn* EAGER, keen, anxious, agog, athirst *Ant* indifferent; averse

**avoid** *Syn* ESCAPE, shun, eschew, evade, elude *Ant* face; meet

**avouch** *Syn* ASSERT, aver, affirm, avow, profess, declare, protest, warrant, predicate

**avow** 1 *Syn* ASSERT, affirm, profess, declare, aver, avouch, warrant, protest, predicate 2 *Syn* ACKNOWLEDGE, own, confess, admit *Ant* disavow

**await** *Syn* EXPECT, hope, look *Ant* despair

**awake** *Syn* AWARE, alive, cognizant, conscious, sensible

**awaken** *Syn* STIR, waken, rouse, arouse, rally *Ant* subdue

**award** *vb Syn* GRANT, accord, vouchsafe, concede

**award** *n Syn* PREMIUM, prize, reward, guerdon, meed, bonus, bounty
**aware** ♦ having knowledge of something *Syn* cognizant, conscious, sensible, alive, awake *Ant* unaware

**awe** *Syn* REVERENCE, fear
**awful** *Syn* FEARFUL, dreadful, frightful, terrible, horrible, shocking, appalling, terrific, horrific
**awkward** ♦ not marked by ease (as of performance, movement, or social conduct) *Syn* clumsy, maladroit, inept, gauche *Ant* handy, deft; graceful
**awry** ♦ deviating from a straight line or direction *Syn* askew, askance
**axiom** *Syn* PRINCIPLE, fundamental, law, theorem

# B

**babble** *Syn* CHAT, gabble, jabber, prattle, chatter, patter, prate, gibber, gab
**babel** *Syn* DIN, hubbub, clamor, racket, uproar, hullabaloo, pandemonium
**baby** *Syn* INDULGE, mollycoddle, humor, pamper, spoil
**back** *n Syn* SPINE, backbone, vertebrae, chine
**back** *adj Syn* POSTERIOR, rear, hind, hinder, after *Ant* front
**back** *vb* 1 *Syn* SUPPORT, uphold, champion, advocate 2 *Syn* RECEDE, retrograde, retreat, retract
**backbiting** *Syn* DETRACTION, slander, scandal, calumny *Ant* vindication
**backbone** 1 *Syn* SPINE, back, vertebrae, chine 2 *Syn* FORTITUDE, grit, guts, sand, pluck *Ant* spinelessness
**backdrop** *Syn* BACKGROUND, setting, milieu, mise-en-scène, environment
**backer** *Syn* SPONSOR, surety, guarantor, patron, angel
**background** ♦ the place, time, and circumstances in which something occurs *Syn* setting, environment, milieu, mise-en-scène, backdrop
**backslide** *Syn* LAPSE, relapse
**backslider** *Syn* RENEGADE, apostate, recreant, turncoat
**backsliding** *Syn* LAPSE, relapse
**backward** ♦ not moving or going ahead *Syn* retrograde, retrogressive, regressive *Ant* advanced
**bad** 1 ♦ deviating from the dictates of moral law *Syn* evil, ill, wicked, naughty *Ant* good 2 ♦ not measuring up to a standard of what is satisfactory *Syn* poor, wrong *Ant* good
**badge** *Syn* SIGN, token, mark, note, symptom
**badger** *Syn* BAIT, hound, chivy, hector, ride, heckle
**badinage** ♦ animated back-and-forth exchange of remarks *Syn* persiflage, raillery
**badlands** *Syn* WASTE, desert, wilderness
**baffle** *Syn* FRUSTRATE, balk, circumvent, outwit, foil, thwart
**bag** *n* ♦ a container made of a flexible material and open or opening at the top *Syn* sack, pouch
**bag** *vb Syn* CATCH, capture, trap, snare, entrap, ensnare
**bail** *n Syn* GUARANTEE, bond, surety, security, guaranty
**bail** *vb Syn* DIP, ladle, scoop, spoon, dish
**bailiwick** *Syn* FIELD, province, domain, territory, sphere
**bait** *vb* ♦ to persist in tormenting or harassing another *Syn* badger, heckle, hector, chivy, hound, ride
**bait** *n Syn* LURE, snare, trap, decoy
**bake** *Syn* DRY, parch, desiccate, dehydrate
**balance** *n* 1 ♦ the stability or efficiency resulting from the equalization or exact adjustment of opposing forces *Syn* equilibrium, equipoise, poise, tension 2 *Syn* SYMMETRY, proportion, harmony 3 *Syn* REMAINDER, rest, residue, residuum, leavings, remnant, remains
**balance** *vb* 1 *Syn* COMPENSATE, counterpoise, counterbalance, countervail, offset 2 *Syn* STABILIZE, poise, ballast, trim, steady
**bald** *Syn* BARE, barren, naked, nude
**balderdash** *Syn* NONSENSE, twaddle, drivel, bunk, poppycock, gobbledygook, trash, rot, bull
**bale** *Syn* BUNDLE, package, pack, parcel, bunch, packet
**baleful** *Syn* SINISTER, maleficent, malefic, malign *Ant* beneficent

**balk** 1 *Syn* FRUSTRATE, thwart, foil, baffle, circumvent, outwit *Ant* forward 2 *Syn* DEMUR, jib, shy, boggle, stickle, scruple, strain, stick
**balky** *Syn* CONTRARY, restive, perverse, froward, wayward
**ballast** *Syn* STABILIZE, steady, balance, trim, poise
**ballot** *Syn* SUFFRAGE, vote, franchise
**ballyhoo** *Syn* PUBLICITY, promotion, propaganda
**balmy** 1 *Syn* ODOROUS, aromatic, fragrant, redolent *Ant* rank, noisome 2 *Syn* SOFT, gentle, smooth, bland, mild, lenient
**bamboozle** *Syn* DUPE, trick, hoodwink, gull, hoax, befool
**ban** *Syn* FORBID, prohibit, interdict, inhibit, enjoin
**banal** *Syn* INSIPID, flat, jejune, inane, vapid, wishy-washy *Ant* original; recherché
**band** 1 *Syn* BOND, tie 2 *Syn* STRIP, stripe, ribbon, fillet 3 *Syn* COMPANY, troop, troupe, party
**bandy** *Syn* EXCHANGE, interchange
**bane** *Syn* POISON, venom, virus, toxin
**baneful** *Syn* PERNICIOUS, noxious, deleterious, detrimental *Ant* beneficial
**banish** ♦ to remove by authority or force from a country, state, or sovereignty *Syn* exile, expatriate, ostracize, deport, transport, extradite
**bank** *n* 1 *Syn* SHOAL, bar, reef 2 *Syn* SHORE, strand, coast, beach, foreshore, littoral 3 *Syn* HEAP, mass, pile, stack, shock, cock
**bank** *vb Syn* HEAP, mass, pile, stack, shock, cock
**bank** *vb Syn* RELY, count, reckon, trust, depend
**bankrupt** *Syn* DEPLETE, impoverish, exhaust, drain
**banner** *Syn* FLAG, standard, ensign, color, streamer, pennant, pendant, pennon, jack
**banquet** *Syn* DINNER, feast
**banter** ♦ to make fun of good-naturedly *Syn* chaff, kid, rag, rib, josh, jolly
**baptize** ♦ to administer the rite of baptism *Syn* christen
**bar** *n* 1 ♦ something which hinders or obstructs *Syn* barrier, barricade 2 *Syn* OBSTACLE, obstruction, impediment, snag *Ant* advantage 3 *Syn* SHOAL, bank, reef
**bar** *vb Syn* HINDER, obstruct, block, dam, impede *Ant* admit; open
**barbarian** ♦ of, relating to, or characteristic of people that are not fully civilized *Syn* barbaric, barbarous, savage *Ant* civilized
**barbaric** *Syn* BARBARIAN, savage, barbarous *Ant* restrained; refined; subdued
**barbarism** ♦ a word or expression which offends against standards of correctness *Syn* corruption, impropriety, solecism, vernacularism, vulgarism
**barbarous** 1 *Syn* BARBARIAN, savage, barbaric *Ant* civilized; humane 2 *Syn* FIERCE, savage, inhuman, ferocious, cruel, fell, truculent *Ant* clement
**bard** *Syn* POET, minstrel, troubadour, rhymer, rhymester, versifier, poetaster
**bare** *adj* 1 ♦ lacking naturally or conventionally appropriate covering or clothing *Syn* naked, nude, bald, barren *Ant* covered 2 *Syn* MERE, very
**bare** *vb Syn* STRIP, denude, divest, dismantle *Ant* cover
**barefaced** *Syn* SHAMELESS, brazen, brash, impudent *Ant* furtive
**bargain** *Syn* CONTRACT, compact, pact
**bark** *vb* ♦ to make the sound of or a sound suggestive of a dog *Syn* bay, howl, growl, snarl, yelp, yap
**bark** *n Syn* SKIN, rind, peel, hide, pelt
**baroque** *Syn* ORNATE, florid, rococo, flamboyant

**barren** 1 *Syn* STERILE, unfruitful, infertile, impotent *Ant* fecund 2 *Syn* BARE, bald, naked, nude
**barricade** *Syn* BAR, barrier
**barrier** *Syn* BAR, barricade
**barrister** *Syn* LAWYER, counselor, counsel, advocate, attorney, solicitor
**basal** 1 *Syn* FUNDAMENTAL, basic, underlying, radical 2 *Syn* ELEMENTARY, beginning, elemental, rudimentary
**base** *n* ♦ something on which another thing is reared or built or by which it is supported or fixed in place *Syn* basis, foundation, ground, groundwork *Ant* top
**base** *vb* ♦ to supply or to serve as a basis *Syn* found, ground, bottom, stay, rest
**base** *adj* ♦ deserving of contempt because of the absence of higher values *Syn* low, vile *Ant* noble
**baseless** ♦ not justified or justifiable in any way *Syn* groundless, unfounded, unwarranted
**bashful** *Syn* SHY, diffident, modest, coy *Ant* forward; brazen
**basic** 1 *Syn* FUNDAMENTAL, basal, underlying, radical *Ant* top; peak 2 *Syn* ALKALINE *Syn* ELEMENTAL, elementary, essential, fundamental, primitive, underlying
**basis** *Syn* BASE, foundation, ground, groundwork
**baste** *Syn* BEAT, pummel, thrash, buffet, pound, belabor
**bastion** *Syn* BULWARK, breastwork, parapet, rampart
**bathos** *Syn* PATHOS, poignancy
**batter** *Syn* MAIM, mangle, mutilate, cripple
**battle** *n* ♦ a hostile meeting between opposing military forces *Syn* engagement, action
**battle** *vb Syn* CONTEND, war, fight
**bawl** *vb* 1 *Syn* ROAR, bellow, bluster, vociferate, clamor, howl, ululate 2 *Syn* SCOLD, rate, berate, tongue-lash, upbraid, chew out, wig, rail, revile, vituperate
**bawl** *n Syn* ROAR, bellow, bluster, vociferation, ululation
**bay** *Syn* BARK, howl, growl, snarl, yelp, yap
**be** ♦ to have actuality or reality *Syn* exist, live, subsist
**beach** *Syn* SHORE, strand, coast, foreshore, bank, littoral
**beak** *Syn* BILL, neb, nib
**beam** *Syn* RAY
**beaming** *Syn* BRIGHT, radiant, refulgent, effulgent, brilliant, luminous, lustrous, lambent, lucent, incandescent
**bear** 1 *Syn* CARRY, convey, transport, transmit 2 ♦ to bring forth as products *Syn* produce, yield, turn out 3 ♦ to sustain something trying or painful *Syn* suffer, endure, abide, tolerate, stand, brook 4 *Syn* PRESS, bear down, squeeze, crowd, jam 5 ♦ to have a connection especially logically *Syn* relate, pertain, appertain, belong, apply
**beard** *Syn* FACE, brave, challenge, dare, defy
**bear down** *Syn* PRESS, bear, squeeze, crowd, jam
**bearing** ♦ the way in which or the quality by which a person outwardly manifests personality *Syn* deportment, demeanor, mien, port, presence
**beastly** *Syn* BRUTAL, bestial, brute, brutish, feral
**beat** *vb* 1 ♦ to strike repeatedly *Syn* pound, pummel, thrash, buffet, baste, belabor 2 *Syn* CONQUER, defeat, lick, vanquish, subdue, subjugate, reduce, overcome, surmount, overthrow, rout 3 *Syn* PULSATE, throb, pulse, palpitate
**beat** *n Syn* PULSATION, pulse, throb, palpitation

**beatitude** *Syn* HAPPINESS, blessedness, bliss, felicity *Ant* despair; dolor

**beau** *Syn* FOP, exquisite, dandy, coxcomb, dude, buck

**beau ideal** *Syn* MODEL, ideal, exemplar, pattern, example, mirror, standard

**beauteous** *Syn* BEAUTIFUL, pulchritudinous, fair, good-looking, handsome, pretty, comely, bonny, lovely

**beautiful** ♦ very pleasing or delightful to look at *Syn* lovely, handsome, pretty, bonny, comely, fair, beauteous, pulchritudinous, good-looking *Ant* ugly

**beautify** *Syn* ADORN, embellish, deck, bedeck, ornament, decorate, garnish *Ant* uglify

**because** ♦ for the reason that *Syn* for, since, as, inasmuch as

**becloud** *Syn* OBSCURE, cloud, eclipse, fog, befog, dim, bedim, darken, obfuscate

**bedeck** *Syn* ADORN, deck, garnish, embellish, beautify, decorate, ornament

**bedim** *Syn* OBSCURE, dim, eclipse, cloud, becloud, fog, befog, obfuscate, darken

**beetle** *Syn* BULGE, overhang, jut, project, protrude, stick out

**befall** *Syn* HAPPEN, betide, occur, chance, transpire

**befog** *Syn* OBSCURE, fog, cloud, becloud, eclipse, darken, dim, bedim, obfuscate

**befool** *Syn* DUPE, trick, hoax, hoodwink, gull, bamboozle

**before** ♦ in advance, especially in place or in time *Syn* ahead, forward *Ant* after

**beforehand** *Syn* EARLY, betimes, soon *Ant* behindhand

**befoul** *Syn* SOIL, foul, dirty, sully, smirch, besmirch, grime, begrime, tarnish

**befuddle** *Syn* CONFUSE, fuddle, addle, muddle *Ant* clarify, clear

**beg** ♦ to ask or request urgently *Syn* entreat, beseech, implore, supplicate, adjure, importune

**beget** *Syn* GENERATE, get, sire, procreate, engender, breed, propagate, reproduce

**beggarly** *Syn* CONTEMPTIBLE, cheap, scurvy, shabby, sorry, despicable, pitiable

**begin** ♦ to take the first step in a course, process, or operation *Syn* commence, start, initiate, inaugurate *Ant* end

**beginning** *n* ♦ the first part or stage of a process or development *Syn* genesis, rise, initiation

**beginning** *adj Syn* ELEMENTARY, basal, elemental, rudimentary

**begrime** *Syn* SOIL, grime, smirch, besmirch, dirty, sully, foul, befoul, tarnish

**begrudge** *Syn* COVET, envy, grudge

**beguile 1** *Syn* DECEIVE, delude, mislead, betray, double-cross **2** *Syn* WHILE, wile, beguile, fleet

**behave 1** ♦ to act or to cause oneself to do something in a certain way *Syn* conduct, comport, demean, deport, acquit, quit *Ant* misbehave **2** *Syn* ACT, react, operate, work, function

**behavior** ♦ one's actions in general or on a particular occasion *Syn* conduct, deportment

**behest** *Syn* COMMAND, bidding, dictate, injunction, order, mandate

**behind** *Syn* AFTER *Ant* ahead

**behindhand** *Syn* TARDY, late, overdue *Ant* beforehand

**behold** *Syn* SEE, view, survey, observe, descry, espy, notice, perceive, discern, remark, note, contemplate

**beholder** *Syn* SPECTATOR, onlooker, looker-on, observer, witness, eyewitness, bystander, kibitzer

**being 1** *Syn* EXISTENCE, actuality *Ant* becoming; nonbeing **2** *Syn* ENTITY, creature, individual, person

**belabor** *Syn* BEAT, pound, pummel, thrash, buffet, baste

**belch** ♦ to eject (gas) from the stomach by way of the mouth or matter from a containing cavity by way of an opening *Syn* burp, vomit, disgorge, regurgitate, spew, throw up

**beleaguer** *Syn* BESIEGE, invest, blockade

**belie** *Syn* MISREPRESENT, falsify, garble *Ant* attest

**belief 1** ♦ the act of one who assents intellectually to something proposed or offered for acceptance as true or the state of mind of one who so assents *Syn* faith, credence, credit *Ant* unbelief, disbelief **2** *Syn* OPINION, conviction, persuasion, view, sentiment

**believable** *Syn* PLAUSIBLE, credible, colorable, specious *Ant* unbelievable

**belittle** *Syn* DECRY, depreciate, disparage, derogate, detract, minimize *Ant* aggrandize, magnify

**bellicose** *Syn* BELLIGERENT, pugnacious, combative, contentious, quarrelsome *Ant* pacific; amicable

**belligerent** ♦ having or taking an aggressive or fighting attitude *Syn* bellicose, pugnacious, combative, quarrelsome, contentious *Ant* friendly

**bellow** *vb Syn* ROAR, bluster, bawl, vociferate, clamor, howl, ululate

**bellow** *n Syn* ROAR, bluster, bawl, vociferation, ululation

**belly** *Syn* ABDOMEN, stomach, paunch, gut

**belong** *Syn* BEAR, pertain, appertain, relate, apply

**belongings** *Syn* POSSESSIONS, effects, means, resources, assets

**below** ♦ in a lower position relative to some other object or place *Syn* under, beneath, underneath *Ant* above

**belt** *Syn* AREA, zone, tract, region

**bemoan** *Syn* DEPLORE, bewail, lament *Ant* exult

**bemuse** *Syn* DAZE, stun, stupefy, benumb, paralyze, petrify

**bend** *Syn* CURVE, twist *Ant* straighten

**beneath** *Syn* BELOW, underneath, under *Ant* above, over

**benefaction** *Syn* DONATION, contribution, alms

**beneficial** ♦ bringing good or gain *Syn* advantageous, profitable *Ant* harmful; detrimental

**benefit** ♦ to do good or to be of advantage to someone *Syn* profit, avail *Ant* harm

**benevolent** *Syn* CHARITABLE, philanthropic, eleemosynary, humanitarian, humane, altruistic *Ant* malevolent

**benign 1** *Syn* KIND, benignant, kindly *Ant* malign **2** *Syn* FAVORABLE, auspicious, propitious *Ant* malign

**benignant** *Syn* KIND, benign, kindly *Ant* malignant

**bent** *Syn* GIFT, turn, talent, aptitude, knack, faculty, genius

**benumb** *Syn* DAZE, stun, bemuse, stupefy, paralyze, petrify

**bequeath** *Syn* WILL, devise, leave, legate

**berate** *Syn* SCOLD, rate, tongue-lash, upbraid, jaw, bawl, chew out, wig, rail, revile, vituperate

**berth 1** *Syn* ROOM, play, elbowroom, leeway, margin, clearance **2** *Syn* WHARF, dock, pier, quay, slip, jetty, levee

**beseech** *Syn* BEG, entreat, implore, supplicate, importune, adjure

**beset** *Syn* INFEST, overrun

**besides** *Syn* ALSO, moreover, furthermore, too, likewise

**besiege** ♦ to surround an enemy in a fortified or strong position so as to prevent ingress or egress *Syn* beleaguer, invest, blockade

**besmirch** *Syn* SOIL, smirch, dirty, sully, foul, befoul, grime, begrime, tarnish *Ant* cleanse

**besotted** *Syn* FOND, infatuated, insensate

**bespangle** *Syn* SPOT, spangle, spatter, sprinkle, mottle, fleck, stipple, marble, speckle

**bespangled** *Syn* SPOTTED, spangled, spattered, sprinkled, mottled, flecked, stippled, marbled, speckled

**bespeak** *Syn* INDICATE, betoken, attest, argue, prove

**bestial** *Syn* BRUTAL, brutish, brute, feral, beastly

**bestow** *Syn* GIVE, confer, present, donate, afford

**bet** ♦ something (as money) staked on a winner-take-all basis on the outcome of an uncertainty *Syn* wager, stake, pot, ante

**bête noire** *Syn* ABOMINATION, bugbear, anathema

**bethink** *Syn* REMEMBER, recollect, remind, recall, reminisce, mind

**betide** *Syn* HAPPEN, befall, chance, occur, transpire

**betimes** *Syn* EARLY, soon, beforehand *Ant* unseasonably, inopportunely

**betoken** *Syn* INDICATE, bespeak, attest, argue, prove

**betray 1** *Syn* DECEIVE, mislead, delude, beguile, double-cross **2** *Syn* REVEAL, discover, disclose, divulge, tell

**better** *adj* ♦ more worthy or more pleasing than another or others *Syn* superior, preferable

**better** *vb Syn* IMPROVE, ameliorate, help *Ant* worsen

**between** ♦ in common to (as in position, in a distribution, or in participation) *Syn* among

**bewail** *Syn* DEPLORE, lament, bemoan *Ant* rejoice

**bewilder** *Syn* PUZZLE, mystify, perplex, distract, confound, nonplus, dumbfound

**bewitch** *Syn* ATTRACT, enchant, captivate, fascinate, charm, allure

**bewitching** *Syn* ATTRACTIVE, enchanting, captivating, fascinating, charming, alluring

**beyond** *Syn* FARTHER further

**bias** *n Syn* PREDILECTION, prejudice, prepossession, partiality

**bias** *vb Syn* INCLINE, dispose, predispose

**bicker** *Syn* QUARREL, squabble, spat, tiff, wrangle, altercate

**bickering** *Syn* QUARREL, spat, tiff, squabble, wrangle, altercation

**bid** *vb* **1** *Syn* COMMAND, order, enjoin, direct, instruct, charge *Ant* forbid **2** *Syn* INVITE, solicit, court, woo

**bid** *n Syn* OVERTURE, tender, advance, approach

**biddable** *Syn* OBEDIENT, docile, amenable, tractable *Ant* willful

**bidding** *Syn* COMMAND, behest, order, injunction, mandate, dictate

**big** *Syn* LARGE, great *Ant* little

**bigot** *Syn* ENTHUSIAST, fanatic, zealot

**bigoted** *Syn* ILLIBERAL, narrow-minded, narrow, intolerant, hidebound

**bill** ♦ the jaws of a bird together with their horny covering *Syn* beak, neb, nib

**billingsgate** *Syn* ABUSE, scurrility, vituperation, invective, obloquy

**bind** *Syn* TIE *Ant* loose; unbind

**biography** ♦ an account of the events and circumstances of a person's life *Syn* life, memoir, autobiography, confessions

**biologic** *Syn* DRUG, simple, medicinal, pharmaceutical

**biotope** *Syn* HABITAT, range, station

**birthright 1** *Syn* RIGHT, appanage, prerogative, privilege, perquisite **2** *Syn* HERITAGE, patrimony, inheritance

**bisexual** ♦ combining male and female qualities *Syn* hermaphroditic, hermaphrodite, androgynous, epicene

**bit** *Syn* PARTICLE, mite, smidgen, whit, atom, iota, jot, tittle

**bite** ♦ to attack with or as if with the teeth *Syn* gnaw, champ, gnash

**biting** *Syn* INCISIVE, cutting, crisp, trenchant, clear-cut

**bitter** ♦ having or being an unusually unpleasant flavor or odor *Syn* acrid *Ant* delicious

**bizarre** *Syn* FANTASTIC, grotesque, antic *Ant* chaste; subdued

**blab** *Syn* GOSSIP, tattle

**blackball** *Syn* EXCLUDE, debar, shut out, eliminate, rule out, disbar, suspend

**blackguard** *Syn* VILLAIN, scoundrel, knave, rascal, rogue, scamp, rapscallion, miscreant

**blame** *vb Syn* CRITICIZE, reprehend, reprobate, condemn, denounce, censure

**blame** *n* ♦ responsibility for misdeed or delinquency *Syn* culpability, guilt, fault

**blameworthy** ♦ deserving reproach and punishment for a wrong, sinful, or criminal act, practice, or condition *Syn* guilty, culpable *Ant* blameless

**blanch** *Syn* WHITEN, bleach, decolorize, etiolate

**bland 1** *Syn* SUAVE, smooth, urbane, diplomatic, politic *Ant* brusque **2** *Syn* SOFT, mild, gentle, smooth, balmy, lenient *Ant* pungent, piquant; savory, tasty, palatable

**blandish** *Syn* COAX, wheedle, cajole

**blank** *Syn* EMPTY, void, vacant, vacuous

**blasé** *Syn* SOPHISTICATED, worldly-wise, worldly, disillusioned

**blasphemous** *Syn* IMPIOUS, profane, sacrilegious *Ant* reverent

**blasphemy 1** ♦ impious or irreverent speech *Syn* profanity, swearing, cursing *Ant* adoration **2** *Syn* PROFANATION, desecration, sacrilege

**blast** *n* ♦ severe, sudden, or surprising ruin or injury *Syn* blight, nip

**blast** *vb* ♦ to ruin or to injure severely, suddenly, or surprisingly *Syn* blight, nip

**blatant** *Syn* VOCIFEROUS, clamorous, strident, boisterous, obstreperous *Ant* decorous; reserved

**blaze** *n* ♦ brightly burning light or fire *Syn* flare, flame, glare, glow

**blaze** *vb* ♦ to burn or appear to burn brightly *Syn* flame, flare, glare, glow

**bleach** *Syn* WHITEN, etiolate, decolorize, blanch *Ant* dye

**bleak** *Syn* DISMAL, cheerless, dispiriting, dreary, desolate

**blemish** ♦ an imperfection (as a spot or crack) *Syn* defect, flaw *Ant* immaculateness

**blench** *Syn* RECOIL, quail, shrink, flinch, wince

**blend** *vb* *Syn* MIX, fuse, merge, coalesce, mingle, commingle, amalgamate *Ant* resolve

**blend** *n* *Syn* MIXTURE, admixture, compound, composite, amalgam

**blessed** *Syn* HOLY, sacred, divine, spiritual, religious *Ant* accursed

**blessedness** *Syn* HAPPINESS, beatitude, bliss, felicity *Ant* misery, dolor

**blight** *n* *Syn* BLAST, nip

**blight** *vb* *Syn* BLAST, nip

**blind** *adj* ♦ lacking or deficient in the power to see or to discriminate objects *Syn* sightless, purblind

**blind** *n* ♦ a device that serves as a screen for a window *Syn* shade, shutter

**blink** *Syn* WINK

**bliss** *Syn* HAPPINESS, beatitude, blessedness, felicity *Ant* anguish; bale

**blithe** *Syn* MERRY, jocund, jovial, jolly *Ant* morose; atrabilious

**bloc** *Syn* COMBINATION, party, faction, ring, combine

**block** *Syn* HINDER, obstruct, bar, dam, impede

**blockade** *n* ♦ the isolation of an enemy area by a belligerent force to prevent the passage of persons or supplies *Syn* siege

**blockade** *vb* *Syn* BESIEGE, beleaguer, invest

**bloodless** *Syn* PALE, anemic *Ant* sanguine; plethoric

**bloody** ♦ affected by or involving the shedding of blood *Syn* sanguinary, sanguine, sanguineous, gory

**bloom** *n* *Syn* BLOSSOM, flower, blow

**bloom** *vb* *Syn* BLOSSOM, flower, blow

**blossom** *n* ♦ the period or state of florescence of a seed plant *Syn* flower, bloom, blow

**blossom** *vb* ♦ to become florescent *Syn* bloom, flower, blow

**blot** *n* *Syn* STIGMA, brand, stain

**blot out** *Syn* ERASE, delete, obliterate, expunge, cancel, efface

**blow** *vb* *Syn* BLOSSOM, bloom, flower

**blow** *n* *Syn* BLOSSOM, bloom, flower

**blowsy** *Syn* SLATTERNLY, frowzy, dowdy *Ant* smart, spruce; dainty

**blubber** *Syn* CRY, weep, wail, keen, whimper

**bluejacket** *Syn* MARINER, sailor, seaman, tar, gob

**blueprint** *n* *Syn* SKETCH, draft, tracing, plot, diagram, delineation, outline

**blueprint** *vb* *Syn* SKETCH, draft, trace, plot, diagram, delineate, outline

**blues** *Syn* SADNESS, dejection, depression, melancholy, gloom, dumps

**bluff** ♦ abrupt and unceremonious in speech or manner *Syn* blunt, brusque, curt, crusty, gruff *Ant* suave, smooth

**blunder** *Syn* STUMBLE, lurch, flounder, trip, lumber, galumph, lollop, bumble

**blunder** *Syn* ERROR, mistake, bull, howler, boner, slip, lapse, faux pas

**blunt 1** *Syn* DULL, obtuse *Ant* keen, sharp **2** *Syn* BLUFF, brusque, curt, gruff, crusty *Ant* tactful; subtle

**blurb** *Syn* CRITICISM, puff, review, critique

**blush** *vb* ♦ to turn or grow red in the face *Syn* flush

**blush** *n* ♦ reddening of the face *Syn* flush

**bluster** *vb* *Syn* ROAR, bellow, bawl, vociferate, clamor, howl, ululate

**bluster** *n* *Syn* ROAR, bellow, bawl, vociferation, ululation

**board** *Syn* HARBOR, house, lodge, shelter, entertain

**boast** ♦ to give vent in speech to one's pride in oneself or something intimately connected with oneself *Syn* brag, vaunt, crow, gasconade *Ant* depreciate (*oneself, one's accomplishments*)

**boat** ♦ a floating structure designed to carry persons or goods over water *Syn* vessel, ship, craft

**bodily** ♦ of or relating to the human body *Syn* physical, corporeal, corporal, somatic

**body** ♦ the dead physical substance of a human being or animal *Syn* corpse, carcass, cadaver

**boggle** *Syn* DEMUR, stickle, stick, strain, scruple, balk, jib, shy *Ant* subscribe (*to*)

**bogus** *Syn* COUNTERFEIT, spurious, fake, sham, pseudo, pinchbeck, phony

**boil** *n* *Syn* ABSCESS, furuncle, carbuncle, pimple, pustule

**boil** *vb* ♦ to prepare (as food) in a liquid heated to the point where it emits considerable steam *Syn* seethe, simmer, parboil, stew

**boisterous** *Syn* VOCIFEROUS, obstreperous, clamorous, blatant, strident

**bold** *Syn* BRAVE, courageous, unafraid, fearless, intrepid, valiant, valorous, dauntless, undaunted, doughty, audacious *Ant* cowardly

**bolster** *Syn* SUPPORT, prop, sustain, buttress, brace

**bombard** *Syn* ATTACK, assail, storm, assault

**bombast** ♦ speech or writing characterized by high-flown pomposity or pretentiousness of language disproportionate to the thought or subject matter *Syn* rhapsody, rant, fustian, rodomontade

**bombastic** *Syn* RHETORICAL, grandiloquent, magniloquent, aureate, flowery, euphuistic

**bona fide** *Syn* AUTHENTIC, genuine, veritable *Ant* counterfeit, bogus

**bond** *adj* *Syn* BOUND, indentured, articled *Ant* free

**bond** *n* **1** ♦ something which serves to bind or bring two or more things firmly together *Syn* band, tie **2** *Syn* GUARANTEE, surety, security, bail, guaranty

**bondage** *Syn* SERVITUDE, slavery

**boner** *Syn* ERROR, blunder, mistake, howler, bull, slip, lapse, faux pas

**bonny** *Syn* BEAUTIFUL, comely, pretty, good-looking, fair, lovely, handsome, beauteous, pulchritudinous *Ant* homely

**bonus** *Syn* PREMIUM, bounty, reward, guerdon, award, prize, meed

**bon vivant** *Syn* EPICURE, gastronome, gourmet, gourmand, glutton *Ant* ascetic

**bookish** *Syn* PEDANTIC, academic, scholastic

**boon** *Syn* GIFT, favor, present, gratuity, largess *Ant* calamity

**boor** ♦ an uncouth ungainly person *Syn* churl, lout, clown, clodhopper, bumpkin, hick, yokel, rube *Ant* gentleman

**boorish** ♦ uncouth in manners, or appearance *Syn* loutish, clownish, churlish *Ant* gentlemanly

**boost** *Syn* LIFT, raise, elevate, hoist, rear, heave

**bootleg** *Syn* SMUGGLED, contraband

**bootless** *Syn* FUTILE, fruitless, vain, abortive

**bootlicker** *Syn* PARASITE, sycophant, toady, lickspittle, hanger-on, favorite, leech, sponge, sponger

**booty** *Syn* SPOIL, loot, plunder, prize, swag

**border** ♦ the line or relatively narrow space which marks the limit or outermost bound of something *Syn* margin, verge, edge, rim, brim, brink

**bore** *Syn* PERFORATE, drill, puncture, punch, prick

**boredom** *Syn* TEDIUM, ennui, doldrums

**boring** *Syn* IRKSOME, tiresome, wearisome, tedious

**botch** ♦ to handle or treat awkwardly or unskillfully *Syn* bungle, fumble, muff, cobble

**bother** *Syn* ANNOY, vex, irk *Ant* comfort

**bottom** *Syn* BASE, found, ground, stay, rest

**bough** *Syn* SHOOT, branch, limb

**bounce** *Syn* DISMISS, drop, sack, fire, discharge, cashier

**bound** *n* *Syn* LIMIT, confine, end, term

**bound** *adj* ♦ obliged to serve a master or in a clearly defined capacity for a certain number of years by the terms of a contract or mutual agreement *Syn* bond, indentured, articled

**bound** *n* *Syn* JUMP, leap, spring, vault

**bound** *vb* **1** *Syn* JUMP, leap, spring, vault **2** *Syn* SKIP, ricochet, hop, curve, lope, lollop

**bounder** *Syn* CAD, rotter

**boundless** *Syn* INFINITE, uncircumscribed, illimitable, eternal, sempiternal

**bountiful, bounteous** *Syn* LIBERAL, generous, openhanded, munificent, handsome *Ant* niggardly

**bounty** *Syn* PREMIUM, award, reward, meed, guerdon, prize, bonus

**bouquet** *Syn* FRAGRANCE, perfume, redolence, incense

**bout** *Syn* SPELL, stint, turn, trick, tour, shift, go

**bow** *vb* *Syn* YIELD, defer, submit, capitulate, succumb, relent, cave

**bow** *n* *Syn* CURVE, arc, arch

**bow** *vb* *Syn* FLEX, crook, buckle

**box** *Syn* STRIKE, hit, smite, punch, slug, slog, swat, clout, slap, cuff

**boyish** *Syn* YOUTHFUL, juvenile, puerile, maiden, virgin, virginal

**brace** *n* *Syn* COUPLE, pair, yoke

**brace** *vb* *Syn* SUPPORT, sustain, buttress, prop, bolster

**brag** *Syn* BOAST, vaunt, crow, gasconade *Ant* apologize

**braid** *Syn* WEAVE, plait, knit, crochet, tat

**brain** *Syn* MIND, intellect, intelligence, wit, psyche, soul

**branch** *Syn* SHOOT, limb, bough

**brand** *n* **1** *Syn* MARK, stamp, label, tag, ticket **2** *Syn* STIGMA, blot, stain

**brand** *vb* *Syn* MARK, stamp, label, tag, ticket

**brandish** *Syn* SWING, flourish, shake, wave, trash

**brash** *Syn* SHAMELESS, brazen, barefaced, impudent *Ant* wary

**brave** *adj* ♦ having or showing no fear when faced with something dangerous, difficult, or unknown *Syn* courageous, unafraid, fearless, intrepid, valiant, valorous, dauntless, undaunted, doughty, bold, audacious *Ant* craven

**brave** *vb* *Syn* FACE, dare, defy, beard, challenge

**bravo** *Syn* ASSASSIN, cutthroat, gunman

**brawl** ♦ a noisy fight or quarrel *Syn* broil, fracas, melee, row, rumpus, scrap

**brawny** *Syn* MUSCULAR, burly, husky, sinewy, athletic *Ant* scrawny

**brazen** *Syn* SHAMELESS, brash, impudent *Ant* bashful

**breach 1** ♦ the act or the offense of failing to keep the law or to do what the law, duty, or obligation requires *Syn* infraction, violation, transgression, trespass, infringement, contravention *Ant* observance **2** ♦ a pulling apart in relations or in connections *Syn* break, split, schism, rent, rupture, rift

**bread, bread and butter** *Syn* LIVING, sustenance, livelihood, subsistence, maintenance, support, keep

**break** *vb* ♦ to come apart or cause to come apart *Syn* crack, burst, bust, snap, shatter, shiver *Ant* cleave (*together*); keep (*of laws*)

**break** *n* **1** ♦ a lapse in continuity *Syn* gap, interruption, interval, interim, hiatus, lacuna **2** *Syn* BREACH, split, schism, rent, rupture, rift **3** *Syn* OPPORTUNITY, chance, occasion, time

**break down** *Syn* ANALYZE, resolve, dissect

**breakdown** *Syn* ANALYSIS, resolution, dissection

**breastwork** *Syn* BULWARK, bastion, parapet, rampart

**breed** *vb Syn* GENERATE, engender, propagate, reproduce, procreate, beget, sire, get

**breed** *n Syn* VARIETY, subspecies, race, cultivar, strain, clone, stock

**breeding** *Syn* CULTURE, cultivation, refinement *Ant* vulgarity

**breeze** *Syn* WIND, gale, hurricane, zephyr

**bridle** **1** *Syn* RESTRAIN, check, curb, inhibit *Ant* vent **2** *Syn* STRUT, bristle, swagger

**brief** *adj* ♦ not long *Syn* short *Ant* prolonged, protracted

**brief** *n Syn* ABRIDGMENT, abstract, epitome, synopsis, conspectus

**bright** **1** ♦ actually or seemingly shining or glowing with light *Syn* brilliant, radiant, luminous, lustrous, effulgent, refulgent, beaming, lambent, lucent, incandescent *Ant* dull; dim **2** *Syn* INTELLIGENT, smart, quick-witted, brilliant, clever, knowing, alert *Ant* dense, dull

**brilliant** **1** *Syn* BRIGHT, radiant, luminous, effulgent, lustrous, refulgent, beaming, lambent, lucent, incandescent *Ant* subdued (*of light, color*) **2** *Syn* INTELLIGENT, clever, bright, smart, alert, quick-witted, knowing *Ant* crass

**brim** *Syn* BORDER, rim, edge, brink, verge, margin

**bring** ♦ to convey from one place to another *Syn* take, fetch *Ant* withdraw, remove

**brink** *Syn* BORDER, rim, brim, verge, edge, margin

**brisk** *Syn* AGILE, nimble, spry *Ant* sluggish

**bristle** *Syn* STRUT, bridle, swagger

**brittle** *Syn* FRAGILE, crisp, frangible, short, friable *Ant* supple

**broach** *Syn* EXPRESS, voice, utter, vent, air, ventilate

**broad** ♦ having horizontal extent *Syn* wide, deep *Ant* narrow

**broadcast** **1** *Syn* STREW, straw, scatter, sow **2** *Syn* DECLARE, promulgate, publish, advertise, announce, proclaim

**broadcasting** *Syn* DECLARATION, promulgation, publication, advertisement, announcement, proclamation

**Brobdingnagian** *Syn* HUGE, vast, immense, enormous, elephantine, mammoth, giant, gigantic, gigantean, colossal, gargantuan, Herculean, cyclopean, titanic *Ant* lilliputian

**broil** *Syn* BRAWL, fracas, melee, row, rumpus, scrap

**bromide** *Syn* COMMONPLACE, cliché, platitude, truism

**brook** *Syn* BEAR, stand, abide, tolerate, suffer, endure

**browbeat** *Syn* INTIMIDATE, bulldoze, bully, cow

**bruise** *vb Syn* CRUSH, mash, smash, squash, macerate

**bruise** *n Syn* WOUND, contusion, trauma, traumatism, lesion

**brush** *vb* ♦ to touch lightly in passing *Syn* graze, glance, shave, skim

**brush** *n Syn* ENCOUNTER, skirmish

**brusque** *Syn* BLUFF, curt, blunt, gruff, crusty *Ant* unctuous; bland

**brutal** ♦ characteristic of an animal in nature, action, or instinct *Syn* brute, brutish, bestial, beastly, feral

**brute** *Syn* BRUTAL, brutish, bestial, beastly, feral

**brutish** *Syn* BRUTAL, brute, bestial, beastly, feral

**buccaneer** *Syn* PIRATE, freebooter, privateer, corsair

**buck** *Syn* FOP, dude, dandy, beau, coxcomb, exquisite

**buckle** *Syn* FLEX, crook, bow

**bucolic** *Syn* RURAL, pastoral, rustic *Ant* urbane

**buffet** *Syn* BEAT, baste, pummel, pound, belabor, thrash

**bugbear** *Syn* ABOMINATION, bête noire, anathema

**build** *vb* ♦ to form or fashion a structure or something comparable to a structure *Syn* construct, erect, frame, raise, rear *Ant* unbuild, destroy

**build** *n Syn* PHYSIQUE, habit, constitution

**building** ♦ a construction (as of wood, brick, or stone) intended to house a family, a business, or an institution *Syn* edifice, structure, pile

**bulge** *vb* ♦ to extend outward beyond the usual and normal line *Syn* jut, stick out, protrude, project, overhang, beetle

**bulge** *n Syn* PROJECTION, protuberance, protrusion

**bulk** ♦ a body of usually material substance that constitutes a thing or unit *Syn* mass, volume

**bulky** *Syn* MASSIVE, massy, monumental, substantial

**bull** **1** *Syn* ERROR, blunder, howler, boner, mistake, slip, lapse, faux pas **2** *Syn* NONSENSE, twaddle, drivel, bunk, balderdash, poppycock, gobbledygook, trash, rot

**bulldoze** *Syn* INTIMIDATE, bully, browbeat, cow

**bullheaded** *Syn* OBSTINATE, pigheaded, stiffnecked, stubborn, mulish, dogged, pertinacious

**bully** *Syn* INTIMIDATE, bulldoze, browbeat, cow *Ant* coax

**bulwark** ♦ an aboveground defensive structure that forms part of a fortification *Syn* breastwork, rampart, parapet, bastion

**bum** *Syn* VAGABOND, vagrant, tramp, hobo, truant

**bumble** *Syn* STUMBLE, trip, blunder, lurch, flounder, lumber, galumph, lollop

**bump** ♦ to come or cause to come into violent contact or close or direct opposition *Syn* clash, collide, conflict

**bumpkin** *Syn* BOOR, hick, yokel, rube, clodhopper, clown, lout, churl

**bunch** **1** *Syn* GROUP, cluster, parcel, lot **2** *Syn* BUNDLE, bale, parcel, pack, package, packet

**bundle** ♦ things done up for storage, sale, or carriage *Syn* bunch, bale, parcel, pack, package, packet

**bungle** *Syn* BOTCH, fumble, muff, cobble

**bunk** *Syn* NONSENSE, twaddle, drivel, balderdash, poppycock, gobbledygook, trash, rot, bull

**buoyant** *Syn* ELASTIC, volatile, expansive, resilient, effervescent *Ant* depressed, dejected

**burden** *n Syn* LOAD, cargo, freight, lading

**burden** *vb* ♦ to lay a heavy load upon or to lie like a heavy load upon a person or thing *Syn* encumber, cumber, weigh, weight, load, lade, tax, charge, saddle

**burden** *n Syn* SUBSTANCE, purport, gist, core, pith

**burdensome** *Syn* ONEROUS, oppressive, exacting *Ant* light

**burglar** *Syn* THIEF, robber, larcener, larcenist

**burglarize** *Syn* ROB, plunder, rifle, loot

**burglary** *Syn* THEFT, larceny, robbery

**burlesque** *n Syn* CARICATURE, parody, travesty

**burlesque** *vb Syn* CARICATURE, parody, travesty

**burly** *Syn* MUSCULAR, husky, brawny, athletic, sinewy *Ant* lanky, lank

**burn** ♦ to injure by exposure to fire or intense heat *Syn* scorch, char, sear, singe

**burp** *Syn* BELCH, vomit, disgorge, regurgitate, spew, throw up

**burst** *Syn* BREAK, crack, bust, snap, shatter, shiver

**bury** *Syn* HIDE, secrete, cache, conceal, screen, ensconce

**business** **1** *Syn* WORK, occupation, pursuit, calling, employment **2** *Syn* AFFAIR, concern, matter, thing **3** ♦ one of the forms or branches of human endeavor which have for their objective the supplying of commodities *Syn* commerce, trade, industry, traffic

**bust** *Syn* BREAK, crack, burst, snap, shatter, shiver

**bustle** *Syn* STIR, flurry, ado, fuss, pother

**busy** ♦ actively engaged or occupied in work or in accomplishing a purpose or intention *Syn* industrious, diligent, assiduous, sedulous *Ant* idle; unoccupied

**butchery** *Syn* MASSACRE, slaughter, carnage, pogrom

**butt in** *Syn* INTRUDE, obtrude, interlope

**buttress** *n* ♦ auxiliary structures designed to serve as a prop, shore, or support for a wall (as of a building) *Syn* pier, abutment

**buttress** *vb Syn* SUPPORT, sustain, prop, bolster, brace

**buy** ♦ to acquire something for money or an equivalent *Syn* purchase

**by** ♦ using as a means of approach or action *Syn* through, with

**bystander** *Syn* SPECTATOR, onlooker, looker-on, witness, eyewitness, observer, beholder

**byword** *Syn* CATCHWORD, shibboleth, slogan

# C

**cabal** *Syn* PLOT, intrigue, conspiracy, machination

**cabalistic** *Syn* MYSTICAL, anagogic, mystic

**cache** *Syn* HIDE, secrete, bury, conceal, ensconce, screen

**cad** ♦ one who shows himself to be no gentleman *Syn* bounder, rotter

**cadaver** *Syn* BODY, corpse, carcass

**cadaverous** *Syn* HAGGARD, wasted, pinched, worn, careworn *Ant* plump, stout

**cadence** *Syn* RHYTHM, meter

**cage** *Syn* ENCLOSE, envelop, fence, pen, coop, corral, wall

**cajole** *Syn* COAX, wheedle, blandish

**cake** *Syn* HARDEN, solidify, indurate, petrify

**calamitous** *Syn* UNLUCKY, disastrous, ill-starred, ill-fated, unfortunate, luckless, hapless

**calamity** *Syn* DISASTER, catastrophe, cataclysm *Ant* boon

**calculate** ♦ to determine something (as cost, speed, or quantity) by mathematical processes *Syn* compute, estimate, reckon

**calculating** *Syn* CAUTIOUS, circumspect, wary, chary *Ant* reckless, rash

**calculation** *Syn* CAUTION, circumspection, wariness, chariness *Ant* recklessness, rashness

**caliber** *Syn* QUALITY, stature

**call** *vb Syn* SUMMON, summons, cite, convoke, convene, muster

**call** *n Syn* VISIT, visitation

**caller** *Syn* VISITOR, visitant, guest

**calling** *Syn* WORK, occupation, pursuit, business, employment

**callous** *Syn* HARDENED, indurated *Ant* tender

**callow** *Syn* RUDE, green, crude, raw, rough, uncouth *Ant* full-fledged, grown-up

**calm** *adj* ♦ quiet and free from all that disturbs or excites *Syn* tranquil, serene, placid, peaceful, halcyon *Ant* stormy; agitated

**calm** *vb* ♦ to relieve or to bring to an end whatever distresses, agitates, or disturbs *Syn* compose, quiet, quieten, still, lull, soothe, settle, tranquilize *Ant* agitate, arouse

**calumniate** *Syn* MALIGN, defame, slander, asperse, traduce, vilify, libel *Ant* eulogize; vindicate

**calumny** *Syn* DETRACTION, slander, backbiting, scandal *Ant* eulogy; vindication

**camouflage** *Syn* DISGUISE, cloak, mask, dissemble

**canal** *Syn* CHANNEL, conduit, duct, aqueduct

**cancel** *Syn* ERASE, efface, obliterate, expunge, delete, blot out

**candid** *Syn* FRANK, open, plain *Ant* evasive

**candidate** ♦ one who seeks an office, honor, position, or award *Syn* aspirant, nominee, applicant

**canon** *Syn* LAW, precept, regulation, rule, statute, ordinance

**cant** 1 *Syn* DIALECT, jargon, argot, lingo, vernacular, slang, patois 2 *Syn* HYPOCRISY, sanctimony, pharisaism

**canting** *Syn* HYPOCRITICAL, sanctimonious, pharisaical

**capability** *Syn* ABILITY, capacity *Ant* incapability, incompetence

**capable** *Syn* ABLE, competent, qualified *Ant* incapable

**capacious** *Syn* SPACIOUS, commodious, ample *Ant* exiguous

**capacity** *Syn* ABILITY, capability *Ant* incapacity

**caper** *Syn* PRANK, monkeyshine, antic, dido

**capital** *Syn* CHIEF, principal, main, leading, foremost

**capitulate** *Syn* YIELD, submit, succumb, relent, defer, bow, cave

**capitulation** *Syn* SURRENDER, submission

**caprice** ♦ an arbitrary notion that usually lacks a logical basis and therefore may be unsound, impractical, or even irrational *Syn* freak, fancy, whim, whimsy, conceit, vagary, crotchet

**capricious** *Syn* INCONSTANT, mercurial, unstable, fickle *Ant* steadfast

**capsize** *Syn* OVERTURN, upset, overthrow, subvert

**caption** *Syn* INSCRIPTION, legend

**captious** *Syn* CRITICAL, caviling, carping, hypercritical, faultfinding, censorious *Ant* appreciative

**captivate** *Syn* ATTRACT, fascinate, bewitch, enchant, charm, allure *Ant* repulse

**captivating** *Syn* ATTRACTIVE, fascinating, bewitching, enchanting, charming, alluring *Ant* repulsive

**captive** *Syn* PRISONER

**capture** *Syn* CATCH, trap, snare, entrap, ensnare, bag

**carbon copy** *Syn* REPRODUCTION, copy, duplicate, transcript, facsimile, replica

**carbuncle** *Syn* ABSCESS, boil, furuncle, pimple, pustule

**carcass** *Syn* BODY, corpse, cadaver

**cardinal** *Syn* ESSENTIAL, vital, fundamental *Ant* negligible

**care** ♦ a troubled or engrossed state of mind or the thing that causes this *Syn* concern, solicitude, anxiety, worry

**careful** ♦ marked by close attention to details or care in execution or performance *Syn* meticulous, scrupulous, punctilious, punctual *Ant* careless

**careless** ♦ showing lack of concern or attention *Syn* heedless, thoughtless, inadvertent *Ant* careful

**caress** ♦ to show affection or love by touching or handling *Syn* fondle, pet, cosset, cuddle, dandle

**careworn** *Syn* HAGGARD, worn, pinched, wasted, cadaverous *Ant* carefree

**cargo** *Syn* LOAD, burden, freight, lading

**caricature** *n* ♦ a grotesque or bizarre imitation of something *Syn* burlesque, parody, travesty

**caricature** *vb* ♦ to make a grotesque or bizarre imitation of something *Syn* burlesque, parody, travesty

**carnage** *Syn* MASSACRE, slaughter, butchery, pogrom

**carnal** ♦ characterized by physical rather than intellectual or spiritual orientation *Syn* fleshly, sensual, animal *Ant* spiritual; intellectual

**carol** *Syn* SING, toll, descant, warble, trill, hymn, chant, intone

**carping** *Syn* CRITICAL, caviling, faultfinding, captious, hypercritical, censorious *Ant* fulsome

**carry** ♦ to be the agent or the means whereby something or someone is moved from one place to another *Syn* bear, convey, transport, transmit

**cartel** 1 *Syn* CONTRACT, compact, pact, convention, bargain, concordat, treaty, entente 2 *Syn* MONOPOLY, pool, syndicate, corner, trust

**carve** 1 *Syn* CUT, slit, hew, chop, slash 2 ♦ to cut an outline or a shape out of or into some substance *Syn* incise, engrave, etch, chisel, sculpture, sculpt, sculp

**case** 1 *Syn* INSTANCE, illustration, example, specimen, sample 2 *Syn* SUIT, cause, action, lawsuit

**casement** *Syn* WINDOW, dormer, oriel

**cash** *Syn* MONEY, currency, legal tender, specie, coin, coinage

**cashier** *Syn* DISMISS, discharge, drop, fire, sack, bounce

**cast** 1 *Syn* THROW, fling, hurl, pitch, toss, sling 2 *Syn* DISCARD, shed, molt, slough, scrap, junk 3 *Syn* ADD, figure, foot, sum, total, tot

**castaway** *Syn* OUTCAST, derelict, reprobate, pariah, untouchable

**castigate** *Syn* PUNISH, chastise, chasten, discipline, correct

**castrate** *Syn* STERILIZE, spay, emasculate, alter, mutilate, geld

**casual** 1 *Syn* ACCIDENTAL, incidental, contingent, fortuitous 2 *Syn* RANDOM, desultory, haphazard, chancy, hit-or-miss, happy-go-lucky *Ant* deliberate

**casualty** *Syn* ACCIDENT, mishap

**casuistical** *Syn* FALLACIOUS, sophistical

**casuistry** *Syn* FALLACY, sophistry, sophism

**cataclysm** *Syn* DISASTER, catastrophe, calamity

**catalog** *n Syn* LIST, inventory, table, schedule, register, roll, roster

**catalog** *vb Syn* RECORD, register, list, enroll

**cataract** *Syn* FLOOD, deluge, inundation, torrent, spate

**catastrophe** *Syn* DISASTER, calamity, cataclysm

**catch** 1 ♦ to come to possess or control by or as if by seizing *Syn* capture, trap, snare, entrap, ensnare, bag *Ant* miss 2 *Syn* INCUR, contract

**catching** *Syn* INFECTIOUS, contagious, communicable

**catchword** ♦ a phrase that catches the eye or the ear and is repeated so often that it becomes a formula *Syn* byword, shibboleth, slogan

**catechize** *Syn* ASK, interrogate, quiz, examine, question, query, inquire

**categorical** 1 *Syn* ULTIMATE, absolute 2 *Syn* EXPLICIT, express, definite, specific

**category** *Syn* CLASS

**cater** ♦ to furnish with what satisfies the appetite or desires *Syn* purvey, pander

**catholic** *Syn* UNIVERSAL, cosmic, ecumenical, cosmopolitan *Ant* parochial; provincial

**catnap** *Syn* SLEEP, nap, snooze, slumber, drowse, doze

**cause** ♦ that (as a person, fact, or condition) which is responsible for an effect *Syn* determinant, antecedent, reason, occasion 2 *Syn* SUIT, lawsuit, action, cause, case

**caustic** ♦ stingingly incisive *Syn* mordant, acrid, scathing *Ant* genial

**caution** *n* ♦ careful prudence esp. in reducing or avoiding risk or danger *Syn* circumspection, wariness, chariness, calculation *Ant* temerity; adventurousness

**caution** *vb Syn* WARN, forewarn

**cautious** ♦ prudently watchful and discreet in the face of danger or risk *Syn* circumspect, wary, chary, calculating *Ant* adventurous, temerarious

**cavalcade** *Syn* PROCESSION, parade, cortege, motorcade

**cave** *Syn* YIELD, succumb, submit, capitulate, relent, defer, bow

**caviling** *Syn* CRITICAL, captious, faultfinding, censorious, carping, hypercritical

**cavity** *Syn* HOLE, hollow, pocket, void, vacuum

**cease** *Syn* STOP, quit, discontinue, desist

**cease-fire** *Syn* TRUCE, armistice, peace

**cede** *Syn* RELINQUISH, surrender, abandon, waive, resign, yield, leave

**celebrate** *Syn* KEEP, commemorate, solemnize, observe

**celebrated** *Syn* FAMOUS, renowned, famed, eminent, illustrious *Ant* obscure

**celebrity** *Syn* FAME, renown, glory, honor, éclat, reputation, repute, notoriety *Ant* obscurity

**celerity** ♦ quickness in movement or action *Syn* alacrity, legerity *Ant* leisureliness

**celestial** ♦ of, relating to, or fit for heaven or the heavens *Syn* heavenly, empyrean, empyreal *Ant* terrestrial

**celibate** *Syn* UNMARRIED, single, virgin, maiden

**cenobite** *Syn* RECLUSE, eremite, hermit, anchorite

**censorious** *Syn* CRITICAL, faultfinding, hypercritical, captious, carping, caviling *Ant* eulogistic

**censure** *Syn* CRITICIZE, reprehend, blame, condemn, denounce, reprobate *Ant* commend

**center** *n* ♦ the point, spot, or portion of a thing which is comparable to a point around which a circle is described *Syn* middle, midst, core, hub, focus, nucleus, heart

**center** *vb* ♦ to draw to or fix upon a center *Syn* focus, centralize, concentrate

**central** ♦ dominant or most important *Syn* focal, pivotal

**centralize** *Syn* CENTER, focus, concentrate

**cerebral** *Syn* MENTAL, intellectual, psychic, intelligent

**ceremonial** *adj* ♦ characterized or marked by attention to the forms, procedures, and details prescribed as right, proper, or requisite *Syn* ceremonious, formal, conventional, solemn

**ceremonial** *n Syn* FORM, ceremony, ritual, rite, liturgy, formality

**ceremonious** *Syn* CEREMONIAL, formal, solemn, conventional *Ant* unceremonious, informal

**ceremony** *Syn* FORM, ceremonial, ritual, liturgy, rite, formality

**certain** 1 *Syn* SURE, positive, cocksure *Ant* uncertain 2 ♦ bound to follow in obedience to the laws of nature or of thought *Syn* inevitable, necessary *Ant* probable; supposed

**certainty** ♦ a state of mind in which one is free from doubt *Syn* certitude, assurance, conviction *Ant* uncertainty

**certify** 1 ♦ to testify to the truth or genuineness of something *Syn* attest, witness, vouch 2 *Syn* APPROVE, endorse, accredit, sanction

**certitude** *Syn* CERTAINTY, assurance, conviction *Ant* doubt

**chafe** *Syn* ABRADE, excoriate, fret, gall

**chaff** *Syn* BANTER, kid, rag, jolly, rib, josh

**chagrined** *Syn* ASHAMED, mortified

**chain** *Syn* SUCCESSION, series, train, string, sequence, progression

**challenge** *Syn* FACE, brave, dare, defy, beard

**chamber** *Syn* ROOM, apartment

**champ** *Syn* BITE, gnaw, gnash

**champion** *n Syn* VICTOR, vanquisher, winner, conqueror

**champion** *vb Syn* SUPPORT, back, advocate, uphold *Ant* combat

**chance** *n* 1 ♦ something that happens without an apparent or determinable cause or as a result of unpredictable forces *Syn* accident, fortune, luck, hap, hazard *Ant* law, principle 2 *Syn* OPPORTUNITY, occasion, break, time

**chance** *vb* 1 *Syn* HAPPEN, befall, betide, occur, transpire 2 *Syn* VENTURE, hazard, risk, jeopardize, endanger, imperil

**chance** *adj Syn* RANDOM, haphazard, chancy, casual, desultory, hit-or-miss, happy-go-lucky

**chancy** *Syn* RANDOM, haphazard, chance, hit-or-miss, happy-go-lucky, casual, desultory

**change** *vb* ♦ to make or become different *Syn* alter, vary, modify

**change** *n* 1 ♦ a making different *Syn* alteration, variation, modification *Ant* uniformity; monotony 2 ♦ a result of a making different *Syn* mutation, permutation, vicissitude, alternation

**changeable** ♦ having or showing a marked capacity for changes or a marked tendency to alter under slight provocation **Syn** changeful, variable, mutable, protean **Ant** stable; unchangeable

**changeful** **Syn** CHANGEABLE, variable, protean, mutable **Ant** changeless; stereotyped

**channel 1 Syn** STRAIT, passage, narrows, sound **2** ♦ something through which a fluid (as water) is led or flows **Syn** canal, conduit, duct, aqueduct **3 Syn** MEAN, vehicle, instrument, instrumentality, organ, agency, agent, medium

**chant** **Syn** SING, troll, carol, descant, warble, trill, hymn, intone

**chaos 1 Syn** CONFUSION, disorder, disarray, jumble, clutter, snarl, muddle **Ant** system **2 Syn** ANARCHY, lawlessness

**chaperone** **Syn** ACCOMPANY, attend, escort, convoy, conduct

**char** **Syn** BURN, scorch, sear, singe

**character 1** ♦ an arbitrary or conventional device that is used in writing and in printing, but is neither a word nor a phrase nor a picture **Syn** symbol, sign, mark **2 Syn** QUALITY, property, attribute, accident **3 Syn** DISPOSITION, individuality, personality, complexion, temperament, temper **4 Syn** TYPE, nature, description, kind, ilk, sort, stripe, kidney **5 Syn** CREDENTIAL, reference, recommendation, testimonial

**characteristic** adj ♦ being or revealing a quality specific or identifying to an individual or group **Syn** individual, peculiar, distinctive

**characteristic** n ♦ something that marks or sets apart a person or thing **Syn** trait, feature

**characterize** ♦ to be a peculiar or significant quality or feature of something **Syn** distinguish, mark, qualify

**charge** vb **1 Syn** BURDEN, encumber, cumber, weigh, weight, load, lade, tax, saddle **2 Syn** COMMAND, direct, instruct, bid, enjoin, order **3 Syn** ACCUSE, incriminate, indict, impeach, arraign **Ant** absolve **4 Syn** ASCRIBE, attribute, impute, assign, refer, credit, accredit **5 Syn** RUSH, dash, tear, shoot

**charge** n **Syn** PRICE, cost, expense

**chargé d'affaires** **Syn** AMBASSADOR, legate, nuncio, minister, envoy, internuncio

**chariness** **Syn** CAUTION, circumspection, wariness, calculation

**charitable** ♦ having or showing interest in or being concerned with the welfare of others **Syn** benevolent, humane, humanitarian, philanthropic, eleemosynary, altruistic **Ant** uncharitable

**charity 1 Syn** MERCY, clemency, grace, lenity **Ant** malice, ill will **2** ♦ love for one's fellowmen and a disposition to help those who are in need **Syn** philanthropy

**charlatan** **Syn** IMPOSTOR, mountebank, quack, faker

**charm** n **Syn** FETISH, talisman, amulet

**charm** vb **Syn** ATTRACT, fascinate, allure, captivate, enchant, bewitch **Ant** disgust

**charming** **Syn** ATTRACTIVE, fascinating, alluring, captivating, enchanting, bewitching **Ant** forbidding

**chart** n ♦ a stylized or symbolic depiction of something incapable of direct verbal or pictorial representation **Syn** map, graph

**chart** vb ♦ to make a representation of something with a chart **Syn** map, graph

**charter** **Syn** HIRE, let, lease, rent

**chary** **Syn** CAUTIOUS, circumspect, wary, calculating

**chase** **Syn** FOLLOW, pursue, trail, tag, tail

**chasm** **Syn** GULF, abyss, abysm

**chaste** ♦ free from all taint of what is lewd or salacious **Syn** pure, modest, decent **Ant** lewd, wanton, immoral; bizarre (of style, effect)

**chasten** **Syn** PUNISH, discipline, correct, chastise, castigate **Ant** pamper, mollycoddle

**chastise** **Syn** PUNISH, discipline, correct, castigate, chasten

**chat** ♦ to emit a loose and ready flow of inconsequential talk **Syn** gab, chatter, patter, prate, prattle, babble, gabble, jabber, gibber

**chatter** **Syn** CHAT, gab, patter, prate, babble, gabble, jabber, gibber

**cheap** **Syn** CONTEMPTIBLE, beggarly, shabby, pitiable, sorry, despicable, scurvy **Ant** noble

**cheat** n **Syn** IMPOSTURE, fraud, fake, deceit, deception, counterfeit, sham, humbug

**cheat** vb ♦ to obtain something and esp. money or valuables from or an advantage over another by dishonesty and trickery **Syn** cozen, defraud, swindle, overreach

**check** n **Syn** CORRECTIVE, control, antidote

**check** vb **1 Syn** ARREST, interrupt **2 Syn** RESTRAIN, bridle, curb, inhibit **Ant** accelerate (of speed); advance (of movements, plans, hopes); release (of feelings, energies)

**checked, checkered** **Syn** VARIEGATED, particolored, motley, pied, piebald, skewbald, dappled, freaked

**cheek** **Syn** TEMERITY, nerve, effrontery, hardihood, gall, audacity **Ant** diffidence

**cheep** vb **Syn** CHIRP, chirrup, peep, tweet, twitter, chitter

**cheep** n **Syn** CHIRP, chirrup, peep, tweet, twitter, chitter

**cheer 1 Syn** ENCOURAGE, inspirit, hearten, embolden, nerve, steel **Ant** deject; dismay **2 Syn** APPLAUD, root

**cheerful** **Syn** GLAD, lighthearted, joyful, joyous, happy **Ant** glum, gloomy

**cheerless** **Syn** DISMAL, dreary, dispiriting, bleak, desolate **Ant** cheerful

**cheeseparing** **Syn** STINGY, close, closefisted, tight, tightfisted, niggardly, penny-pinching, parsimonious, penurious, miserly

**chemist** **Syn** DRUGGIST, apothecary, pharmacist

**cherish 1 Syn** APPRECIATE, prize, treasure, value **Ant** neglect **2 Syn** NURSE, foster, nurture, cultivate **Ant** abandon

**chew out** **Syn** SCOLD, upbraid, rate, berate, tonguelash, jaw, bawl, wig, rail, revile, vituperate

**chic** **Syn** STYLISH, smart, fashionable, modish, dashing

**chicane, chicanery** **Syn** DECEPTION, trickery, double-dealing, fraud

**chide** **Syn** REPROVE, reproach, rebuke, reprimand, admonish **Ant** commend

**chief** n ♦ the person in whom resides authority or ruling power **Syn** chieftain, head, headman, leader, master

**chief** adj ♦ first in importance or in standing **Syn** principal, main, leading, foremost, capital **Ant** subordinate

**chiefly** **Syn** LARGELY, greatly, mostly, mainly, principally, generally

**chieftain** **Syn** CHIEF, head, leader, master

**childish** **Syn** CHILDLIKE **Ant** mature, grown-up

**childlike** ♦ having or showing the manner, spirit, or disposition of a child **Syn** childish

**chilly** **Syn** COLD, cool, frigid, freezing, frosty, gelid, icy, glacial, arctic **Ant** balmy

**chimerical** **Syn** IMAGINARY, fantastic, fanciful, visionary, quixotic **Ant** feasible

**chine** **Syn** SPINE, backbone, back, vertebrae

**chink** **Syn** CRACK, cleft, fissure, crevasse, crevice, cranny

**chirp** vb ♦ to make a short, sharp, and usu. repetitive sound **Syn** chirrup, cheep, peep, tweet, twitter, chitter

**chirp** n ♦ the little sounds characteristic of small animals or sounds that suggest such small animal sounds **Syn** chirrup, cheep, peep, tweet, twitter, chitter

**chirrup** vb **Syn** CHIRP, cheep, peep, tweet, twitter, chitter

**chirrup** n **Syn** CHIRP, cheep, peep, tweet, twitter, chitter

**chisel** **Syn** CARVE, sculpture, sculpt, sculp, incise, engrave, etch

**chitter** vb **Syn** CHIRP, chirrup, cheep, peep, tweet, twitter

**chitter** n **Syn** CHIRP, chirrup, cheep, peep, tweet, twitter

**chivalrous** **Syn** CIVIL, gallant, courtly, courteous, polite **Ant** churlish

**chivy** **Syn** BAIT, badger, heckle, hector, hound, ride

**choice** n ♦ the act or opportunity of choosing or the thing chosen **Syn** option, alternative, preference, selection, election

**choice** adj ♦ having qualities that appeal to a fine or highly refined taste **Syn** exquisite, elegant, recherché, rare, dainty, delicate **Ant** indifferent; medium

**choke** **Syn** SUFFOCATE, asphyxiate, stifle, smother, strangle, throttle

**choleric** **Syn** IRASCIBLE, splenetic, testy, touchy, cranky, cross **Ant** placid; imperturbable

**choose** ♦ to fix upon one of a number of things as the one to be taken, accepted, or adopted **Syn** select, elect, opt, pick, cull, prefer, single **Ant** reject; eschew

**chop** **Syn** CUT, hew, slit, slash, carve

**chore** **Syn** TASK, duty, assignment, job, stint

**christen** **Syn** BAPTIZE

**chronic** **Syn** INVETERATE, confirmed, deep-seated, deep-rooted **Ant** acute (of illness)

**chronicle 1 Syn** HISTORY, annals **2 Syn** ACCOUNT, story, report, version

**chthonic, chthonian** **Syn** INFERNAL, Hadean, stygian, hellish, Tartarean

**chubby** **Syn** FLESHY, rotund, plump, fat, stout, portly, corpulent, obese **Ant** slim

**chummy** **Syn** FAMILIAR, intimate, close, thick, confidential

**chunky** **Syn** STOCKY, thickset, thick, stubby, squat, dumpy

**church** **Syn** RELIGION, denomination, sect, communion, creed, faith, cult, persuasion

**churl** **Syn** BOOR, lout, clown, clodhopper, bumpkin, hick, yokel, rube

**churlish** **Syn** BOORISH, loutish, clownish **Ant** courtly

**cinders** **Syn** ASH, clinkers, embers

**circadian** **Syn** DAILY, diurnal, quotidian

**circle** n **Syn** SET, coterie, clique

**circle** vb **1 Syn** SURROUND, environ, encircle, encompass, compass, hem, gird, girdle, ring **2 Syn** TURN, revolve, rotate, gyrate, wheel, spin, twirl, whirl, eddy, swirl, pirouette

**circuit** **Syn** CIRCUMFERENCE, compass, perimeter, periphery

**circuitous** **Syn** INDIRECT, roundabout **Ant** straight

**circulate** **Syn** SPREAD, disseminate, diffuse, propagate, radiate

**circumference** ♦ a continuous line enclosing an area or space **Syn** perimeter, periphery, circuit, compass

**circumlocution** **Syn** VERBIAGE, periphrasis, pleonasm, redundancy, tautology

**circumscribe** **Syn** LIMIT, confine, restrict **Ant** expand, dilate

**circumspect** **Syn** CAUTIOUS, wary, calculating, chary **Ant** audacious

**circumspection** **Syn** CAUTION, wariness, calculation, chariness **Ant** audacity

**circumstance** **Syn** OCCURRENCE, event, incident, episode

**circumstantial** ♦ dealing with a matter fully and usu. point by point **Syn** minute, particular, particularized, detailed, itemized **Ant** abridged; summary

**circumvent** **Syn** FRUSTRATE, outwit, baffle, balk, thwart, foil **Ant** conform (to laws, orders); cooperate (with persons)

**citadel** **Syn** FORT, stronghold, fortress, fastness

**citation** **Syn** ENCOMIUM, eulogy, tribute, panegyric

**cite 1 Syn** SUMMON, summons, call, convoke, convene, muster **2 Syn** QUOTE, repeat **3 Syn** ADDUCE, advance, allege

**citizen 1 Syn** INHABITANT, resident, denizen **2** ♦ a person who is regarded as a member of a sovereign state, entitled to its protection, and subject to its laws **Syn** subject, national **Ant** alien

**civil** ♦ observant of the forms required by good breeding *Syn* polite, courteous, courtly, gallant, chivalrous *Ant* uncivil, rude

**claim** *vb Syn* DEMAND, exact, require *Ant* disclaim; renounce

**claim** *n* ♦ an actual or alleged right to demand something as one's possession, quality, power, or prerogative *Syn* title, pretension, pretense

**clamor** *n Syn* DIN, uproar, pandemonium, hullabaloo, babel, hubbub, racket

**clamor** *vb Syn* ROAR, bellow, bluster, bawl, vociferate, howl, ululate

**clamorous** *Syn* VOCIFEROUS, blatant, strident, boisterous, obstreperous *Ant* taciturn

**clandestine** *Syn* SECRET, covert, surreptitious, furtive, underhand, underhanded, stealthy *Ant* open

**clash** *vb Syn* BUMP, collide, conflict *Ant* blend

**clash** *n Syn* IMPACT, collision, impingement, shock, concussion, percussion, jar, jolt

**class** *n* ♦ a group including all individuals with a common characteristic *Syn* category

**class** *vb* ♦ to order a number of things according to a scale or to place a thing in its due order *Syn* grade, rank, rate, graduate, gradate

**classify** *Syn* ASSORT, pigeonhole, sort

**clause** *Syn* PARAGRAPH, verse, article, plank, count

**clean** ♦ to remove whatever soils, stains, or contaminates *Syn* cleanse *Ant* soil

**cleanse** *Syn* CLEAN *Ant* defile, besmirch

**clear** *adj* 1 ♦ having the property of being literally or figuratively seen through *Syn* transparent, translucent, lucid, pellucid, diaphanous, limpid *Ant* turbid; confused 2 ♦ quickly and easily understood *Syn* perspicuous, lucid *Ant* unintelligible; abstruse 3 *Syn* EVIDENT, manifest, obvious, distinct, apparent, patent, palpable, plain

**clear** *vb Syn* RID, unburden, disabuse, purge

**clearance** *Syn* ROOM, berth, play, elbowroom, leeway, margin

**clear-cut** *Syn* INCISIVE, trenchant, cutting, biting, crisp

**cleave** *vb Syn* STICK, cling, adhere, cohere *Ant* part

**cleave** *vb Syn* TEAR, split, rive, rend, rip

**cleft** *Syn* CRACK, fissure, crevasse, crevice, cranny, chink

**clemency** 1 *Syn* MERCY, lenity, charity, grace *Ant* harshness 2 *Syn* FORBEARANCE, mercifulness, leniency, indulgence, tolerance

**clement** *Syn* FORBEARING, merciful, lenient, indulgent, tolerant *Ant* harsh; barbarous

**clemently** *Syn* FORBEARINGLY, tolerantly, mercifully, leniently, indulgently

**clever** 1 *Syn* INTELLIGENT, quick-witted, brilliant, bright, smart, alert, knowing *Ant* dull 2 ♦ having or showing a high degree of practical intelligence or skill in contrivance *Syn* adroit, cunning, ingenious

**cliché** *Syn* COMMONPLACE, platitude, truism, bromide

**clientele** *Syn* FOLLOWING, public, audience

**climax** *Syn* SUMMIT, culmination, peak, apex, acme, zenith, apogee, pinnacle, meridian

**climb** *Syn* ASCEND, mount, scale *Ant* descend

**cling** *Syn* STICK, cleave, adhere, cohere

**clinkers** *Syn* ASH, cinders, embers

**clip** *Syn* SHEAR, poll, trim, prune, lop, snip, crop

**clique** *Syn* SET, circle, coterie

**cloak** *Syn* DISGUISE, mask, dissemble, camouflage *Ant* uncloak

**clodhopper** *Syn* BOOR, bumpkin, hick, yokel, rube, lout, clown, churl

**clog** *Syn* HAMPER, fetter, hog-tie, shackle, manacle, trammel *Ant* expedite, facilitate

**cloister** 1 ♦ a place of retirement from the world for members of a religious community *Syn* convent, monastery, nunnery, abbey, priory 2 *Syn* PASSAGE, arcade, passageway, ambulatory, gallery, corridor, aisle, hall, hallway

**clone** *Syn* VARIETY, subspecies, race, breed, cultivar, strain, stock

**close** *vb* 1 ♦ to stop or fill in an opening by means of a closure *Syn* shut *Ant* open 2 ♦ to bring or come to a limit or a natural or appropriate stopping point *Syn* end, conclude, finish, complete, terminate

**close** *adj* 1 ♦ not far (as in place, time, or relationship) from the point, position, or relation that is indicated or understood *Syn* near, nigh, nearby *Ant* remote, remotely 2 ♦ having constituent parts that are massed tightly together *Syn* dense, compact, thick *Ant* open 3 *Syn* SILENT, close-lipped, closemouthed, tight-lipped, secretive, reserved, taciturn, reticent, uncommunicative *Ant* open, frank 4 *Syn* FAMILIAR, intimate, confidential, chummy, thick *Ant* aloof 5 *Syn* STINGY, closefisted, tight, tightfisted, niggardly, parsimonious, penurious, cheeseparing, penny-pinching *Ant* liberal

**closefisted** *Syn* STINGY, close, tight, tightfisted, niggardly, parsimonious, penurious, miserly, cheeseparing, penny-pinching

**close-lipped** *Syn* SILENT, close, closemouthed, uncommunicative, taciturn, reserved, reticent, secretive, tight-lipped

**closemouthed** *Syn* SILENT, close, close-lipped, tight-lipped, reticent, reserved, uncommunicative, taciturn, secretive

**clot** *Syn* COAGULATE, congeal, curdle, set, jelly, jell

**clothe** ♦ to cover with or as if with garments *Syn* attire, dress, apparel, array, robe *Ant* unclothe

**clothes** ♦ a person's garments considered collectively *Syn* clothing, dress, attire, apparel, raiment

**clothing** *Syn* CLOTHES, dress, attire, apparel, raiment

**cloud** *Syn* OBSCURE, dim, bedim, darken, eclipse, becloud, fog, befog, obfuscate

**clout** *Syn* STRIKE, hit, smite, punch, slug, slog, swat, slap, cuff, box

**clown** *Syn* BOOR, clodhopper, lout, bumpkin, hick, yokel, rube, churl

**clownish** *Syn* BOORISH, loutish, churlish *Ant* urbane

**cloy** *Syn* SATIATE, sate, surfeit, pall, glut, gorge

**club** *Syn* ASSOCIATION, society, order

**clumsy** *Syn* AWKWARD, gauche, maladroit, inept *Ant* dexterous, adroit; facile

**cluster** *Syn* GROUP, bunch, parcel, lot

**clutch** *vb Syn* TAKE, grasp, grab, seize, snatch

**clutch** *n Syn* HOLD, grip, grasp

**clutter** *Syn* CONFUSION, disorder, disarray, jumble, chaos, muddle, snarl

**coadjutor** *Syn* ASSISTANT, helper, aid, aide, aide-de-camp

**coagulate** ♦ to alter by chemical reaction from a liquid to a more or less firm jelly *Syn* congeal, set, curdle, clot, jelly, jell

**coalesce** *Syn* MIX, merge, fuse, blend, mingle, commingle, amalgamate

**coalition** *Syn* ALLIANCE, fusion, confederacy, confederation, federation, league

**coarse** ♦ offensive to good taste or morals *Syn* vulgar, gross, obscene, ribald *Ant* fine; refined

**coast** *n Syn* SHORE, strand, beach, bank, foreshore, littoral

**coast** *vb Syn* SLIDE, toboggan, glide, slip, skid, glissade, slither

**coax** ♦ to use ingratiating art in persuading or attempting to persuade *Syn* cajole, wheedle, blandish *Ant* bully

**cobble** *Syn* BOTCH, bungle, fumble, muff

**cock** *vb Syn* HEAP, stack, shock, pile, mass, bank

**cock** *n Syn* HEAP, stack, shock, pile, mass, bank

**cocksure** *Syn* SURE, positive, certain *Ant* dubious, doubtful

**coerce** *Syn* FORCE, compel, constrain, oblige

**coercion** *Syn* FORCE, compulsion, violence, duress, constraint, restraint

**coetaneous** *Syn* CONTEMPORARY, coeval, contemporaneous, synchronous, simultaneous, coincident, concomitant, concurrent

**coeval** *Syn* CONTEMPORARY, coetaneous, synchro-

nous, concurrent, simultaneous, coincident, concomitant, contemporaneous

**cogent** *Syn* VALID, convincing, compelling, telling, sound

**cogitate** *Syn* THINK, reflect, deliberate, reason, speculate

**cognate** *Syn* RELATED, allied, kindred, affiliated

**cognizant** *Syn* AWARE, conscious, sensible, alive, awake *Ant* ignorant

**cohere** *Syn* STICK, adhere, cleave, cling

**coherence** ♦ the quality or character of a whole all of whose parts cohere or stick together *Syn* cohesion *Ant* incoherence

**cohesion** *Syn* COHERENCE

**coil** *Syn* WIND, curl, twist, twine, wreathe, entwine

**coin** *Syn* MONEY, coinage, currency, specie, legal tender, cash

**coinage** *Syn* MONEY, coin, currency, cash, specie, legal tender

**coincide** *Syn* AGREE, concur *Ant* differ

**coincident** *Syn* CONTEMPORARY, synchronous, simultaneous, concurrent, concomitant, coeval, coetaneous, contemporaneous

**cold** ♦ having a temperature below that which is normal or comfortable *Syn* cool, chilly, frigid, freezing, frosty, gelid, icy, glacial, arctic *Ant* hot

**collate** *Syn* COMPARE, contrast

**collateral** *Syn* SUBORDINATE, secondary, dependent, subject, tributary

**collation** *Syn* COMPARISON, parallel, contrast, antithesis

**colleague** *Syn* PARTNER, copartner, ally, confederate

**collect** *Syn* GATHER, assemble, congregate *Ant* disperse; distribute

**collected** *Syn* COOL, composed, unruffled, imperturbable, unflappable, nonchalant *Ant* distracted, distraught

**collection** *Syn* GATHERING, assemblage, assembly, congregation

**collide** *Syn* BUMP, clash, conflict

**collision** *Syn* IMPACT, impingement, clash, shock, concussion, percussion, jar, jolt

**color** 1 ♦ a property or attribute of a visible thing recognizable only when rays of light fall upon it and serving to distinguish things otherwise visually identical (as shape or size) *Syn* hue, shade, tint, tinge, tone 2 *usu pl* colors *Syn* FLAG, ensign, standard, banner, streamer, pennant, pendant, pennon, jack

**colorable** *Syn* PLAUSIBLE, credible, believable, specious

**colorless** ♦ without color *Syn* uncolored, achromatic *Ant* colorful

**colossal** *Syn* HUGE, vast, immense, enormous, elephantine, mammoth, giant, gigantic, gigantean, gargantuan, Herculean, cyclopean, titanic, Brobdingnagian

**column** *Syn* PILLAR, pilaster

**comatose** *Syn* LETHARGIC, torpid, sluggish *Ant* awake

**comb** *Syn* SEEK, search, scour, hunt, ferret out, ransack, rummage

**combat** *vb Syn* RESIST, withstand, contest, oppose, fight, conflict, antagonize *Ant* champion; defend

**combat** *n Syn* CONTEST, conflict, fight, affray, fray

**combative** *Syn* BELLIGERENT, bellicose, pugnacious, quarrelsome, contentious *Ant* pacifistic

**combination** ♦ a union, either of individuals or of organized interests, for mutual support in obtaining common political or private ends *Syn* combine, party, bloc, faction, ring

**combine** *vb* 1 *Syn* JOIN, unite, associate, link, conjoin, connect, relate *Ant* separate 2 *Syn* UNITE, cooperate, concur, conjoin

**combine** *n Syn* COMBINATION, party, bloc, faction, ring

**combustible** ♦ showing a tendency to catch or be set on fire *Syn* inflammable, flammable, incendiary, inflammatory

**come** ♦ to get to one point from another more or

less distant in space, time, relation, or development *Syn* arrive *Ant* go

**comely** *Syn* BEAUTIFUL, fair, pretty, bonny, handsome, lovely, good-looking, beauteous, pulchritudinous *Ant* homely

**comestibles** *Syn* FOOD, provisions, viands, victuals, feed, provender, fodder, forage

**comfort** *n Syn* REST, ease, repose, relaxation, leisure *Ant* discomfort

**comfort** *vb* ♦ to give or offer a person help or assistance in relieving his suffering or sorrow *Syn* console, solace *Ant* afflict; bother

**comfortable** ♦ enjoying or providing condition or circumstances which make for one's contentment and security *Syn* cozy, snug, easy, restful *Ant* uncomfortable; miserable

**comic** *Syn* LAUGHABLE, comical, farcical, funny, droll, risible, ludicrous, ridiculous *Ant* tragic

**comical** *Syn* LAUGHABLE, comic, farcical, ludicrous, ridiculous, risible, droll, funny *Ant* pathetic

**comity** *Syn* FRIENDSHIP, amity, goodwill

**command** *vb* ♦ to issue orders to someone to give, get, or do something *Syn* order, bid, enjoin, direct, instruct, charge *Ant* comply, obey

**command** *n* 1 ♦ a direction that must or should be obeyed *Syn* order, injunction, bidding, behest, mandate, dictate 2 *Syn* POWER, control, authority, jurisdiction, sway, dominion

**commemorate** *Syn* KEEP, celebrate, observe, solemnize

**commence** *Syn* BEGIN, start, initiate, inaugurate

**commend** ♦ to voice or otherwise manifest to others one's warm approval *Syn* recommend, applaud, compliment *Ant* censure; admonish

**commensurable** *Syn* PROPORTIONAL, commensurate, proportionate *Ant* incommensurable

**commensurate** *Syn* PROPORTIONAL, commensurable, proportionate *Ant* incommensurate

**comment** *n Syn* REMARK, commentary, observation, note, obiter dictum

**comment** *vb Syn* REMARK, commentate, animadvert

**commentary** *Syn* REMARK, comment, observation, note, obiter dictum

**commentate** *Syn* REMARK, comment, animadvert

**commerce** 1 *Syn* BUSINESS, trade, industry, traffic 2 *Syn* INTERCOURSE, traffic, dealings, communication, communion, conversation, converse, correspondence

**commercial** ♦ of, relating to, or dealing with the supplying of commodities *Syn* mercantile

**commingle** *Syn* MIX, mingle, blend, merge, coalesce, fuse, amalgamate

**commiseration** *Syn* SYMPATHY, compassion, pity, condolence, ruth, empathy *Ant* ruthlessness, pitilessness

**commission** *Syn* AUTHORIZE, accredit, license

**commit** 1 ♦ to assign to a person or place for some definite end or purpose (as custody or safekeeping) *Syn* entrust, confide, consign, relegate 2 ♦ to be responsible for or to be guilty of some offense or mistake *Syn* perpetrate

**commodious** *Syn* SPACIOUS, capacious, ample

**common** 1 *Syn* UNIVERSAL, general, generic *Ant* individual 2 *Syn* RECIPROCAL, mutual 3 ♦ generally met with and not in any way special, strange, or unusual *Syn* ordinary, familiar, popular, vulgar *Ant* uncommon; exceptional

**commonplace** ♦ an idea or expression lacking in originality or freshness *Syn* platitude, truism, bromide, cliché

**common sense** *Syn* — see SENSE 2

**commotion** ♦ great physical, mental, or emotional excitement *Syn* agitation, tumult, turmoil, turbulence, confusion, convulsion, upheaval

**commune** *Syn* CONFER, consult, advise, parley, treat, negotiate

**communicable** *Syn* INFECTIOUS, contagious, catching

**communicate** ♦ to convey or transfer something (as information, feelings, or qualities) neither tangible nor concrete *Syn* impart

**communication** *Syn* INTERCOURSE, commerce, traffic, dealings, conversation, converse, correspondence, communion

**communion** 1 *Syn* INTERCOURSE, commerce, traffic, converse, dealings, communication, conversation, correspondence 2 *Syn* RELIGION, denomination, faith, church, creed, sect, cult, persuasion

**compact** *adj Syn* CLOSE, dense, thick

**compact** *vb* ♦ to bring or gather together the parts, particles, elements, or units of a thing so as to form a close mass or an integral whole *Syn* consolidate, unify, concentrate

**compact** *n Syn* CONTRACT, pact, entente, convention, concordat, treat, cartel, bargain

**companion** *Syn* ASSOCIATE, comrade, crony

**companionable** *Syn* SOCIAL, cooperative, convivial, gregarious, hospitable

**company** ♦ a group of persons who are associated in a joint endeavor or who are assembled for a common end *Syn* party, band, troop, troupe

**comparable** *Syn* LIKE, alike, similar, analogous, akin, parallel, uniform, identical *Ant* disparate

**compare** ♦ to set two or more things side by side in order to show likenesses and differences *Syn* contrast, collate

**comparison** ♦ a setting of things side by side so as to discover or exhibit their likenesses and differences *Syn* contrast, antithesis, collation, parallel

**compass** *vb* 1 *Syn* SURROUND, environ, encircle, circle, encompass, hem, gird, girdle, ring 2 *Syn* REACH, gain, attain, achieve

**compass** *n* 1 *Syn* CIRCUMFERENCE, perimeter, periphery, circuit 2 *Syn* RANGE, gamut, reach, radius, sweep, scope, orbit, horizon, ken, purview

**compassion** *Syn* SYMPATHY, pity, commiseration, ruth, empathy, condolence

**compassionate** *Syn* TENDER, sympathetic, warmhearted, warm, responsive

**compatible** *Syn* CONSONANT, congruous, consistent, congenial, sympathetic *Ant* incompatible

**compel** *Syn* FORCE, coerce, constrain, oblige

**compelling** *Syn* VALID, telling, convincing, cogent, sound

**compendious** *Syn* CONCISE, summary, pithy, succinct, terse, laconic

**compendium** ♦ a condensed treatment of a subject *Syn* syllabus, digest, pandect, survey, sketch, précis, aperçu

**compensate** 1 ♦ to make up for or to undo the effects of *Syn* countervail, balance, offset, counterbalance, counterpoise 2 *Syn* PAY, remunerate, recompense, repay, reimburse, satisfy, indemnify

**compete** 1 ♦ to strive to gain the mastery or upper hand *Syn* contend, contest 2 *Syn* RIVAL, vie, emulate

**competent** 1 *Syn* ABLE, capable, qualified *Ant* incompetent 2 *Syn* sufficient, enough, adequate

**compile** *Syn* EDIT, revise, redact, rewrite, adapt

**complacent** ♦ feeling or showing an often excessive or unjustified satisfaction in one's possessions, attainments, accomplishments, or virtues *Syn* self-complacent, self-satisfied, smug, priggish

**complaint** *Syn* DISEASE, ailment, disorder, condition, affection, malady, distemper, syndrome

**complaisant** *Syn* AMIABLE, obliging, good-natured *Ant* contrary, perverse

**complement** *n* ♦ something that makes up for a want or deficiency in another thing *Syn* supplement

**complement** *vb* ♦ to supply what is needed to make up for a want or deficiency *Syn* supplement

**complementary, complemental** *Syn* RECIPROCAL, correlative, corresponding, convertible

**complete** *adj Syn* FULL, plenary, replete *Ant* incomplete

**complete** *vb Syn* CLOSE, finish, conclude, end, terminate

**complex** *adj* ♦ having parts or elements that are more or less confusingly interrelated *Syn* complicated, intricate, involved, knotty *Ant* simple

**complex** *n Syn* SYSTEM, network, organism, scheme *Ant* component

**complexion** *Syn* DISPOSITION, temperament, temper, character, personality, individuality

**compliance** ♦ passive or weak agreement to what is asked or demanded *Syn* acquiescence, resignation *Ant* forwardness

**compliant** ♦ manifesting acceptance (as of another's will or something disagreeable) *Syn* acquiescent, resigned *Ant* forward

**complicated** *Syn* COMPLEX, intricate, involved, knotty *Ant* simple

**compliment** *n* ♦ praise addressed directly to a person *Syn* flattery, adulation *Ant* taunt

**compliment** *vb Syn* COMMEND, applaud, recommend

**comply** *Syn* OBEY, mind *Ant* command, enjoin

**component** *Syn* ELEMENT, constituent, ingredient, factor *Ant* composite; complex

**comport** *Syn* BEHAVE, acquit, quit, demean, conduct, deport

**compose** *Syn* CALM, quiet, quieten, still, lull, soothe, settle, tranquilize *Ant* discompose

**composed** *Syn* COOL, collected, unruffled, imperturbable, unflappable, nonchalant *Ant* discomposed; anxious

**composite** *Syn* MIXTURE, admixture, blend, compound, amalgam

**composition** *Syn* ESSAY, theme, paper, article

**composure** *Syn* EQUANIMITY, sangfroid, phlegm *Ant* discomposure, perturbation

**compound** *Syn* MIXTURE, amalgam, composite, admixture, blend *Ant* element

**comprehend** 1 *Syn* UNDERSTAND, appreciate 2 *Syn* APPREHEND 3 *Syn* INCLUDE, embrace, involve, imply, subsume

**comprehension** *Syn* APPREHENSION,

**compress** *Syn* CONTRACT, constrict, deflate, condense, shrink *Ant* stretch; spread

**compulsion** *Syn* FORCE, coercion, constraint, duress, violence, restraint

**compunction** 1 *Syn* PENITENCE, remorse, repentance, contrition, attrition 2 *Syn* QUALM, scruple, demur

**compute** *Syn* CALCULATE, reckon, estimate

**comrade** *Syn* ASSOCIATE, companion, crony

**conation** *Syn* WILL, volition

**concatenate** *Syn* INTEGRATE, articulate

**concatenation** *Syn* INTEGRATION, articulation

**conceal** *Syn* HIDE, screen, secrete, bury, cache, ensconce *Ant* reveal

**concede** 1 *Syn* GRANT, allow *Ant* dispute 2 *Syn* GRANT, vouchsafe, accord, award *Ant* deny (*something to somebody*)

**conceit** 1 ♦ an attitude of regarding oneself with favor *Syn* egotism, egoism, self-esteem, self-love, amour propre *Ant* humility 2 *Syn* CAPRICE, freak, fancy, whim, whimsy, vagary, crotchet

**conceive** *Syn* THINK, imagine, fancy, realize, envisage, envision

**concentrate** 1 *Syn* CENTER, focus, centralize 2 *Syn* COMPACT, consolidate, unify *Ant* dissipate

**concentration** *Syn* ATTENTION, application, study *Ant* distraction

**concept** *Syn* IDEA, conception, notion, thought, impression

**conception** *Syn* IDEA, concept, thought, notion, impression

**concern** 1 *Syn* AFFAIR, business, matter, thing 2 *Syn* CARE, solicitude, anxiety, worry *Ant* unconcern

**concerned** *Syn* WORRIED, solicitous, anxious *Ant* unconcerned

**concerning** *Syn* ABOUT, regarding, respecting

**concert** *Syn* NEGOTIATE, arrange

**concession** *Syn* ALLOWANCE

**conciliate** *Syn* PACIFY, appease, placate, propitiate, mollify *Ant* antagonize

**concise** ♦ presented with or given to brevity of expression *Syn* terse, succinct, laconic, summary, pithy, compendious *Ant* redundant

**conclude** 1 *Syn* CLOSE, finish, terminate, end,

complete *Ant* open **2** *Syn* INFER, judge, gather, deduce

**concluding** *Syn* LAST, final, terminal, latest, ultimate *Ant* opening

**conclusion** *Syn* INFERENCE, judgment, deduction

**conclusive** ♦ having or manifesting qualities that bring something to a finish or end *Syn* decisive, determinative, definitive *Ant* inconclusive

**concoct** *Syn* CONTRIVE, devise, invent, frame

**concomitant** *adj Syn* CONTEMPORARY, coincident, concurrent, synchronous, simultaneous, contemporaneous, coeval, coetaneous

**concomitant** *n Syn* ACCOMPANIMENT

**concord** *Syn* HARMONY, consonance, accord *Ant* discord

**concordat** *Syn* CONTRACT, compact, pact, treaty, entente, convention, cartel, bargain

**concourse** *Syn* JUNCTION, confluence

**concur 1** *Syn* UNITE, conjoin, combine, cooperate **2** *Syn* AGREE, coincide *Ant* contend; altercate

**concurrent** *Syn* CONTEMPORARY, coincident, simultaneous, synchronous, concomitant, contemporaneous, coeval, coetaneous

**concussion** *Syn* IMPACT, shock, percussion, impingement, collision, clash, jar, jolt

**condemn 1** *Syn* CRITICIZE, denounce, censure, blame, reprobate, reprehend **2** *Syn* SENTENCE, doom, damn, proscribe

**condense** *Syn* CONTRACT, shrink, compress, constrict, deflate *Ant* amplify

**condescend** *Syn* STOOP, deign *Ant* presume

**condign** *Syn* DUE, rightful

**condition** *n* **1** ♦ something that limits or qualifies an agreement or offer *Syn* stipulation, terms, provision, proviso, reservation, strings **2** *Syn* STATE, situation, mode, posture, status **3** *Syn* DISEASE, disorder, affection, ailment, malady, complaint, distemper, syndrome

**condition** *vb Syn* PREPARE, fit, qualify, ready

**conditional** *Syn* DEPENDENT, contingent, relative *Ant* unconditional

**condolence** *Syn* SYMPATHY, pity, commiseration, compassion, ruth, empathy

**condone** *Syn* EXCUSE, forgive, pardon, remit

**conduct** *n Syn* BEHAVIOR, deportment

**conduct** *vb* **1** *Syn* ACCOMPANY, escort, convoy, attend, chaperone **2** ♦ to use one's skill, authority, or other powers in order to lead, guide, command, or dominate persons or things *Syn* manage, control, direct **3** *Syn* BEHAVE, demean, deport, comport, acquit, quit

**conduit** *Syn* CHANNEL, canal, duct, aqueduct

**confederacy, confederation** *Syn* ALLIANCE, federation, coalition, fusion, league

**confederate 1** *Syn* PARTNER, copartner, colleague, ally **2** ♦ one associated with another or others in a wrong or unlawful act *Syn* conspirator, accessory, abettor, accomplice

**confer 1** *Syn* GIVE, bestow, present, donate, afford **2** ♦ to carry on a conversation or discussion esp. in order to reach a decision or settlement *Syn* commune, consult, advise, parley, treat, negotiate

**confess** *Syn* ACKNOWLEDGE, avow, admit, own *Ant* renounce (*one's beliefs, principles*)

**confessions** *Syn* BIOGRAPHY, life, memoir, autobiography

**confidant** *Syn* FRIEND, intimate, acquaintance

**confide** *Syn* COMMIT, entrust, consign, relegate

**confidence 1** *Syn* TRUST, reliance, dependence, faith *Ant* doubt; apprehension **2** ♦ a feeling or showing of adequacy or reliance on oneself and one's powers *Syn* self-confidence, assurance, self-assurance, self-possession, aplomb *Ant* diffidence

**confident** ♦ not inhibited by doubts, fears, or a sense of inferiority *Syn* assured, sanguine, sure, presumptuous *Ant* apprehensive; diffident

**confidential** *Syn* FAMILIAR, close, intimate, chummy, thick

**configuration** *Syn* FORM, conformation, figure, shape

**confine** *vb Syn* LIMIT, circumscribe, restrict

**confine** *n Syn* LIMIT, bound, end, term

**confirm 1** *Syn* RATIFY **2** ♦ to attest to the truth, genuineness, accuracy, or validity of something *Syn* corroborate, substantiate, verify, authenticate, validate *Ant* deny; contradict

**confirmed** *Syn* INVETERATE, chronic, deep-seated, deep-rooted

**confiscate** *Syn* ARROGATE, appropriate, usurp, preempt

**conflagration** *Syn* FIRE, holocaust

**conflict** *n* **1** *Syn* CONTEST, combat, fight, affray, fray **2** *Syn* DISCORD, strife, contention, dissension, difference, variance *Ant* harmony

**conflict** *vb* **1** *Syn* RESIST, withstand, contest, oppose, fight, combat, antagonize **2** *Syn* BUMP, clash, collide *Ant* accord

**confluence** *Syn* JUNCTION, concourse

**conform 1** *Syn* ADAPT, adjust, accommodate, reconcile **2** *Syn* AGREE, accord, harmonize, correspond, square, tally, jibe *Ant* diverge

**conformation** *Syn* FORM, configuration, shape, figure

**confound 1** *Syn* PUZZLE, dumbfound, nonplus, bewilder, mystify, perplex, distract **2** *Syn* MISTAKE, confuse *Ant* distinguish, discriminate

**confront** *Syn* MEET, face, encounter *Ant* recoil

**confuse 1** ♦ to make unclear in mind or purpose *Syn* muddle, addle, fuddle, befuddle *Ant* enlighten **2** *Syn* MISTAKE, confound *Ant* differentiate

**confusion 1** ♦ a condition in which things are not in their normal or proper places or relationships *Syn* disorder, chaos, disarray, jumble, clutter, snarl, muddle **2** *Syn* COMMOTION, agitation, tumult, turmoil, turbulence, convulsion, upheaval

**confute** *Syn* DISPROVE, controvert, refute, rebut

**congeal** *Syn* COAGULATE, set, curdle, clot, jelly, jell

**congenial** *Syn* CONSONANT, consistent, compatible, congruous, sympathetic *Ant* uncongenial; antipathetic (*of persons*); abhorrent (*of tasks, duties*)

**congenital** *Syn* INNATE, inborn, hereditary, inherited, inbred

**conglomerate, conglomeration** *Syn* AGGREGATE, agglomerate, agglomeration, aggregation

**congratulate** *Syn* FELICITATE

**congregate** *Syn* GATHER, assemble, collect *Ant* disperse

**congregation** *Syn* GATHERING, assembly, assemblage, collection

**congruous** *Syn* CONSONANT, compatible, congenial, sympathetic, consistent *Ant* incongruous

**conjectural** *Syn* SUPPOSED, hypothetical, suppositious, reputed, putative, purported

**conjecture** *vb* ♦ to draw an inference from slight evidence *Syn* surmise, guess

**conjecture** *n* ♦ an inference based on slight evidence *Syn* surmise, guess *Ant* fact

**conjoin 1** *Syn* JOIN, combine, unite, connect, link, associate, relate **2** *Syn* UNITE, combine, concur, cooperate

**conjugal** *Syn* MATRIMONIAL, marital, connubial, nuptial, hymeneal *Ant* single

**connect** *Syn* JOIN, link, associate, relate, unite, conjoin, combine *Ant* disconnect

**connoisseur** *Syn* AESTHETE, dilettante

**connubial** *Syn* MATRIMONIAL, conjugal, marital, nuptial, hymeneal

**conquer** ♦ to get the better of or to bring into subjection by force or strategy *Syn* defeat, vanquish, overcome, surmount, subdue, subjugate, reduce, overthrow, rout, beat, lick

**conqueror** *Syn* VICTOR, vanquisher, winner, champion

**conquest** *Syn* VICTORY, triumph

**conscientious** *Syn* UPRIGHT, scrupulous, honorable, honest, just *Ant* unconscientious, unscrupulous

**conscious** *Syn* AWARE, sensible, cognizant, alive, awake *Ant* unconscious

**consecrate** *Syn* DEVOTE, hallow, dedicate

**consecutive** ♦ following one after the other in order *Syn* successive, sequent, sequential, serial *Ant* inconsecutive

**consent** *Syn* ASSENT, accede, acquiesce, agree, subscribe *Ant* dissent

**consequence 1** *Syn* EFFECT, result, upshot, aftereffect, aftermath, sequel, issue, outcome, event *Ant* antecedent **2** *Syn* IMPORTANCE, moment, weight, significance, import

**consequently** *Syn* THEREFORE, hence, then, accordingly, so

**conserve** *Syn* SAVE, preserve *Ant* waste, squander

**consider 1** ♦ to give serious thought to *Syn* study, contemplate, weigh, excogitate **2** ♦ to come to view, judge, or classify *Syn* regard, account, reckon, deem

**considerate** *Syn* THOUGHTFUL, attentive *Ant* inconsiderate

**considered** *Syn* DELIBERATE, premeditated, advised, designed, studied *Ant* unconsidered

**consign** *Syn* COMMIT, entrust, confide, relegate

**consistent** *Syn* CONSONANT, congruous, compatible, congenial, sympathetic *Ant* inconsistent

**console** *Syn* COMFORT, solace

**consolidate** *Syn* COMPACT, unify, concentrate

**consolidation** ♦ a union of two or more business corporations *Syn* merger, amalgamation *Ant* dissolution

**consonance** *Syn* HARMONY, concord, accord *Ant* dissonance (*in music*); discord

**consonant** ♦ conforming (as to a pattern, standard, or relationship) without discord or difficulty *Syn* consistent, compatible, congruous, congenial, sympathetic *Ant* inconstant; dissonant (*in music*)

**conspectus** *Syn* ABRIDGMENT, synopsis, epitome, abstract, brief

**conspicuous** *Syn* NOTICEABLE, prominent, salient, signal, remarkable, striking, arresting, outstanding *Ant* inconspicuous

**conspiracy** *Syn* PLOT, cabal, intrigue, machination

**conspirator** *Syn* CONFEDERATE, accessory, accomplice, abettor

**constant 1** *Syn* FAITHFUL, true, loyal, staunch, steadfast, resolute *Ant* inconstant, fickle **2** *Syn* STEADY, uniform, even, equable *Ant* variable **3** *Syn* CONTINUAL, incessant, unremitting, continuous, perpetual, perennial *Ant* fitful

**consternation** *Syn* FEAR, panic, terror, alarm, fright, dread, dismay, horror, trepidation

**constituent** *Syn* ELEMENT, component, ingredient, factor *Ant* whole, aggregate

**constitution** *Syn* PHYSIQUE, build, habit

**constitutional** *Syn* INHERENT, intrinsic, essential, ingrained

**constrain** *Syn* FORCE, oblige, coerce, compel

**constraint** *Syn* FORCE, compulsion, coercion, duress, restraint, violence

**constrict** *Syn* CONTRACT, compress, shrink, condense, deflate

**construct** *Syn* BUILD, erect, frame, raise, rear *Ant* demolish; analyze

**constructive** *Syn* IMPLICIT, virtual *Ant* manifest

**construe** *Syn* EXPLAIN, explicate, elucidate, interpret, expound

**consult** *Syn* CONFER, advise, parley, commune, treat, negotiate

**consume 1** *Syn* WASTE, squander, dissipate, fritter **2** *Syn* EAT, swallow, ingest, devour **3** *Syn* MONOPOLIZE, engross, absorb

**consummate** ♦ brought to completion or perfection *Syn* finished, accomplished *Ant* crude

**contact** ♦ the state of coming into direct connection or close association *Syn* touch

**contagious** *Syn* INFECTIOUS, communicable, catching

**contain** ♦ to have or be capable of having within *Syn* hold, accommodate

**contaminate** ♦ to debase by making impure or unclean *Syn* taint, attaint, pollute, defile

**contemn** *Syn* DESPISE, disdain, scorn, scout

**contemplate 1** *Syn* CONSIDER, study, weigh, excogitate **2** *Syn* SEE, observe, survey, notice, remark, note, perceive, discern, view, behold, decry, espy

**contemplative** *Syn* THOUGHTFUL, meditative, reflective, speculative, pensive

**contemporaneous** *Syn* CONTEMPORARY, coeval, coetaneous, synchronous, simultaneous, coincident, concomitant, concurrent

**contemporary** ♦ existing, living, or occurring at the same time *Syn* contemporaneous, coeval, coetaneous, synchronous, simultaneous, coincident, concomitant, concurrent

**contempt** *Syn* DESPITE, disdain, scorn *Ant* respect

**contemptible** ♦ arousing or deserving scorn or disdain *Syn* despicable, pitiable, sorry, scurvy, cheap, beggarly, shabby *Ant* admirable, estimable; formidable

**contend** 1 ♦ to strive in opposition to someone or something *Syn* fight, battle, war 2 *Syn* COMPETE, contest

**content** **contented** *adj Syn* SATISFIED,

**content** *vb Syn* SATISFY

**contention** *Syn* DISCORD, dissension, difference, variance, strife, conflict

**contentious** *Syn* BELLIGERENT, quarrelsome, bellicose, pugnacious, combative *Ant* peaceable

**conterminous** *Syn* ADJACENT, contiguous, abutting, adjoining, tangent, juxtaposed

**contest** *vb* 1 *Syn* COMPETE, contend 2 *Syn* RESIST, withstand, oppose, fight, combat, conflict, antagonize

**contest** *n* ♦ a battle between opposing forces for supremacy, for power, or for possessions *Syn* conflict, combat, fight, affray, fray

**contiguous** *Syn* ADJACENT, adjoining, abutting, conterminous, tangent, juxtaposed

**continence** *Syn* TEMPERANCE, abstemiousness, sobriety, abstinence *Ant* incontinence

**continent** *Syn* SOBER, temperate, unimpassioned *Ant* incontinent

**contingency** *Syn* JUNCTURE, emergency, exigency, pinch, pass, strait, crisis

**contingent** 1 *Syn* ACCIDENTAL, fortuitous, casual, incidental 2 *Syn* DEPENDENT, conditional, relative

**continual** ♦ characterized by continued occurrence or recurrence over a relatively long period of time *Syn* continuous, constant, incessant, unremitting, perpetual, perennial *Ant* intermittent

**continuance** *Syn* CONTINUATION, continuity

**continuation** ♦ the quality, the act, or the state of continuing or of being continued *Syn* continuance, continuity *Ant* cessation

**continue** ♦ to remain indefinitely in existence or in a given condition or course *Syn* last, endure, abide, persist

**continuity** *Syn* CONTINUATION, continuance

**continuous** *Syn* CONTINUAL, constant, perpetual, perennial, incessant, unremitting *Ant* interrupted

**contort** *Syn* DEFORM, distort, warp

**contour** *Syn* OUTLINE, silhouette, skyline, profile

**contraband** *Syn* SMUGGLED, bootleg

**contract** *n* ♦ an agreement reached after negotiation and ending in an exchange of promises between the parties concerned *Syn* bargain, compact, pact, treaty, entente, convention, cartel, concordat

**contract** *vb* 1 *Syn* PROMISE, pledge, covenant, engage, plight 2 *Syn* INCUR, catch 3 ♦ to decrease in bulk, volume, or content *Syn* shrink, condense, compress, constrict, deflate *Ant* expand

**contradict** *Syn* DENY, gainsay, negative, contravene, traverse, impugn *Ant* corroborate

**contradictory** *n Syn* OPPOSITE, contrary, antithesis, antonym, antipode

**contradictory** *adj Syn* OPPOSITE, contrary, antithetical, antonymous, antipodal, antipodean, converse, counter, reverse

**contraption** *Syn* DEVICE, gadget, contrivance

**contrary** *n Syn* OPPOSITE, antithesis, contradictory, antonym, antipode

**contrary** *adj* 1 *Syn* OPPOSITE, antithetical, contradictory, antonymous, antipodal, antipodean, converse, counter, reverse 2 ♦ given to opposing or resisting wishes, commands, conditions, or circumstances *Syn* perverse, restive, balky, froward, wayward *Ant* good-natured, complaisant

**contrast** *n Syn* COMPARISON, collation, parallel, antithesis

**contrast** *vb Syn* COMPARE, collate

**contravene** *Syn* DENY, contradict, traverse, impugn, negative *Ant* uphold (*law*, *principle*); allege (*right*, *claim*, *privilege*)

**contravention** *Syn* BREACH, trespass, transgression, violation, infringement, infraction

**contribution** *Syn* DONATION, benefaction, alms

**contributory** *Syn* AUXILIARY, ancillary, adjuvant, subservient, accessory

**contrition** *Syn* PENITENCE, attrition, repentance, compunction, remorse

**contrivance** *Syn* DEVICE, gadget, contraption

**contrive** ♦ to find a way of making or doing something or of achieving an end by the exercise of one's mind *Syn* devise, invent, frame, concoct

**control** *vb Syn* CONDUCT, direct, manage

**control** *n* 1 *Syn* POWER, command, dominion, authority, jurisdiction, sway 2 *Syn* CORRECTIVE, check, antidote

**controversy** *Syn* ARGUMENT, dispute

**controvert** *Syn* DISPROVE, rebut, refute, confute *Ant* assert

**contumacious** *Syn* INSUBORDINATE, rebellious, mutinous, seditious, factious *Ant* obedient

**contumelious** *Syn* ABUSIVE, opprobrious, vituperative, scurrilous *Ant* obsequious

**contusion** *Syn* WOUND, bruise, trauma, traumatism, lesion

**conundrum** *Syn* MYSTERY, puzzle, riddle, enigma, problem

**convalesce** *Syn* IMPROVE, recover, recuperate, gain

**convenance** *Syn* FORM, convention, usage

**convene** *Syn* SUMMON, convoke, muster, summons, call, cite *Ant* adjourn

**convent** *Syn* CLOISTER, nunnery, monastery, abbey, priory

**convention** 1 *Syn* CONTRACT, entente, compact, pact, treaty, cartel, concordat, bargain 2 *Syn* FORM, convenance, usage

**conventional** *Syn* CEREMONIAL, formal, ceremonious, solemn *Ant* unconventional

**conversant** ♦ familiar with something *Syn* versed *Ant* ignorant

**conversation, converse** *Syn* INTERCOURSE, communion, communication, commerce, traffic, dealings, correspondence

**converse** *vb Syn* SPEAK, talk

**converse** *n Syn* OPPOSITE, contrary, antithesis, contradictory, antipode, antonym, counter, reverse

**conversion** *Syn* TRANSFORMATION, metamorphosis, transmutation, transmogrification, transfiguration

**convert** *vb Syn* TRANSFORM, metamorphose, transmute, transmogrify, transfigure

**convert** *n* ♦ a person who has embraced another creed, opinion, or doctrine than the one he or she has previously accepted or adhered to *Syn* proselyte

**convertible** *Syn* RECIPROCAL, corresponding, correlative, complementary, complemental

**convey** 1 *Syn* CARRY, transport, transmit, bear 2 *Syn* TRANSFER, deed, alienate

**convict** *Syn* CRIMINAL, felon, malefactor, culprit, delinquent

**conviction** 1 *Syn* CERTAINTY, assurance, certitude 2 *Syn* OPINION, belief, persuasion, view, sentiment

**convincing** *Syn* VALID, compelling, telling, cogent, sound

**convivial** *Syn* SOCIAL, companionable, gregarious, hospitable, cooperative *Ant* taciturn; staid

**convoke** *Syn* SUMMON, convene, muster, summons, call, cite *Ant* prorogue, dissolve

**convoy** *Syn* ACCOMPANY, escort, conduct, attend, chaperone

**convulse** *Syn* SHAKE, rock, agitate

**convulsion** 1 *Syn* FIT, spasm, paroxysm, attack, access, accession 2 *Syn* COMMOTION, agitation, tumult, turmoil, turbulence, confusion, upheaval

**convulsive** *Syn* FITFUL, spasmodic

**cool** 1 *Syn* COLD, chilly, frigid, freezing, frosty, gelid, icy, glacial, arctic *Ant* warm 2 ♦ showing or seeming to show freedom from agitation or excitement *Syn* composed, collected, unruffled, imperturbable, unflappable, nonchalant *Ant* ardent; agitated

**coop** *Syn* ENCLOSE, envelop, fence, pen, corral, cage, wall

**cooperate** *Syn* UNITE, conjoin, combine *Ant* counteract

**cooperative** *Syn* SOCIAL, companionable, gregarious, convivial, hospitable *Ant* uncooperative

**cop** *Syn* STEAL, filch, pinch, snitch, swipe, lift, pilfer, purloin

**copartner** *Syn* PARTNER, colleague, ally, confederate

**copious** *Syn* PLENTIFUL, abundant, ample, plenteous *Ant* meager

**copy** *n Syn* REPRODUCTION, duplicate, carbon, carbon copy, transcript, facsimile, replica *Ant* original

**copy** *vb* ♦ to make something like an already existing thing in form, appearance, or obvious or salient characteristics *Syn* imitate, mimic, ape, mock *Ant* originate

**coquet** *Syn* TRIFLE, flirt, dally, toy

**cordial** *Syn* GRACIOUS, genial, affable, sociable

**core** 1 *Syn* CENTER, middle, midst, hub, focus, nucleus, heart 2 *Syn* SUBSTANCE, purport, gist, burden, pith

**corner** *Syn* MONOPOLY, pool, syndicate, trust, cartel

**corporal** *Syn* BODILY, corporeal, physical, somatic

**corporeal** 1 *Syn* MATERIAL, physical, sensible, phenomenal, objective *Ant* incorporeal 2 *Syn* BODILY, physical, corporal, somatic

**corpse** *Syn* BODY, carcass, cadaver

**corpulent** *Syn* FLESHY, portly, fat, stout, obese, rotund, plump, chubby *Ant* spare

**corral** *Syn* ENCLOSE, envelop, fence, pen, coop, cage, wall

**correct** *vb* 1 ♦ to set or make right something which is wrong *Syn* rectify, emend, remedy, redress, amend, reform, revise 2 *Syn* PUNISH, discipline, chastise, chasten, castigate

**correct** *adj* ♦ conforming to standard, fact, or truth *Syn* accurate, exact, precise, nice, right *Ant* incorrect

**corrective** *adj Syn* CURATIVE, remedial, restorative, sanative

**corrective** *n* ♦ something which serves to keep another thing in its desired place or condition *Syn* control, check, antidote

**correlate** *Syn* PARALLEL, analogue, counterpart

**correlative** *Syn* RECIPROCAL, corresponding, complementary, complemental, convertible

**correspond** *Syn* AGREE, square, accord, tally, jibe, harmonize, conform

**correspondence** *Syn* INTERCOURSE, communication, conversation, converse, communion, commerce, traffic, dealings

**corresponding** *Syn* RECIPROCAL, correlative, complementary, complemental, convertible

**corridor** *Syn* PASSAGE, passageway, hall, hallway, gallery, arcade, cloister, aisle, ambulatory

**corroborate** *Syn* CONFIRM, substantiate, verify, authenticate, validate *Ant* contradict

**corrupt** *vb Syn* DEBASE, deprave, debauch, pervert

**corrupt** *adj Syn* VICIOUS, iniquitous, nefarious, flagitious, infamous, villainous, degenerate

**corrupted** *Syn* DEBASED, corrupt, vitiated, depraved, debauched, perverted

**corruption** *Syn* BARBARISM, impropriety, solecism, vulgarism, vernacular

**corsair** *Syn* PIRATE, freebooter, buccaneer, privateer

**cortege** *Syn* PROCESSION, cavalcade, parade, motorcade

**coruscate** *Syn* FLASH, gleam, scintillate, glance, glint, sparkle, glitter, glisten, twinkle

**cosmic** *Syn* UNIVERSAL, catholic, ecumenical, cosmopolitan

**cosmopolitan** *Syn* UNIVERSAL, catholic, ecumenical, cosmic *Ant* provincial; insular; parochial

**cosset** *Syn* CARESS, fondle, pet, cuddle, dandle

**cost** *Syn* PRICE, expense, charge

**costly** ♦ having a high value or valuation, esp. in terms of money *Syn* expensive, dear, valuable, precious, invaluable, priceless *Ant* cheap

**coterie** *Syn* SET, circle, clique

**couchant** *Syn* PRONE, recumbent, dormant, supine, prostrate

**counsel** *n* 1 *Syn* ADVICE 2 *Syn* LAWYER, counselor, barrister, advocate, attorney, solicitor

**counsel** *vb* *Syn* ADVISE

**counselor** *Syn* LAWYER, barrister, counsel, advocate, attorney, solicitor

**count** *vb* 1 ♦ to ascertain the total of units in a collection by noting one after another *Syn* tell, enumerate, number 2 *Syn* RELY, depend, bank, trust, reckon

**count** *n* *Syn* PARAGRAPH, verse, article, clause, plank

**countenance** *n* *Syn* FACE, visage, physiognomy, mug, puss

**countenance** *vb* *Syn* FAVOR, encourage

**counter** *adj* *Syn* ADVERSE, antagonistic, counteractive

**counter** *n* *Syn* OPPOSITE, contradictory, contrary, antithesis, antipode, antonym, converse, reverse

**counteract** *Syn* NEUTRALIZE, negative *Ant* cooperate

**counteractive** *Syn* ADVERSE, counter, antagonistic

**counterbalance** *Syn* COMPENSATE, offset, countervail, balance, counterpoise

**counterfeit** *vb* *Syn* ASSUME, feign, sham, simulate, pretend, affect

**counterfeit** *adj* ♦ being an imitation intended to mislead or deceive *Syn* spurious, bogus, fake, sham, pseudo, pinchbeck, phony *Ant* bona fide, genuine

**counterfeit** *n* *Syn* IMPOSTURE, fraud, sham, fake, cheat, humbug, deceit, deception

**counterpart** *Syn* PARALLEL, correlate, analogue

**counterpoise** *Syn* COMPENSATE, balance, countervail, counterbalance, offset

**countervail** *Syn* COMPENSATE, offset, balance, counterbalance, counterpoise

**county** *Syn* ARISTOCRACY, gentry, elite, nobility, society

**coup, coup d'etat** *Syn* REBELLION, revolution, uprising, revolt, insurrection, mutiny, putsch

**couple** ♦ two things of the same kind *Syn* pair, brace, yoke

**courage** ♦ a quality of mind or temperament that enables one to stand fast in the face of opposition, danger, or hardship *Syn* mettle, spirit, resolution, tenacity *Ant* cowardice

**courageous** *Syn* BRAVE, unafraid, fearless, intrepid, valiant, valorous, dauntless, undaunted, doughty, bold, audacious *Ant* pusillanimous

**course** *Syn* WAY, route, passage, pass, artery

**court** *Syn* INVITE, woo, bid, solicit

**courteous** *Syn* CIVIL, polite, courtly, gallant, chivalrous *Ant* discourteous

**courtesy** ♦ a manner or an act which promotes agreeable or pleasant social relations *Syn* amenity, attention, gallantry *Ant* discourtesy

**courtly** *Syn* CIVIL, courteous, gallant, chivalrous, polite *Ant* churlish

**covenant** *Syn* PROMISE, pledge, engage, plight, contract

**cover** *vb* ♦ to put or place or to be put or placed over or around *Syn* overspread, envelop, wrap, shroud, veil *Ant* bare

**cover** *n* *Syn* SHELTER, retreat, refuge, asylum, sanctuary *Ant* exposure

**covert** *Syn* SECRET, clandestine, surreptitious, underhand, underhanded, stealthy, furtive *Ant* overt

**covet** 1 ♦ to desire selfishly to have something for one's own *Syn* envy, grudge, begrudge 2

*Syn* DESIRE, crave, wish, want *Ant* renounce (*something desirable*)

**covetous** ♦ having or manifesting a strong desire for esp. material possessions *Syn* greedy, acquisitive, grasping, avaricious

**cow** *Syn* INTIMIDATE, browbeat, bulldoze, bully

**cower** *Syn* FAWN, cringe, truckle, toady

**coxcomb** *Syn* FOP, dandy, beau, exquisite, dude, buck

**coy** *Syn* SHY, bashful, diffident, modest *Ant* pert

**cozen** *Syn* CHEAT, defraud, swindle, overreach

**cozy** *Syn* COMFORTABLE, snug, easy, restful

**crabbed** *Syn* SULLEN, surly, glum, morose, gloomy, sulky, saturnine, dour

**crack** *vb* *Syn* BREAK, burst, bust, snap, shatter, shiver

**crack** *n* 1 ♦ an opening, break, or discontinuity made by or as if by splitting or rupture *Syn* cleft, fissure, crevasse, crevice, cranny, chink 2 *Syn* JOKE, wisecrack, witticism, jest, jape, quip, gag

**craft** 1 *Syn* ART, skill, cunning, artifice 2 *Syn* TRADE, handicraft, art, profession 3 *Syn* BOAT, ship, vessel

**craftsman** *Syn* WORKER, handicraftsman, mechanic, artisan, workman, workingman, laborer, hand, operative, roustabout

**crafty** *Syn* SLY, tricky, cunning, insidious, foxy, guileful, wily, artful

**cram** *Syn* PACK, crowd, stuff, ram, tamp

**cranky** *Syn* IRASCIBLE, cross, choleric, splenetic, testy, touchy

**cranny** *Syn* CRACK, cleft, fissure, crevasse, crevice, chink

**crass** *Syn* STUPID, dense, slow, dull, dumb *Ant* brilliant

**crave** *Syn* DESIRE, covet, wish, want *Ant* spurn

**crawl** *Syn* CREEP

**craze** *Syn* FASHION, vogue, fad, rage, style, mode, dernier cri, cry

**crazy, crazed** *Syn* INSANE, mad, demented, lunatic, maniac, deranged, non compos mentis

**cream** *Syn* OIL, grease, lubricate, anoint

**create** *Syn* ESTABLISH, institute, organize

**creator** *Syn* MAKER, author

**creature** *Syn* ENTITY, being, individual, person

**credence** *Syn* BELIEF, credit, faith

**credential** ♦ something presented by one person to another in proof that he is what or who he claims to be *Syn* testimonial, recommendation, character, reference

**credible** *Syn* PLAUSIBLE, believable, colorable, specious *Ant* incredible

**credit** *n* 1 *Syn* BELIEF, faith, credence 2 *Syn* INFLUENCE, prestige, authority, weight *Ant* discredit 3 ♦ a person or thing that enhances another *Syn* asset

**credit** *vb* *Syn* ASCRIBE, accredit, assign, attribute, impute, refer, charge

**credulity** ♦ undue trust or confidence *Syn* gullibility *Ant* incredulity; skepticism

**credulous** ♦ unduly trusting or confiding *Syn* gullible *Ant* incredulous; skeptical

**creed** *Syn* RELIGION, faith, persuasion, denomination, sect, cult, communion, church

**creep** ♦ to move slowly along a surface in a prone or crouching position *Syn* crawl

**crevasse** *Syn* CRACK, cleft, fissure, crevice, cranny, chink

**crevice** *Syn* CRACK, cleft, fissure, crevasse, cranny, chink

**crime** *Syn* OFFENSE, vice, sin, scandal

**criminal** ♦ one who has committed a usu. serious offense esp. against the law *Syn* felon, convict, malefactor, culprit, delinquent

**cringe** *Syn* FAWN, cower, truckle, toady

**cripple** 1 *Syn* MAIM, mutilate, batter, mangle 2 *Syn* WEAKEN, disable, enfeeble, debilitate, undermine, sap

**crisis** *Syn* JUNCTURE, exigency, emergency, pinch, pass, contingency, strait

**crisp** 1 *Syn* FRAGILE, brittle, short, friable, frangi-

ble 2 *Syn* INCISIVE, clear-cut, cutting, trenchant, biting

**criterion** *Syn* STANDARD, touchstone, yardstick, gauge

**critical** 1 ♦ exhibiting the spirit of one who detects and points out faults or defects *Syn* hypercritical, faultfinding, captious, caviling, carping, censorious *Ant* uncritical 2 *Syn* ACUTE, crucial

**criticism** ♦ a discourse presenting one's conclusions after examining a work of art and esp. of literature *Syn* critique, review, blurb, puff

**criticize** ♦ to find fault with someone or something openly, often publicly, and with varying degrees of severity *Syn* reprehend, blame, censure, reprobate, condemn, denounce

**critique** *Syn* CRITICISM, review, blurb, puff

**crochet** *Syn* WEAVE, knit, plait, braid, tat

**crony** *Syn* ASSOCIATE, comrade, companion

**crook** *Syn* FLEX, bow, buckle

**crooked** ♦ not straight or straightforward *Syn* devious, oblique *Ant* straight

**crop** *Syn* SHEAR, poll, clip, trim, prune, lop, snip

**cross** *n* *Syn* TRIAL, tribulation, affliction, visitation

**cross** *adj* *Syn* IRASCIBLE, cranky, testy, touchy, choleric, splenetic

**crosswise, crossways** *Syn* ACROSS, athwart

**crotchet** *Syn* CAPRICE, freak, fancy, whim, whimsy, conceit, vagary

**crow** *Syn* BOAST, brag, vaunt, gasconade

**crowd** *vb* 1 *Syn* PRESS, bear, bear down, squeeze, jam 2 *Syn* PACK, cram, stuff, ram, tamp

**crowd** *n* ♦ a more or less closely assembled multitude usually of persons *Syn* throng, press, crush, mob, rout, horde

**crucial** *Syn* ACUTE, critical

**crude** *Syn* RUDE, rough, uncouth, raw, callow, green *Ant* consummate, finished

**cruel** *Syn* FIERCE, inhuman, fell, truculent, ferocious, barbarous, savage *Ant* pitiful

**cruise** *Syn* JOURNEY, voyage, tour, trip, jaunt, excursion, expedition, pilgrimage

**crumble** *Syn* DECAY, disintegrate, decompose, rot, putrefy, spoil

**crush** *vb* 1 ♦ to reduce or be reduced to a pulpy or broken mass *Syn* mash, smash, bruise, squash, macerate 2 ♦ to bring to an end by destroying or defeating *Syn* quell, extinguish, suppress, quench, quash

**crush** *n* *Syn* CROWD, press, throng, horde, mob, rout

**crusty** *Syn* BLUFF, brusque, gruff, blunt, curt

**cry** *vb* ♦ to show grief, pain, or distress by tears and usu. inarticulate utterances *Syn* weep, wail, keen, whimper, blubber

**cry** *Syn* FASHION, vogue, rage, style, mode, fad, craze, dernier cri

**crying** *Syn* PRESSING, urgent, imperative, importunate, insistent, exigent, instant

**cryptic** *Syn* OBSCURE, enigmatic, dark, vague, ambiguous, equivocal

**cuddle** *Syn* CARESS, fondle, dandle, pet, cosset

**cuff** *Syn* STRIKE, hit, smite, punch, slug, slog, swat, clout, slap, box

**cull** *Syn* CHOOSE, pick, single, select, elect, opt, prefer

**culmination** *Syn* SUMMIT, peak, climax, apex, acme, pinnacle, meridian, zenith, apogee

**culpability** *Syn* BLAME, guilt, fault

**culpable** *Syn* BLAMEWORTHY, guilty

**culprit** *Syn* CRIMINAL, felon, convict, malefactor, delinquent

**cult** *Syn* RELIGION, sect, denomination, communion, faith, creed, persuasion, church

**cultivar** *Syn* VARIETY, subspecies, race, breed, strain, clone, stock

**cultivate** *Syn* NURSE, nurture, foster, cherish

**cultivation** *Syn* CULTURE, breeding, refinement

**culture** ♦ enlightenment and excellence of taste acquired by intellectual and aesthetic training *Syn* cultivation, breeding, refinement

**cumber** *Syn* BURDEN, encumber, weigh, weight, load, lade, tax, charge, saddle

**cumbersome, cumbrous** *Syn* HEAVY, ponderous, weighty, hefty

**cumulative** ♦ increasing or produced by the addition of like or assimilable things *Syn* accumulative, additive, summative

**cunning** *adj* **1** *Syn* CLEVER, ingenious, adroit **2** *Syn* SLY, crafty, tricky, artful, foxy, insidious, wily, guileful *Ant* ingenuous

**cunning** *n* **1** *Syn* ART, skill, craft, artifice **2** *Syn* DECEIT, guile, duplicity, dissimulation *Ant* ingenuousness

**cupidity** ♦ intense desire for wealth or possessions *Syn* greed, rapacity, avarice

**curative** ♦ returning or tending to return to a state of normalcy or health *Syn* sanative, restorative, remedial, corrective

**curb** *Syn* RESTRAIN, check, bridle, inhibit *Ant* spur

**curdle** *Syn* COAGULATE, congeal, set, clot, jelly, jell

**cure** *n* *Syn* REMEDY, medicine, medicament, medication, specific, physic

**cure** *vb* ♦ to rectify an unhealthy or undesirable condition especially by some specific treatment *Syn* heal, remedy

**curious 1**♦ interested in what is not one's personal or proper concern *Syn* inquisitive, prying, snoopy, nosy *Ant* incurious; uninterested **2** *Syn* STRANGE, singular, peculiar, unique, odd, queer, quaint, outlandish, eccentric, erratic

**curl** *Syn* WIND, coil, twist, twine, wreathe, entwine

**currency** *Syn* MONEY, cash, legal tender, specie, coin, coinage

**current** *adj* *Syn* PREVAILING, prevalent, rife *Ant* antique, antiquated; obsolete

**current** *n* *Syn* FLOW, stream, flood, tide, flux

**curse** *n* ♦ a denunciation that conveys a wish or threat of evil *Syn* imprecation, malediction, anathema *Ant* blessing

**curse** *vb* *Syn* EXECRATE, damn, anathematize, objurgate *Ant* bless

**cursed** *Syn* EXECRABLE, accursed, damnable

**cursing** *Syn* BLASPHEMY, profanity, swearing

**cursory** *Syn* SUPERFICIAL, shallow, uncritical *Ant* painstaking

**curt** *Syn* BLUFF, brusque, blunt, crusty, gruff *Ant* voluble

**curtail** *Syn* SHORTEN, abbreviate, abridge, retrench *Ant* protract, prolong

**curve** *vb* ♦ to swerve or cause to swerve from a straight line or course *Syn* bend, twist

**curve** *n* ♦ a line or something which follows a line that is neither straight nor angular but rounded *Syn* arc, bow, arch

**curvet** *Syn* SKIP, bound, hop, lope, lollop, ricochet

**custom** *Syn* HABIT, usage, habitude, practice, use, wont

**customary** *Syn* USUAL, wonted, accustomed, habitual *Ant* occasional

**cut** ♦ to penetrate and divide something with a sharp-bladed tool or instrument *Syn* hew, chop, carve, slit, slash

**cutthroat** *Syn* ASSASSIN, gunman, bravo

**cutting** *Syn* INCISIVE, trenchant, clear-cut, biting, crisp

**cyclone** *Syn* TORNADO, twister

**cyclopean** *Syn* HUGE, vast, immense, enormous, elephantine, mammoth, giant, gigantic, gigantean, colossal, gargantuan, Herculean, titanic, Brobdingnagian

**cynical** ♦ deeply and often contemptuously distrustful *Syn* misanthropic, pessimistic

# D

**dabbler** *Syn* AMATEUR, tyro, dilettante

**daily** ♦ of each or every day *Syn* diurnal, quotidian, circadian

**dainty 1** *Syn* CHOICE, delicate, exquisite, elegant, recherché, rare *Ant* gross **2** *Syn* NICE, fastidious, finicky, finicking, finical, particular, fussy, squeamish, persnickety, pernickety

**dally** *Syn* TRIFLE, flirt, coquet, toy

**dam** *Syn* HINDER, bar, block, obstruct, impede

**damage** *n* *Syn* INJURY, harm, hurt, mischief

**damage** *vb* *Syn* INJURE, harm, impair, mar, hurt, spoil

**damn 1** *Syn* SENTENCE, doom, condemn, proscribe *Ant* save (*from eternal punishment*) **2** *Syn* EXECRATE, curse, anathematize, objurgate

**damnable** *Syn* EXECRABLE, accursed, cursed

**damp** *Syn* WET, moist, dank, humid

**dandle** *Syn* CARESS, cuddle, pet, cosset, fondle

**dandy** *Syn* FOP, beau, coxcomb, exquisite, dude, buck *Ant* sloven

**danger** ♦ the state of being exposed to injury, pain, or loss *Syn* peril, jeopardy, hazard, risk *Ant* security

**dangerous** ♦ attended by or involving the possibility of loss, evil, injury, or harm *Syn* hazardous, precarious, perilous, risky *Ant* safe, secure

**dangle** *Syn* HANG, suspend, sling

**dank** *Syn* WET, damp, humid, moist

**dappled** *Syn* VARIEGATED, parti-colored, motley, checkered, checked, pied, piebald, skewbald, freaked

**dare** *Syn* FACE, brave, challenge, defy, beard

**daredevil** *Syn* ADVENTUROUS, daring, rash, reckless, foolhardy, venturesome

**daring** *Syn* ADVENTUROUS, rash, reckless, daredevil, foolhardy, venturesome

**dark 1** ♦ deficient in light *Syn* dim, dusky, obscure, murky, gloomy *Ant* light **2** *Syn* OBSCURE, vague, enigmatic, cryptic, ambiguous, equivocal *Ant* lucid

**darken** *Syn* OBSCURE, dim, bedim, eclipse, cloud, becloud, fog, befog, obfuscate *Ant* illuminate

**dart** *Syn* FLY, scud, skim, float, shoot, sail

**dash** *vb* *Syn* RUSH, tear, shoot, charge

**dash** *n* **1** *Syn* VIGOR, vim, spirit, esprit, verve, punch, élan, drive **2** *Syn* TOUCH, suggestion, suspicion, soupçon, tincture, tinge, shade, smack, spice, vein, strain, streak

**dashing** *Syn* STYLISH, smart, fashionable, modish, chic

**date** *Syn* ENGAGEMENT, rendezvous, tryst, appointment, assignation

**daunt** *Syn* DISMAY, appall, horrify

**dauntless** *Syn* BRAVE, courageous, unafraid, fearless, intrepid, valiant, valorous, undaunted, doughty, bold, audacious *Ant* poltroon

**dawdle** *Syn* DELAY, procrastinate, loiter, lag

**daydream** *Syn* FANCY, dream, fantasy, phantasy, phantasm, vision, nightmare

**daze** ♦ to dull or deaden the powers of the mind through some disturbing experience or influence *Syn* stun, bemuse, stupefy, benumb, paralyze, petrify

**dazzled** *Syn* GIDDY, dizzy, vertiginous, swimming

**dead** ♦ devoid of life *Syn* defunct, deceased, departed, late, lifeless, inanimate

**deadlock** *Syn* DRAW, tie, stalemate, standoff

**deadly** ♦ causing or causative of death *Syn* mortal, fatal, lethal

**deal 1** *Syn* DISTRIBUTE, divide, dispense, dole **2** *Syn* TREAT, handle

**dealings** *Syn* INTERCOURSE, commerce, traffic, communication, communion, conversation, converse, correspondence

**dear** ♦ *Syn* COSTLY, expensive, precious, valuable, invaluable, priceless *Ant* cheap

**dearth** *Syn* LACK, want, absence, defect, privation *Ant* excess

**death** ♦ the end or the ending of life *Syn* decease, demise, passing *Ant* life

**deathless** *Syn* IMMORTAL, undying, unfading

**debar** *Syn* EXCLUDE, blackball, disbar, suspend, shut out, eliminate, rule out

**debase 1** ♦ to cause a person or thing to become impaired and lowered in quality or character *Syn* vitiate, deprave, corrupt, debauch, pervert *Ant* elevate (*taste, character*); amend (*morals, way of life*) **2** *Syn* ABASE, degrade, demean, humble, humiliate

**debased** ♦ being lowered in quality or character *Syn* vitiated, depraved, corrupted, debauched, perverted

**debate** *n* *Syn* ARGUMENTATION, disputation, forensic, dialectic

**debate** *vb* *Syn* DISCUSS, dispute, argue, agitate

**debauch** *Syn* DEBASE, corrupt, deprave, pervert, vitiate

**debauched** *Syn* DEBASED, corrupted, depraved, perverted, vitiated

**debilitate** *Syn* WEAKEN, enfeeble, undermine, sap, cripple, disable *Ant* invigorate

**debit** *Syn* DEBT, indebtedness, liability, obligation, arrear *Ant* credit

**debris** *Syn* REFUSE, waste, rubbish, trash, garbage, offal

**debt** ♦ something, and esp. a sum of money, that is owed *Syn* indebtedness, obligation, liability, debit, arrear

**decadence** *Syn* DETERIORATION, decline, declension, degeneration, devolution *Ant* rise; flourishing

**decamp** *Syn* ESCAPE, flee, fly, abscond

**decay** ♦ to undergo or to cause to undergo destructive changes *Syn* decompose, rot, putrefy, spoil, disintegrate, crumble

**decease** *Syn* DEATH, demise, passing

**deceased** *Syn* DEAD, departed, late, defunct, lifeless, inanimate

**deceit 1** ♦ the act or practice of imposing upon the credulity of others by dishonesty, fraud, or trickery *Syn* duplicity, dissimulation, cunning, guile **2** *Syn* IMPOSTURE, cheat, fraud, sham, fake, deception, counterfeit, humbug

**deceitful** *Syn* DISHONEST, mendacious, lying, untruthful *Ant* trustworthy

**deceive** ♦ to lead astray or into evil or to frustrate by underhandedness or craft *Syn* mislead, delude, beguile, betray, double-cross *Ant* undeceive; enlighten

**decency** *Syn* DECORUM, propriety, dignity, etiquette

**decent 1** *Syn* DECOROUS, seemly, proper, nice **2** *Syn* CHASTE, modest, pure *Ant* indecent; obscene

**deception 1** ♦ the act or practice of deliberately deceiving *Syn* fraud, double-dealing, trickery, chicane, chicanery **2** *Syn* IMPOSTURE, cheat, fraud, sham, fake, humbug, counterfeit, deceit

**deceptive** *Syn* MISLEADING, delusory, delusive

**decide** ♦ to come or to cause to come to a conclusion *Syn* determine, settle, rule, resolve

**decided** ♦ free from any doubt, wavering, or ambiguity *Syn* decisive, determined, resolved

**decipher** *Syn* SOLVE, resolve, unfold, unravel

**decisive 1** *Syn* CONCLUSIVE, determinative, definitive *Ant* indecisive **2** *Syn* DECIDED, determined, resolved *Ant* irresolute

**deck** *Syn* ADORN, bedeck, decorate, ornament, garnish, embellish, beautify

**declaration** ♦ the act of making known openly or publicly *Syn* announcement, publication, advertisement, proclamation, promulgation, broadcasting

**declare 1** ♦ to make known explicitly or plainly

*Syn* announce, publish, advertise, proclaim, promulgate, broadcast 2 *Syn* ASSERT, profess, affirm, aver, avouch, avow, protest, predicate, warrant

**declass** *Syn* DEGRADE, demote, reduce, disrate

**declension** *Syn* DETERIORATION, decline, decadence, degeneration, devolution

**decline** *vb* ♦ to turn away by not accepting, receiving, or considering *Syn* refuse, reject, repudiate, spurn *Ant* accept

**decline** *n Syn* DETERIORATION, declension, decadence, degeneration, devolution

**decolorize** *Syn* WHITEN, blanch, bleach, etiolate

**decompose** *Syn* DECAY, rot, putrefy, spoil, disintegrate, crumble

**decorate** *Syn* ADORN, ornament, embellish, beautify, deck, bedeck, garnish

**decorous** ♦ conforming to an accepted standard of what is right or fitting or is regarded as good form *Syn* decent, seemly, proper, nice *Ant* indecorous; blatant

**decorticate** *Syn* SKIN, peel, pare, flay

**decorum** ♦ the quality or character of rightness, fitness, or honorableness in behavior or conduct *Syn* decency, propriety, dignity, etiquette *Ant* indecorum; license

**decoy** *n Syn* LURE, bait, snare, trap

**decoy** *vb Syn* LURE, entice, inveigle, tempt, seduce

**decrease** ♦ to make or grow less esp. gradually *Syn* lessen, diminish, reduce, abate, dwindle *Ant* increase

**decree** *Syn* DICTATE, prescribe, ordain, impose

**decrepit** *Syn* WEAK, infirm, feeble, frail, fragile *Ant* sturdy

**decry** ♦ to indicate one's low opinion of something *Syn* deprecate, disparage, derogate, detract, belittle, minimize *Ant* extol

**dedicate** *Syn* DEVOTE, consecrate, hallow

**deduce** *Syn* INFER, gather, conclude, judge

**deduct** ♦ to take away one quantity from another *Syn* subtract *Ant* add

**deduction** 1 ♦ an amount subtracted from a gross sum *Syn* abatement, rebate, discount 2 *Syn* INFERENCE, conclusion, judgment

**deed** *n Syn* ACTION, act

**deed** *vb Syn* TRANSFER, convey, alienate

**deem** *Syn* CONSIDER, regard, account, reckon

**deep** 1 ♦ having great extension downward or inward *Syn* profound, abysmal 2 *Syn* BROAD, wide

**deep-rooted** *Syn* INVETERATE, deep-seated, chronic, confirmed

**deep-seated** *Syn* INVETERATE, chronic, deep-rooted, confirmed

**deface** ♦ to mar the appearance of *Syn* disfigure

**defame** *Syn* MALIGN, vilify, calumniate, traduce, asperse, slander, libel

**default** *Syn* FAILURE, neglect, miscarriage, dereliction

**defeat** *Syn* CONQUER, beat, vanquish, lick, subdue, subjugate, reduce, overcome, surmount, overthrow, rout

**defect** 1 *Syn* LACK, want, dearth, absence, privation 2 *Syn* BLEMISH, flaw

**defection** ♦ conscious abandonment of allegiance or duty *Syn* desertion, apostasy

**defective** *Syn* DEFICIENT *Ant* intact

**defend** 1 ♦ to keep secure from danger or against attack *Syn* protect, shield, guard, safeguard *Ant* combat; attack 2 *Syn* MAINTAIN, assert, vindicate

**defer** *vb* ♦ to a delay an action, activity, or proceeding *Syn* postpone, intermit, suspend, stay

**defer** *vb Syn* YIELD, bow, submit, cave, capitulate, succumb, relent

**deference** *Syn* HONOR, reverence, homage, obeisance *Ant* disrespect

**deficiency** *Syn* IMPERFECTION, shortcoming, fault *Ant* excess

**deficient** ♦ showing lack of something necessary *Syn* defective *Ant* sufficient, adequate; excessive

**defile** *Syn* CONTAMINATE, pollute, taint, attaint *Ant* cleanse; purify

**define** *Syn* PRESCRIBE, assign

**definite** *Syn* EXPLICIT, express, specific, categorical *Ant* indefinite; equivocal

**definitive** *Syn* CONCLUSIVE, determinative, decisive *Ant* tentative, provisional

**deflate** *Syn* CONTRACT, compress, shrink, condense, constrict *Ant* inflate

**deflect** *Syn* TURN, divert, avert, sheer

**deflection** *Syn* DEVIATION, aberration, divergence

**deform** ♦ to mar or spoil by or as if by twisting *Syn* distort, contort, warp

**defraud** *Syn* CHEAT, swindle, overreach, cozen

**deft** *Syn* DEXTEROUS, adroit, handy *Ant* awkward

**defunct** *Syn* DEAD, deceased, departed, late, lifeless, inanimate *Ant* alive; live

**defy** *Syn* FACE, brave, challenge, dare, beard *Ant* recoil

**degenerate** *Syn* VICIOUS, corrupt, infamous, villainous, iniquitous, nefarious, flagitious

**degeneration** *Syn* DETERIORATION, devolution, decadence, decline, declension

**degrade** 1 ♦ to lower in station, rank, or grade *Syn* demote, reduce, declass, disrate *Ant* elevate 2 *Syn* ABASE, debase, demean, humble, humiliate *Ant* uplift

**dehydrate** *Syn* DRY, desiccate, parch, bake

**deign** *Syn* STOOP, condescend

**deject** *Syn* DISCOURAGE, dishearten, dispirit *Ant* exhilarate; cheer

**dejected** *Syn* DOWNCAST, depressed, dispirited, disconsolate, woebegone

**dejection** *Syn* SADNESS, depression, melancholy, melancholia, gloom, blues, dumps *Ant* exhilaration

**delay** 1 ♦ to cause to be late or behind in movement or progress *Syn* retard, slow, slacken, detain *Ant* expedite; hasten 2 ♦ to move or act slowly so that progress is hindered or work remains undone or unfinished *Syn* procrastinate, lag, loiter, dawdle *Ant* hasten, hurry

**delectable** *Syn* DELIGHTFUL, delicious, luscious

**delectation** *Syn* PLEASURE, enjoyment, delight, joy, fruition

**delegate** ♦ a person who stands in place of another or others *Syn* deputy, representative

**delete** *Syn* ERASE, cancel, efface, obliterate, blot out, expunge

**deleterious** *Syn* PERNICIOUS, detrimental, baneful, noxious *Ant* salutary

**deliberate** *adj* 1 *Syn* VOLUNTARY, willful, intentional, willing *Ant* impulsive 2 ♦ arrived at after due thought *Syn* considered, advised, premeditated, designed, studied *Ant* casual 3 *Syn* SLOW, leisurely, dilatory, laggard *Ant* precipitate, abrupt

**deliberate** *vb Syn* THINK, reflect, cogitate, reason, speculate

**delicate** *Syn* CHOICE, exquisite, dainty, rare, recherché, elegant *Ant* gross

**delicious** *Syn* DELIGHTFUL, delectable, luscious

**delight** *n Syn* PLEASURE, delectation, enjoyment, joy, fruition *Ant* disappointment; discontent

**delight** *vb Syn* PLEASE, gratify, rejoice, gladden, tickle, regale *Ant* distress; bore

**delightful** ♦ highly pleasing to the senses or to aesthetic taste *Syn* delicious, delectable, luscious *Ant* distressing; boring; horrid

**delineate** 1 *Syn* SKETCH, trace, outline, diagram, draft, plot, blueprint 2 *Syn* REPRESENT, depict, portray, picture, limn

**delineation** *Syn* SKETCH, tracing, outline, sketch, diagram, plot, blueprint

**delinquent** *Syn* CRIMINAL, felon, convict, malefactor, culprit

**deliquesce** *Syn* LIQUEFY, melt, fuse, thaw

**delirious** *Syn* FURIOUS, frantic, frenzied, wild, frenetic, rabid

**delirium** *Syn* MANIA, frenzy, hysteria

**deliver** *Syn* RESCUE, redeem, save, ransom, reclaim

**delude** *Syn* DECEIVE, beguile, mislead, betray, double-cross *Ant* enlighten

**deluge** *Syn* FLOOD, inundation, torrent, spate, cataract

**delusion** ♦ something which is believed to be or is accepted as being true or real but which is actually false or unreal *Syn* illusion, hallucination, mirage

**delusive, delusory** *Syn* MISLEADING, deceptive

**delve** *Syn* DIG, spade, grub, excavate

**demand** ♦ to ask or call for something as due or as necessary or as strongly desired *Syn* claim, require, exact

**demarcate** *Syn* DISTINGUISH, differentiate, discriminate

**demean** *vb Syn* BEHAVE, deport, comport, conduct, acquit, quit

**demean** *vb Syn* ABASE, degrade, debase, humble, humiliate

**demeanor** *Syn* BEARING, deportment, mien, port, presence

**demented** *Syn* INSANE, mad, crazy, crazed, deranged, lunatic, maniac, non compos mentis *Ant* rational

**dementia** *Syn* INSANITY, lunacy, mania, psychosis

**demise** *Syn* DEATH, decease, passing

**demolish** *Syn* DESTROY, raze *Ant* construct

**demoniac, demonic** *Syn* FIENDISH, diabolic, diabolical, devilish

**demonstrate** 1 *Syn* SHOW, manifest, evince, evidence 2 *Syn* PROVE, try, test

**demonstration** *Syn* PROOF, trial, test

**demote** *Syn* DEGRADE, reduce, declass, disrate *Ant* promote (*in rank, grade*)

**demur** *vb* ♦ to hesitate or show reluctance because of difficulties in the way *Syn* scruple, balk, jib, shy, boggle, stick, stickle, strain *Ant* accede

**demur** *n Syn* QUALM, compunction, scruple

**denizen** *Syn* INHABITANT, resident, citizen

**denomination** 1 *Syn* NAME, designation, appellation, title, style 2 *Syn* RELIGION, sect, communion, faith, creed, cult, persuasion, church

**denote** *Syn* MEAN, signify, import

**denounce** *Syn* CRITICIZE, condemn, censure, reprobate, reprehend, blame *Ant* eulogize

**dense** 1 *Syn* CLOSE, compact, thick *Ant* sparse (*of population, forests*); tenuous (*of clouds, air, masses*) 2 *Syn* STUPID, crass, slow, dull, dumb *Ant* subtle; bright

**denude** *Syn* STRIP, bare, divest, dismantle *Ant* clothe

**deny** ♦ to refuse to accept as true or valid *Syn* gainsay, contradict, negative, traverse, impugn, contravene *Ant* confirm; concede

**depart** 1 *Syn* GO, leave, withdraw, retire, quit *Ant* arrive; remain, abide 2 *Syn* SWERVE, digress, deviate, diverge, veer

**departed** *Syn* DEAD, deceased, late, defunct, lifeless, inanimate

**depend** 1 ♦ (on *or* upon) *Syn* RELY, trust, count, reckon, bank 2 ♦ to rest or to be contingent upon something uncertain, variable, or indeterminable *Syn* hinge, hang, turn

**dependable** *Syn* RELIABLE, trustworthy, trusty, tried

**dependence** *Syn* TRUST, reliance, confidence, faith

**dependent** 1 ♦ determined or conditioned by another *Syn* contingent, conditional, relative *Ant* absolute; infinite; original 2 *Syn* SUBORDINATE, subject, tributary, secondary, collateral *Ant* independent

**depict** *Syn* REPRESENT, portray, delineate, picture, limn

**deplete** ♦ to bring to a low estate by depriving of something essential *Syn* drain, exhaust, impoverish, bankrupt

**deplore** ♦ to manifest grief or sorrow for something *Syn* lament, bewail, bemoan

**deport** 1 *Syn* BEHAVE, demean, comport, conduct, acquit, quit 2 *Syn* BANISH, transport, exile, expatriate, ostracize, extradite

**deportment** 1 *Syn* BEHAVIOR, conduct 2 *Syn* BEARING, demeanor, mien, port, presence

**deposit** ♦ matter which settles to the bottom of a

liquid *Syn* precipitate, sediment, dregs, lees, grounds

**deprave** *Syn* DEBASE, vitiate, corrupt, debauch, pervert

**depraved** *Syn* DEBASED, vitiated, corrupted, debauched, perverted

**deprecate** *Syn* DISAPPROVE *Ant* endorse

**depreciate** *Syn* DECRY, disparage, derogate, detract, belittle, minimize *Ant* appreciate

**depreciative, depreciatory** *Syn* DEROGATORY, disparaging, slighting, pejorative

**depress** ♦ to lower in spirit or mood *Syn* weigh, oppress *Ant* elate; cheer

**depressed** *Syn* DOWNCAST, dejected, dispirited, disconsolate, woebegone

**depression** *Syn* SADNESS, dejection, gloom, blues, dumps, melancholy, melancholia *Ant* buoyancy

**deputy 1** *Syn* AGENT, attorney, factor, proxy **2** *Syn* DELEGATE, representative

**deracinate** *Syn* EXTERMINATE, uproot, eradicate, extirpate, wipe

**derange** *Syn* DISORDER, disarrange, unsettle, disturb, disorganize *Ant* arrange; adjust

**deranged** *Syn* INSANE, demented, non compos mentis, crazed, crazy, mad, lunatic, maniac

**derangement** *Syn* ABERRATION, alienation

**derelict** *Syn* OUTCAST, castaway, reprobate, pariah, untouchable

**dereliction** *Syn* FAILURE, neglect, default, miscarriage

**deride** *Syn* RIDICULE, mock, taunt, twit, rally

**derive** *Syn* SPRING, originate, arise, rise, emanate, issue, stem, flow, proceed

**dernier cri** *Syn* FASHION, style, mode, vogue, fad, rage, craze, cry

**derogate** *Syn* DECRY, disparage, detract, belittle, minimize, depreciate

**derogatory** ♦ designed or tending to belittle *Syn* depreciatory, depreciative, disparaging, slighting, pejorative

**descant 1** *Syn* SING, troll, carol, warble, trill, hymn, chant, intone **2** *Syn* DISCOURSE, expatiate, dilate

**descend** ♦ to get or come down from a height *Syn* dismount, alight *Ant* ascend; climb

**descendant** *Syn* OFFSPRING, young, progeny, issue, posterity

**describe** *Syn* RELATE, narrate, state, report, rehearse, recite, recount

**description** *Syn* TYPE, kind, sort, character, nature, stripe, kidney, ilk

**descry** *Syn* SEE, espy, behold, observe, notice, remark, note, perceive, discern, view, survey, contemplate

**desecration** *Syn* PROFANATION, sacrilege, blasphemy

**desert** *n Syn* WASTE, badlands, wilderness

**desert** *n Syn* DUE, merit

**desert** *vb Syn* ABANDON, forsake *Ant* stick to, cleave to

**desertion** *Syn* DEFECTION, apostasy

**deserve** ♦ to be or become worthy of *Syn* merit, earn, rate

**desiccate** *Syn* DRY, dehydrate, parch, bake

**design** *vb* **1** *Syn* INTEND, mean, propose, purpose **2** *Syn* PLAN, plot, scheme, project

**design** *n* **1** *Syn* PLAN, plot, scheme, project **2** *Syn* INTENTION, intent, purpose, aim, end, object, objective, goal *Ant* accident **3** *Syn* FIGURE, pattern, motif, device

**designate** ♦ to declare a person one's choice *Syn* name, nominate, elect, appoint

**designation** *Syn* NAME, denomination, appellation, title, style

**designed** *Syn* DELIBERATE, premeditated, considered, advised, studied *Ant* accidental

**desire** *vb* ♦ to have a longing for something *Syn* wish, want, crave, covet

**desire** *n* ♦ a longing for something that promises enjoyment or satisfaction *Syn* appetite, lust, passion, urge *Ant* distaste

**desist** *Syn* STOP, discontinue, cease, quit *Ant* persist

**desolate 1** *Syn* ALONE, forlorn, lorn, lonesome, lone, solitary, lonely **2** *Syn* DISMAL, dreary, cheerless, dispiriting, bleak

**despair** *Syn* DESPONDENCY, hopelessness, desperation, forlornness *Ant* hope; optimism; beatitude

**despairing** *Syn* DESPONDENT, hopeless, desperate, forlorn *Ant* hopeful

**desperate** *Syn* DESPONDENT, hopeless, despairing, forlorn

**desperation** *Syn* DESPONDENCY, hopelessness, despair, forlornness

**despicable** *Syn* CONTEMPTIBLE, pitiable, sorry, scurvy, cheap, beggarly, shabby *Ant* praiseworthy, laudable

**despise** ♦ to regard as beneath one's notice and as unworthy of attention or interest *Syn* contemn, scorn, disdain, scout *Ant* appreciate

**despite** *n* **1** *Syn* MALICE, spite, ill will, malevolence, spleen, grudge, malignity, malignancy *Ant* appreciation; regard **2** ♦ the feeling or attitude of despising *Syn* contempt, scorn, disdain

**despite** *prep Syn* NOTWITHSTANDING, in spite of

**despoil** *Syn* RAVAGE, devastate, waste, sack, pillage, spoliate

**despondency** ♦ the state or feeling of having lost hope *Syn* despair, desperation, hopelessness, forlornness *Ant* lightheartedness

**despondent** ♦ having lost all or nearly all hope *Syn* despairing, desperate, hopeless, forlorn *Ant* lighthearted

**despotic** *Syn* ABSOLUTE, tyrannical, tyrannous, arbitrary, autocratic

**destiny** *Syn* FATE, lot, doom, portion

**destitute 1** *Syn* DEVOID, void **2** *Syn* POOR, indigent, needy, penniless, impecunious, poverty-stricken, necessitous *Ant* opulent

**destitution** *Syn* POVERTY, want, indigence, penury, privation *Ant* opulence

**destroy** ♦ to bring to ruin *Syn* demolish, raze

**destruction** *Syn* RUIN, havoc, devastation

**desultory** *Syn* RANDOM, casual, hit or miss, haphazard, happy-go-lucky, chance, chancy *Ant* assiduous; methodical

**detach** ♦ to remove one thing from another with which it is in union or association *Syn* disengage, abstract *Ant* attach, affix

**detached** *Syn* INDIFFERENT, aloof, uninterested, disinterested, unconcerned, incurious *Ant* interested; selfish

**detail 1** *Syn* ITEM, particular **2** *Syn* PART, portion, piece, parcel, member, division, segment, sector, fraction, fragment

**detailed** *Syn* CIRCUMSTANTIAL, itemized, particularized, minute, particular

**detain 1** *Syn* ARREST, apprehend, attach **2** *Syn* KEEP, withhold, hold, hold back, keep back, keep out, retain, reserve **3** *Syn* DELAY, retard, slow, slacken

**detention** *Syn* ARREST, apprehension, attachment

**deter** *Syn* DISSUADE, discourage, divert *Ant* abet; actuate, motivate

**deterioration** ♦ a falling from a higher to a lower level in quality, character, or vitality *Syn* degeneration, devolution, decadence, decline, declension *Ant* improvement, amelioration

**determinant** *Syn* CAUSE, antecedent, reason, occasion

**determinative** *Syn* CONCLUSIVE, decisive, definitive

**determine 1** *Syn* DECIDE, settle, rule, resolve **2** *Syn* DISCOVER, ascertain, unearth, learn

**determined** *Syn* DECIDED, decisive, resolved

**detest** *Syn* HATE, abhor, abominate, loathe *Ant* adore

**detestable** *Syn* HATEFUL, odious, abominable, abhorrent

**detestation** *Syn* ABHORRENCE, hate, hatred, abomination, loathing

**detract** *Syn* DECRY, belittle, minimize, disparage, derogate, depreciate

**detraction** ♦ the expression of damaging or malicious opinions *Syn* backbiting, calumny, slander, scandal

**detriment** *Syn* DISADVANTAGE, handicap, drawback *Ant* advantage, benefit

**detrimental** *Syn* PERNICIOUS, deleterious, noxious, baneful *Ant* beneficial

**devastate** *Syn* RAVAGE, waste, sack, pillage, despoil, spoliate

**devastation** *Syn* RUIN, havoc, destruction

**develop 1** *Syn* UNFOLD, evolve, elaborate, perfect **2** *Syn* MATURE, ripen, age

**development** ♦ advance from a lower to a higher form *Syn* evolution

**deviate** *Syn* SWERVE, digress, diverge, veer, depart

**deviation** ♦ departure from a straight course or procedure or from a norm or standard *Syn* aberration, divergence, deflection

**device 1** ♦ something usu. of a mechanical character that performs a function or effects a desired end *Syn* contrivance, gadget, contraption **2** *Syn* FIGURE, design, motif, pattern

**devilish** *Syn* FIENDISH, diabolical, diabolic, demoniac, demonic *Ant* angelic

**devious** *Syn* CROOKED, oblique *Ant* straightforward

**devise 1** *Syn* CONTRIVE, invent, frame, concoct **2** *Syn* WILL, bequeath, leave, legate

**devoid** ♦ showing a want or lack *Syn* void, destitute

**devolution** *Syn* DETERIORATION, decadence, decline, declension, degeneration *Ant* evolution

**devote 1** ♦ to set apart for a particular and often a better or higher use or end *Syn* dedicate, consecrate, hallow **2** *Syn* DIRECT, apply, address

**devoted** *Syn* LOVING, affectionate, fond, doting

**devotee** *Syn* ADDICT, votary, habitué

**devotion** *Syn* FIDELITY, loyalty, fealty, piety, allegiance

**devour** *Syn* EAT, swallow, ingest, consume

**devout** ♦ showing fervor and reverence in the practice of religion *Syn* pious, religious, pietistic, sanctimonious

**dexterity** *Syn* READINESS, facility, ease *Ant* clumsiness

**dexterous** ♦ ready and skilled in physical movements *Syn* adroit, deft, handy *Ant* clumsy

**diabolical, diabolic** *Syn* FIENDISH, demonic, devilish, demoniac

**diagram** *n Syn* SKETCH, outline, draft, tracing, delineation, plot, blueprint

**diagram** *vb Syn* SKETCH, outline, plot, blueprint, draft, trace, delineate

**dialect 1** ♦ a form of language that is not recognized as standard *Syn* vernacular, patois, lingo, jargon, cant, argot, slang **2** *Syn* LANGUAGE, tongue, speech, idiom

**dialectic** *Syn* ARGUMENTATION, disputation, debate, forensic

**diaphanous** *Syn* CLEAR, limpid, pellucid, transparent, translucent, lucid

**diatribe** *Syn* TIRADE, jeremiad, philippic

**dictate** *vb* ♦ to lay down expressly something to be followed, observed, obeyed, or accepted *Syn* prescribe, ordain, decree, impose

**dictate** *n Syn* COMMAND, behest, bidding, injunction, order, mandate

**dictatorial** ♦ imposing one's will or opinions on others *Syn* magisterial, authoritarian, dogmatic, doctrinaire, oracular

**diction** *Syn* LANGUAGE, vocabulary, phraseology, phrasing, style

**dido** *Syn* PRANK, caper, antic, monkeyshine

**differ** ♦ to be unlike or out of harmony *Syn* vary, disagree, dissent *Ant* agree

**difference 1** *Syn* DISSIMILARITY, unlikeness, divergence, divergency, distinction *Ant* resemblance **2** *Syn* DISCORD, strife, conflict, contention, dissension, variance

**different** ♦ unlike in kind or character *Syn* diverse, divergent, disparate, various *Ant* identical, alike, same

**differentiate** *Syn* DISTINGUISH, discriminate, demarcate *Ant* confuse

**difficult** *Syn* HARD, arduous *Ant* simple

**difficulty** ♦ something which demands effort and

endurance if it is to be overcome or one's end achieved **Syn** hardship, rigor, vicissitude

**diffident** *Syn* SHY, modest, bashful, coy *Ant* confident

**diffuse** *adj Syn* WORDY, prolix, redundant, verbose *Ant* succinct

**diffuse** *vb Syn* SPREAD, circulate, disseminate, propagate, radiate *Ant* concentrate

**dig** ♦ to loosen and turn over or remove (as soil) with or as if with a spade *Syn* delve, spade, grub, excavate

**digest** *Syn* COMPENDIUM, syllabus, pandect, survey, sketch, précis, aperçu

**digit** *Syn* NUMBER, numeral, figure, integer

**dignify** ♦ to enhance the status of or raise in human estimation *Syn* ennoble, honor, glorify

**dignity 1** *Syn* DECORUM, decency, propriety, etiquette **2** *Syn* ELEGANCE, grace

**digress** *Syn* SWERVE, deviate, diverge, depart, veer

**digression** ♦ a departure from a subject or theme *Syn* episode, excursus, divagation

**dilapidate** *Syn* RUIN, wreck

**dilapidated** *Syn* SHABBY, dingy, faded, seedy, threadbare

**dilate 1** *Syn* DISCOURSE, expatiate, descant **2** *Syn* EXPAND, distend, swell, amplify, inflate *Ant* constrict; circumscribe; attenuate

**dilatory** *Syn* SLOW, laggard, deliberate, leisurely *Ant* diligent

**dilemma** *Syn* PREDICAMENT, quandary, plight, scrape, fix, jam, pickle

**dilettante 1** *Syn* AMATEUR, dabbler, tyro **2** *Syn* AESTHETE, connoisseur

**diligent** *Syn* BUSY, assiduous, sedulous, industrious *Ant* dilatory

**dilute** *Syn* THIN, attenuate, rarefy *Ant* condense; concentrate

**dim** *adj Syn* DARK, dusky, obscure, murky, gloomy *Ant* bright; distinct

**dim** *vb Syn* OBSCURE, bedim, darken, eclipse, cloud, becloud, fog, befog, obfuscate *Ant* illustrate

**dimensions** *Syn* SIZE, extent, area, magnitude, volume

**diminish** *Syn* DECREASE, reduce, lessen, abate, dwindle

**diminutive** *Syn* SMALL, little, wee, tiny, minute, miniature

**din** *n* ♦ a disturbing or confusing welter of sounds *Syn* uproar, pandemonium, hullabaloo, babel, hubbub, clamor, racket *Ant* quiet

**dingy** *Syn* SHABBY, dilapidated, faded, seedy, threadbare

**dinner** ♦ a usu. elaborate meal served to guests or to a group often to mark an occasion or honor an individual *Syn* banquet, feast

**dip 1** ♦ to plunge a person or thing into or as if into liquid *Syn* immerse, submerge, duck, souse, dunk **2** ♦ to remove a liquid or a loose or soft substance from a container by means of an implement shaped to hold liquid *Syn* bail, scoop, ladle, spoon, dish

**diplomatic** *Syn* SUAVE, politic, smooth, bland, urbane

**dipsomaniac** *Syn* DRUNKARD, alcoholic, inebriate, sot, soak, toper, tosspot, tippler

**direct** *vb* **1** ♦ to turn or bend one's attention or efforts toward a certain object or objective *Syn* address, devote, apply **2** ♦ to turn something toward its appointed or intended mark or goal *Syn* aim, point, level, train, lay *Ant* misdirect **3** *Syn* CONDUCT, manage, control **4** *Syn* COMMAND, order, bid, enjoin, instruct, charge

**direct** *adj* ♦ marked by the absence of interruption (as between the cause and the effect, the source and the issue, or the beginning and the end) *Syn* immediate

**directly** *Syn* PRESENTLY, shortly, soon

**dirty** *adj* ♦ conspicuously unclean or impure *Syn* filthy, foul, nasty, squalid *Ant* clean

**dirty** *vb Syn* SOIL, sully, tarnish, foul, befoul, smirch, besmirch, grime, begrime

**disable** *Syn* WEAKEN, cripple, undermine, enfeeble, debilitate, sap *Ant* rehabilitate

**disabuse** *Syn* RID, clear, unburden, purge

**disadvantage** ♦ something which interferes with the success or well-being of a person or thing *Syn* detriment, handicap, drawback *Ant* advantage

**disaffect** *Syn* ESTRANGE, alienate, wean *Ant* win over

**disagree** *Syn* DIFFER, vary, dissent *Ant* agree

**disallow** *Syn* DISCLAIM, disavow, repudiate, disown *Ant* allow

**disappear** *Syn* VANISH, evanesce, evaporate, fade *Ant* appear

**disapprove** ♦ to feel or to express an objection to or condemnation of *Syn* deprecate *Ant* approve

**disarrange** *Syn* DISORDER, derange, disorganize, unsettle, disturb *Ant* arrange

**disarray** *Syn* CONFUSION, disorder, chaos, jumble, clutter, snarl, muddle

**disaster** ♦ an event bringing great damage, loss, or destruction *Syn* calamity, catastrophe, cataclysm

**disastrous** *Syn* UNLUCKY, ill-starred, ill-fated, unfortunate, calamitous, luckless, hapless

**disavow** *Syn* DISCLAIM, repudiate, disown, disallow *Ant* avow

**disbar** *Syn* EXCLUDE, shut out, eliminate, rule out, suspend, debar, blackball

**disbelief** *Syn* UNBELIEF, incredulity *Ant* belief

**disburse** *Syn* SPEND, expend

**discard** ♦ to get rid of *Syn* cast, shed, molt, slough, scrap, junk

**discern** *Syn* SEE, perceive, descry, observe, notice, remark, note, espy, behold, view, survey, contemplate

**discernment** ♦ a power to see what is not evident to the average mind *Syn* discrimination, perception, penetration, insight, acumen

**discharge 1** *Syn* FREE, release, liberate, emancipate, manumit **2** *Syn* DISMISS, cashier, drop, sack, fire, bounce **3** *Syn* PERFORM, execute, accomplish, achieve, effect, fulfill

**disciple** *Syn* FOLLOWER, adherent, henchman, satellite, sectary, partisan

**discipline** *n Syn* MORALE, esprit de corps *Ant* anarchy, lawlessness

**discipline** *vb* **1** *Syn* TEACH, train, educate, instruct, school **2** *Syn* PUNISH, chastise, castigate, chasten, correct

**disclaim** ♦ to refuse to admit, accept, or approve *Syn* disavow, repudiate, disown, disallow *Ant* claim

**disclose** *Syn* REVEAL, divulge, tell, discover, betray

**discomfit** *Syn* EMBARRASS, disconcert, faze, abash, rattle

**discommode** *Syn* INCONVENIENCE, incommode, trouble

**discompose** ♦ to excite one so as to destroy one's capacity for clear or collected thought or prompt action *Syn* disquiet, disturb, perturb, agitate, upset, fluster, flurry

**disconcert** *Syn* EMBARRASS, rattle, faze, discomfit, abash

**disconsolate** *Syn* DOWNCAST, woebegone, dejected, depressed, dispirited

**discontinue** *Syn* STOP, desist, cease, quit *Ant* continue

**discord** ♦ a state or condition marked by disagreement and lack of harmony *Syn* strife, conflict, contention, dissension, difference, variance

**discordant** *Syn* INCONSONANT, incongruous, uncongenial, unsympathetic, incompatible, inconsistent, discrepant

**discount** *Syn* DEDUCTION, rebate, abatement

**discourage 1** ♦ to weaken the stamina, interest, or zeal of *Syn* dishearten, dispirit, deject *Ant* encourage **2** *Syn* DISSUADE, deter, divert

**discourse** *n* ♦ a systematic, serious, and often learned exposition of a subject or topic *Syn* treatise, disquisition, dissertation, thesis, monograph

**discourse** *vb* ♦ to talk or sometimes write esp.

formally and at length upon a subject *Syn* expatiate, dilate, descant

**discourteous** *Syn* RUDE, impolite, uncivil, ungracious, ill-mannered *Ant* courteous

**discover 1** *Syn* REVEAL, disclose, divulge, tell, betray **2** ♦ to find out something not previously known *Syn* ascertain, determine, unearth, learn

**discreet** *Syn* PRUDENT, forethoughtful, foresighted, provident *Ant* indiscreet

**discrepant** *Syn* INCONSONANT, inconsistent, discordant, incompatible, incongruous, uncongenial, unsympathetic *Ant* identical (*as accounts, explanations*)

**discrete** *Syn* DISTINCT, separate, several

**discretion** *Syn* PRUDENCE, forethought, foresight, providence *Ant* indiscretion

**discriminate** *Syn* DISTINGUISH, differentiate, demarcate *Ant* confound

**discrimination** *Syn* DISCERNMENT, penetration, insight, perception, acumen

**discuss** ♦ to exchange views about something in order to arrive at the truth or to convince others *Syn* argue, debate, dispute, agitate

**disdain** *n Syn* DESPITE, scorn, contempt

**disdain** *vb Syn* DESPISE, scorn, scout, contemn *Ant* favor; admit

**disdainful** *Syn* PROUD, supercilious, overbearing, insolent, arrogant, lordly, haughty

**disease** ♦ an impairment of the normal state of the living body that interferes with normal bodily functions *Syn* disorder, condition, affection, ailment, malady, complaint, distemper, syndrome

**diseased** *Syn* UNWHOLESOME, morbid, sickly, pathological

**disembarrass** *Syn* EXTRICATE, disencumber, disentangle, untangle

**disencumber** *Syn* EXTRICATE, disembarrass, disentangle, untangle

**disengage** *Syn* DETACH, abstract *Ant* engage

**disentangle** *Syn* EXTRICATE, untangle, disembarrass, disencumber *Ant* entangle

**disfavor** *Syn* DISLIKE, distaste, aversion

**disfigure** *Syn* DEFACE, *Ant* adorn

**disgorge** *Syn* BELCH, burp, vomit, regurgitate, spew, throw up

**disgrace** ♦ the state of suffering loss of esteem and of enduring reproach *Syn* dishonor, disrepute, shame, infamy, ignominy, opprobrium, obloquy, odium *Ant* respect, esteem

**disguise** ♦ to alter so as to hide the true appearance or character of *Syn* cloak, mask, dissemble, camouflage

**disgust** ♦ to arouse an extreme distaste in *Syn* sicken, nauseate *Ant* charm

**dish** *Syn* DIP, ladle, spoon, bail, scoop

**dishearten** *Syn* DISCOURAGE, dispirit, deject *Ant* hearten

**disheveled** *Syn* SLIPSHOD, unkempt, sloppy, slovenly

**dishonest** ♦ unworthy of trust or belief *Syn* DECEITFUL, mendacious, lying, untruthful *Ant* honest

**dishonor** *Syn* DISGRACE, disrepute, shame, infamy, ignominy, opprobrium, obloquy, odium *Ant* honor

**disillusioned** *Syn* SOPHISTICATED, worldly-wise, worldly, blasé

**disinclined** ♦ lacking the will or the desire to do something *Syn* indisposed, hesitant, reluctant, loath, averse

**disinfect** *Syn* STERILIZE, sanitize, fumigate *Ant* infect

**disintegrate** *Syn* DECAY, crumble, decompose, rot, putrefy, spoil *Ant* integrate

**disinterested** *Syn* INDIFFERENT, uninterested, detached, aloof, unconcerned, incurious *Ant* interested; prejudiced, biased

**dislike** ♦ a feeling of aversion or disapproval *Syn* distaste, aversion, disfavor *Ant* liking

**disloyal** *Syn* FAITHLESS, false, perfidious, traitorous, treacherous *Ant* loyal

**dismal** ♦ devoid of all that makes for cheer or

comfort *Syn* dreary, cheerless, dispiriting, bleak, desolate

**dismantle** *Syn* STRIP, divest, denude, bare

**dismay** *vb* ♦ to unnerve and check by arousing fear, apprehension, or aversion *Syn* appall, horrify, daunt *Ant* cheer

**dismay** *n Syn* FEAR, alarm, consternation, panic, dread, fright, terror, horror, trepidation

**dismiss 1** ♦ to let go from one's employ or service *Syn* discharge, cashier, drop, sack, fire, bounce **2** *Syn* EJECT, oust, expel, evict

**dismount** *Syn* DESCEND, alight

**disorder** *vb* ♦ to undo the fixed or proper order of something *Syn* derange, disarrange, disorganize, unsettle, disturb

**disorder** *n* **1** *Syn* CONFUSION, disarray, clutter, jumble, chaos, snarl, muddle *Ant* order **2** *Syn* DISEASE, condition, affection, ailment, malady, complaint, distemper, syndrome

**disorganize** *Syn* DISORDER, disturb, unsettle, derange, disarrange

**disown** *Syn* DISCLAIM, disavow, repudiate, disallow *Ant* own

**disparage** *Syn* DECRY, depreciate, derogate, detract, belittle, minimize *Ant* applaud

**disparaging** *Syn* DEROGATORY, depreciatory, depreciative, slighting, pejorative

**disparate** *Syn* DIFFERENT, diverse, divergent, various *Ant* comparable, analogous

**dispassionate** *Syn* FAIR, unbiased, impartial, objective, uncolored, just, equitable *Ant* passionate; intemperate

**dispatch** *vb* **1** *Syn* SEND, forward, transmit, remit, route, ship **2** *Syn* KILL, slay, murder, assassinate, execute

**dispatch** *n* **1** *Syn* HASTE, speed, expedition, hurry *Ant* delay **2** *Syn* LETTER, message, note, epistle, report, memorandum, missive

**dispel** *Syn* SCATTER, dissipate, disperse

**dispense** *Syn* DISTRIBUTE, divide, deal, dole **2** *Syn* ADMINISTER

**disperse** *Syn* SCATTER, dissipate, dispel *Ant* assemble, congregate; collect

**dispirit** *Syn* DISCOURAGE, dishearten, deject *Ant* inspirit

**dispirited** *Syn* DOWNCAST, depressed, dejected, disconsolate, woebegone *Ant* high-spirited

**dispiriting** *Syn* DISMAL, dreary, cheerless, bleak, desolate *Ant* inspiriting

**displace** *Syn* REPLACE, supplant, supersede

**display** *vb Syn* SHOW, exhibit, expose, parade, flaunt

**display** *n* ♦ a striking or spectacular show or exhibition for the sake of effect *Syn* parade, array, pomp

**disport** *n Syn* PLAY, sport, frolic, rollick, romp, gambol

**disport** *vb Syn* PLAY, sport, frolic, rollick, romp, gambol

**disposal** ♦ the act or the power of disposing of something *Syn* disposition

**dispose** *Syn* INCLINE, predispose, bias

**disposition 1** *Syn* DISPOSAL **2** ♦ the prevailing and dominant quality or qualities which distinguish or identify a person or group *Syn* temperament, temper, complexion, character, personality, individuality

**disprove** ♦ to show by presenting evidence that something is not true *Syn* refute, confute, rebut, controvert *Ant* prove, demonstrate

**disputation** *Syn* ARGUMENTATION, debate, forensic, dialectic

**dispute** *vb Syn* DISCUSS, argue, debate, agitate *Ant* concede

**dispute** *n Syn* ARGUMENT, controversy

**disquiet** *Syn* DISCOMPOSE, disturb, agitate, perturb, upset, fluster, flurry *Ant* tranquilize, soothe

**disquisition** *Syn* DISCOURSE, dissertation, thesis, treatise, monograph

**disrate** *Syn* DEGRADE, demote, reduce, declass

**disregard** *Syn* NEGLECT, ignore, overlook, slight, forget, omit

**disrepute** *Syn* DISGRACE, dishonor, shame, infamy, ignominy, opprobrium, obloquy, odium

**dissect** *Syn* ANALYZE, break down, resolve

**dissection** *Syn* ANALYSIS, breakdown, resolution

**dissemble** *Syn* DISGUISE, mask, cloak, camouflage *Ant* betray

**disseminate** *Syn* SPREAD, circulate, diffuse, propagate, radiate

**dissension** *Syn* DISCORD, difference, variance, strife, conflict, contention *Ant* accord; comity

**dissent** *Syn* DIFFER, vary, disagree *Ant* concur; assent; consent

**dissenter** *Syn* HERETIC, nonconformist, sectarian, sectary, schismatic

**dissertation** *Syn* DISCOURSE, disquisition, thesis, treatise, monograph

**dissimilarity** ♦ lack of agreement or correspondence or an instance of this *Syn* unlikeness, difference, divergence, divergency, distinction *Ant* similarity

**dissimulation** *Syn* DECEIT, duplicity, cunning, guile

**dissipate 1** *Syn* SCATTER, dispel, disperse *Ant* accumulate; absorb; concentrate **2** *Syn* WASTE, squander, fritter, consume

**dissolute** *Syn* ABANDONED, profligate, reprobate

**dissuade** ♦ to turn one aside from a purpose, a project, or a plan *Syn* deter, discourage, divert *Ant* persuade

**distant** ♦ not close in space, time, or relationship *Syn* far, faraway, far-off, remote, removed

**distaste** *Syn* DISLIKE, aversion, disfavor *Ant* taste

**distasteful** *Syn* REPUGNANT, obnoxious, repellent, abhorrent, invidious *Ant* agreeable; palatable

**distemper** *Syn* DISEASE, complaint, syndrome, malady, ailment, disorder, condition, affection

**distend** *Syn* EXPAND, swell, dilate, inflate, amplify *Ant* constrict

**distinct 1** ♦ capable of being distinguished as differing *Syn* separate, several, discrete **2** *Syn* EVIDENT, manifest, patent, obvious, apparent, palpable, plain, clear *Ant* indistinct; nebulous

**distinction** *Syn* DISSIMILARITY, difference, divergence, divergency, unlikeness

**distinctive** *Syn* CHARACTERISTIC, peculiar, individual *Ant* typical

**distinguish 1** ♦ to recognize the differences between *Syn* differentiate, discriminate, demarcate *Ant* confound **2** *Syn* CHARACTERIZE, mark, qualify

**distort** *Syn* DEFORM, contort, warp

**distract** *Syn* PUZZLE, bewilder, nonplus, confound, dumbfound, mystify, perplex *Ant* collect (*one's thoughts, one's powers*)

**distraught** *Syn* ABSTRACTED, absentminded, absent, preoccupied *Ant* collected

**distress** *n* ♦ the state of being in great trouble or in mental or physical anguish *Syn* suffering, misery, agony, dolor, passion

**distress** *vb Syn* TROUBLE, ail

**distribute** ♦ to give out, usu. in shares, to each member of a group *Syn* dispense, divide, deal, dole *Ant* collect; amass

**district** *Syn* LOCALITY, vicinity, neighborhood

**distrust** *vb* ♦ to lack trust or confidence in *Syn* mistrust, doubt, misdoubt, suspect

**distrust** *n* ♦ a lack of trust or confidence *Syn* mistrust

**disturb 1** *Syn* DISORDER, unsettle, derange, disarrange, disorganize **2** *Syn* DISCOMPOSE, perturb, upset, disquiet, agitate, fluster, flurry

**dither** *Syn* SHAKE, tremble, quake, quiver, shiver, quaver, wobble, teeter, shimmy, shudder, totter

**diurnal** *Syn* DAILY, quotidian

**divagation** *Syn* DIGRESSION, episode, excursus

**dive** *Syn* PLUNGE, pitch

**diverge** *Syn* SWERVE, veer, deviate, depart, digress *Ant* converge; conform

**divergence 1** *Syn* DEVIATION, deflection, aberration *Ant* convergence **2** *Syn* DISSIMILARITY, divergency, difference, unlikeness, distinction *Ant* conformity, correspondence

**divergency** *Syn* DISSIMILARITY, divergence, difference, unlikeness, distinction

**divergent** *Syn* DIFFERENT, diverse, disparate, various *Ant* convergent

**divers** *Syn* MANY, several, sundry, various, numerous, multifarious

**diverse** *Syn* DIFFERENT, divergent, disparate, various *Ant* identical, selfsame

**diversion** *Syn* AMUSEMENT, recreation, entertainment

**diversity** *Syn* VARIETY *Ant* uniformity; identity

**divert 1** *Syn* TURN, deflect, avert, sheer **2** *Syn* AMUSE, entertain, recreate **3** *Syn* DISSUADE, deter, discourage

**divest** *Syn* STRIP, denude, bare, dismantle *Ant* invest, vest (*in robes of office, with power or authority*); apparel, clothe

**divide 1** *Syn* SEPARATE, part, sever, sunder, divorce *Ant* unite **2** *Syn* DISTRIBUTE, dispense, deal, dole

**divine** *adj Syn* HOLY, sacred, spiritual, religious, blessed

**divine** *vb Syn* FORESEE, foreknow, apprehend, anticipate

**division** *Syn* PART, section, segment, sector, portion, piece, detail, member, fraction, fragment, parcel

**divorce** *Syn* SEPARATE, sever, sunder, part, divide

**divulge** *Syn* REVEAL, tell, disclose, betray, discover

**dizzy** *Syn* GIDDY, vertiginous, swimming, dazzled

**docile** *Syn* OBEDIENT, biddable, tractable, amenable *Ant* indocile; unruly, ungovernable

**dock** *Syn* WHARF, pier, quay, slip, berth, jetty, levee

**doctor** *Syn* ADULTERATE, sophisticate, load, weight

**doctrinaire** *Syn* DICTATORIAL, dogmatic, magisterial, oracular, authoritarian

**doctrine** ♦ a principle accepted as valid and authoritative *Syn* dogma, tenet

**document** ♦ something preserved and serving as evidence (as of an event, a situation, or the culture of the period) *Syn* monument, record, archive

**dodge** ♦ to avoid or evade by some maneuver or shift *Syn* parry, sidestep, duck, shirk, fence, malinger *Ant* face

**dogged** *Syn* OBSTINATE, pertinacious, mulish, stubborn, stiff-necked, pigheaded, bullheaded *Ant* faltering

**dogma** *Syn* DOCTRINE, tenet

**dogmatic** *Syn* DICTATORIAL, magisterial, doctrinaire, oracular, authoritarian

**doldrums** *Syn* TEDIUM, boredom, ennui *Ant* spirits, high spirits

**dole** *n Syn* RATION, allowance, pittance

**dole** *vb Syn* DISTRIBUTE, dispense, deal, divide

**doleful** *Syn* MELANCHOLY, lugubrious, dolorous, plaintive, rueful *Ant* cheerful, cheery

**dolor** *Syn* DISTRESS, agony, suffering, passion, misery *Ant* beatitude, blessedness

**dolorous** *Syn* MELANCHOLY, doleful, plaintive, lugubrious, rueful

**domain** *Syn* FIELD, sphere, province, territory, bailiwick

**domicile** *Syn* HABITATION, dwelling, abode, residence, house, home

**dominant** ♦ superior to all others in power, influence, position, or rank *Syn* predominant, paramount, preponderant, preponderating, sovereign *Ant* subordinate

**domineering** *Syn* MASTERFUL, imperious, imperative, peremptory *Ant* subservient

**dominion** *Syn* POWER, control, command, sway, authority, jurisdiction

**donate** *Syn* GIVE, present, bestow, confer, afford

**donation** ♦ a gift of money or its equivalent for a charitable, philanthropic, or humanitarian object *Syn* benefaction, contribution, alms

**doom** *n Syn* FATE, destiny, lot, portion

**doom** *vb Syn* SENTENCE, damn, condemn, proscribe

**door** ♦ an entrance to a place *Syn* gate, portal, postern, doorway, gateway

**doorway** *Syn* DOOR, portal, postern, gate, gateway

**dormant** 1 *Syn* LATENT, quiescent, abeyant, potential *Ant* active, live 2 *Syn* PRONE, couchant, recumbent, supine, prostrate

**dormer** *Syn* WINDOW, casement, oriel

**dotage** *Syn* AGE, senility, senescence *Ant* infancy

**dote** *Syn* LIKE, love, relish, enjoy, fancy *Ant* loathe

**doting** *Syn* LOVING, fond, devoted, affectionate

**double** *Syn* SUBSTITUTE, understudy, stand-in, supply, locum tenens, alternate, pinch hitter

**double-cross** *Syn* DECEIVE, delude, betray, beguile, mislead

**double-dealing** *Syn* DECEPTION, chicanery, chicane, trickery, fraud

**double entendre** *Syn* AMBIGUITY, equivocation, tergiversation

**doubt** *n Syn* UNCERTAINTY, skepticism, suspicion, mistrust, dubiety, dubiosity *Ant* certitude; confidence

**doubt** *vb Syn* DISTRUST, mistrust, misdoubt, suspect

**doubtful** ♦ not affording assurance of the worth, soundness, success, or certainty of something or someone *Syn* dubious, problematic, questionable *Ant* cocksure, positive

**doughty** *Syn* BRAVE, courageous, unafraid, fearless, intrepid, valiant, valorous, dauntless, undaunted, bold, audacious

**dour** *Syn* SULLEN, saturnine, glum, gloomy, morose, surly, sulky, crabbed

**dowdy** *Syn* SLATTERNLY, frowzy, blowsy *Ant* smart (*in dress, appearance*)

**dower** ♦ to furnish or provide with a gift *Syn* endow, endue

**downcast** ♦ very low in spirits *Syn* dispirited, dejected, depressed, disconsolate, woebegone *Ant* elated

**downright** *Syn* FORTHRIGHT

**doze** *Syn* SLEEP, drowse, snooze, slumber, nap, catnap

**draft** *n Syn* SKETCH, outline, diagram, delineation, tracing, plot, blueprint

**draft** *vb Syn* SKETCH, outline, diagram, delineate, trace, plot, blueprint

**drag** *Syn* PULL, draw, haul, hale, tug, tow

**drain** *Syn* DEPLETE, exhaust, impoverish, bankrupt

**dramatic** ♦ of, relating to, or suggestive of plays, or the performance of a play *Syn* theatrical, dramaturgic, melodramatic, histrionic

**dramaturgic** *Syn* DRAMATIC, theatrical, histrionic, melodramatic

**draw** *vb Syn* PULL, drag, tug, tow, haul, hale

**draw** *n* ♦ an indecisive ending to a contest or competition *Syn* tie, stalemate, deadlock, standoff

**drawback** *Syn* DISADVANTAGE, detriment, handicap

**dread** *Syn* FEAR, horror, terror, fright, alarm, trepidation, panic, consternation, dismay

**dreadful** *Syn* FEARFUL, horrible, horrific, appalling, awful, frightful, terrible, terrific, shocking

**dream** *Syn* FANCY, fantasy, phantasy, phantasm, vision, daydream, nightmare

**dreary** 1 *Syn* DISMAL, cheerless, dispiriting, bleak, desolate 2 *Syn* DULL, humdrum, monotonous, pedestrian, stodgy

**dregs** *Syn* DEPOSIT, sediment, precipitate, lees, grounds

**drench** *Syn* SOAK, saturate, sop, steep, impregnate, waterlog

**dress** *vb Syn* CLOTHE, attire, apparel, array, robe *Ant* undress

**dress** *n Syn* CLOTHES, clothing, attire, apparel, raiment

**drift** *Syn* TENDENCY, trend, tenor

**drill** *vb* 1 *Syn* PERFORATE, bore, punch, puncture, prick 2 *Syn* PRACTICE, exercise

**drill** *n Syn* PRACTICE, exercise

**drive** *vb Syn* MOVE, impel, actuate

**drive** *n* 1 *Syn* RIDE 2 *Syn* VIGOR, vim, spirit, dash, esprit, verve, punch, élan

**drivel** *Syn* NONSENSE, twaddle, bunk, balderdash, poppycock, gobbledygook, trash, rot, bull

**droll** *Syn* LAUGHABLE, risible, comic, comical, funny, ludicrous, ridiculous, farcical

**droop** ♦ to become literally or figuratively limp through loss of vigor or freshness *Syn* wilt, flag, sag

**drop** 1 *Syn* FALL, sink, slump, subside *Ant* mount 2 *Syn* DISMISS, discharge, cashier, sack, fire, bounce

**drowse** *Syn* SLEEP, doze, snooze, slumber, nap, catnap

**drowsy** *Syn* SLEEPY, somnolent, slumberous

**drudgery** *Syn* WORK, toil, travail, labor, grind

**drug** ♦ a substance used by itself or in a mixture for the treatment or in the diagnosis of disease *Syn* medicinal, pharmaceutical, biologic, simple

**druggist** ♦ one who deals in medicinal drugs *Syn* pharmacist, apothecary, chemist

**drunk** ♦ having the faculties impaired by alcohol *Syn* drunken, intoxicated, inebriated, tipsy, tight *Ant* sober

**drunkard** ♦ one who is habitually drunk *Syn* inebriate, alcoholic, dipsomaniac, sot, soak, toper, tosspot, tippler *Ant* teetotaler

**drunken** *Syn* DRUNK, intoxicated, inebriated, tipsy, tight

**dry** *adj* 1 ♦ devoid of moisture *Syn* arid *Ant* wet 2 *Syn* SOUR, acid, acidulous, tart *Ant* sweet (*wine*)

**dry** *vb* ♦ to treat or to affect so as to deprive of moisture *Syn* desiccate, dehydrate, bake, parch *Ant* moisten, wet

**dubiety** *Syn* UNCERTAINTY, dubiosity, doubt, skepticism, suspicion, mistrust *Ant* decision

**dubiosity** *Syn* UNCERTAINTY, dubiety, doubt, skepticism, suspicion, mistrust *Ant* decidedness

**dubious** *Syn* DOUBTFUL, questionable, problematic *Ant* cocksure; reliable; trustworthy

**duck** 1 *Syn* DIP, immerse, submerge, souse, dunk 2 *Syn* DODGE, parry, shirk, sidestep, fence, malinger

**duct** *Syn* CHANNEL, canal, conduit, aqueduct

**ductile** *Syn* PLASTIC, pliable, pliant, malleable, adaptable

**dude** *Syn* FOP, dandy, beau, coxcomb, exquisite, buck

**dudgeon** *Syn* OFFENSE, umbrage, huff, pique, resentment

**due** *adj* ♦ being in accordance with what is just and appropriate *Syn* rightful, condign

**due** *n* ♦ what is justly owed to a person (sometimes a thing), esp. as a recompense or compensation *Syn* desert, merit

**dulcet** *Syn* SWEET, engaging, winning, winsome *Ant* grating

**dull** 1 *Syn* STUPID, slow, dumb, dense, crass *Ant* clever, bright 2 ♦ lacking sharpness of edge or point *Syn* blunt, obtuse *Ant* sharp; poignant (*sensation, feeling, reaction*) 3 ♦ being so unvaried and uninteresting as to provoke boredom or tedium *Syn* humdrum, dreary, monotonous, pedestrian, stodgy *Ant* lively

**dumb** 1 ♦ lacking the power to speak *Syn* mute, speechless, inarticulate 2 *Syn* STUPID, dull, slow, dense, crass *Ant* articulate

**dumbfound** *Syn* PUZZLE, confound, nonplus, bewilder, distract, mystify, perplex

**dumps** *Syn* SADNESS, dejection, gloom, blues, depression, melancholy, melancholia

**dumpy** *Syn* STOCKY, thickset, thick, chunky, stubby, squat

**dunk** *Syn* DIP, immerse, souse, submerge, duck

**dupe** ♦ mean to delude by underhanded means or methods *Syn* gull, befool, trick, hoax, hoodwink, bamboozle

**duplicate** *Syn* REPRODUCTION, facsimile, copy, carbon copy, transcript, replica

**duplicity** *Syn* DECEIT, dissimulation, cunning, guile

**durable** *Syn* LASTING, perdurable, permanent, stable, perpetual

**duress** *Syn* FORCE, constraint, coercion, compulsion, violence, restraint

**dusky** *Syn* DARK, dim, obscure, murky, gloomy

**duty** 1 *Syn* OBLIGATION 2 *Syn* FUNCTION, office, province 3 *Syn* TASK, assignment, job, stint, chore

**dwarf** ♦ an individual and usu. a person of very small size *Syn* pygmy, midget, manikin, homunculus, runt

**dwell** *Syn* RESIDE, live, lodge, sojourn, stay, put up, stop

**dwelling** *Syn* HABITATION, abode, residence, domicile, home, house

**dwindle** *Syn* DECREASE, diminish, lessen, reduce

**dynamic** *Syn* ACTIVE, live, operative

# E

**each** *adj Syn* ALL, every

**each** *adv* ♦ by, for, or to every one of the many *Syn* apiece, severally, individually, respectively

**eager** ♦ moved by a strong and urgent desire or interest *Syn* avid, keen, anxious, agog, athirst *Ant* listless

**early** ♦ at or nearly at the beginning of a specified or implied period of time *Syn* soon, beforehand, betimes *Ant* late

**earn** *Syn* DESERVE, merit, rate

**earnest** *adj Syn* SERIOUS, solemn, grave, somber, sober, sedate, staid *Ant* frivolous

**earnest** *n Syn* PLEDGE, token, pawn, hostage

**earsplitting** *Syn* LOUD, stentorian, hoarse, raucous, strident, stertorous

**earth** ♦ the entire area or extent of space in which human beings think of themselves as living and acting *Syn* world, globe, planet

**earthly** ♦ of, belonging to, or characteristic of the earth or life on earth *Syn* terrestrial, earthy, mundane, worldly, sublunary

**earthy** *Syn* EARTHLY, mundane, worldly, terrestrial, sublunary

**ease** 1 *Syn* REST, comfort, relaxation, repose, leisure 2 *Syn* READINESS, facility, dexterity *Ant* effort

**easy** 1 *Syn* COMFORTABLE, restful, cozy, snug *Ant* disquieting, disquieted 2 ♦ causing or involving little or no difficulty *Syn* facile, simple, light, effortless, smooth *Ant* hard

**eat** ♦ to take food into the stomach through the mouth *Syn* swallow, ingest, devour, consume

**ebb** *Syn* ABATE, subside, wane *Ant* flow

**eccentric** *Syn* STRANGE, erratic, odd, queer, peculiar, singular, unique, quaint, outlandish, curious

**eccentricity** ♦ an act, a practice, or a characteristic that impresses the observer as strange or singular *Syn* idiosyncrasy

**echelon** *Syn* LINE, row, rank, file, tier

**éclat** *Syn* FAME, renown, glory, celebrity, notoriety, repute, reputation, honor

**eclipse** *Syn* OBSCURE, dim, bedim, darken, cloud, becloud, fog, befog, obfuscate

**economical** *Syn* SPARING, frugal, thrifty *Ant* extravagant

**ecstasy** ♦ a feeling or a state of intense, sometimes excessive or extreme, mental and emotional exaltation *Syn* rapture, transport

**ecumenical** *Syn* UNIVERSAL, cosmic, catholic, cosmopolitan *Ant* provincial; diocesan

**eddy** *n* ♦ a swirling mass esp. of water *Syn* whirlpool, maelstrom, vortex

**eddy** *vb Syn* TURN, rotate, gyrate, circle, spin, whirl, revolve, twirl, wheel, swirl, pirouette

**edge 1** *Syn* BORDER, verge, rim, brink, margin, brim **2** *Syn* ADVANTAGE, odds, handicap, allowance

**edifice** *Syn* BUILDING, structure, pile

**edit** ♦ to prepare material for publication *Syn* compile, revise, redact, rewrite, adapt

**edition** ♦ the total number of copies of the same work printed during a stretch of time *Syn* impression, reprinting, printing, reissue

**educate** *Syn* TEACH, train, discipline, school, instruct

**educe** ♦ to bring or draw out what is hidden, latent, or reserved *Syn* evoke, elicit, extract, extort

**eerie** *Syn* WEIRD, uncanny

**efface** *Syn* ERASE, obliterate, expunge, blot out, delete, cancel

**effect** *n* **1** ♦ a condition, situation, or occurrence, ascribable to a cause *Syn* result, consequence, upshot, aftereffect, aftermath, sequel, issue, outcome, event *Ant* cause **2** *pl* **effects** *Syn* POSSESSIONS, belongings, means, resources, assets

**effect** *vb Syn* PERFORM, accomplish, achieve, execute, discharge, fulfill

**effective** ♦ producing or capable of producing a result *Syn* effectual, efficient, efficacious *Ant* ineffective; futile

**effectual** *Syn* EFFECTIVE, efficacious, efficient *Ant* ineffectual; fruitless

**effervescent** *Syn* ELASTIC, volatile, buoyant, expansive, resilient *Ant* subdued

**efficacious** *Syn* EFFECTIVE, effectual, efficient *Ant* inefficacious; powerless

**efficient** *Syn* EFFECTIVE, effectual, efficacious *Ant* inefficient

**effort** ♦ the active use or expenditure of physical or mental power to produce a desired result *Syn* exertion, pains, trouble *Ant* ease

**effortless** *Syn* EASY, smooth, facile, simple, light *Ant* painstaking

**effrontery** *Syn* TEMERITY, audacity, hardihood, nerve, cheek, gall

**effulgent** *Syn* BRIGHT, radiant, luminous, brilliant, lustrous, refulgent, beaming, lambent, lucent, incandescent

**egg** *Syn* URGE, exhort, goad, spur, prod, prick, sic

**egoism** *Syn* CONCEIT, egotism, amour propre, self-love, self-esteem *Ant* altruism

**egotism** *Syn* CONCEIT, egoism, self-love, amour propre, self-esteem *Ant* modesty

**eject** ♦ to force or thrust something or someone out *Syn* expel, oust, evict, dismiss *Ant* admit

**elaborate** *Syn* UNFOLD, evolve, develop, perfect

**élan** *Syn* VIGOR, vim, spirit, dash, esprit, verve, punch, drive

**elapse** *Syn* PASS, pass away, expire

**elastic** **1** ♦ able to endure strain without being permanently affected or injured *Syn* resilient, springy, flexible, supple *Ant* rigid **2** ♦ able to recover quickly from depression and maintain high spirits *Syn* expansive, resilient, buoyant, volatile, effervescent *Ant* depressed

**elbowroom** *Syn* ROOM, berth, play, leeway, margin, clearance

**elderly** *Syn* AGED, old, superannuated *Ant* youthful

**elect** *adj Syn* SELECT, picked, exclusive *Ant* reprobate (*in theology*)

**elect** *vb* **1** *Syn* CHOOSE, select, pick, prefer, single, opt, cull *Ant* abjure **2** *Syn* DESIGNATE, name, nominate, appoint

**election** *Syn* CHOICE, selection, option, preference, alternative

**electrify** *Syn* THRILL, enthuse

**eleemosynary** *Syn* CHARITABLE, benevolent, humane, humanitarian, philanthropic, altruistic

**elegance** ♦ impressive beauty of form, appearance, or behavior *Syn* grace, dignity

**elegant** *Syn* CHOICE, exquisite, recherché, rare, dainty, delicate

**element** ♦ one of the parts of a compound or complex whole *Syn* component, constituent, ingredient, factor *Ant* compound (*in science*); composite

**elemental** **1** ♦ of, relating to, or being an ultimate or irreducible element *Syn* basic, elementary, essential, fundamental, primitive, underlying **2** *Syn* ELEMENTARY, basal, beginning, rudimentary

**elementary** **1** ♦ of, relating to, or dealing with the simplest principles *Syn* basal, beginning, elemental, rudimentary **2** *Syn* ELEMENTAL, basic, essential, fundamental, primitive, underlying

**elephantine** *Syn* HUGE, vast, immense, enormous, mammoth, giant, gigantic, gigantean, colossal, gargantuan, Herculean, cyclopean, titanic, Brobdingnagian

**elevate** *Syn* LIFT, raise, rear, hoist, heave, boost *Ant* lower

**elevation 1** *Syn* HEIGHT, altitude **2** *Syn* ADVANCEMENT, promotion, preferment *Ant* degradation

**elicit** *Syn* EDUCE, evoke, extract, extort

**eliminate** *Syn* EXCLUDE, rule out, debar, blackball, disbar, suspend, shut out

**elite** *Syn* ARISTOCRACY, society, nobility, gentry, county *Ant* rabble

**ell** *Syn* ANNEX, wing, extension

**elongate** *Syn* EXTEND, lengthen, prolong, protract *Ant* abbreviate, shorten

**eloquent 1** *Syn* VOCAL, articulate, voluble, fluent, glib **2** *Syn* EXPRESSIVE, significant, meaningful, pregnant, sententious

**elucidate** *Syn* EXPLAIN, interpret, construe, expound, explicate

**elude** *Syn* ESCAPE, evade, avoid, shun, eschew

**emanate** *Syn* SPRING, issue, proceed, rise, arise, originate, derive, flow, stem

**emancipate** *Syn* FREE, manumit, liberate, release, discharge

**emasculate 1** *Syn* STERILIZE, castrate, spay, alter, mutilate, geld **2** *Syn* UNNERVE, enervate, unman

**embarrass** ♦ to distress by confusing or confounding *Syn* discomfit, abash, disconcert, rattle, faze *Ant* relieve; facilitate

**embellish** *Syn* ADORN, beautify, deck, bedeck, garnish, decorate, ornament

**embers** *Syn* ASH, cinders, clinkers

**emblem** *Syn* SYMBOL, attribute, type

**embody 1** *Syn* REALIZE, incarnate, materialize, externalize, objectify, actualize, hypostatize, reify *Ant* disembody **2** *Syn* IDENTIFY, incorporate, assimilate

**embolden** *Syn* ENCOURAGE, inspirit, hearten, cheer, nerve, steel *Ant* abash

**embrace 1** *Syn* ADOPT, espouse *Ant* spurn **2** *Syn* INCLUDE, comprehend, involve, imply, subsume

**emend** *Syn* CORRECT, rectify, revise, amend, remedy, redress, reform *Ant* corrupt (*a text, passage*)

**emerge** *Syn* APPEAR, loom

**emergency** *Syn* JUNCTURE, exigency, contingency, crisis, pass, pinch, strait

**emigrant** ♦ a person who leaves one country in order to settle in another *Syn* immigrant, migrant

**emigrate** *Syn* MIGRATE immigrate

**émigré** *Syn* STRANGER, immigrant, alien, foreigner, outlander, outsider

**eminent** *Syn* FAMOUS, illustrious, renowned, celebrated, famed

**emolument** *Syn* WAGE, stipend, salary, fee, pay, hire

**emotion** *Syn* FEELING, affection, passion, sentiment

**empathy** *Syn* SYMPATHY, pity, compassion, commiseration, ruth, condolence

**emphasis** ♦ exerted force or special stress that gives impressiveness or importance to something *Syn* stress, accent, accentuation

**employ** *Syn* USE, utilize, apply, avail

**employment** *Syn* WORK, occupation, business, calling, pursuit

**empower** *Syn* ENABLE

**empty 1** ♦ lacking the contents that could or

should be present *Syn* vacant, blank, void, vacuous *Ant* full **2** *Syn* VAIN, idle, hollow, nugatory, otiose

**empyrean empyreal** *Syn* CELESTIAL, heavenly

**emulate** *Syn* RIVAL, compete, vie

**emulous** *Syn* AMBITIOUS

**enable** ♦ to render able often by giving power, strength, or means to *Syn* empower

**enamored** ♦ possessed by a strong or unreasoning love or admiration *Syn* infatuated

**enchant** *Syn* ATTRACT, charm, captivate, allure, fascinate, bewitch *Ant* disenchant

**enchanting** *Syn* ATTRACTIVE, charming, captivating, alluring, fascinating, bewitching

**encircle** *Syn* SURROUND, environ, circle, encompass, compass, hem, gird, girdle, ring

**enclose** ♦ to shut in or confine by or as if by barriers *Syn* envelop, fence, pen, coop, corral, cage, wall

**encomium** ♦ a more or less formal and public expression of praise *Syn* eulogy, panegyric, tribute, citation

**encompass** *Syn* SURROUND, environ, encircle, circle, compass, hem, gird, girdle, ring

**encounter** *vb Syn* MEET, face, confront

**encounter** *n* ♦ a sudden, hostile, and usu. brief confrontation or dispute between factions or persons *Syn* skirmish, brush

**encourage 1** ♦ to fill with courage or strength of purpose esp. in preparation for a hard task *Syn* inspirit, hearten, embolden, cheer, nerve, steel *Ant* discourage **2** *Syn* FAVOR, countenance *Ant* discourage

**encroach** *Syn* TRESPASS, entrench, infringe, invade

**encumber** *Syn* BURDEN, cumber, weigh, weight, load, lade, tax, charge, saddle

**end** *n* **1** *Syn* LIMIT, bound, term, confine **2** ♦ the point at which something ceases *Syn* termination, ending, terminus *Ant* beginning **3** *Syn* INTENTION, objective, goal, aim, object, intent, purpose, design

**end** *vb Syn* CLOSE, conclude, terminate, finish, complete *Ant* begin

**endanger** *Syn* VENTURE, hazard, risk, chance, jeopardize, imperil

**endeavor** *vb Syn* ATTEMPT, try, essay, strive, struggle

**endeavor** *n Syn* ATTEMPT, essay, striving, struggle, try

**endemic** *Syn* NATIVE, indigenous, autochthonous, aboriginal *Ant* exotic; pandemic

**ending** *Syn* END, terminus, termination

**endless** *Syn* EVERLASTING, interminable, unceasing

**endorse** *Syn* APPROVE, sanction, accredit, certify

**endow** *Syn* DOWER, endue

**endue** *Syn* DOWER, endow

**endure 1** *Syn* CONTINUE, last, abide, persist *Ant* perish **2** *Syn* BEAR, abide, tolerate, suffer, stand, brook

**enemy** ♦ an individual or a group that is hostile toward another *Syn* foe

**energetic** *Syn* VIGOROUS, strenuous, lusty, nervous *Ant* lethargic

**energize 1** *Syn* VITALIZE, activate **2** *Syn* STRENGTHEN, invigorate, fortify, reinforce

**energy** *Syn* POWER, force, strength, might, puissance *Ant* inertia

**enervate** *Syn* UNNERVE, emasculate, unman *Ant* harden, inure

**enervated** *Syn* LANGUID, languishing, languorous, lackadaisical, spiritless, listless

**enfeeble** *Syn* WEAKEN, debilitate, sap, undermine, cripple, disable *Ant* fortify

**enforce** ♦ to put something into effect or operation *Syn* implement *Ant* relax (*discipline, rules, demands*)

**engage** *Syn* PROMISE, pledge, plight, covenant, contract

**engagement 1** ♦ a promise to be in an agreed place at a specified time, usu. for a particular purpose *Syn* appointment, rendezvous, tryst, assignation, date **2** *Syn* BATTLE, action

**engaging** *Syn* SWEET, winning, winsome, dulcet *Ant* loathsome

**engender** *Syn* GENERATE, breed, beget, get, sire, procreate, propagate, reproduce

**engine** *Syn* MACHINE, mechanism, machinery, apparatus, motor

**engineer** *Syn* GUIDE, pilot, lead, steer

**engrave** *Syn* CARVE, incise, etch, sculpture, sculpt, sculp, chisel

**engross** *Syn* MONOPOLIZE, absorb, consume

**engrossed** *Syn* INTENT, absorbed, rapt

**engrossing** *Syn* INTERESTING, absorbing, intriguing *Ant* irksome

**enhance** *Syn* INTENSIFY, heighten, aggravate

**enigma** *Syn* MYSTERY, riddle, puzzle, conundrum, problem

**enigmatic** *Syn* OBSCURE, cryptic, dark, vague, ambiguous, equivocal *Ant* explicit

**enjoin 1** *Syn* COMMAND, direct, order, bid, instruct, charge **2** *Syn* FORBID, interdict, prohibit, inhibit, ban

**enjoy 1** *Syn* LIKE, love, relish, fancy, dote *Ant* loathe, abhor, abominate **2** *Syn* HAVE, possess, own, hold

**enjoyment** *Syn* PLEASURE, delight, joy, delectation, fruition *Ant* abhorrence

**enlarge** *Syn* INCREASE, augment, multiply

**enlighten** *Syn* ILLUMINATE, illustrate, illume, light, lighten *Ant* confuse, muddle

**enliven** *Syn* QUICKEN, animate, vivify *Ant* deaden; subdue

**enmesh** *Syn* ENTANGLE, involve

**enmity** ♦ deep-seated dislike or ill will or a manifestation of such a feeling *Syn* hostility, antipathy, antagonism, animosity, rancor, animus *Ant* amity

**ennoble** *Syn* DIGNIFY, honor, glorify

**ennui** *Syn* TEDIUM, doldrums, boredom

**enormous** *Syn* HUGE, vast, immense, elephantine, mammoth, giant, gigantic, gigantean, colossal, gargantuan, Herculean, cyclopean, titanic, Brobdingnagian

**enough** *Syn* SUFFICIENT, adequate, competent

**enrage** *Syn* ANGER, infuriate, madden, incense *Ant* placate

**enrapture** *Syn* TRANSPORT, ravish, entrance

**enroll** *Syn* RECORD, register, list, catalog

**ensconce** *Syn* HIDE, screen, secrete, conceal, cache, bury

**ensign** *Syn* FLAG, standard, banner, color, streamer, pennant, pendant, pennon, jack

**ensnare** *Syn* CATCH, snare, entrap, trap, bag, capture

**ensue** *Syn* FOLLOW, succeed, supervene

**ensure** ♦ to make a person or thing certain or sure *Syn* insure, assure, secure

**entangle** ♦ to catch or hold as if in a net from which it is difficult to escape *Syn* involve, enmesh *Ant* disentangle

**entente** *Syn* CONTRACT, treaty, pact, compact, concordat, convention, cartel, bargain

**enter 1** ♦ to make way into something so as to reach or pass through the interior *Syn* penetrate, pierce, probe *Ant* issue from **2** ♦ to cause or permit to go in or get in *Syn* introduce, admit

**enterprise** *Syn* ADVENTURE, quest

**entertain 1** *Syn* HARBOR, shelter, lodge, house, board **2** *Syn* AMUSE, divert, recreate

**entertainment** *Syn* AMUSEMENT, diversion, recreation

**enthuse** *Syn* THRILL, electrify

**enthusiasm** *Syn* PASSION, fervor, ardor, zeal *Ant* apathy

**enthusiast** ♦ a person who manifests excessive ardor, fervor, or devotion in an attachment to some cause, idea, party, or church *Syn* fanatic, zealot, bigot

**entice** *Syn* LURE, inveigle, decoy, tempt, seduce *Ant* scare

**entire 1** *Syn* WHOLE, total, all, gross *Ant* partial **2** *Syn* PERFECT, whole, intact *Ant* impaired

**entity** ♦ one that has real and independent existence *Syn* being, creature, individual, person

**entrance** *n* ♦ the act or fact of going in or coming in *Syn* entry, entrée, ingress, access *Ant* exit

**entrance** *vb* *Syn* TRANSPORT, ravish, enrapture

**entrap** *Syn* CATCH, trap, snare, ensnare, bag, capture

**entreat** *Syn* BEG, beseech, implore, supplicate, importune, adjure

**entrée** *Syn* ENTRANCE, entry, ingress, access

**entrench** *Syn* TRESPASS, encroach, infringe, invade

**entrust** *Syn* COMMIT, confide, consign, relegate

**entry** *Syn* ENTRANCE, entrée, ingress, access

**entwine** *Syn* WIND, coil, curl, twist, twine, wreathe

**enumerate** *Syn* COUNT, tell, number

**enunciate** *Syn* ARTICULATE, pronounce

**envelop 1** *Syn* COVER, overspread, wrap, shroud, veil **2** *Syn* ENCLOSE, fence, pen, coop, corral, cage, wall

**envious** ♦ maliciously grudging another's advantages *Syn* jealous

**environ** *Syn* SURROUND, encircle, circle, encompass, compass, hem, gird, girdle, ring

**environment** *Syn* BACKGROUND, setting, milieu, backdrop, mise-en-scène

**envisage envision** *Syn* THINK, conceive, imagine, realize, fancy

**envoy** *Syn* AMBASSADOR, legate, minister, nuncio, internuncio, chargé d'affaires

**envy** *Syn* COVET, grudge, begrudge

**ephemeral** *Syn* TRANSIENT, transitory, passing, fugitive, fleeting, evanescent, momentary, short-lived

**epicene** *Syn* BISEXUAL, hermaphroditic, hermaphrodite, androgynous

**epicure** ♦ one who takes great pleasure in eating and drinking *Syn* gourmet, gourmand, glutton, bon vivant, gastronome

**epicurean** *Syn* SENSUOUS, sybaritic, luxurious, sensual, voluptuous *Ant* gross

**epigram** *Syn* SAYING, aphorism, apothegm, saw, maxim, adage, proverb, motto

**episode 1** *Syn* DIGRESSION, divagation, excursus **2** *Syn* OCCURRENCE, incident, event, circumstance

**epistle** *Syn* LETTER, missive, note, message, dispatch, report, memorandum

**epitome** *Syn* ABRIDGMENT, conspectus, synopsis, abstract, brief

**epoch** *Syn* PERIOD, era, age, aeon

**equable** *Syn* STEADY, even, constant, uniform *Ant* variable, changeable

**equal** *adj* *Syn* SAME, equivalent, very, identical, identic, tantamount *Ant* unequal

**equal** *vb* *Syn* MATCH, rival, approach, touch

**equanimity** ♦ the characteristic quality of one who is self-possessed or not easily disturbed or perturbed *Syn* composure, sangfroid, phlegm

**equilibrium** *Syn* BALANCE, equipoise, poise, tension

**equip** *Syn* FURNISH, outfit, appoint, accouter, arm

**equipment** ♦ items needed for the performance of a task or useful in effecting a given end *Syn* apparatus, machinery, paraphernalia, outfit, tackle, gear, matériel

**equipoise** *Syn* BALANCE, equilibrium, poise, tension

**equitable** *Syn* FAIR, just, impartial, unbiased, dispassionate, uncolored, objective *Ant* inequitable, unfair

**equity** *Syn* JUSTICE

**equivalent** *Syn* SAME, equal, identical, identic, selfsame, very, tantamount *Ant* different

**equivocal** *Syn* OBSCURE, ambiguous, dark, vague, enigmatic, cryptic *Ant* unequivocal

**equivocate** *Syn* LIE, prevaricate, palter, fib

**equivocation** *Syn* AMBIGUITY, tergiversation, double entendre

**era** *Syn* PERIOD, age, epoch, aeon

**eradicate** *Syn* EXTERMINATE, uproot, deracinate, extirpate, wipe

**erase** ♦ to strike, rub, or scrape out something so that it no longer has effect or existence *Syn* expunge, cancel, efface, obliterate, blot out, delete

**erect** *Syn* BUILD, construct, frame, raise, rear *Ant* raze

**eremite** *Syn* RECLUSE, hermit, anchorite, cenobite

**erotic** ♦ of, devoted to, affected by, or tending to arouse sexual love or desire *Syn* amatory, amorous, amative, aphrodisiac

**erratic** *Syn* STRANGE, eccentric, odd, queer, singular, peculiar, unique, quaint, outlandish, curious

**error** ♦ something (as an act, statement, or belief) that departs from what is or is generally held to be acceptable *Syn* mistake, blunder, slip, lapse, faux pas, bull, howler, boner

**errorless** *Syn* IMPECCABLE, flawless, faultless

**ersatz** *Syn* ARTIFICIAL, synthetic, factitious

**erudite** *Syn* LEARNED, scholarly

**erudition** *Syn* KNOWLEDGE, learning, scholarship, science, information, lore

**escape 1** ♦ to run away esp. from something that limits one's freedom or threatens one's well-being *Syn* flee, fly, decamp, abscond **2** ♦ to get away or keep away from what one does not wish to incur, endure, or encounter *Syn* avoid, evade, elude, shun, eschew

**eschew 1** *Syn* ESCAPE, shun, elude, avoid, evade *Ant* choose **2** *Syn* FORGO, forbear, abnegate, sacrifice

**escort** *Syn* ACCOMPANY, conduct, convoy, chaperone, attend

**esoteric** *Syn* RECONDITE, occult, abstruse

**especial** *Syn* SPECIAL, specific, particular, individual

**espousal** *Syn* MARRIAGE, matrimony, nuptial, wedding, wedlock

**espouse** *Syn* ADOPT, embrace

**esprit** *Syn* VIGOR, vim, spirit, dash, verve, punch, élan, drive

**esprit de corps** *Syn* MORALE, discipline

**espy** *Syn* SEE, descry, behold, perceive, discern, notice, remark, note, observe, survey, view, contemplate

**essay** *vb* *Syn* ATTEMPT, endeavor, strive, struggle, try

**essay** *n* **1** *Syn* ATTEMPT, endeavor, striving, struggle, try **2** ♦ a relatively brief discourse written for others' reading or consideration *Syn* article, paper, theme, composition

**essential 1** *Syn* INHERENT, intrinsic, constitutional, ingrained *Ant* accidental **2** ♦ so important as to be indispensable *Syn* fundamental, vital, cardinal **3** *Syn* NEEDFUL, indispensable, requisite, necessary *Ant* nonessential **4** *Syn* ELEMENTAL, basic, elementary, fundamental, primitive, underlying

**establish 1** *Syn* SET, settle, fix *Ant* uproot; abrogate **2** *Syn* FOUND, institute, organize, create *Ant* abolish

**esteem** *n* *Syn* REGARD, respect, admiration *Ant* abomination; contempt

**esteem** *vb* *Syn* REGARD, respect, admire *Ant* abominate

**estimate** *vb* **1** ♦ to judge a thing with respect to its worth *Syn* appraise, evaluate, value, rate, assess, assay **2** *Syn* CALCULATE, reckon, compute

**estimate** *n* *Syn* ESTIMATION

**estimation** ♦ the act of valuing or appraising *Syn* estimate

**estrange** ♦ to cause one to break a bond or tie of affection or loyalty *Syn* alienate, disaffect, wean *Ant* reconcile

**etch** *Syn* CARVE, incise, engrave, chisel, sculpture, sculpt, sculp

**eternal** *Syn* INFINITE, sempiternal, boundless, illimitable, uncircumscribed *Ant* mortal

**ethereal** *Syn* AIRY, aerial *Ant* substantial

**ethical** *Syn* MORAL, righteous, virtuous, noble *Ant* unethical

**etiolate** *Syn* WHITEN, decolorize, blanch, bleach

**etiquette** *Syn* DECORUM, propriety, decency, dignity

**eulogize** *Syn* PRAISE, extol, acclaim, laud *Ant* calumniate, vilify

**eulogy** *Syn* ENCOMIUM, panegyric, tribute, citation *Ant* calumny; tirade

**euphuistic** *Syn* RHETORICAL, flowery, aureate, grandiloquent, magniloquent, bombastic

**evade** *Syn* ESCAPE, elude, avoid, shun, eschew

**evaluate** *Syn* ESTIMATE, appraise, value, rate, assess, assay

**evanesce** *Syn* VANISH, evaporate, disappear, fade

**evanescent** *Syn* TRANSIENT, ephemeral, passing, fugitive, fleeting, transitory, momentary, short-lived

**evaporate** *Syn* VANISH, evanesce, disappear, fade

**even 1** *Syn* LEVEL, smooth, flat, plane, plain, flush *Ant* uneven **2** *Syn* STEADY, uniform, equable, constant

**event 1** *Syn* OCCURRENCE, incident, episode, circumstance **2** *Syn* EFFECT, result, consequence, upshot, aftereffect, aftermath, sequel, issue, outcome

**eventual** *Syn* LAST, ultimate, concluding, terminal, final, latest

**everlasting** ♦ continuing on and on without end *Syn* endless, interminable, unceasing *Ant* transitory

**every** *Syn* ALL, each

**evict** *Syn* EJECT, oust, expel, dismiss

**evidence** *Syn* SHOW, evince, manifest, demonstrate

**evident** ♦ readily perceived or apprehended *Syn* manifest, patent, distinct, obvious, apparent, palpable, plain, clear

**evil** *adj Syn* BAD, ill, wicked, naughty *Ant* exemplary; salutary

**evil** *n* ♦ whatever is harmful or disastrous to morals or well-being *Syn* ill *Ant* good

**evince** *Syn* SHOW, manifest, evidence, demonstrate

**evoke** *Syn* EDUCE, elicit, extract, extort

**evolution** *Syn* DEVELOPMENT

**evolve** *Syn* UNFOLD, develop, elaborate, perfect

**exact** *vb Syn* DEMAND, require, claim

**exact** *adj Syn* CORRECT, accurate, right, precise, nice

**exacting** *Syn* ONEROUS, burdensome, oppressive *Ant* easy; lenient

**exaggeration** ♦ an overstepping of the bounds of truth, especially in describing the goodness or badness or the greatness or the smallness of something *Syn* overstatement, hyperbole

**exalt** ♦ to increase in importance or in prestige *Syn* magnify, aggrandize *Ant* abase

**examination** *Syn* SCRUTINY, inspection, scanning, audit

**examine 1** *Syn* SCRUTINIZE, inspect, scan, audit **2** *Syn* ASK, question, interrogate, quiz, catechize, query, inquire

**example 1** *Syn* INSTANCE, sample, specimen, case, illustration **2** *Syn* MODEL, exemplar, pattern, ideal, standard, beau ideal, mirror

**exasperate** *Syn* IRRITATE, provoke, nettle, aggravate, rile, peeve *Ant* mollify

**excavate** *Syn* DIG, delve, spade, grub

**exceed** ♦ to go or to be beyond a stated or implied limit, measure, or degree *Syn* surpass, transcend, excel, outdo, outstrip

**excel** *Syn* EXCEED, surpass, transcend, outdo, outstrip

**excellence** ♦ the quality of especial worth or value *Syn* merit, virtue, perfection *Ant* fault

**exceptionable** *Syn* OBJECTIONABLE, unacceptable, undesirable, unwanted, unwelcome *Ant* unexceptionable; exemplary

**exceptional** ♦ being out of the ordinary *Syn* extraordinary, phenomenal, unusual, unwonted *Ant* common; average

**excerpt** *Syn* EXTRACT

**excess** ♦ whatever exceeds a limit, measure, bound, or usual degree *Syn* superfluity, surplus, surplusage, overplus *Ant* deficiency; dearth, paucity

**excessive** ♦ going beyond a normal or acceptable limit *Syn* immoderate, inordinate, extravagant, exorbitant, extreme *Ant* deficient

**exchange** ♦ to give and receive reciprocally *Syn* interchange, bandy

**excitant** *Syn* STIMULUS, stimulant, incitement, impetus

**excite** *Syn* PROVOKE, stimulate, pique, quicken, galvanize *Ant* soothe, quiet; allay (*fears, anxiety*)

**exclude** ♦ to prevent the participation, consideration, or inclusion of *Syn* debar, blackball, eliminate, rule out, shut out, disbar, suspend *Ant* admit; include

**exclusive** *Syn* SELECT, elect, picked *Ant* inclusive

**excogitate** *Syn* CONSIDER, weigh, study, contemplate

**excoriate** *Syn* ABRADE, chafe, fret, gall

**excruciating** ♦ intensely or unbearably painful *Syn* agonizing, racking

**exculpate** ♦ to free from alleged fault or guilt *Syn* absolve, exonerate, acquit, vindicate *Ant* inculpate; accuse

**excursion** *Syn* JOURNEY, trip, jaunt, tour, cruise, voyage, expedition, pilgrimage

**excursus** *Syn* DIGRESSION, divagation, episode

**excuse** *vb* ♦ to exact neither punishment nor redress for or from *Syn* condone, pardon, forgive, remit *Ant* punish

**excuse** *n Syn* APOLOGY, plea, pretext, apologia, alibi

**execrable** ♦ so odious as to be utterly detestable *Syn* damnable, accursed, cursed

**execrate** ♦ to denounce violently *Syn* curse, damn, anathematize, objurgate

**execute 1** *Syn* PERFORM, effect, fulfill, discharge, accomplish, achieve **2** *Syn* KILL, dispatch, slay, murder, assassinate

**exemplar** *Syn* MODEL, pattern, ideal, beau ideal, example, mirror, standard

**exemplify** ♦ to use examples or show instances of in order to clarify *Syn* illustrate

**exemption** ♦ freeing or the state of being free or freed from a charge or obligation to which others are subject *Syn* immunity

**exercise** *n* ♦ repeated activity or exertion *Syn* practice, drill

**exercise** *vb Syn* PRACTICE, drill

**exertion** *Syn* EFFORT, pains, trouble

**exhaust 1** *Syn* DEPLETE, drain, impoverish, bankrupt **2** *Syn* TIRE, fatigue, jade, weary, fag, tucker

**exhibit** *vb Syn* SHOW, display, expose, parade, flaunt

**exhibit** *n Syn* EXHIBITION, show, exposition, fair

**exhibition** ♦ a public display of objects of interest *Syn* show, exhibit, exposition, fair

**exhort** *Syn* URGE, egg, goad, spur, prod, prick, sic

**exigency 1** *Syn* JUNCTURE, pass, emergency, pinch, strait, crisis, contingency **2** *Syn* NEED, necessity

**exigent** *Syn* PRESSING, urgent, imperative, crying, importunate, insistent, instant

**exiguous** *Syn* MEAGER, scant, scanty, skimpy, scrimpy, spare, sparse *Ant* capacious, ample

**exile** *Syn* BANISH, expatriate, ostracize, deport, transport, extradite

**exist** *Syn* BE, live, subsist

**existence** ♦ the state or fact of having independent reality *Syn* being, actuality *Ant* nonexistence

**exonerate** *Syn* EXCULPATE, acquit, vindicate, absolve *Ant* charge

**exorbitant** *Syn* EXCESSIVE, inordinate, extravagant, immoderate, extreme *Ant* just

**exordium** *Syn* INTRODUCTION, preamble, preface, foreword, prologue, prelude

**expand** ♦ to increase or become increased in size, bulk, or volume *Syn* amplify, swell, distend, inflate, dilate *Ant* contract; abridge; circumscribe

**expanse** ♦ a significantly large area or range *Syn* amplitude, spread, stretch

**expansive** *Syn* ELASTIC, resilient, buoyant, volatile, effervescent *Ant* tense; reserved

**expatiate** *Syn* DISCOURSE, descant, dilate

**expatriate** *Syn* BANISH, exile, ostracize, deport, transport, extradite *Ant* repatriate

**expect** ♦ to anticipate in the mind *Syn* hope, look, await *Ant* despair of

**expedient** *adj* ♦ dictated by practical wisdom or by motives of prudence *Syn* politic, advisable *Ant* inexpedient

**expedient** *n Syn* RESOURCE, resort, shift, makeshift, stopgap, substitute, surrogate

**expedition 1** *Syn* HASTE, dispatch, speed, hurry *Ant* procrastination **2** *Syn* JOURNEY, voyage, tour, trip, jaunt, excursion, cruise, pilgrimage

**expeditious** *Syn* FAST, speedy, swift, rapid, fleet, quick, hasty *Ant* sluggish

**expel** *Syn* EJECT, oust, dismiss, evict *Ant* admit

**expend** *Syn* SPEND, disburse

**expense** *Syn* PRICE, cost, charge

**expensive** *Syn* COSTLY, dear, valuable, precious, invaluable, priceless *Ant* inexpensive

**experience** ♦ to pass through the process of actually coming to know or to feel *Syn* undergo, sustain, suffer

**expert** *adj Syn* PROFICIENT, adept, skilled, skillful, masterly *Ant* amateurish

**expert** *n* ♦ one who shows mastery in a subject, an art, or a profession or who reveals extraordinary skill in execution, performance, or technique *Syn* adept, artist, artiste, virtuoso, wizard *Ant* amateur

**expiate** ♦ to make amends or give satisfaction for wrong done *Syn* atone

**expiation** ♦ the making of amends or the giving of satisfaction for wrongs done *Syn* atonement

**expire** *Syn* PASS, pass away, elapse

**explain 1** ♦ to make the meaning of something understood or more comprehensible *Syn* expound, explicate, elucidate, interpret, construe **2** ♦ to give the reason for or cause of *Syn* account, justify, rationalize

**explicate** *Syn* EXPLAIN, expound, elucidate, interpret, construe

**explicit** ♦ characterized by full precise expression and meaning that is perfectly clear *Syn* express, specific, definite, categorical *Ant* ambiguous

**exploit** *Syn* FEAT, achievement

**expose** *Syn* SHOW, display, exhibit, parade, flaunt

**exposé** *Syn* EXPOSITION, exposure

**exposed** *Syn* LIABLE, open, subject, prone, susceptible, sensitive

**exposition 1** *Syn* EXHIBITION, fair, exhibit, show **2** ♦ a setting forth or laying open of a thing or things hitherto not known or fully understood *Syn* exposure, exposé

**expostulate** *Syn* OBJECT, remonstrate, protest, kick

**exposure** *Syn* EXPOSITION, exposé *Ant* cover; covering

**expound** *Syn* EXPLAIN, explicate, elucidate, interpret, construe

**express** *adj Syn* EXPLICIT, definite, specific, categorical

**express** *vb* ♦ to let out what one feels or thinks *Syn* vent, utter, voice, broach, air, ventilate *Ant* imply

**expression** *Syn* PHRASE, locution, idiom

**expressive** ♦ clearly conveying or manifesting a thought, idea, or feeling or a combination of these *Syn* eloquent, significant, meaningful, pregnant, sententious

**expunge** *Syn* ERASE, cancel, efface, obliterate, blot out, delete

**exquisite** *adj* **1** *Syn* CHOICE, recherché, rare, dainty, delicate, elegant **2** *Syn* INTENSE, vehement, fierce, violent

**exquisite** *n Syn* FOP, coxcomb, beau, dandy, dude, buck

**extemporaneous** ♦ composed, devised, or done at the moment rather than beforehand *Syn* extempore, extemporary, improvised, impromptu, offhand, unpremeditated

**extemporary, extempore** *Syn* EXTEMPORANEOUS, improvised, impromptu, offhand, unpremeditated

**extend** ♦ to make or become longer *Syn* lengthen, elongate, prolong, protract *Ant* abridge, shorten

**extension** *Syn* ANNEX, wing, ell

**extent** *Syn* SIZE, dimensions, area, magnitude, volume

**extenuate** *Syn* THIN, attenuate, dilute, rarefy *Ant* intensify **2** *Syn* PALLIATE, gloze, gloss, whitewash, whiten

**exterior** *Syn* OUTER, external, outward, outside *Ant* interior

**exterminate** ♦ to destroy utterly *Syn* extirpate, eradicate, uproot, deracinate, wipe

**external** *Syn* OUTER, exterior, outward, outside *Ant* internal

**externalize** *Syn* REALIZE, materialize, actualize, embody, incarnate, objectify, hypostatize, reify

**extinguish** 1 *Syn* CRUSH, quell, suppress, quench, quash *Ant* inflame 2 *Syn* ABOLISH, annihilate, abate

**extirpate** *Syn* EXTERMINATE, eradicate, uproot, deracinate, wipe out

**extol** *Syn* PRAISE, laud, eulogize, acclaim *Ant* decry; abase (*oneself*)

**extort** *Syn* EDUCE, extract, elicit, evoke

**extra** *Syn* SUPERFLUOUS, supernumerary, spare, surplus

**extract** *vb Syn* EDUCE, extort, elicit, evoke

**extract** *n* ♦ a passage transcribed or quoted from a book or document *Syn* excerpt

**extradite** *Syn* BANISH, deport, transport, expatriate, exile, ostracize

**extraneous** *Syn* EXTRINSIC, foreign, alien *Ant* relevant

**extraordinary** *Syn* EXCEPTIONAL, phenomenal, unusual, unwonted

**extravagant** *Syn* EXCESSIVE, inordinate, immoderate, exorbitant, extreme *Ant* restrained

**extreme** *adj Syn* EXCESSIVE, exorbitant, inordinate, immoderate, extravagant

**extreme** *n* ♦ the utmost limit or degree of something *Syn* extremity

**extremity** *Syn* EXTREME

**extricate** ♦ to free or release from what binds or holds back *Syn* disentangle, untangle, disencumber, disembarrass

**extrinsic** ♦ external to a thing, its essential nature, or its original character *Syn* extraneous, foreign, alien *Ant* intrinsic

**exuberant** *Syn* PROFUSE, lavish, prodigal, luxuriant, lush *Ant* austere; sterile

**eyewitness** *Syn* SPECTATOR, witness, onlooker, looker-on, observer, beholder, bystander, kibitzer

# F

**fable** 1 *Syn* FICTION, fabrication, figment 2 *Syn* ALLEGORY, myth, parable

**fabricate** *Syn* MAKE, fashion, forge, form, shape, manufacture

**fabrication** *Syn* FICTION, figment, fable

**fabulous** *Syn* FICTITIOUS, mythical, legendary, apocryphal

**face** *n* ♦ the front part of a human or, sometimes, animal head including the mouth, nose, eyes, forehead, and cheeks *Syn* countenance, visage, physiognomy, mug, puss

**face** *vb* 1 *Syn* MEET, encounter, confront 2 ♦ to confront with courage or boldness *Syn* brave, challenge, dare, defy, beard *Ant* avoid

**facet** *Syn* PHASE, aspect, side, angle

**facetious** *Syn* WITTY, humorous, jocose, jocular *Ant* lugubrious

**facile** *Syn* EASY, smooth, light, simple, effortless *Ant* arduous; constrained, clumsy

**facility** *Syn* READINESS, ease, dexterity

**facsimile** *Syn* REPRODUCTION, copy, carbon copy, duplicate, replica, transcript

**faction** *Syn* COMBINATION, bloc, party, combine, ring

**factious** *Syn* INSUBORDINATE, contumacious, seditious, mutinous, rebellious *Ant* cooperative

**factitious** *Syn* ARTIFICIAL, synthetic, ersatz *Ant* bona fide, veritable

**factor** 1 *Syn* AGENT, attorney, deputy, proxy 2 *Syn* ELEMENT, constituent, component, ingredient

**faculty** 1 *Syn* POWER, function 2 *Syn* GIFT, aptitude, knack, bent, turn, genius, talent

**fad** *Syn* FASHION, vogue, style, rage, craze, mode, dernier cri, cry

**fade** *Syn* VANISH, evanesce, evaporate, disappear

**faded** *Syn* SHABBY, dilapidated, dingy, seedy, threadbare

**fag** *Syn* TIRE, exhaust, jade, fatigue, weary, tucker

**failing** *Syn* FAULT, frailty, foible, vice *Ant* perfection

**failure** ♦ an omission on the part of someone or something of what is expected or required *Syn* neglect, default, miscarriage, dereliction

**faineant** *Syn* LAZY, indolent, slothful

**fair** *adj* 1 *Syn* BEAUTIFUL, comely, lovely, pretty, bonny, handsome, beauteous, pulchritudinous, good-looking *Ant* foul; ill-favored 2 ♦ characterized by honesty, justice, and freedom from improper influence *Syn* just, equitable, impartial, unbiased, dispassionate, uncolored, objective *Ant* unfair 3 *Syn* MEDIUM, average, middling, mediocre, second-rate, moderate, indifferent

**fair** *n Syn* EXHIBITION, exposition, show, exhibit

**faith** 1 *Syn* BELIEF, credence, credit *Ant* doubt 2 *Syn* TRUST, dependence, reliance, confidence 3 *Syn* RELIGION, creed, persuasion, church, denomination, sect, cult, communion

**faithful** ♦ firm in adherence to whatever one is bound to by duty or promise *Syn* loyal, true, constant, staunch, steadfast, resolute *Ant* faithless

**faithless** ♦ not true to allegiance or duty *Syn* false, disloyal, traitorous, treacherous, perfidious *Ant* faithful

**fake** *n Syn* IMPOSTURE, sham, humbug, counterfeit, cheat, fraud, deceit, deception

**fake** *adj Syn* COUNTERFEIT, spurious, bogus, sham, pseudo, pinchbeck, phony

**faker** *Syn* IMPOSTOR, mountebank, charlatan, quack

**fall** ♦ to go or to let go downward freely *Syn* drop, sink, slump, subside *Ant* rise

**fallacious** ♦ contrary to or devoid of logic *Syn* sophistical, casuistical *Ant* sound, valid

**fallacy** ♦ unsound and misleading reasoning or line of argument *Syn* sophism, sophistry, casuistry

**false** 1 ♦ not in conformity with what is true or right *Syn* wrong *Ant* true 2 *Syn* FAITHLESS, perfidious, disloyal, traitorous, treacherous *Ant* true

**falsehood** *Syn* LIE, untruth, fib, misrepresentation, story *Ant* truth

**falsify** *Syn* MISREPRESENT, belie, garble

**falter** *Syn* HESITATE, waver, vacillate

**fame** ♦ the state of being widely known for one's deeds *Syn* renown, honor, glory, celebrity, reputation, repute, notoriety, éclat *Ant* infamy; obscurity

**famed** *Syn* FAMOUS, renowned, celebrated, eminent, illustrious *Ant* obscure

**familiar** 1 ♦ near to one another because of frequent association or shared interests *Syn* intimate, close, confidential, chummy, thick *Ant* aloof 2 *Syn* COMMON, ordinary, popular, vulgar *Ant* unfamiliar; strange

**famous** ♦ widely known and honored for achievement *Syn* famed, renowned, celebrated, eminent, illustrious *Ant* obscure

**fanatic** *Syn* ENTHUSIAST, bigot, zealot

**fanciful** *Syn* IMAGINARY, visionary, fantastic, chimerical, quixotic *Ant* realistic

**fancy** *n* 1 *Syn* CAPRICE, freak, whim, whimsy, conceit, vagary, crotchet 2 *Syn* IMAGINATION, fantasy *Ant* experience 3 ♦ a vivid idea or image present in the mind but having no concrete or objective reality *Syn* fantasy, phantasy, phantasm, vision, dream, daydream, nightmare *Ant* reality

**fancy** *vb* 1 *Syn* LIKE, dote, love, enjoy, relish 2 *Syn* THINK, imagine, conceive, envisage, envision, realize

**fantastic** 1 *Syn* IMAGINARY, chimerical, visionary, fanciful, quixotic 2 ♦ conceived or made without reference to reality *Syn* bizarre, grotesque, antic

**fantasy** 1 *Syn* IMAGINATION, fancy 2 *Syn* FANCY, phantasy, phantasm, vision, dream, daydream, nightmare

**far faraway, far-off** *Syn* DISTANT, remote, removed *Ant* near, nigh, nearly

**farcical** *Syn* LAUGHABLE, comical, comic, ludicrous, ridiculous, risible, droll, funny

**farfetched** *Syn* FORCED, labored, strained

**farming** *Syn* AGRICULTURE, husbandry

**farther** ♦ at or to a greater distance or more advanced point *Syn* further, beyond

**fascinate** *Syn* ATTRACT, charm, bewitch, enchant, captivate, allure

**fascinating** *Syn* ATTRACTIVE, charming, bewitching, enchanting, captivating, alluring

**fashion** *n* 1 *Syn* METHOD, manner, way, mode, system 2 ♦ the prevailing or accepted custom *Syn* style, mode, vogue, fad, rage, craze, dernier cri, cry

**fashion** *vb Syn* MAKE, form, shape, fabricate, manufacture, forge

**fashionable** *Syn* STYLISH, modish, smart, chic, dashing *Ant* unfashionable; old-fashioned

**fast** ♦ moving, proceeding, or acting with great celerity *Syn* rapid, swift, fleet, quick, speedy, hasty, expeditious *Ant* slow

**fasten** ♦ to cause one thing to hold to another *Syn* fix, attach, affix *Ant* unfasten; loosen, loose

**fastidious** *Syn* NICE, finicky, finicking, finical, particular, fussy, dainty, squeamish, persnickety, pernickety

**fastness** *Syn* FORT, stronghold, fortress, citadel

**fat** *Syn* FLESHY, stout, portly, plump, corpulent, obese, rotund, chubby *Ant* lean

**fatal** *Syn* DEADLY, mortal, lethal

**fate** ♦ whatever is destined or inevitably decreed for one *Syn* destiny, lot, portion, doom

**fateful** *Syn* OMINOUS, portentous, inauspicious, unpropitious

**fathom** ♦ to measure depth typically with a weighted line *Syn* sound, plumb

**fatigue** *Syn* TIRE, exhaust, jade, weary, fag, tucker *Ant* rest

**fatuous** *Syn* SIMPLE, asinine, silly, foolish *Ant* sensible

**fault** 1 *Syn* IMPERFECTION, deficiency, shortcoming *Ant* excellence 2 ♦ an imperfection in character or an ingrained moral weakness *Syn* failing, frailty, foible, vice *Ant* merit 3 *Syn* BLAME, culpability, guilt

**faultfinding** *Syn* CRITICAL, captious, caviling, carping, censorious, hypercritical

**faultless** *Syn* IMPECCABLE, flawless, errorless *Ant* faulty

**faux pas** *Syn* ERROR, blunder, slip, mistake, lapse, bull, howler, boner

**favor** *n Syn* GIFT, boon, largess, present, gratuity

**favor** *vb* 1 ♦ to give the support of one's approval to *Syn* countenance, encourage *Ant* disapprove 2 *Syn* OBLIGE, accommodate

**favorable** ♦ being of good omen or presaging a happy or successful outcome *Syn* benign, auspicious, propitious *Ant* unfavorable; antagonistic

**favorite** *Syn* PARASITE, sycophant, toady, lickspittle, bootlicker, hanger-on, leech, sponge, sponger

**fawn** ♦ to behave abjectly before a superior *Syn* toady, truckle, cringe, cower *Ant* domineer

**faze** *Syn* EMBARRASS, disconcert, discomfit, rattle, abash

**fealty** *Syn* FIDELITY, loyalty, devotion, allegiance, piety *Ant* perfidy

**fear** 1 ♦ agitation or dismay which overcomes one in the anticipation or in the presence of danger *Syn* dread, fright, alarm, dismay, consternation, panic, terror, horror, trepidation *Ant* fearlessness 2 *Syn* REVERENCE, awe *Ant* contempt

**fearful 1** ♦ inspired or moved by fear *Syn* apprehensive, afraid *Ant* fearless; intrepid **2** ♦ causing fear *Syn* awful, dreadful, frightful, terrible, terrific, horrible, horrific, shocking, appalling

**fearless** *Syn* BRAVE, unafraid, dauntless, undaunted, bold, intrepid, audacious, courageous, valiant, valorous, doughty *Ant* fearful

**feasible** *Syn* POSSIBLE, practicable *Ant* unfeasible, infeasible; chimerical

**feast** *Syn* DINNER, banquet

**feat** ♦ a remarkable deed or performance *Syn* exploit, achievement

**feature** *Syn* CHARACTERISTIC, trait

**fecund** *Syn* FERTILE, fruitful, prolific *Ant* barren

**fecundity** *Syn* FERTILITY, fruitfulness, prolificacy *Ant* barrenness

**federation** *Syn* ALLIANCE, confederacy, confederation, coalition, fusion

**fee** *Syn* WAGE, stipend, emolument, salary, wages, pay, hire

**feeble** *Syn* WEAK, infirm, decrepit, frail, fragile *Ant* robust

**feed** *vb* ♦ to provide the food that one needs or desires *Syn* nourish, pasture, graze *Ant* starve

**feed** *n Syn* FOOD, fodder, forage, provender, victuals, viands, provisions, comestibles

**feel** *vb Syn* TOUCH, palpate, handle, paw

**feel** *n Syn* ATMOSPHERE, feeling, aura

**feeling 1** *Syn* SENSATION, sensibility, sense **2** ♦ subjective response or reaction *Syn* affection, emotion, sentiment, passion **3** *Syn* ATMOSPHERE, feel, aura

**feign** *Syn* ASSUME, simulate, counterfeit, sham, pretend, affect

**feint** *Syn* TRICK, artifice, wile, ruse, gambit, ploy, stratagem, maneuver

**felicitate** ♦ to express one's pleasure in the joy, success, elevation, or prospects of another *Syn* congratulate

**felicitous** *Syn* FIT, happy, apt, fitting, appropriate, suitable, meet, proper *Ant* infelicitous; inept, maladroit

**felicity** *Syn* HAPPINESS, bliss, beatitude, blessedness *Ant* misery

**fell** *Syn* FIERCE, cruel, inhuman, savage, barbarous, ferocious, truculent

**felon** *Syn* CRIMINAL, convict, malefactor, culprit, delinquent

**female** *n* ♦ a person and esp. an adult who belongs to the sex that is the counterpart of the male sex *Syn* woman, lady

**female** *adj* ♦ of, characteristic of, or like a female esp. of the human species *Syn* feminine, womanly, womanlike, womanish, ladylike *Ant* male

**feminine** *Syn* FEMALE, womanly, womanish, ladylike, womanlike *Ant* masculine

**fence 1** *Syn* ENCLOSE, envelop, pen, coop, corral, cage, wall **2** *Syn* DODGE, parry, sidestep, duck, shirk, malinger

**feral** *Syn* BRUTAL, brute, brutish, bestial, beastly

**ferocious** *Syn* FIERCE, truculent, barbarous, savage, inhuman, cruel, fell

**ferret out** *Syn* SEEK, search, scour, hunt, comb, ransack, rummage

**fertile** ♦ marked by abundant productivity *Syn* fecund, fruitful, prolific *Ant* infertile, sterile

**fertility** ♦ the quality or state of being fertile *Syn* fruitfulness, fecundity, prolificacy *Ant* infertility, sterility

**fervent** *Syn* IMPASSIONED, ardent, fervid, perfervid, passionate

**fervid** *Syn* IMPASSIONED, fervent, ardent, perfervid, passionate

**fervor** *Syn* PASSION, ardor, enthusiasm, zeal

**fetch** *Syn* BRING, take

**fetid** *Syn* MALODOROUS, noisome, stinking, putrid, rank, rancid, fusty, musty *Ant* fragrant

**fetish** ♦ an object believed to be endowed with the virtue of averting evil or of bringing good fortune *Syn* talisman, charm, amulet

**fetter** *Syn* HAMPER, shackle, trammel, clog, manacle, hog-tie

**fib** *n Syn* LIE, untruth, falsehood, misrepresentation, story

**fib** *vb Syn* LIE, equivocate, palter, prevaricate

**fickle** *Syn* INCONSTANT, unstable, capricious, mercurial *Ant* constant, true

**fiction** ♦ a story, account, explanation, or conception which is an invention of the human mind *Syn* figment, fabrication, fable

**fictitious** ♦ having the character of something invented or imagined as opposed to something true or genuine *Syn* fabulous, legendary, mythical, apocryphal *Ant* historical

**fidelity** ♦ faithfulness to something to which one is bound by a pledge or duty *Syn* allegiance, fealty, loyalty, devotion, piety *Ant* faithlessness; perfidy

**fidgety** *Syn* IMPATIENT, restless, restive, uneasy, jumpy, jittery, nervous, unquiet

**field** ♦ a limited area of knowledge or endeavor to which pursuits, activities, and interests are confined *Syn* domain, province, sphere, territory, bailiwick

**fiendish** ♦ having or manifesting qualities associated with devils, demons, and fiends *Syn* devilish, diabolical, diabolic, demoniac, demonic

**fierce 1** ♦ displaying fury or malignity in looks or actions *Syn* truculent, ferocious, barbarous, savage, inhuman, cruel, fell *Ant* tame; mild **2** *Syn* INTENSE, vehement, exquisite, violent

**fiery** *Syn* SPIRITED, high-spirited, peppery, gingery, mettlesome, spunky

**fight** *vb* **1** *Syn* CONTEND, battle, war **2** *Syn* RESIST, withstand, contest, oppose, combat, conflict, antagonize

**fight** *n Syn* CONTEST, combat, fray, affray, conflict

**figment** *Syn* FICTION, fabrication, fable

**figure** *n* **1** *Syn* NUMBER, numeral, digit, integer **2** *Syn* FORM, shape, configuration, conformation **3** ♦ a unit in a decorative composition (as in fabric) *Syn* pattern, design, motif, device

**figure** *vb Syn* ADD, cast, sum, total, tot, foot

**filch** *Syn* STEAL, purloin, lift, pilfer, pinch, snitch, swipe, cop

**file** *Syn* LINE, row, rank, echelon, tier

**fillet** *Syn* STRIP, band, ribbon, stripe

**filthy** *Syn* DIRTY, foul, squalid, nasty *Ant* neat, spick-and-span

**final** *Syn* LAST, terminal, concluding, latest, ultimate, eventual

**financial** ♦ of or relating to the possession, making, borrowing, lending, or expenditure of money *Syn* monetary, pecuniary, fiscal

**fine** *n* ♦ a pecuniary penalty exacted by an authority *Syn* amercement

**fine** *vb Syn* PENALIZE, amerce, mulct

**finicky, finicking, finical** *Syn* NICE, particular, fussy, fastidious, dainty, squeamish, persnickety, pernickety

**finish** *Syn* CLOSE, complete, conclude, end, terminate

**finished** *Syn* CONSUMMATE, accomplished *Ant* crude

**fire** *n* ♦ a destructive burning *Syn* conflagration, holocaust

**fire** *vb* **1** *Syn* LIGHT, kindle, ignite **2** *Syn* INFORM, animate, inspire *Ant* daunt **3** *Syn* DISMISS, discharge, cashier, drop, sack, bounce

**firm** ♦ having a texture or consistency that resists deformation by external force *Syn* hard, solid *Ant* loose, flabby

**fiscal** *Syn* FINANCIAL, monetary, pecuniary

**fish** ♦ to attempt to catch fish *Syn* angle

**fissure** *Syn* CRACK, cleft, crevasse, crevice, cranny, chink

**fit** *n* ♦ an episode of bodily or mental disorder or excess *Syn* attack, access, accession, paroxysm, spasm, convulsion

**fit** *adj* ♦ right with respect to some end, need, use, or circumstances *Syn* suitable, meet, proper, appropriate, fitting, apt, happy, felicitous *Ant* unfit

**fit** *vb Syn* PREPARE, qualify, condition, ready

**fitful** ♦ lacking steadiness or regularity in course, movement, or succession *Syn* spasmodic, convulsive *Ant* constant

**fitting** *Syn* FIT, appropriate, proper, meet, suitable, apt, happy, felicitous *Ant* unfitting

**fix** *vb* **1** *Syn* SET, settle, establish *Ant* alter; abrogate (*a custom, rule, law*) **2** *Syn* FASTEN, attach, affix **3** *Syn* ADJUST, regulate

**fix** *n Syn* PREDICAMENT, plight, dilemma, quandary, scrape, jam, pickle

**flabbergast** *Syn* SURPRISE, amaze, astound, astonish

**flabby** *Syn* LIMP, flaccid, floppy, flimsy, sleazy *Ant* firm

**flaccid** *Syn* LIMP, flabby, floppy, flimsy, sleazy *Ant* resilient

**flag** *n* ♦ a piece of fabric that is used as a symbol (as of a nation) or as a signaling device *Syn* ensign, standard, banner, color, streamer, pennant, pendant, pennon, jack

**flag** *vb Syn* DROOP, wilt, sag

**flagitious** *Syn* VICIOUS, nefarious, infamous, iniquitous, villainous, corrupt, degenerate

**flagrant** ♦ bad or objectionable *Syn* glaring, gross, rank

**flair** *Syn* LEANING, proclivity, propensity, penchant

**flamboyant** *Syn* ORNATE, florid, rococo, baroque

**flame** *n Syn* BLAZE, flare, glare, glow

**flame** *vb Syn* BLAZE, flare, glare, glow

**flammable** *Syn* COMBUSTIBLE, inflammable, incendiary, inflammatory

**flare** *vb Syn* BLAZE, glare, flame, glow *Ant* gutter out

**flare** *n Syn* BLAZE, glare, flame, glow

**flash** *vb* ♦ to shoot forth light (as in rays or sparks) *Syn* gleam, glance, glint, sparkle, glitter, glisten, scintillate, coruscate, twinkle

**flash** *n Syn* INSTANT, second, moment, minute, jiffy, twinkling, split second

**flashy** *Syn* GAUDY, garish, tawdry, meretricious

**flat 1** *Syn* LEVEL, plane, plain, even, smooth, flush **2** *Syn* INSIPID, vapid, jejune, banal, wishy-washy, inane

**flattery** *Syn* COMPLIMENT, adulation

**flatulent** *Syn* INFLATED, tumid, turgid

**flaunt** *Syn* SHOW, parade, expose, display, exhibit

**flavor** *Syn* TASTE, savor, tang, relish, smack

**flavorsome** *Syn* PALATABLE, toothsome, tasty, savory, sapid, relishing, appetizing

**flaw** *Syn* BLEMISH, defect

**flawless** *Syn* IMPECCABLE, faultless, errorless

**flay** *Syn* SKIN, decorticate, peel, pare

**fleck** *Syn* SPOT, spatter, sprinkle, mottle, stipple, marble, speckle, spangle, bespangle

**flecked** *Syn* SPOTTED, spattered, sprinkled, mottled, stippled, marbled, speckled, spangled, bespangled

**flee** *Syn* ESCAPE, fly, decamp, abscond

**fleer** *Syn* SCOFF, jeer, gibe, gird, sneer, flout

**fleet** *vb Syn* WHILE, wile, beguile

**fleet** *adj Syn* FAST, swift, rapid, quick, speedy, hasty, expeditious

**fleeting** *Syn* TRANSIENT, evanescent, fugitive, passing, transitory, ephemeral, momentary, short-lived *Ant* lasting

**fleshly** *Syn* CARNAL, sensual, animal

**fleshy** ♦ thick and heavy in body because of superfluous fat *Syn* fat, stout, portly, plump, rotund, chubby, corpulent, obese *Ant* skinny, scrawny

**flex** ♦ to bend *Syn* crook, bow, buckle *Ant* extend

**flexible** *Syn* ELASTIC, supple, resilient, springy *Ant* inflexible

**flexuous** *Syn* WINDING, sinuous, serpentine, tortuous

**flicker** *Syn* FLIT, flutter, flitter, hover

**flightiness** *Syn* LIGHTNESS, light-mindedness, volatility, levity, frivolity, flippancy *Ant* steadiness; steadfastness

**flimsy** *Syn* LIMP, sleazy, floppy, flaccid, flabby

**flinch** *Syn* RECOIL, shrink, wince, blench, quail

**fling** *Syn* THROW, hurl, sling, toss, cast, pitch

**flippancy** *Syn* LIGHTNESS, levity, light-mindedness, frivolity, volatility, flightiness *Ant* seriousness

**flirt** *Syn* TRIFLE, coquet, dally, toy

**flit** ♦ to move or fly briskly, irregularly, and usu. intermittently *Syn* flutter, flitter, flicker, hover

**flitter** *Syn* FLIT, flutter, flicker, hover

**float** *Syn* FLY, skim, sail, dart, scud, shoot

**flood 1** *Syn* FLOW, stream, current, tide, flux **2** ♦ a great or overwhelming flow of or as if of water *Syn* deluge, inundation, torrent, spate, cataract

**floppy** *Syn* LIMP, flabby, flaccid, flimsy, sleazy

**florid** *Syn* ORNATE, flamboyant, rococo, baroque *Ant* chaste (*in style, decoration*)

**flounder** *Syn* STUMBLE, trip, blunder, lurch, lumber, galumph, lollop, bumble

**flourish 1** *Syn* SUCCEED, prosper, thrive *Ant* languish **2** *Syn* SWING, brandish, shake, wave, thrash

**flout** *Syn* SCOFF, jeer, gibe, fleer, gird, sneer *Ant* revere

**flow** *vb Syn* SPRING, issue, emanate, proceed, stem, derive, arise, rise, originate

**flow** *n* ♦ something suggestive of running water *Syn* stream, current, flood, tide, flux

**flower** *n Syn* BLOSSOM, bloom, blow

**flower** *vb Syn* BLOSSOM, bloom, blow

**flowery** *Syn* RHETORICAL, aureate, grandiloquent, magniloquent, euphuistic, bombastic

**fluctuate** *Syn* SWING, oscillate, sway, vibrate, pendulate, waver, undulate

**fluent** *Syn* VOCAL, eloquent, voluble, glib, articulate

**fluid** *Syn* LIQUID

**flurry** *n Syn* STIR, bustle, fuss, ado, pother

**flurry** *vb Syn* DISCOMPOSE, fluster, agitate, perturb, disturb, disquiet

**flush** *n Syn* BLUSH

**flush** *vb Syn* BLUSH

**flush** *adj Syn* LEVEL, even, flat, plane, plain, smooth

**fluster** *Syn* DISCOMPOSE, upset, agitate, perturb, flurry, disturb, disquiet

**flutter** *Syn* FLIT, flitter, flicker, hover

**flux** *Syn* FLOW, current, tide, stream, flood

**fly 1** ♦ to pass lightly or quickly over or above a surface *Syn* dart, float, skim, scud, shoot, sail **2** *Syn* ESCAPE, flee, decamp, abscond

**flying field** *Syn* AIRPORT, airdrome, airfield, airstrip, landing strip, landing field

**foam** ♦ a mass of bubbles gathering in or on the surface of a liquid or something as insubstantial as such a mass *Syn* froth, spume, scum, lather, suds, yeast

**focal** *Syn* CENTRAL, pivotal

**focus** *n Syn* CENTER, heart, nucleus, core, middle, midst, hub

**focus** *vb Syn* CENTER, centralize, concentrate

**fodder** *Syn* FOOD, forage, feed, provender, provisions, comestibles, victuals, viands

**foe** *Syn* ENEMY *Ant* friend

**fog** *n Syn* HAZE, smog, mist

**fog** *vb Syn* OBSCURE, dim, bedim, darken, eclipse, cloud, becloud, befog, obfuscate

**foible** *Syn* FAULT, failing, frailty, vice

**foil** *Syn* FRUSTRATE, thwart, circumvent, balk, baffle, outwit

**follow 1** ♦ to come after in time *Syn* succeed, ensue, supervene **2** ♦ to go after or on the trail of *Syn* pursue, chase, trail, tag, tail *Ant* precede; forsake (*a teacher or teachings*)

**follower** ♦ one who attaches himself to another *Syn* adherent, disciple, sectary, partisan, henchman, satellite *Ant* leader

**following** ♦ the body of persons who attach themselves to another esp. as disciples, patrons, or admirers *Syn* clientele, public, audience

**foment** *Syn* INCITE, abet, instigate *Ant* quell

**fond 1** ♦ made blindly or stupidly foolish *Syn* infatuated, besotted, insensate **2** *Syn* LOVING, devoted, affectionate, doting

**fondle** *Syn* CARESS, pet, cosset, cuddle, dandle

**food 1** ♦ things that are edible for human beings or animals *Syn* feed, victuals, viands, provisions, comestibles, provender, fodder, forage **2** ♦ material which feeds and supports the mind or

the spirit *Syn* aliment, pabulum, nutriment, nourishment, sustenance, pap

**fool** ♦ one regarded as lacking sense or good judgment *Syn* idiot, imbecile, moron, simpleton, natural

**foolhardy** *Syn* ADVENTUROUS, daring, daredevil, rash, reckless, venturesome *Ant* wary

**foolish 1** *Syn* SIMPLE, silly, fatuous, asinine **2** ♦ felt to be ridiculous because not exhibiting good sense *Syn* silly, absurd, preposterous *Ant* sensible

**foot** *Syn* ADD, figure, cast, sum, total, tot

**fop** ♦ a man who is conspicuously fashionable or elegant in dress or manners *Syn* dandy, beau, coxcomb, exquisite, dude, buck

**for** *Syn* BECAUSE, since, as, inasmuch as

**forage** *Syn* FOOD, fodder, provender, feed, provisions, comestibles, victuals, viands

**forbear 1** *Syn* FORGO, abnegate, eschew, sacrifice **2** *Syn* REFRAIN, abstain

**forbearance 1** *Syn* PATIENCE, long-suffering, longanimity, resignation **2** ♦ a disinclination to be severe or rigorous *Syn* tolerance, clemency, mercifulness, leniency, indulgence *Ant* vindictiveness; anger

**forbearing** ♦ disinclined by nature, disposition, or circumstances to be severe or rigorous *Syn* tolerant, clement, merciful, lenient, indulgent *Ant* unrelenting

**forbearingly** ♦ in a forbearing manner *Syn* tolerantly, clemently, mercifully, leniently, indulgently

**forbid** ♦ to debar one from using, doing, or entering or something from being used, done, or entered *Syn* prohibit, enjoin, interdict, inhibit, ban *Ant* permit; bid

**force** *n* **1** *Syn* POWER, energy, strength, might, puissance **2** ♦ the exercise of power in order to impose one's will on a person or to have one's will with a thing *Syn* violence, compulsion, coercion, duress, constraint, restraint

**force** *vb* ♦ to cause a person or thing to yield to pressure *Syn* compel, coerce, constrain, oblige

**forced** ♦ produced or kept up through effort *Syn* labored, strained, farfetched

**forceful** *Syn* POWERFUL, potent, forcible, puissant *Ant* feeble

**forcible** *Syn* POWERFUL, forceful, potent, puissant

**forebear** *Syn* ANCESTOR, forefather, progenitor

**forebode** *Syn* FORETELL, portend, presage, augur, prognosticate, predict, forecast, prophesy

**foreboding** *Syn* APPREHENSION, misgiving, presentiment

**forecast** *Syn* FORETELL, predict, prophesy, prognosticate, augur, presage, portend, forebode

**forefather** *Syn* ANCESTOR, forebear, progenitor

**foregoing** *Syn* PRECEDING, antecedent, precedent, previous, prior, former, anterior *Ant* following

**foreign** *Syn* EXTRINSIC, alien, extraneous *Ant* germane

**foreigner** *Syn* STRANGER, alien, outlander, outsider, immigrant, émigré

**foreknow** *Syn* FORESEE, divine, anticipate, apprehend

**foremost** *Syn* CHIEF, leading, principal, main, capital

**forensic** *Syn* ARGUMENTATION, debate, disputation, dialectic

**forerunner** ♦ one that goes before or in some way announces the coming of another *Syn* precursor, harbinger, herald

**foresee** ♦ to know or expect in advance that something will happen or come into existence or be made manifest *Syn* foreknow, divine, apprehend, anticipate

**foreshore** *Syn* SHORE, beach, strand, coast, littoral

**foresight** *Syn* PRUDENCE, forethought, providence, discretion *Ant* hindsight

**foresighted** *Syn* PRUDENT, forethoughtful, provident, discreet *Ant* hindsighted

**forestall** *Syn* PREVENT, anticipate

**foretaste** *Syn* PROSPECT, anticipation, outlook

**foretell** ♦ to tell something before it happens through special knowledge or occult power *Syn* predict, forecast, prophesy, prognosticate, augur, presage, portend, forebode

**forethought** *Syn* PRUDENCE, foresight, providence, discretion

**forethoughtful** *Syn* PRUDENT, foresighted, provident, discreet

**foretoken** ♦ something that serves as a sign of future happenings *Syn* presage, prognostic, omen, augury, portent

**forewarn** *Syn* WARN, caution

**foreword** *Syn* INTRODUCTION, preface, exordium, prologue, prelude, preamble

**forge** *Syn* MAKE, fabricate, fashion, manufacture, form, shape

**forget** *Syn* NEGLECT, overlook, ignore, disregard, omit, slight *Ant* remember

**forgetful** ♦ losing or letting go from one's mind something once known or learned *Syn* oblivious, unmindful

**forgive** *Syn* EXCUSE, pardon, remit, condone

**forgo** ♦ to deny oneself something for the sake of an end *Syn* forbear, abnegate, eschew, sacrifice

**forlorn 1** *Syn* ALONE, lorn, lone, desolate, lonesome, lonely, solitary **2** *Syn* DESPONDENT, hopeless, despairing, desperate

**forlornness** *Syn* DESPONDENCY, hopelessness, despair, desperation

**form** *n* **1** ♦ outward appearance of something as distinguished from the substance of which it is made *Syn* figure, shape, conformation, configuration **2** ♦ conduct regulated by an external control (as custom or a formal protocol of procedure) *Syn* formality, ceremony, ceremonial, rite, ritual, liturgy **3** ♦ a fixed or accepted way of doing or sometimes of expressing something *Syn* usage, convention, convenance

**form** *vb Syn* MAKE, shape, fashion, fabricate, manufacture, forge

**formal** *Syn* CEREMONIAL, conventional, ceremonious, solemn *Ant* informal

**formality** *Syn* FORM, ceremony, ceremonial, rite, liturgy, ritual

**former** *Syn* PRECEDING, prior, previous, antecedent, precedent, foregoing, anterior *Ant* latter

**formless** ♦ having no definite or recognizable form *Syn* unformed, shapeless

**forsake** *Syn* ABANDON, desert *Ant* return to; revert to

**forswear 1** *Syn* ABJURE, renounce, recant, retract **2** *Syn* PERJURE

**fort** ♦ a structure or place offering resistance to a hostile force *Syn* fortress, citadel, stronghold, fastness

**forth** *Syn* ONWARD, forward

**forthright** *Syn* STRAIGHTFORWARD, aboveboard *Ant* furtive

**fortify** *Syn* STRENGTHEN, invigorate, energize, reinforce *Ant* enfeeble

**fortitude** ♦ a quality of character combining courage and staying power *Syn* grit, backbone, pluck, guts, sand *Ant* pusillanimity

**fortress** *Syn* FORT, citadel, stronghold, fastness

**fortuitous** *Syn* ACCIDENTAL, contingent, casual, incidental

**fortunate** *Syn* LUCKY, providential, happy *Ant* unfortunate; disastrous

**fortune** *Syn* CHANCE, accident, luck, haphazard

**forward** *adj Syn* PREMATURE, advanced, untimely, precocious *Ant* backward

**forward** *adv* **1** *Syn* BEFORE, ahead *Ant* backward **2** *Syn* ONWARD, forth *Ant* backward

**forward** *vb* **1** *Syn* ADVANCE, promote, further *Ant* hinder; balk **2** *Syn* SEND, dispatch, transmit, remit, route, ship

**foster** *Syn* NURSE, nurture, cherish, cultivate

**foul** *adj Syn* DIRTY, filthy, nasty, squalid *Ant* fair; undefiled

**foul** *vb Syn* SOIL, dirty, sully, tarnish, befoul, smirch, besmirch, grime, begrime

**found 1** *Syn* BASE, ground, bottom, stay, rest **2** ♦

to set going or to bring into existence **Syn** establish, institute, organize, create

**foundation** **Syn** BASE, basis, ground, groundwork **Ant** superstructure

**foxy** **Syn** SLY, insidious, wily, guileful, tricky, crafty, cunning, artful

**fracas** **Syn** BRAWL, broil, melee, row, rumpus, scrap

**fraction** **Syn** PART, fragment, piece, portion, section, segment, sector, detail, member, division, parcel

**fractious** **Syn** IRRITABLE, peevish, snappish, waspish, petulant, pettish, huffy, fretful, querulous

**fragile** 1 ♦ easily broken **Syn** frangible, brittle, crisp, short, friable **Ant** tough 2 **Syn** WEAK, frail, feeble, decrepit, infirm **Ant** durable

**fragment** **Syn** PART, fraction, piece, portion, section, segment, sector, division, detail, member, parcel

**fragrance** ♦ a sweet or pleasant odor **Syn** perfume, incense, redolence, bouquet **Ant** stench, stink

**fragrant** **Syn** ODOROUS, aromatic, redolent, balmy **Ant** fetid

**frail** **Syn** WEAK, fragile, feeble, infirm, decrepit **Ant** robust

**frailty** **Syn** FAULT, failing, foible, vice

**frame** 1 **Syn** BUILD, construct, erect, raise, rear 2 **Syn** CONTRIVE, devise, invent, concoct

**framework** **Syn** STRUCTURE, skeleton, anatomy

**franchise** **Syn** SUFFRAGE, vote, ballot

**frangible** **Syn** FRAGILE, brittle, crisp, short, friable

**frank** ♦ marked by free, forthright, and sincere expression **Syn** candid, open, plain **Ant** reticent

**frantic** **Syn** FURIOUS, frenzied, wild, frenetic, delirious, rabid

**fraud** 1 **Syn** DECEPTION, trickery, chicanery, chicane, double-dealing 2 **Syn** IMPOSTURE, cheat, sham, fake, humbug, deceit, deception, counterfeit

**fray** **Syn** CONTEST, affray, fight, conflict, combat

**freak** **Syn** CAPRICE, fancy, whim, whimsy, conceit, vagary, crotchet

**freaked** **Syn** VARIEGATED, parti-colored, motley, checkered, checked, pied, piebald, skewbald, dappled

**free** *adj* ♦ not subject to the rule or control of another **Syn** independent, sovereign, autonomous, autarchic, autarkic **Ant** bond

**free** *vb* ♦ to relieve from constraint or restraint **Syn** release, liberate, emancipate, manumit, discharge

**freebooter** **Syn** PIRATE, buccaneer, privateer, corsair

**freedom** 1 ♦ the state or condition of not being subject to external rule or control **Syn** independence, autonomy, sovereignty, autarchy, autarky **Ant** bondage 2 ♦ the power or condition of acting without compulsion **Syn** liberty, license **Ant** necessity

**freethinker** **Syn** ATHEIST, unbeliever, agnostic, deist, infidel

**freezing** **Syn** COLD, frigid, frosty, gelid, icy, glacial, arctic, chilly, cool

**freight** **Syn** LOAD, cargo, burden, lading

**frenetic** **Syn** FURIOUS, frantic, frenzied, wild, delirious, rabid

**frenzied** **Syn** FURIOUS, frantic, wild, frenetic, delirious, rabid

**frenzy** 1 **Syn** MANIA, delirium, hysteria 2 **Syn** INSPIRATION, fury, afflatus

**frequently** **Syn** OFTEN, oft, oftentimes **Ant** rarely, seldom

**fresh** **Syn** NEW, novel, new-fashioned, newfangled, modern, modernistic, original **Ant** stale

**fret** **Syn** ABRADE, excoriate, chafe, gall

**fretful** **Syn** IRRITABLE, peevish, petulant, querulous, fractious, snappish, waspish, pettish, huffy

**friable** **Syn** FRAGILE, short, frangible, crisp, brittle

**friar** **Syn** RELIGIOUS, monk, nun

**friend** ♦ a person, esp. not related by blood, with whom one is on good and usu. familiar terms **Syn** acquaintance, intimate, confidant **Ant** foe

**friendly** **Syn** AMICABLE, neighborly **Ant** unfriendly; belligerent

**friendship** ♦ the relation existing between persons, communities, states, or peoples that are in accord and in sympathy with each other **Syn** amity, comity, goodwill **Ant** animosity

**fright** *n* **Syn** FEAR, alarm, consternation, panic, dread, dismay, terror, horror, trepidation

**fright** *vb* **Syn** FRIGHTEN, scare, alarm, terrify, terrorize, startle, affray, affright

**frighten** ♦ to strike or to fill with fear or dread **Syn** fright, scare, alarm, terrify, terrorize, startle, affray, affright

**frightful** **Syn** FEARFUL, dreadful, awful, terrible, terrific, horrible, horrific, shocking, appalling

**frigid** **Syn** COLD, freezing, gelid, icy, glacial, arctic, cool, chilly, frosty **Ant** torrid (*temperature*); amorous (*persons*)

**fritter** **Syn** WASTE, squander, dissipate, consume

**frivolity** **Syn** LIGHTNESS, levity, flippancy, lightmindedness, volatility, flightiness **Ant** seriousness, staidness

**frolic** *vb* **Syn** PLAY, sport, disport, rollick, romp, gambol

**frolic** *n* **Syn** PLAY, sport, disport, rollick, romp, gambol

**frolicsome** **Syn** PLAYFUL, sportive, roguish, waggish, impish, mischievous

**frosty** **Syn** COLD, chilly, cool, frigid, freezing, gelid, icy, glacial, arctic

**froth** **Syn** FOAM, spume, scum, lather, suds, yeast

**froward** **Syn** CONTRARY, perverse, balky, restive, wayward **Ant** compliant

**frown** ♦ to put on a dark or malignant countenance or aspect **Syn** scowl, glower, lower, gloom **Ant** smile

**frowzy** **Syn** SLATTERNLY, blowsy, dowdy **Ant** trim; smart

**frugal** **Syn** SPARING, thrifty, economical **Ant** wasteful

**fruitful** **Syn** FERTILE, fecund, prolific **Ant** unfruitful; fruitless

**fruitfulness** **Syn** FERTILITY, prolificacy, fecundity

**fruition** **Syn** PLEASURE, enjoyment, delectation, delight, joy

**fruitless** **Syn** FUTILE, vain, bootless, abortive **Ant** fruitful

**frustrate** ♦ to come between a person and his or her aim or desire or to defeat another's plan **Syn**

thwart, foil, baffle, balk, circumvent, outwit **Ant** fulfill

**fuddle** **Syn** CONFUSE, muddle, addle

**fugitive** **Syn** TRANSIENT, evanescent, transitory, fleeting, passing, ephemeral, momentary, short-lived

**fulfill** 1 **Syn** PERFORM, effect, achieve, accomplish, execute, discharge **Ant** frustrate; fail (in) 2 **Syn** SATISFY, meet, answer **Ant** fall short (of)

**full** ♦ containing all that is wanted or needed or possible **Syn** complete, plenary, replete **Ant** empty

**fulsome** ♦ too obviously extravagant or ingratiating to be accepted as genuine or sincere **Syn** oily, unctuous, oleaginous, slick, soapy

**fumble** **Syn** BOTCH, bungle, muff, cobble

**fumigate** **Syn** STERILIZE, disinfect, sanitize

**fun** ♦ action or speech that is intended to amuse or arouse laughter **Syn** jest, sport, game, play

**function** *n* 1 ♦ acts or operations expected of a person or thing **Syn** office, duty, province 2 **Syn** POWER, faculty

**function** *vb* **Syn** ACT, operate, work, behave, react

**fundamental** *adj* 1 ♦ forming or affecting the groundwork, roots, or lowest part of something **Syn** basic, basal, underlying, radical 2 **Syn** ESSENTIAL, vital, cardinal 3 **Syn** ELEMENTAL, basic, elementary, essential, primitive, underlying

**fundamental** *n* **Syn** PRINCIPLE, axiom, law, theorem

**funny** **Syn** LAUGHABLE, risible, ludicrous, ridiculous, comic, comical, farcical, droll

**furious** ♦ marked by uncontrollable excitement esp. under the stress of a powerful emotion **Syn** frantic, frenzied, wild, frenetic, delirious, rabid

**furnish** 1 **Syn** PROVIDE, supply **Ant** strip 2 ♦ to supply one with what is needed (as for daily living or a particular activity) **Syn** equip, outfit, appoint, accouter, arm

**further** *adv* **Syn** FARTHER, beyond

**further** *vb* **Syn** ADVANCE, forward, promote **Ant** hinder; retard

**furthermore** **Syn** ALSO, moreover, besides, likewise, too

**furtive** **Syn** SECRET, stealthy, clandestine, surreptitious, underhand, underhanded, covert **Ant** forthright; brazen

**furuncle** **Syn** ABSCESS, boil, carbuncle, pimple, pustule

**fury** 1 **Syn** ANGER, rage, ire, wrath, indignation 2 **Syn** INSPIRATION, frenzy, afflatus

**fuse** 1 **Syn** LIQUEFY, melt, deliquesce, thaw 2 **Syn** MIX, amalgamate, merge, coalesce, blend, mingle, commingle

**fusion** **Syn** ALLIANCE, coalition, league, federation, confederation, confederacy

**fuss** **Syn** STIR, pother, ado, flurry, bustle

**fussy** **Syn** NICE, finicky, finicking, finical, particular, persnickety, pernickety, dainty, fastidious, squeamish

**fustian** **Syn** BOMBAST, rant, rodomontade, rhapsody

**fusty** **Syn** MALODOROUS, musty, rancid, putrid, fetid, stinking, noisome, rank

**futile** ♦ barren of result **Syn** vain, fruitless, bootless, abortive

# G

**gab** **Syn** CHAT, chatter, patter, prate, prattle, babble, gabble, jabber, gibber

**gabble** **Syn** CHAT, babble, gab, chatter, patter, prate, prattle, jabber, gibber

**gad** **Syn** WANDER, stray, roam, ramble, rove, range, prowl, gallivant, traipse, meander

**gadget** **Syn** DEVICE, contraption, contrivance

**gag** **Syn** JOKE, jest, jape, quip, witticism, wisecrack, crack

**gain** 1 **Syn** GET, win, obtain, procure, secure, acquire **Ant** forfeit; lose 2 **Syn** REACH, compass,

achieve, attain 3 **Syn** IMPROVE, recover, recuperate, convalesce

**gainful** **Syn** PAYING, remunerative, lucrative, profitable

**gainsay** **Syn** DENY, contradict, impugn, contravene, negative, traverse **Ant** admit

**gall** *n* **Syn** TEMERITY, effrontery, nerve, cheek, hardihood, audacity

**gall** *vb* **Syn** ABRADE, chafe, excoriate, fret

**gallant** **Syn** CIVIL, courtly, chivalrous, courteous, polite

**gallantry** 1 **Syn** HEROISM, valor, prowess **Ant** dastardliness 2 **Syn** COURTESY, attention, amenity

**gallery** **Syn** PASSAGE, passageway, corridor, arcade, cloister, ambulatory, aisle, hall, hallway

**gallivant** **Syn** WANDER, stray, roam, ramble, rove, range, prowl, gad, traipse, meander

**galumph** **Syn** STUMBLE, trip, blunder, lurch, flounder, lumber, lollop, bumble

**galvanize** **Syn** PROVOKE, excite, stimulate, quicken, pique

**gambit** *Syn* TRICK, ruse, stratagem, maneuver, ploy, artifice, wile, feint

**gambol** *n Syn* PLAY, frolic, disport, sport, rollick, romp

**gambol** *vb Syn* PLAY, frolic, disport, sport, rollick, romp

**game 1** *Syn* FUN, sport, play, jest **2** *pl* **games** *Syn* ATHLETICS, sports

**gamut** *Syn* RANGE, reach, radius, compass, sweep, scope, orbit, horizon, ken, purview

**gap** *Syn* BREAK, interruption, interval, interim, hiatus, lacuna

**gape** *Syn* GAZE, stare, glare, gloat, peer

**garbage** *Syn* REFUSE, waste, offal, rubbish, trash, debris

**garble** *Syn* MISREPRESENT, falsify, belie

**gargantuan** *Syn* HUGE, vast, immense, enormous, elephantine, mammoth, giant, gigantic, gigantean, colossal, Herculean, cyclopean, titanic, Brobdingnagian

**garish** *Syn* GAUDY, tawdry, flashy, meretricious *Ant* somber

**garner** *Syn* REAP, glean, gather, harvest

**garnish** *Syn* ADORN, embellish, beautify, deck, bedeck, decorate, ornament

**garrulity, garrulousness** *Syn* TALKATIVENESS, loquacity, volubility, glibness

**garrulous** *Syn* TALKATIVE, loquacious, voluble, glib *Ant* taciturn

**gasconade** *Syn* BOAST, vaunt, brag, crow

**gastronome** *Syn* EPICURE, gourmet, gourmand, bon vivant, glutton

**gate** *Syn* DOOR, portal, gateway, postern, doorway

**gateway** *Syn* DOOR, gate, portal, postern, doorway

**gather 1** ♦ to come or bring together *Syn* collect, assemble, congregate **2** *Syn* REAP, glean, garner, harvest **3** *Syn* INFER, deduce, conclude, judge

**gathering** ♦ a number of individuals come or brought together *Syn* collection, assemblage, assembly, congregation

**gauche** *Syn* AWKWARD, maladroit, clumsy, inept

**gaudy** ♦ vulgar or cheap in its showiness *Syn* tawdry, garish, flashy, meretricious *Ant* quiet (*in taste or style*)

**gauge** *Syn* STANDARD, criterion, yardstick, touchstone

**gaunt** *Syn* LEAN, rawboned, angular, lank, lanky, spare, scrawny, skinny

**gay** *Syn* LIVELY, vivacious, sprightly, animated *Ant* grave, sober

**gaze** ♦ to look at long and attentively *Syn* gape, stare, glare, peer, gloat

**gear** *Syn* EQUIPMENT, tackle, paraphernalia, outfit, apparatus, machinery

**geld** *Syn* STERILIZE, castrate, spay, emasculate, alter, mutilate

**gelid** *Syn* COLD, icy, frigid, freezing, frosty, glacial, arctic, cool, chilly

**general** *Syn* UNIVERSAL, generic, common

**generally** *Syn* LARGELY, mostly, chiefly, mainly, principally, greatly

**generate** ♦ to give life or origin to or to bring into existence by or as if by natural processes *Syn* engender, breed, beget, get, sire, procreate, propagate, reproduce

**generic** *Syn* UNIVERSAL, general, common

**generous** *Syn* LIBERAL, bountiful, bounteous, openhanded, munificent, handsome *Ant* stingy

**genesis** *Syn* BEGINNING, rise, initiation

**genial** *Syn* GRACIOUS, sociable, affable, cordial *Ant* saturnine; caustic

**genius** *Syn* GIFT, talent, faculty, aptitude, knack, bent, turn

**gentle** *Syn* SOFT, mild, smooth, lenient, bland, balmy *Ant* rough, harsh

**gentleman** ♦ a person of good or noble birth *Syn* patrician, aristocrat *Ant* boor

**gentry** *Syn* ARISTOCRACY, county, nobility, elite, society

**genuine** *Syn* AUTHENTIC, bona fide, veritable *Ant* counterfeit; fraudulent

**germane** *Syn* RELEVANT, pertinent, material, apposite, applicable, apropos *Ant* foreign

**gesticulation** *Syn* GESTURE

**gesture** ♦ an expressive movement of the body or the use of such a movement *Syn* gesticulation

**get 1** ♦ to come into possession of *Syn* obtain, procure, secure, acquire, gain, win **2** *Syn* GENERATE, beget, procreate, sire, engender, breed, propagate, reproduce **3** *Syn* INDUCE, persuade, prevail

**ghastly** ♦ horrifying and repellent in appearance or aspect *Syn* grisly, gruesome, macabre, grim, lurid

**ghost** *Syn* APPARITION, spirit, specter, shade, phantasm, phantom, wraith, revenant

**giant** *Syn* HUGE, vast, immense, enormous, elephantine, mammoth, gigantic, gigantean, colossal, gargantuan, Herculean, cyclopean, titanic, Brobdingnagian

**gibber** *Syn* CHAT, prate, chatter, gab, patter, prattle, babble, gabble, jabber

**gibberish** ♦ speech or actions that are esoteric in nature and suggest the magical, strange, or unknown *Syn* mummery, hocus-pocus, abracadabra

**gibe** *Syn* SCOFF, jeer, sneer, flout, gird, fleer

**giddy** ♦ affected by a sensation of being whirled about or around *Syn* dizzy, vertiginous, swimming, dazzled

**gift 1** ♦ something, often of value but not necessarily material, given freely to another for his benefit or pleasure *Syn* present, gratuity, favor, boon, largess **2** ♦ a special ability or a capacity for a definite kind of activity or achievement *Syn* faculty, aptitude, genius, talent, knack, bent, turn

**gigantic, gigantean** *Syn* HUGE, vast, immense, enormous, elephantine, mammoth, giant, colossal, gargantuan, Herculean, cyclopean, titanic, Brobdingnagian

**gingery** *Syn* SPIRITED, fiery, peppery, high-spirited, mettlesome, spunky

**gird** *vb Syn* SURROUND, environ, encircle, circle, encompass, compass, hem, girdle, ring

**gird** *vb Syn* SCOFF, sneer, flout, jeer, gibe, fleer

**girdle** *Syn* SURROUND, environ, encircle, circle, encompass, compass, hem, gird, ring

**gist** *Syn* SUBSTANCE, purport, burden, core, pith

**give** ♦ to convey something or make something over or available to another *Syn* present, donate, bestow, confer, afford

**glacial** *Syn* COLD, arctic, icy, gelid, frigid, freezing, frosty, cool, chilly

**glad** ♦ characterized by or expressing the mood of one who is pleased or delighted *Syn* happy, cheerful, lighthearted, joyful, joyous *Ant* sad

**gladden** *Syn* PLEASE, delight, rejoice, gratify, tickle, regale *Ant* sadden

**glance** *vb* **1** *Syn* BRUSH, graze, shave, skim **2** *Syn* FLASH, glint, gleam, sparkle, glitter, glisten, scintillate, coruscate, twinkle

**glance** *n Syn* LOOK, glimpse, peep, peek, sight, view

**glare** *vb* **1** *Syn* BLAZE, glow, flare, flame **2** *Syn* GAZE, stare, peer, gloat, gape

**glare** *n Syn* BLAZE, flare, glow, flame

**glaring** *Syn* FLAGRANT, gross, rank

**glaze** *Syn* LUSTER, gloss, sheen

**gleam** *Syn* FLASH, glance, glint, sparkle, glitter, glisten, scintillate, coruscate, twinkle

**glean** *Syn* REAP, gather, garner, harvest

**glee** *Syn* MIRTH, jollity, hilarity *Ant* gloom

**glib 1** *Syn* VOCAL, fluent, voluble, articulate, eloquent **2** *Syn* TALKATIVE, loquacious, garrulous, voluble

**glibness** *Syn* TALKATIVENESS, loquacity, garrulity, volubility

**glide** *Syn* SLIDE, slip, skid, glissade, slither, coast, toboggan

**glimpse** *Syn* LOOK, glance, peep, peek, sight, view

**glint** *Syn* FLASH, glance, gleam, sparkle, glitter, glisten, scintillate, coruscate, twinkle

**glissade** *Syn* SLIDE, glide, slip, skid, slither, coast, toboggan

**glisten** *Syn* FLASH, sparkle, glitter, gleam, glance, glint, scintillate, coruscate, twinkle

**glitter** *Syn* FLASH, glisten, sparkle, gleam, glance, glint, scintillate, coruscate, twinkle

**gloat** *Syn* GAZE, gape, stare, glare, peer

**globe** *Syn* EARTH, world, planet

**gloom** *vb Syn* FROWN, lower, glower, scowl

**gloom** *n Syn* SADNESS, dejection, depression, melancholy, melancholia, blues, dumps *Ant* glee

**gloomy 1** *Syn* DARK, murky, obscure, dim, dusky *Ant* brilliant **2** *Syn* SULLEN, glum, morose, saturnine, dour, surly, sulky, crabbed *Ant* cheerful

**glorify** *Syn* DIGNIFY, ennoble, honor

**glorious** *Syn* SPLENDID, resplendent, sublime, superb, gorgeous *Ant* inglorious

**glory** *Syn* FAME, renown, honor, celebrity, éclat, reputation, repute, notoriety *Ant* ignominy, shame

**gloss** *n Syn* LUSTER, sheen, glaze

**gloss** *vb Syn* PALLIATE, gloze, extenuate, whitewash, whiten

**gloss** *n Syn* ANNOTATION

**gloss** *vb Syn* ANNOTATE

**glossy** *Syn* SLEEK, slick, velvety, silken, silky, satiny

**glow** *vb Syn* BLAZE, flame, flare, glare

**glow** *n Syn* BLAZE, flame, flare, glare

**glower** *Syn* FROWN, lower, scowl, gloom

**gloze** *Syn* PALLIATE, gloss, whitewash, extenuate, whiten

**glum** *Syn* SULLEN, gloomy, morose, saturnine, dour, surly, sulky, crabbed *Ant* cheerful

**glut** *Syn* SATIATE, gorge, surfeit, sate, cloy, pall

**glutton** *Syn* EPICURE, gourmand, gastronome, bon vivant, gourmet

**gluttonous** *Syn* VORACIOUS, ravenous, ravening, rapacious *Ant* abstemious

**gnash** *Syn* BITE, gnaw, champ

**gnaw** *Syn* BITE, champ, gnash

**go** *vb* **1** ♦ to move out of or away from where one is *Syn* leave, depart, quit, withdraw, retire *Ant* come **2** *Syn* RESORT, refer, apply, turn

**go** *n Syn* SPELL, shift, tour, trick, turn, stint, bout

**goad** *n Syn* MOTIVE, spur, incentive, inducement, spring, impulse *Ant* curb

**goad** *vb Syn* URGE, egg, exhort, spur, prod, prick, sic

**goal** *Syn* INTENTION, objective, object, end, aim, intent, purpose, design

**gob** *Syn* MARINER, sailor, seaman, tar, bluejacket

**gobbledygook** *Syn* NONSENSE, twaddle, drivel, bunk, balderdash, poppycock, trash, rot, bull

**godless** *Syn* IRRELIGIOUS, ungodly, unreligious, nonreligious

**good** ♦ in accordance with one's standard of what is satisfactory *Syn* right *Ant* bad; poor

**good-looking** *Syn* BEAUTIFUL, comely, pretty, bonny, fair, beauteous, pulchritudinous, handsome, lovely

**good-natured** *Syn* AMIABLE, obliging, complaisant *Ant* contrary

**goodness** ♦ moral excellence *Syn* virtue, rectitude, morality *Ant* badness, evil

**good sense** *Syn* SENSE

**goodwill** *Syn* FRIENDSHIP, amity, comity *Ant* animosity

**gorge** *Syn* SATIATE, surfeit, sate, glut, cloy, pall

**gorgeous** *Syn* SPLENDID, resplendent, glorious, sublime, superb

**gory** *Syn* BLOODY, sanguinary, sanguine, sanguineous

**gossip** *n Syn* REPORT, rumor, hearsay

**gossip** *vb* ♦ to disclose something, often of questionable veracity, that is better kept to oneself *Syn* blab, tattle

**gourmand** *Syn* EPICURE, glutton, gastronome, bon vivant, gourmet

**gourmet** *Syn* EPICURE, bon vivant, gastronome, gourmand, glutton

**govern** ♦ to exercise sovereign authority *Syn* rule

**grab** *Syn* TAKE, grasp, clutch, seize, snatch

**grace 1** *Syn* MERCY, clemency, lenity, charity **2** *Syn* ELEGANCE, dignity

**gracious** ♦ marked by kindly courtesy *Syn* cordial, affable, genial, sociable *Ant* ungracious

**gradate** *Syn* CLASS, grade, rank, rate, graduate

**gradation** ♦ difference or variation between two things that are nearly alike *Syn* shade, nuance

**grade** *Syn* CLASS, rank, rate, graduate, gradate

**graduate** *Syn* CLASS, grade, rank, rate, gradate

**grand** ♦ large, handsome, dignified, and impressive *Syn* magnificent, imposing, stately, majestic, august, noble, grandiose

**grandiloquent** *Syn* RHETORICAL, magniloquent, aureate, flowery, euphuistic, bombastic

**grandiose** *Syn* GRAND, imposing, stately, august, magnificent, majestic, noble

**grant** *vb* **1** ♦ to give as a favor or as a right *Syn* concede, vouchsafe, accord, award **2** ♦ to admit something in question, esp. a contention of one's opponent in an argument *Syn* concede, allow

**grant** *n* *Syn* APPROPRIATION, subvention, subsidy

**graph** *n* *Syn* CHART, map

**graph** *vb* *Syn* CHART, map

**graphic** ♦ giving a clear visual impression esp. in words *Syn* vivid, picturesque, pictorial

**grapple** *Syn* WRESTLE, tussle, scuffle

**grasp** *vb* *Syn* TAKE, clutch, grab, seize, snatch

**grasp** *n* *Syn* HOLD, grip, clutch

**grasping** *Syn* COVETOUS, greedy, avaricious, acquisitive

**grate** *Syn* SCRAPE, scratch, rasp, grind

**grateful 1** ♦ feeling or expressing gratitude *Syn* thankful *Ant* ungrateful **2** *Syn* PLEASANT, agreeable, gratifying, pleasing, welcome *Ant* obnoxious

**gratify** *Syn* PLEASE, delight, rejoice, gladden, tickle, regale *Ant* anger; offend, affront; disappoint

**gratifying** *Syn* PLEASANT, grateful, agreeable, pleasing, welcome

**gratuitous** *Syn* SUPEREROGATORY, uncalled-for, wanton

**gratuity** *Syn* GIFT, largess, boon, favor, present

**grave** *Syn* SERIOUS, solemn, somber, sedate, sober, earnest, staid *Ant* gay

**graze** *vb* *Syn* FEED, pasture, nourish

**graze** *vb* *Syn* BRUSH, glance, shave, skim

**grease** *Syn* OIL, lubricate, anoint, cream

**great** *Syn* LARGE, big *Ant* little

**greatly** *Syn* LARGELY, mostly, chiefly, mainly, principally, generally

**greed** *Syn* CUPIDITY, rapacity, avarice

**greedy** *Syn* COVETOUS, acquisitive, grasping, avaricious

**green** *Syn* RUDE, callow, raw, crude, rough, uncouth *Ant* experienced; seasoned

**greet** *Syn* ADDRESS, salute, hail, accost

**greeting** ♦ the ceremonial words or acts of one who meets, welcomes, or formally addresses another *Syn* salutation, salute

**gregarious** *Syn* SOCIAL, cooperative, convivial, companionable, hospitable

**grief** *Syn* SORROW, anguish, woe, heartache, heartbreak, regret

**grievance** *Syn* INJUSTICE, wrong, injury

**grieve** ♦ to feel or express sorrow or grief *Syn* mourn, sorrow *Ant* rejoice

**grim 1** ♦ being extremely obdurate or firm in action or purpose *Syn* implacable, relentless, unrelenting, merciless *Ant* lenient **2** *Syn* GHASTLY, grisly, gruesome, macabre, lurid

**grime** *Syn* SOIL, dirty, sully, tarnish, foul, befoul, smirch, besmirch, begrime

**grin** *vb* *Syn* SMILE, smirk, simper

**grin** *n* *Syn* SMILE, smirk, simper

**grind** *vb* *Syn* SCRAPE, scratch, grate, rasp

**grind** *n* *Syn* WORK, drudgery, toil, travail, labor

**grip** *Syn* HOLD, grasp, clutch

**grisly** *Syn* GHASTLY, gruesome, macabre, grim, lurid

**grit** *Syn* FORTITUDE, pluck, backbone, guts, sand *Ant* faintheartedness

**groan** *vb* *Syn* SIGH, moan, sob

**groan** *n* *Syn* SIGH, moan, sob

**gross 1** *Syn* WHOLE, total, entire, all *Ant* net **2** *Syn* COARSE, vulgar, obscene, ribald *Ant* delicate, dainty; ethereal **3** *Syn* FLAGRANT, glaring, rank *Ant* petty

**grotesque** *Syn* FANTASTIC, bizarre, antic

**ground** *n* **1** *Syn* BASE, basis, foundation, groundwork **2** *Syn* REASON, argument, proof **3** *pl* **grounds** *Syn* DEPOSIT, precipitate, sediment, dregs, lees

**ground** *vb* *Syn* BASE, found, bottom, stay, rest

**groundless** *Syn* BASELESS, unfounded, unwarranted

**groundwork** *Syn* BASE, foundation, basis, ground *Ant* superstructure

**group** ♦ a collection or assemblage of persons or things *Syn* cluster, bunch, parcel, lot

**grovel** *Syn* WALLOW, welter

**growl** *Syn* BARK, bay, howl, snarl, yelp, yap

**grown-up** *Syn* MATURE, adult, matured, ripe, mellow *Ant* childish; callow

**grub** *Syn* DIG, delve, spade, excavate

**grudge** *vb* *Syn* COVET, begrudge, envy

**grudge** *n* *Syn* MALICE, ill will, malevolence, spite, despite, malignity, malignancy, spleen

**gruesome** *Syn* GHASTLY, macabre, grisly, grim, lurid

**gruff** *Syn* BLUFF, crusty, brusque, blunt, curt

**guarantee** ♦ an assurance for the fulfillment of a condition or a person who provides such assurance *Syn* guaranty, surety, security, bond, bail

**guarantor** *Syn* SPONSOR, surety, patron, backer, angel

**guaranty** *Syn* GUARANTEE, surety, security, bond, bail

**guard** *Syn* DEFEND, shield, protect, safeguard

**guerdon** *Syn* PREMIUM, reward, meed, bounty, award, prize, bonus

**guess** *vb* *Syn* CONJECTURE, surmise

**guess** *n* *Syn* CONJECTURE, surmise *Ant* certainty

**guest** *Syn* VISITOR, caller, visitant

**guide** ♦ to put or lead on a course or into the way to be followed *Syn* lead, steer, pilot, engineer *Ant* misguide

**guile** *Syn* DECEIT, duplicity, dissimulation, cunning *Ant* ingenuousness; candor

**guileful** *Syn* SLY, cunning, crafty, tricky, foxy, insidious, wily, artful

**guilt** *Syn* BLAME, culpability, fault *Ant* innocence; guiltlessness

**guilty** *Syn* BLAMEWORTHY, culpable *Ant* innocent

**gulf** ♦ a hollow place of vast width and depth *Syn* chasm, abysm, abyss

**gull** *Syn* DUPE, befool, trick, hoax, hoodwink, bamboozle

**gullibility** *Syn* CREDULITY *Ant* astuteness

**gullible** *Syn* CREDULOUS *Ant* astute

**gumption** *Syn* SENSE, common sense, good sense, judgment, wisdom

**gunman** *Syn* ASSASSIN, cutthroat, bravo

**gush** *Syn* POUR, stream, sluice

**gusto** *Syn* TASTE, relish, zest, palate

**gut 1** *Syn* ABDOMEN, belly, stomach, paunch **2** *pl* **guts** *Syn* FORTITUDE, grit, pluck, backbone, sand

**gyrate** *Syn* TURN, rotate, revolve, spin, whirl, wheel, circle, twirl, eddy, swirl, pirouette

# H

**habit 1** ♦ a mode of behaving or doing that has become fixed by constant repetition *Syn* habitude, practice, usage, custom, use, wont **2** *Syn* PHYSIQUE, build, constitution

**habitat** ♦ the place in which a particular kind of organism lives or grows *Syn* biotope, range, station

**habitation** ♦ the place where one lives *Syn* dwelling, abode, residence, domicile, home, house

**habitual** *Syn* USUAL, customary, wonted, accustomed *Ant* occasional

**habituate** ♦ to make used to something *Syn* accustom, addict, inure

**habitude** *Syn* HABIT, practice, usage, custom, use, wont

**habitué** *Syn* ADDICT, votary, devotee

**hack** *Syn* MERCENARY, hireling, venal

**hackneyed** *Syn* TRITE, stereotyped, threadbare, shopworn

**Hadean** *Syn* INFERNAL, chthonian, Tartarean, stygian, hellish, chthonic

**haggard** ♦ thin and drawn by or as if by worry, fatigue, hunger, or illness *Syn* worn, careworn, pinched, wasted, cadaverous

**hail** *Syn* ADDRESS, salute, greet, accost

**halcyon** *Syn* CALM, serene, placid, tranquil, peaceful

**hale** *adj* *Syn* HEALTHY, robust, sound, wholesome, well *Ant* infirm

**hale** *vb* *Syn* PULL, haul, draw, drag, tug, tow

**hall hallway** *Syn* PASSAGE, passageway, corridor, gallery, arcade, cloister, aisle, ambulatory

**hallow** *Syn* DEVOTE, consecrate, dedicate

**hallucination** *Syn* DELUSION, mirage, illusion

**hamper** ♦ to hinder or impede in moving, progressing, or acting freely *Syn* trammel, clog, fetter, shackle, manacle, hog-tie *Ant* assist (*persons*); expedite (*work, projects*)

**hand** *Syn* WORKER, operative, workman, workingman, laborer, craftsman, handicraftsman, mechanic, artisan, roustabout

**handicap 1** *Syn* ADVANTAGE, allowance, odds, edge **2** *Syn* DISADVANTAGE, detriment, drawback *Ant* asset, advantage

**handicraft** *Syn* TRADE, craft, art, profession

**handicraftsman** *Syn* WORKER, craftsman, workman, artisan, mechanic, workingman, laborer, operative, hand, roustabout

**handle 1** ♦ to deal with or manage usu. with dexterity or efficiency *Syn* manipulate, wield, swing, ply **2** *Syn* TREAT, deal **3** *Syn* TOUCH, feel, palpate, paw

**handsome 1** *Syn* LIBERAL, generous, bountiful, bounteous, openhanded, munificent **2** *Syn* BEAUTIFUL, pulchritudinous, beauteous, comely, good-looking, lovely, pretty, bonny, fair

**handy** *Syn* DEXTEROUS, deft, adroit

**hang 1** ♦ to place or be placed so as to be supported at one point or side usu. at the top *Syn* suspend, sling, dangle **2** *Syn* DEPEND, hinge, turn

**hanger-on** *Syn* PARASITE, sycophant, leech, sponge, sponger, favorite, toady, lickspittle, bootlicker

**hanker** *Syn* LONG, yearn, pine, hunger, thirst

**hap** *Syn* CHANCE, fortune, luck, accident, hazard

**haphazard** *Syn* RANDOM, chance, chancy, casual, desultory, hit-or-miss, happy-go-lucky

**hapless** *Syn* UNLUCKY, disastrous, ill-starred, ill-fated, unfortunate, calamitous, luckless

**happen** ♦ to come to pass or to come about *Syn* chance, occur, befall, betide, transpire

**happiness** ♦ a state of well-being or pleasurable satisfaction *Syn* felicity, beatitude, blessedness, bliss *Ant* unhappiness

**happy 1** *Syn* LUCKY, fortunate, providential *Ant* unhappy **2** *Syn* FIT, felicitous, apt, appropriate, fitting, suitable, meet, proper *Ant* unhappy **3**

*Syn* GLAD, cheerful, lighthearted, joyful, joyous *Ant* unhappy; disconsolate

**happy-go-lucky** *Syn* RANDOM, haphazard, hit-or-miss, chance, chancy, casual, desultory

**harangue** *Syn* SPEECH, oration, address, lecture, talk, sermon, homily

**harass** *Syn* WORRY, harry, annoy, plague, pester, tease, tantalize

**harbinger** *Syn* FORERUNNER, precursor, herald

**harbor** *n* ♦ a place where seacraft may ride secure *Syn* haven, port

**harbor** *vb* ♦ to provide with shelter or refuge *Syn* shelter, entertain, lodge, house, board

**hard 1** *Syn* FIRM, solid *Ant* soft **2** ♦ demanding great toil or effort *Syn* difficult, arduous *Ant* easy

**harden 1** ♦ to make or to become physically hard or solid *Syn* solidify, indurate, petrify, cake *Ant* soften **2** ♦ to make proof against hardship, strain, or exposure *Syn* season, acclimatize, acclimate *Ant* soften

**hardened** ♦ grown or become hard *Syn* indurated, callous *Ant* softened.

**hardihood** *Syn* TEMERITY, audacity, effrontery, nerve, cheek, gall

**hardship** *Syn* DIFFICULTY, rigor, vicissitude

**harm** *n Syn* INJURY, damage, hurt, mischief *Ant* benefit

**harm** *vb Syn* INJURE, impair, hurt, damage, mar, spoil *Ant* benefit

**harmless** ♦ not having hurtful or injurious qualities *Syn* innocuous, innocent, inoffensive, unoffending *Ant* harmful

**harmonize 1** *Syn* AGREE, accord, correspond, square, conform, tally, jibe *Ant* clash; conflict **2** ♦ to bring into consonance or accord *Syn* tune, attune

**harmony 1** ♦ the effect produced when different things come together without clashing or disagreement *Syn* consonance, accord, concord *Ant* conflict **2** *Syn* SYMMETRY, proportion, balance

**harry** *Syn* WORRY, harass, annoy, plague, pester, tease, tantalize

**harsh** *Syn* ROUGH, rugged, scabrous, uneven *Ant* pleasant; mild

**harvest** *Syn* REAP, glean, gather, garner

**haste** ♦ rapidity of motion or action *Syn* hurry, speed, expedition, dispatch *Ant* deliberation

**hasten** *Syn* SPEED, accelerate, quicken, hurry, precipitate *Ant* delay

**hasty 1** *Syn* FAST, speedy, quick, expeditious, rapid, swift, fleet **2** *Syn* PRECIPITATE, headlong, abrupt, impetuous, sudden

**hate** *n Syn* ABHORRENCE, hatred, detestation, abomination, loathing *Ant* love

**hate** *vb* ♦ to feel extreme enmity or dislike *Syn* detest, abhor, abominate, loathe *Ant* love

**hateful** ♦ deserving of or arousing hate *Syn* odious, abhorrent, detestable, abominable *Ant* lovable; sympathetic

**hatred** *Syn* ABHORRENCE, hate, detestation, abomination, loathing

**haughty** *Syn* PROUD, arrogant, insolent, lordly, overbearing, supercilious, disdainful *Ant* lowly

**haul** *Syn* PULL, hale, draw, drag, tug, tow

**have** ♦ to keep, control, or experience as one's own *Syn* hold, own, possess, enjoy

**haven** *Syn* HARBOR, port

**havoc** *Syn* RUIN, devastation, destruction

**hazard** *n* **1** *Syn* CHANCE, accident, fortune, luck, hap **2** *Syn* DANGER, jeopardy, peril, risk

**hazard** *vb Syn* VENTURE, risk, chance, jeopardize, endanger, imperil

**hazardous** *Syn* DANGEROUS, precarious, risky, perilous

**haze** ♦ an atmospheric condition that is characterized by the presence of fine particulate material in the air and that deprives the air of its transparency *Syn* mist, fog, smog

**head, headman** *Syn* CHIEF, leader, chieftain, master

**headlong** *Syn* PRECIPITATE, impetuous, abrupt, hasty, sudden

**headstrong** *Syn* UNRULY, ungovernable, intractable, refractory, recalcitrant, willful

**headway** *Syn* SPEED, pace, velocity, momentum, impetus

**heal** *Syn* CURE, remedy

**healthful** ♦ conducive or beneficial to the health or soundness of body or mind *Syn* healthy, wholesome, salubrious, salutary, hygienic, sanitary

**healthy 1** *Syn* HEALTHFUL, wholesome, salubrious, salutary, hygienic, sanitary **2** ♦ having or manifesting health of mind or body or indicative of such health *Syn* sound, wholesome, robust, hale, well *Ant* unhealthy

**heap** *n* ♦ a quantity of things brought together into a more or less compact group *Syn* pile, stack, shock, cock, mass, bank

**heap** *vb* ♦ to bring a number of things together into a more or less compact group or collection *Syn* pile, stack, shock, cock, mass, bank

**hearing** ♦ an opportunity to be heard *Syn* audience, audition

**hearsay** *Syn* REPORT, rumor, gossip

**heart** *Syn* CENTER, middle, core, hub, nucleus, midst, focus

**heartache, heartbreak** *Syn* SORROW, grief, anguish, woe, regret

**hearten** *Syn* ENCOURAGE, inspirit, embolden, cheer, nerve, steel *Ant* dishearten

**heartfelt** *Syn* SINCERE, hearty, unfeigned, wholehearted, whole-souled

**hearty** *Syn* SINCERE, heartfelt, unfeigned, wholehearted, whole-souled *Ant* hollow

**heave** *Syn* LIFT, raise, hoist, elevate, boost, rear

**heavenly** *Syn* CELESTIAL, empyrean, empyreal

**heavy** ♦ having great weight *Syn* weighty, ponderous, cumbrous, cumbersome, hefty *Ant* light

**heckle** *Syn* BAIT, badger, hector, chivy, hound, ride

**hector** *Syn* BAIT, badger, chivy, heckle, hound, ride

**heedless** *Syn* CARELESS, thoughtless, inadvertent *Ant* heedful

**hefty** *Syn* HEAVY, weighty, ponderous, cumbrous, cumbersome

**height** ♦ the distance a thing rises above the level on which it stands *Syn* altitude, elevation

**heighten** *Syn* INTENSIFY, enhance, aggravate

**heinous** *Syn* OUTRAGEOUS, atrocious, monstrous *Ant* venial

**hellish** *Syn* INFERNAL, chthonian, chthonic, Hadean, Tartarean, stygian

**help** *vb* **1** ♦ to give assistance or support *Syn* aid, assist *Ant* hinder **2** *Syn* IMPROVE, better, ameliorate

**help** *n* ♦ an act or instance of giving what will benefit or assist *Syn* aid, assistance

**helper** *Syn* ASSISTANT, coadjutor, aid, aide, aide-de-camp

**hem** *Syn* SURROUND, environ, encircle, circle, encompass, compass, gird, girdle, ring

**hence** *Syn* THEREFORE, consequently, then, accordingly, so

**henchman** *Syn* FOLLOWER, adherent, disciple, partisan, satellite, sectary

**herald** *Syn* FORERUNNER, harbinger, precursor

**Herculean** *Syn* HUGE, vast, immense, enormous, elephantine, mammoth, giant, gigantic, gigantean, colossal, gargantuan, cyclopean, titanic, Brobdingnagian

**hereditary** *Syn* INNATE, congenital, inborn, inherited, inbred

**heretic** ♦ one who is not orthodox in his beliefs *Syn* schismatic, sectarian, sectary, dissenter, nonconformist

**heretical** *Syn* HETERODOX

**heritage** ♦ something which one receives or is entitled to receive by succession *Syn* inheritance, patrimony, birthright

**hermaphroditic, hermaphrodite** *Syn* BISEXUAL, androgynous, epicene

**hermit** *Syn* RECLUSE, eremite, anchorite, cenobite

**heroism** ♦ conspicuous courage or bravery *Syn* valor, prowess, gallantry

**hesitancy** *Syn* HESITATION

**hesitant** *Syn* DISINCLINED, reluctant, loath, averse, indisposed

**hesitate** ♦ to show irresolution or uncertainty *Syn* waver, vacillate, falter

**hesitation** ♦ an act or action of hesitating *Syn* hesitancy

**heterodox** ♦ not in conformity with orthodox beliefs or teachings *Syn* heretical *Ant* orthodox

**heterogeneous** *Syn* MISCELLANEOUS, motley, promiscuous, assorted *Ant* homogeneous

**hew** *Syn* CUT, chop, carve, slit, slash

**hiatus** *Syn* BREAK, gap, interruption, interval, interim, lacuna

**hick** *Syn* BOOR, bumpkin, yokel, rube, clodhopper, clown, lout, churl

**hide** *vb* ♦ to withdraw or to withhold from sight or observation *Syn* conceal, screen, secrete, cache, bury, ensconce

**hide** *n Syn* SKIN, pelt, rind, bark, peel

**hidebound** *Syn* ILLIBERAL, narrow-minded, narrow, intolerant, bigoted

**hideous** *Syn* UGLY, ill-favored, unsightly *Ant* fair

**high** ♦ having a relatively great upward extension *Syn* tall, lofty *Ant* low

**high-spirited** *Syn* SPIRITED, mettlesome, spunky, fiery, peppery, gingery

**hilarity** *Syn* MIRTH, jollity, glee

**hind** *Syn* POSTERIOR, hinder, rear, after, back *Ant* fore, front

**hinder** *vb* ♦ to put obstacles in the way *Syn* impede, obstruct, block, bar, dam *Ant* further

**hinder** *adj Syn* POSTERIOR, hind, rear, after, back *Ant* front, fore

**hinge** *Syn* DEPEND, hang, turn

**hint** *Syn* SUGGEST, intimate, insinuate, imply

**hire** *n Syn* WAGE, wages, pay, salary, stipend, fee, emolument

**hire** *vb* ♦ to take or engage something or grant the use of something for a stipulated price or rate *Syn* let, lease, rent, charter

**hireling** *Syn* MERCENARY, venal, hack

**history** ♦ a chronological record of events *Syn* chronicle, annals

**histrionic** *Syn* DRAMATIC, theatrical, dramaturgic, melodramatic

**hit** *Syn* STRIKE, smite, punch, slug, slog, swat, clout, slap, cuff, box

**hit-or-miss** *Syn* RANDOM, haphazard, happy-go-lucky, desultory, casual, chance, chancy

**hoard** *Syn* ACCUMULATE, amass

**hoarse** *Syn* LOUD, raucous, strident, stentorian, earsplitting, stertorous

**hoax** *Syn* DUPE, hoodwink, bamboozle, gull, befool, trick

**hobo** *Syn* VAGABOND, tramp, vagrant, truant, bum

**hocus-pocus** *Syn* GIBBERISH, mummery, abracadabra

**hog-tie** *Syn* HAMPER, trammel, clog, fetter, shackle, manacle

**hoist** *Syn* LIFT, raise, elevate, boost, heave, rear

**hold** *vb* **1** *Syn* KEEP, hold back, withhold, reserve, detain, retain, keep back, keep out **2** *Syn* CONTAIN, accommodate **3** *Syn* HAVE, own, possess, enjoy

**hold** *n* ♦ the act or manner of grasping or holding *Syn* grip, grasp, clutch

**hold back** *Syn* KEEP, hold, withhold, reserve, detain, retain, keep back, keep out

**hole** ♦ a space within the substance of a body or mass *Syn* hollow, cavity, pocket, void, vacuum

**holiness** ♦ a state of spiritual soundness and unimpaired virtue *Syn* sanctity

**holler** *vb Syn* SHOUT, yell, shriek, scream, screech, squeal, whoop

**holler** *n Syn* SHOUT, yell, shriek, scream, screech, squeal, whoop

**hollow** *adj Syn* VAIN, empty, nugatory, otiose, idle

**hollow** *n Syn* HOLE, cavity, pocket, void, vacuum

**holocaust** *Syn* FIRE, conflagration

**holy** ♦ dedicated to the service of or set apart by religion *Syn* sacred, divine, spiritual, religious, blessed *Ant* unholy

**homage** *Syn* HONOR, reverence, deference, obeisance

**home** *Syn* HABITATION, house, dwelling, abode, residence, domicile

**homely** *Syn* PLAIN, simple, unpretentious *Ant* comely, bonny

**homily** *Syn* SPEECH, sermon, talk, address, oration, harangue, lecture

**homunculus** *Syn* DWARF, manikin, midget, pygmy, runt

**honest** *Syn* UPRIGHT, just, conscientious, scrupulous, honorable *Ant* dishonest

**honesty** ♦ uprightness as evidenced in character and actions *Syn* honor, integrity, probity *Ant* dishonesty

**honor** *n* 1 *Syn* FAME, glory, renown, celebrity, éclat, reputation, repute, notoriety *Ant* dishonor 2 ♦ respect or esteem shown one as his or her due or claimed by one as a right *Syn* homage, reverence, deference, obeisance 3 *Syn* HONESTY, integrity, probity

**honor** *vb Syn* DIGNIFY, ennoble, glorify

**honorable** *Syn* UPRIGHT, just, scrupulous, conscientious, honest *Ant* dishonorable

**hoodwink** *Syn* DUPE, hoax, trick, gull, befool, bamboozle

**hop** *Syn* SKIP, bound, curvet, lope, lollop, ricochet

**hope** *Syn* EXPECT, look, await *Ant* despair (*of*); despond

**hopeful** ♦ having or showing confidence that the end or outcome will be favorable *Syn* optimistic, roseate, rose-colored *Ant* hopeless, despairing

**hopeless** *Syn* DESPONDENT, despairing, desperate, forlorn *Ant* hopeful

**hopelessness** *Syn* DESPONDENCY, despair, desperation, forlornness *Ant* hopefulness

**horde** *Syn* CROWD, mob, throng, crush, press, rout

**horizon** *Syn* RANGE, gamut, reach, radius, compass, sweep, scope, orbit, ken, purview

**horrendous** *Syn* HORRIBLE, horrific, horrid

**horrible** 1 ♦ inspiring horror or abhorrence *Syn* horrid, horrific, horrendous *Ant* fascinating 2 *Syn* FEARFUL, horrific, shocking, appalling, awful, dreadful, frightful, terrible, terrific

**horrid** *Syn* HORRIBLE, horrific, horrendous *Ant* delightful

**horrific** 1 *Syn* HORRIBLE, horrid, horrendous 2 *Syn* FEARFUL, horrible, terrible, terrific, shocking, appalling, awful, dreadful, frightful

**horrify** *Syn* DISMAY, daunt, appall

**horror** *Syn* FEAR, terror, dread, fright, alarm, dismay, consternation, panic, trepidation *Ant* fascination

**hors d'oeuvre** *Syn* APPETIZER, aperitif

**horse sense** *Syn* SENSE, common sense, good sense, gumption, judgment, wisdom

**hospitable** *Syn* SOCIAL, gregarious, convivial, cooperative, companionable *Ant* inhospitable

**host** *Syn* MULTITUDE, army, legion

**hostage** *Syn* PLEDGE, pawn, earnest, token

**hostility** *Syn* ENMITY, animosity, antagonism, antipathy, rancor, animus

**hound** *Syn* BAIT, ride, hector, badger, heckle, chivy

**house** *n Syn* HABITATION, home, dwelling, abode, residence, domicile

**house** *vb Syn* HARBOR, lodge, board, shelter, entertain

**hover** *Syn* FLIT, flutter, flitter, flicker

**howl** 1 *Syn* BARK, bay, growl, snarl, yelp, yap 2 *Syn* ROAR, bellow, bluster, bawl, vociferate, clamor, ululate

**howler** *Syn* ERROR, boner, mistake, blunder, slip, lapse, faux pas, bull

**hub** *Syn* CENTER, core, middle, nucleus, heart, focus, midst

**hubbub** *Syn* DIN, uproar, pandemonium, hullabaloo, babel, clamor, racket

**hue** *Syn* COLOR, shade, tint, tinge, tone

**huff** *Syn* OFFENSE, dudgeon, pique, resentment, umbrage

**huffy** *Syn* IRRITABLE, petulant, pettish, fractious, peevish, snappish, waspish, fretful, querulous

**huge** ♦ exceedingly or excessively large *Syn* vast, immense, enormous, elephantine, mammoth, giant, gigantic, gigantean, colossal, gargantuan, Herculean, cyclopean, titanic, Brobdingnagian

**hullabaloo** *Syn* DIN, uproar, pandemonium, babel, hubbub, clamor, racket

**humane** *Syn* CHARITABLE, humanitarian, benevolent, philanthropic, eleemosynary, altruistic *Ant* barbarous, inhuman; atrocious

**humanitarian** *Syn* CHARITABLE, humane, benevolent, philanthropic, eleemosynary, altruistic

**humble** *adj* ♦ lacking all signs of pride, aggressiveness, or self-assertiveness *Syn* meek, modest, lowly

**humble** *vb Syn* ABASE, humiliate, demean, debase, degrade

**humbug** *Syn* IMPOSTURE, fake, sham, cheat, fraud, deceit, deception, counterfeit

**humdrum** *Syn* DULL, dreary, monotonous, pedestrian, stodgy

**humid** *Syn* WET, moist, damp, dank

**humiliate** *Syn* ABASE, humble, degrade, debase, demean

**humor** *n* 1 *Syn* MOOD, temper, vein 2 *Syn* WIT, irony, satire, sarcasm, repartee

**humor** *vb Syn* INDULGE, pamper, spoil, baby, mollycoddle

**humorous** *Syn* WITTY, facetious, jocular, jocose

**hunger** *Syn* LONG, yearn, hanker, pine, thirst

**hunt** *Syn* SEEK, search, ransack, rummage, scour, comb, ferret out

**hurl** *Syn* THROW, fling, cast, pitch, toss, sling

**hurricane** ♦ a violent rotating storm originating in the tropics and often moving into temperate latitudes *Syn* tropical storm, typhoon

**hurry** *vb Syn* SPEED, quicken, precipitate, hasten *Ant* delay

**hurry** *n Syn* HASTE, speed, dispatch, expedition

**hurt** *vb Syn* INJURE, harm, damage, impair, mar, spoil

**hurt** *n Syn* INJURY, harm, damage, mischief

**husbandry** *Syn* AGRICULTURE, farming

**husky** *Syn* MUSCULAR, brawny, sinewy, athletic, burly

**hygienic** *Syn* HEALTHFUL, sanitary, healthy, wholesome, salubrious, salutary

**hymeneal** *Syn* MATRIMONIAL, nuptial, marital, connubial, conjugal

**hymn** *Syn* SING, troll, carol, descant, warble, trill, chant, intone

**hyperbole** *Syn* EXAGGERATION, overstatement

**hypercritical** *Syn* CRITICAL, captious, caviling, carping, censorious, faultfinding

**hypochondriac** *Syn* MELANCHOLIC, melancholy, atrabilious

**hypocrisy** ♦ the pretense or affectation of having virtues, principles, or beliefs that one does not actually have *Syn* sanctimony, pharisaism, cant

**hypocritical** ♦ characterized by hypocrisy *Syn* sanctimonious, pharisaical, canting

**hypostatize** *Syn* REALIZE, reify, externalize, materialize, incarnate, actualize, embody, objectify

**hypothetical** *Syn* SUPPOSED, conjectural, suppositious, reputed, putative, purported

**hysteria** *Syn* MANIA, delirium, frenzy

# I

**icon** *Syn* IMAGE, portrait, effigy, statue, photograph, mask

**iconoclast** *Syn* REBEL, insurgent

**icy** *Syn* COLD, glacial, arctic, gelid, frigid, freezing, frosty, cool, chilly *Ant* fiery

**idea** ♦ what exists in the mind as a representation as of something comprehended or as a formulation as of a plan *Syn* concept, conception, thought, notion, impression

**ideal** *adj Syn* ABSTRACT, transcendent, transcendental *Ant* actual

**ideal** *n Syn* MODEL, pattern, exemplar, example, standard, beau ideal, mirror

**identical** 1 *also* identic *Syn* SAME, selfsame, very, equivalent, equal, tantamount *Ant* diverse 2 *Syn* LIKE, alike, similar, analogous, comparable, akin, parallel, uniform *Ant* different

**identification** *Syn* RECOGNITION, apperception, assimilation

**identify** ♦ to bring (one or more things) into union with another thing *Syn* incorporate, embody, assimilate

**idiom** 1 *Syn* LANGUAGE, dialect, speech, tongue 2 *Syn* PHRASE, expression, locution

**idiosyncrasy** *Syn* ECCENTRICITY

**idiot** *Syn* FOOL, imbecile, moron, simpleton, natural

**idle** *adj* 1 *Syn* VAIN, nugatory, otiose, empty, hollow 2 *Syn* INACTIVE, inert, passive, supine *Ant* busy

**idle** *vb* ♦ to spend time not in work but in idleness *Syn* loaf, lounge, loll, laze

**idolize** *Syn* ADORE, worship

**ignite** *Syn* LIGHT, kindle, fire *Ant* stifle; extinguish

**ignoble** *Syn* MEAN, sordid, abject *Ant* noble; magnanimous

**ignominy** *Syn* DISGRACE, infamy, shame, opprobrium, dishonor, disrepute, obloquy, odium

**ignorant** ♦ lacking knowledge or education *Syn* illiterate, unlettered, uneducated, untaught, untutored, unlearned *Ant* cognizant (*of something*); conversant; informed

**ignore** *Syn* NEGLECT, disregard, overlook, slight, omit, forget *Ant* heed (*a warning, a sign, a symptom*); acknowledge

**ilk** *Syn* TYPE, kind, sort, nature, description, character, stripe, kidney

**ill** *adj Syn* BAD, evil, wicked, naughty *Ant* good

**ill** *n Syn* EVIL *Ant* good

**illegal** *Syn* UNLAWFUL, illegitimate, illicit *Ant* legal

**illegitimate** *Syn* UNLAWFUL, illegal, illicit *Ant* legitimate

**ill-fated** *Syn* UNLUCKY, ill-starred, disastrous, unfortunate, calamitous, luckless, hapless

**ill-favored** *Syn* UGLY, hideous, unsightly *Ant* well-favored; fair

**illiberal** ♦ unwilling or unable to understand the point of view of others *Syn* narrow-minded, narrow, intolerant, bigoted, hidebound *Ant* liberal

**illicit** *Syn* UNLAWFUL, illegal, illegitimate *Ant* licit

**illimitable** *Syn* INFINITE, boundless, uncircumscribed, eternal, sempiternal

**illiterate** *Syn* IGNORANT, unlettered, uneducated, untaught, untutored, unlearned *Ant* literate

**ill-mannered** *Syn* RUDE, uncivil, ungracious, impolite, discourteous *Ant* well-bred

**ill-starred** *Syn* UNLUCKY, ill-fated, disastrous, unfortunate, calamitous, luckless, hapless

**ill-treat** *Syn* ABUSE, maltreat, mistreat, misuse, outrage

**illuminate, illumine** ♦ to fill with or to throw light upon *Syn* light, lighten, enlighten, illustrate *Ant* darken, obscure

**illusion** *Syn* DELUSION, mirage, hallucination

**illusory** *Syn* APPARENT, seeming, ostensible *Ant* factual; matter-of-fact

**illustrate 1** *Syn* ILLUMINATE, enlighten, illumine, light, lighten *Ant* dim **2** *Syn* EXEMPLIFY

**illustration** *Syn* INSTANCE, example, case, sample, specimen

**illustrious** *Syn* FAMOUS, eminent, renowned, celebrated, famed *Ant* infamous

**ill will** *Syn* MALICE, malevolence, malignity, malignancy, spite, despite, spleen, grudge *Ant* goodwill; charity

**image 1** ♦ a lifelike representation esp. of a living being *Syn* effigy, statue, icon, portrait, photograph, mask **2** *Syn* SENSATION, percept, sensedatum, sensum

**imaginary** ♦ unreal or unbelievable or conceiving such unreal or unbelievable things *Syn* fanciful, visionary, fantastic, chimerical, quixotic *Ant* real, actual

**imagination** ♦ the power or function of the mind by which mental images of things are formed or the exercise of that power *Syn* fancy, fantasy

**imagine** *Syn* THINK, conceive, fancy, realize, envisage, envision

**imbecile** *Syn* FOOL, idiot, moron, simpleton, natural

**imbibe** *Syn* ABSORB, assimilate *Ant* ooze, exude

**imbue** *Syn* INFUSE, inoculate, leaven, ingrain, suffuse

**imitate** *Syn* COPY, mimic, ape, mock

**immaterial** ♦ not composed of matter *Syn* spiritual, incorporeal *Ant* material

**immature** ♦ not fully developed *Syn* unmatured, unripe, unmellow *Ant* mature

**immediate** *Syn* DIRECT *Ant* mediate (*knowledge, relation, operation*); distant (*relatives*)

**immense** *Syn* HUGE, vast, enormous, elephantine, mammoth, giant, gigantic, gigantean, colossal, gargantuan, Herculean, cyclopean, titanic, Brobdingnagian

**immerse** *Syn* DIP, submerge, duck, souse, dunk

**immigrant 1** *Syn* STRANGER, alien, foreigner, outlander, outsider, émigré **2** *Syn* EMIGRANT, migrant

**immigrate** *Syn* MIGRATE, emigrate

**imminent** *Syn* IMPENDING

**immobile** *Syn* IMMOVABLE, immotive *Ant* mobile

**immoderate** *Syn* EXCESSIVE, inordinate, exorbitant, extreme, extravagant *Ant* moderate

**immortal** ♦ not subject to death or decay *Syn* deathless, undying, unfading *Ant* mortal

**immotive** *Syn* IMMOVABLE, immobile

**immovable** ♦ incapable of moving or being moved *Syn* immobile, immotive *Ant* movable

**immunity** *Syn* EXEMPTION *Ant* susceptibility

**immure** *Syn* IMPRISON, incarcerate, jail, intern

**impact** ♦ a forcible or enforced contact between two or more things *Syn* impingement, collision, clash, shock, concussion, percussion, jar, jolt

**impair** *Syn* INJURE, damage, mar, harm, hurt, spoil *Ant* improve, amend; repair

**impalpable** *Syn* IMPERCEPTIBLE, insensible, intangible, inappreciable, imponderable *Ant* palpable

**impart** *Syn* COMMUNICATE

**impartial** *Syn* FAIR, equitable, unbiased, objective, just, dispassionate, uncolored *Ant* partial

**impassable** ♦ not allowing passage *Syn* impenetrable, impervious, impermeable *Ant* passable

**impassible** *Syn* INSENSIBLE, insensitive, anesthetic

**impassioned** ♦ actuated by or showing intense feeling *Syn* passionate, ardent, fervent, fervid, perfervid *Ant* unimpassioned

**impassive** ♦ unresponsive to what might normally excite interest or emotion *Syn* stoic, phlegmatic, apathetic, stolid *Ant* responsive

**impassivity, impassiveness** ♦ unresponsiveness to something that might normally excite interest or emotion *Syn* apathy, stolidity, phlegm, stoicism

**impatient** ♦ manifesting signs of unrest or an inability to keep still or quiet *Syn* nervous, unquiet, restless, restive, uneasy, fidgety, jumpy, jittery *Ant* patient

**impeach** *Syn* ACCUSE, indict, incriminate, charge, arraign

**impeccable** ♦ absolutely correct and beyond criticism *Syn* faultless, flawless, errorless

**impecunious** *Syn* POOR, indigent, needy, destitute, penniless, poverty-stricken, necessitous *Ant* flush

**impede** *Syn* HINDER, obstruct, block, bar, dam *Ant* assist; promote

**impediment** *Syn* OBSTACLE, obstruction, bar, snag *Ant* aid, assistance; advantage

**impel** *Syn* MOVE, drive, actuate *Ant* restrain

**impending** ♦ likely to occur soon or without further warning *Syn* imminent

**impenetrable** *Syn* IMPASSABLE, impervious, impermeable *Ant* penetrable

**impenetrate** *Syn* PERMEATE, interpenetrate, penetrate, pervade, impregnate, saturate

**imperative 1** *Syn* MASTERFUL, peremptory, imperious, domineering **2** *Syn* PRESSING, urgent, crying, importunate, insistent, exigent, instant

**imperceptible** ♦ incapable of being apprehended by the senses or intellect *Syn* insensible, impalpable, intangible, inappreciable, imponderable *Ant* perceptible

**imperfection** ♦ an instance of failure to reach a standard of excellence or perfection *Syn* deficiency, shortcoming, fault *Ant* perfection

**imperial** *Syn* KINGLY, regal, royal, queenly, princely

**imperil** *Syn* VENTURE, hazard, risk, chance, jeopardize, endanger

**imperious** *Syn* MASTERFUL, domineering, peremptory, imperative *Ant* abject

**impermeable** *Syn* IMPASSABLE, impervious, impenetrable

**impersonate** *Syn* ACT, play

**impersonator** *Syn* ACTOR, player, mummer, mime, mimic, performer, thespian, trouper

**impertinent** ♦ given to thrusting oneself into the affairs of others *Syn* officious, meddlesome, intrusive, obtrusive

**imperturbable** *Syn* COOL, composed, collected, unruffled, unflappable, nonchalant *Ant* choleric, touchy

**impervious** *Syn* IMPASSABLE, impenetrable, impermeable

**impetuous** *Syn* PRECIPITATE, headlong, abrupt, hasty, sudden

**impetus 1** *Syn* SPEED, momentum, velocity, pace **2** *Syn* STIMULUS, excitant, incitement, stimulant

**impingement** *Syn* IMPACT, collision, clash, shock, concussion, percussion, jar, jolt

**impious** ♦ lacking in reverence for what is sacred or divine *Syn* profane, blasphemous, sacrilegious *Ant* pious; reverent

**impish** *Syn* PLAYFUL, roguish, waggish, mischievous, frolicsome, sportive

**implacable** *Syn* GRIM, relentless, unrelenting, merciless

**implant** ♦ to introduce into the mind *Syn* inculcate, instill

**implement** *n* ♦ a relatively simple device for performing work *Syn* tool, instrument, appliance, utensil

**implement** *vb* *Syn* ENFORCE

**implicate** *Syn* INVOLVE

**implication** ♦ something hinted at but not explicitly stated *Syn* inference

**implicit** ♦ understood though not directly stated *Syn* virtual, constructive *Ant* explicit

**implore** *Syn* BEG, entreat, beseech, supplicate, importune, adjure

**imply 1** *Syn* INCLUDE, involve, comprehend, embrace, subsume **2** *Syn* SUGGEST, hint, intimate, insinuate *Ant* express

**impolite** *Syn* RUDE, uncivil, discourteous, ill-mannered, ungracious *Ant* polite

**imponderable** *Syn* IMPERCEPTIBLE, impalpable, inappreciable, insensible, intangible *Ant* ponderable, appreciable

**import** *vb* *Syn* MEAN, denote, signify

**import** *n* **1** *Syn* MEANING, significance, sense, ac-

ceptation, signification **2** *Syn* IMPORTANCE, significance, consequence, moment, weight

**importance** ♦ the quality or state of being of notable worth or influence *Syn* consequence, moment, weight, significance, import *Ant* unimportance

**importunate** *Syn* PRESSING, urgent, imperative, crying, insistent, exigent, instant

**importune** *Syn* BEG, entreat, beseech, implore, supplicate, adjure

**impose** *Syn* DICTATE, prescribe, ordain, decree

**imposing** *Syn* GRAND, stately, majestic, august, noble, magnificent, grandiose *Ant* unimposing

**impostor** ♦ a person who fraudulently pretends to be someone or something else *Syn* faker, quack, mountebank, charlatan

**imposture** ♦ a thing made to seem other than it is *Syn* cheat, fraud, sham, fake, humbug, deceit, deception, counterfeit

**impotent 1** *Syn* POWERLESS *Ant* potent **2** *Syn* STERILE, barren, unfruitful, infertile *Ant* virile

**impoverish** *Syn* DEPLETE, bankrupt, exhaust, drain *Ant* enrich

**imprecation** *Syn* CURSE, malediction, anathema *Ant* prayer

**impregnable** *Syn* INVINCIBLE, inexpugnable, unassailable, invulnerable, unconquerable, indomitable

**impregnate 1** *Syn* PERMEATE, saturate, pervade, penetrate, impenetrate, interpenetrate **2** *Syn* SOAK, saturate, drench, steep, sop, waterlog

**impress** *vb* *Syn* AFFECT, touch, strike, influence, sway

**impress** *n* *Syn* IMPRESSION, imprint, print, stamp

**impressible** *Syn* SENTIENT, sensitive, impressionable, responsive, susceptible

**impression 1** ♦ the perceptible trace or traces left by pressure *Syn* impress, imprint, print, stamp **2** *Syn* IDEA, notion, thought, concept, conception **3** *Syn* EDITION, reprinting, printing, reissue

**impressionable** *Syn* SENTIENT, sensitive, impressible, responsive, susceptible

**impressive** *Syn* MOVING, affecting, poignant, touching, pathetic *Ant* unimpressive

**imprint** *Syn* IMPRESSION, print, impress, stamp

**imprison** ♦ to confine closely so that escape is impossible or unlikely *Syn* incarcerate, jail, immure, intern

**impromptu** *Syn* EXTEMPORANEOUS, unpremeditated, offhand, improvised, extempore, extemporary

**improper 1** *Syn* UNFIT, inappropriate, unfitting, unsuitable, inapt, unhappy, infelicitous *Ant* proper **2** *Syn* INDECOROUS, indecent, unseemly, unbecoming, indelicate *Ant* proper

**impropriety** *Syn* BARBARISM, corruption, solecism, vulgarism, vernacular

**improve 1** ♦ to make more acceptable or bring nearer to some standard *Syn* better, help, ameliorate *Ant* impair; worsen **2** ♦ to grow or become better (as in health or well-being) *Syn* recover, recuperate, convalesce, gain

**improvised** *Syn* EXTEMPORANEOUS, unpremeditated, impromptu, offhand, extempore, extemporary

**impudent** *Syn* SHAMELESS, brazen, barefaced, brash *Ant* respectful

**impugn** *Syn* DENY, gainsay, contradict, negative, traverse, contravene *Ant* authenticate; advocate

**impulse** *Syn* MOTIVE, spring, incentive, inducement, spur, goad

**impulsive** *Syn* SPONTANEOUS, instinctive, automatic, mechanical *Ant* deliberate

**impute** *Syn* ASCRIBE, attribute, assign, refer, credit, accredit, charge

**inactive** ♦ not engaged in work or activity *Syn* idle, inert, passive, supine *Ant* active, live

**inadvertent** *Syn* CARELESS, heedless, thoughtless

**inane** *Syn* INSIPID, banal, wishy-washy, jejune, vapid, flat

**inanimate** *Syn* DEAD, lifeless, defunct, deceased, departed, late *Ant* animate

**inappreciable** *Syn* IMPERCEPTIBLE, imponderable,

impalpable, insensible, intangible *Ant* appreciable, ponderable

**inappropriate** *Syn* UNFIT, unfitting, inapt, improper, unsuitable, unhappy, infelicitous *Ant* appropriate

**inapt** *Syn* UNFIT, unhappy, infelicitous, inappropriate, unfitting, unsuitable, improper *Ant* apt

**inarticulate** *Syn* DUMB, speechless, mute *Ant* articulate

**inasmuch as** *Syn* BECAUSE, since, for, as

**inaugurate 1** *Syn* INITIATE, install, induct, invest **2** *Syn* BEGIN, start, commence

**inauspicious** *Syn* OMINOUS, unpropitious, portentous, fateful *Ant* auspicious

**inborn** *Syn* INNATE, congenital, hereditary, inherited, inbred *Ant* acquired

**inbred** *Syn* INNATE, inborn, congenital, hereditary, inherited

**incapable** ♦ mentally or physically unfit, or untrained to do a given kind of work *Syn* incompetent, unqualified *Ant* capable

**incarcerate** *Syn* IMPRISON, jail, immure, intern

**incarnate** *Syn* REALIZE, embody, hypostatize, materialize, externalize, objectify, actualize, reify

**incendiary** *Syn* COMBUSTIBLE, inflammable, flammable, inflammatory

**incense** *n Syn* FRAGRANCE, redolence, perfume, bouquet

**incense** *vb Syn* ANGER, enrage, infuriate, madden *Ant* placate

**incentive** *Syn* MOTIVE, inducement, spring, spur, goad, impulse

**inception** *Syn* ORIGIN, source, root, provenance, provenience *Ant* termination

**incessant** *Syn* CONTINUAL, continuous, constant, unremitting, perpetual, perennial *Ant* intermittent

**incident** *Syn* OCCURRENCE, episode, event, circumstance

**incidental** *Syn* ACCIDENTAL, casual, fortuitous, contingent *Ant* essential

**incise** *Syn* CARVE, engrave, etch, chisel, sculpture, sculpt, sculp

**incisive** ♦ having, manifesting, or suggesting a keen alertness of mind *Syn* trenchant, clear-cut, cutting, biting, crisp

**incite** ♦ to spur to action *Syn* instigate, abet, foment *Ant* restrain

**incitement** *Syn* STIMULUS, stimulant, excitant, impetus *Ant* restraint; inhibition

**incline 1** *Syn* SLANT, lean, slope **2** ♦ to influence one to have or to take an attitude toward something *Syn* bias, dispose, predispose *Ant* disincline, indispose

**include** ♦ to contain within as part of the whole *Syn* comprehend, embrace, involve, imply, subsume *Ant* exclude

**incognito** *Syn* PSEUDONYM, alias, nom de guerre, pen name, nom de plume

**incommode** *Syn* INCONVENIENCE, discommode, trouble *Ant* accommodate

**incomparable** *Syn* SUPREME, peerless, superlative, transcendent, surpassing, preeminent

**incompatible** *Syn* INCONSONANT, incongruous, inconsistent, discordant, discrepant, uncongenial, unsympathetic *Ant* compatible

**incompetent** *Syn* INCAPABLE, unqualified *Ant* competent

**incongruous** *Syn* INCONSONANT, uncongenial, incompatible, inconsistent, discordant, discrepant, unsympathetic *Ant* congruous

**inconsistent** *Syn* INCONSONANT, incompatible, incongruous, uncongenial, unsympathetic, discordant, discrepant *Ant* consistent

**inconsonant** ♦ not in agreement with or not agreeable to *Syn* inconsistent, incompatible, incongruous, uncongenial, unsympathetic, discordant, discrepant *Ant* consonant

**inconstant** ♦ lacking firmness or steadiness (as in purpose or devotion) *Syn* fickle, capricious, mercurial, unstable *Ant* constant

**inconvenience** ♦ to subject to disturbance or discomfort *Syn* incommode, discommode, trouble

**incorporate** *Syn* IDENTIFY, embody, assimilate

**incorporeal** *Syn* IMMATERIAL, spiritual *Ant* corporeal

**increase** ♦ to make or become greater *Syn* enlarge, augment, multiply *Ant* decrease

**incredulity** *Syn* UNBELIEF, disbelief *Ant* credulity

**increment** *Syn* ADDITION, accretion, accession

**incriminate** *Syn* ACCUSE, impeach, indict, charge, arraign

**inculcate** *Syn* IMPLANT, instill

**incur** ♦ to bring upon oneself something usu. unpleasant or injurious *Syn* contract, catch

**incurious** *Syn* INDIFFERENT, unconcerned, aloof, detached, uninterested, disinterested *Ant* curious, inquisitive

**incursion** *Syn* INVASION, raid, inroad

**indebtedness** *Syn* DEBT, debit, obligation, liability, arrear

**indecent** *Syn* INDECOROUS, unseemly, indelicate, improper, unbecoming *Ant* decent

**indecorous** ♦ not conforming to what is accepted as right, fitting, or in good taste *Syn* improper, unseemly, indecent, unbecoming, indelicate *Ant* decorous

**indefatigable** ♦ capable of prolonged and arduous effort *Syn* tireless, weariless, untiring, unwearying, unwearied, unflagging

**indefinable** *Syn* UNUTTERABLE, inexpressible, unspeakable, ineffable, indescribable

**indelicate** *Syn* INDECOROUS, indecent, unseemly, improper, unbecoming *Ant* delicate, refined

**indemnify** *Syn* PAY, reimburse, recompense, compensate, remunerate, repay, satisfy

**indemnity** *Syn* REPARATION, redress, amends, restitution

**indentured** *Syn* BOUND, articled, bond

**independence** *Syn* FREEDOM, autonomy, sovereignty, autarchy, autarky *Ant* dependence

**independent** *Syn* FREE, autonomous, sovereign, autarchic, autarkic *Ant* dependent

**indescribable** *Syn* UNUTTERABLE, inexpressible, ineffable, unspeakable, indefinable

**indicate** ♦ to give evidence of or to serve as ground for a valid or reasonable inference *Syn* betoken, attest, bespeak, argue, prove

**indict** *Syn* ACCUSE, incriminate, impeach, charge, arraign

**indifferent 1** ♦ not showing or feeling interest *Syn* unconcerned, incurious, aloof, detached, uninterested, disinterested *Ant* avid **2** *Syn* MEDIUM, average, moderate, middling, fair, mediocre, second-rate *Ant* choice **3** *Syn* NEUTRAL

**indigence** *Syn* POVERTY, penury, want, destitution, privation *Ant* affluence, opulence

**indigenous** *Syn* NATIVE, autochthonous, endemic, aboriginal *Ant* naturalized; exotic

**indigent** *Syn* POOR, needy, destitute, penniless, impecunious, poverty-stricken, necessitous *Ant* opulent

**indignant** *Syn* ANGRY, irate, wrathful, wroth, acrimonious, mad

**indignation** *Syn* ANGER, wrath, ire, rage, fury

**indignity** *Syn* AFFRONT, insult

**indirect** ♦ deviating from a direct line or straightforward course *Syn* circuitous, roundabout *Ant* direct; forthright, straightforward

**indiscriminate** ♦ including all or nearly all within the range of choice, operation, or effectiveness *Syn* wholesale, sweeping *Ant* selective; discriminating

**indispensable** *Syn* NEEDFUL, essential, necessary, requisite *Ant* dispensable

**indisposed** *Syn* DISINCLINED, loath, averse, hesitant, reluctant *Ant* disposed

**individual** *adj* **1** *Syn* SPECIAL, particular, specific, especial *Ant* general **2** *Syn* CHARACTERISTIC, peculiar, distinctive *Ant* common

**individual** *n Syn* ENTITY, being, creature, person

**individuality** *Syn* DISPOSITION, personality, temperament, temper, complexion, character

**individually** *Syn* EACH, apiece, severally, respectively

**indolent** *Syn* LAZY, faineant, slothful *Ant* industrious

**indomitable** *Syn* INVINCIBLE, unconquerable, impregnable, inexpugnable, unassailable, invulnerable

**induce** ♦ to move another to do or agree to something *Syn* persuade, prevail, get

**inducement** *Syn* MOTIVE, incentive, spur, goad, spring, impulse

**induct** *Syn* INITIATE, inaugurate, install, invest

**indulge** ♦ to show undue favor to a person's desires and feelings *Syn* pamper, humor, spoil, baby, mollycoddle *Ant* discipline (*others*); abstain (*with reference to oneself, one's appetite*)

**indulgence** *Syn* FORBEARANCE, tolerance, clemency, mercifulness, leniency *Ant* strictness

**indulgent** *Syn* FORBEARING, lenient, tolerant, clement, merciful *Ant* strict

**indulgently** *Syn* FORBEARINGLY, tolerantly, clemently, mercifully, leniently

**indurate** *Syn* HARDEN, solidify, petrify, cake

**indurated** *Syn* HARDENED, callous *Ant* pliable

**industrious** *Syn* BUSY, diligent, assiduous, sedulous *Ant* slothful, indolent

**industry** *Syn* BUSINESS, trade, commerce, traffic

**inebriate** *Syn* DRUNKARD, alcoholic, dipsomaniac, sot, soak, toper, tosspot, tippler *Ant* teetotaler

**inebriated** *Syn* DRUNK, drunken, intoxicated, tipsy, tight

**ineffable** *Syn* UNUTTERABLE, inexpressible, unspeakable, indescribable, indefinable

**ineffective** ♦ not producing or incapable of producing an intended result *Syn* ineffectual, inefficient, inefficacious *Ant* effective

**ineffectual** *Syn* INEFFECTIVE, inefficacious, inefficient *Ant* effectual

**inefficacious** *Syn* INEFFECTIVE, ineffectual, inefficient *Ant* efficacious

**inefficient** *Syn* INEFFECTIVE, ineffectual, inefficacious *Ant* efficient

**ineluctable** *Syn* INEVITABLE, inescapable, unescapable, unavoidable

**inept** *Syn* AWKWARD, clumsy, maladroit, gauche *Ant* apt; adept; able

**inerrable** *Syn* INFALLIBLE, inerrant, unerring

**inerrant** *Syn* INFALLIBLE, unerring

**inert** *Syn* INACTIVE, passive, idle, supine *Ant* dynamic; animated

**inescapable** *Syn* INEVITABLE, ineluctable, unescapable, unavoidable *Ant* escapable

**inevitable 1** ♦ incapable of being avoided or escaped *Syn* ineluctable, inescapable, unescapable, unavoidable *Ant* evitable **2** *Syn* CERTAIN, necessary

**inexorable** *Syn* INFLEXIBLE, obdurate, adamant, adamantine *Ant* exorable

**inexpressible** *Syn* UNUTTERABLE, ineffable, unspeakable, indescribable, indefinable *Ant* expressible

**inexpugnable** *Syn* INVINCIBLE, unassailable, impregnable, unconquerable, invulnerable, indomitable *Ant* expugnable

**infallible** ♦ incapable of making mistakes or errors *Syn* inerrable, inerrant, unerring *Ant* fallible

**infamous** *Syn* VICIOUS, nefarious, flagitious, iniquitous, villainous, corrupt, degenerate *Ant* illustrious

**infamy** *Syn* DISGRACE, ignominy, shame, dishonor, disrepute, opprobrium, obloquy, odium

**infancy** ♦ the state or period of being under the age established by law for the attainment of full civil rights *Syn* minority, nonage

**infatuated 1** *Syn* FOND, besotted, insensate **2** *Syn* ENAMORED

**infectious 1** ♦ transmissible by infection *Syn* contagious, communicable, catching **2** ♦ capable of infecting or tending to infect *Syn* infective

**infective** *Syn* INFECTIOUS

**infelicitous** *Syn* UNFIT, unhappy, inapt, inappropriate, unfitting, unsuitable, improper *Ant* felicitous

**infer** ♦ to arrive at by reasoning from evidence or

from premises *Syn* deduce, conclude, judge, gather

**inference 1** ♦ the deriving of a conclusion by reasoning *Syn* deduction, conclusion, judgment **2** ♦ the process of arriving at conclusions from data or premises *Syn* ratiocination **3** *Syn* IMPLICATION

**inferential** ♦ deduced or deducible by reasoning *Syn* ratiocinative

**inferior** ♦ one who is lower than another esp. in station or rank *Syn* underling, subordinate *Ant* superior

**infernal** ♦ of or relating to a nether world of the dead *Syn* chthonian, chthonic, hellish, Hadean, Tartarean, stygian *Ant* supernal

**infertile** *Syn* STERILE, barren, impotent, unfruitful *Ant* fertile

**infest** ♦ to spread or swarm over in a troublesome manner *Syn* overrun, beset *Ant* disinfest

**infidel** *Syn* ATHEIST, unbeliever, freethinker, agnostic, deist

**infinite** ♦ being without known limits *Syn* eternal, sempiternal, boundless, illimitable, uncircumscribed *Ant* finite

**infirm** *Syn* WEAK, feeble, decrepit, frail, fragile *Ant* hale

**inflammable** *Syn* COMBUSTIBLE, flammable, incendiary, inflammatory *Ant* extinguishable

**inflammatory** *Syn* COMBUSTIBLE, inflammable, flammable, incendiary

**inflate** *Syn* EXPAND, distend, swell, amplify, dilate *Ant* deflate

**inflated** ♦ swollen with or as if with something insubstantial *Syn* flatulent, tumid, turgid *Ant* pithy

**inflection** ♦ a particular manner of employing the sounds of the voice in speech *Syn* intonation, accent

**inflexible 1** *Syn* STIFF, rigid, tense, stark, wooden *Ant* flexible **2** ♦ unwilling to alter a predetermined course or purpose *Syn* inexorable, obdurate, adamant, adamantine *Ant* flexible

**influence** *n* ♦ power exerted over the minds or behavior of others *Syn* authority, prestige, weight, credit

**influence** *vb Syn* AFFECT, sway, impress, touch, strike

**inform 1** ♦ to stimulate (as mental powers) to higher or more intense activity *Syn* animate, inspire, fire **2** ♦ to make one aware of something *Syn* acquaint, apprise, advise, notify

**information** *Syn* KNOWLEDGE, lore, learning, science, erudition, scholarship

**infraction** *Syn* BREACH, violation, transgression, infringement, trespass, contravention *Ant* observance

**infrequent** ♦ not common or abundant *Syn* uncommon, scarce, rare, occasional, sporadic *Ant* frequent

**infringe** *Syn* TRESPASS, encroach, entrench, invade

**infringement** *Syn* BREACH, infraction, violation, trespass, transgression, contravention

**infuriate** *Syn* ANGER, enrage, incense, madden

**infuse** ♦ to introduce one thing into another so as to affect it throughout *Syn* suffuse, imbue, ingrain, inoculate, leaven

**ingeminate** *Syn* REPEAT, iterate, reiterate

**ingenious** *Syn* CLEVER, cunning, adroit

**ingenuous** *Syn* NATURAL, simple, naïve, unsophisticated, artless *Ant* disingenuous; cunning

**ingest** *Syn* EAT, swallow, devour, consume

**ingrain** *Syn* INFUSE, suffuse, imbue, inoculate, leaven

**ingrained** *Syn* INHERENT, constitutional, essential, intrinsic

**ingredient** *Syn* ELEMENT, constituent, component, factor

**ingress** *Syn* ENTRANCE, entry, entrée, access *Ant* egress

**inhabitant** ♦ one that occupies a particular place regularly *Syn* denizen, resident, citizen

**inherent** ♦ being a part, element, or quality of a

thing's inmost being *Syn* ingrained, intrinsic, essential, constitutional *Ant* adventitious

**inheritance** *Syn* HERITAGE, patrimony, birthright

**inherited** *Syn* INNATE, hereditary, inborn, inbred, congenital

**inhibit 1** *Syn* FORBID, prohibit, interdict, ban, enjoin *Ant* allow **2** *Syn* RESTRAIN, curb, check, bridle *Ant* animate; activate

**inhuman** *Syn* FIERCE, savage, barbarous, truculent, ferocious, cruel, fell *Ant* humane

**iniquitous** *Syn* VICIOUS, nefarious, flagitious, villainous, infamous, corrupt, degenerate *Ant* righteous

**initial** ♦ marking a beginning or constituting a start *Syn* original, primordial *Ant* final

**initiate 1** *Syn* BEGIN, commence, start, inaugurate *Ant* consummate **2** ♦ to put through the formalities for becoming a member or an official *Syn* induct, inaugurate, install, invest

**initiation** *Syn* BEGINNING, genesis, rise

**initiative** *Syn* MANDATE, referendum, plebiscite

**injunction** *Syn* COMMAND, order, bidding, behest, mandate, dictate

**injure** ♦ to deplete the soundness, strength, effectiveness, or perfection of something *Syn* harm, hurt, damage, impair, mar, spoil *Ant* aid

**injury 1** ♦ the act or the result of inflicting something that causes loss or pain *Syn* hurt, damage, harm, mischief **2** *Syn* INJUSTICE, wrong, grievance

**injustice** ♦ an act that inflicts undeserved hurt *Syn* injury, wrong, grievance

**innate** ♦ not acquired after birth *Syn* inborn, inbred, congenital, hereditary, inherited *Ant* acquired

**inner** ♦ situated further in *Syn* inward, inside, interior, internal, intestine *Ant* outer

**innocent** *Syn* HARMLESS, innocuous, inoffensive, unoffending

**innocuous** *Syn* HARMLESS, innocent, inoffensive, unoffending *Ant* pernicious

**innuendo** *Syn* INSINUATION

**inoculate** *Syn* INFUSE, imbue, ingrain, leaven, suffuse

**inoffensive** *Syn* HARMLESS, innocuous, innocent, unoffending *Ant* offensive

**inordinate** *Syn* EXCESSIVE, immoderate, exorbitant, extreme, extravagant *Ant* temperate

**inquest** *Syn* INQUIRY, investigation, probe, inquisition, research

**inquire** *Syn* ASK, query, question, interrogate, catechize, quiz, examine

**inquiry** ♦ a search for truth, knowledge, or information *Syn* inquisition, investigation, inquest, probe, research

**inquisition** *Syn* INQUIRY, inquest, probe, investigation, research

**inquisitive** *Syn* CURIOUS, prying, snoopy, nosy *Ant* incurious

**inroad** *Syn* INVASION, incursion, raid

**insane** ♦ afflicted by or manifesting unsoundness of mind or an inability to control one's rational processes *Syn* mad, crazy, crazed, demented, deranged, lunatic, maniac, non compos mentis *Ant* sane

**insanity** ♦ a deranged state of mind or serious mental disorder *Syn* lunacy, psychosis, mania, dementia *Ant* sanity

**inscription** ♦ something written, printed, or engraved (as on a coin or a medal or under or over a picture) to indicate or describe the purpose or the nature of the thing *Syn* legend, caption

**inscrutable** *Syn* MYSTERIOUS, arcane

**insensate** *Syn* FOND, besotted, infatuated

**insensible 1** ♦ unresponsive to stimuli or to external influences *Syn* insensitive, impassible, anesthetic *Ant* sensible (*to or of something*) **2** *Syn* IMPERCEPTIBLE, impalpable, intangible, inappreciable, imponderable *Ant* sensible, palpable

**insensitive** *Syn* INSENSIBLE, impassible, anesthetic *Ant* sensitive

**insert** *Syn* INTRODUCE, interpolate, intercalate, insinuate, interpose, interject *Ant* abstract; extract

**inside** *Syn* INNER, interior, internal, intestine, inward *Ant* outside

**insidious** *Syn* SLY, cunning, crafty, tricky, foxy, wily, guileful, artful

**insight** *Syn* DISCERNMENT, penetration, acumen, discrimination, perception *Ant* obtuseness

**insinuate 1** *Syn* INTRODUCE, insert, interject, interpolate, intercalate, interpose **2** *Syn* SUGGEST, intimate, hint, imply

**insinuation** ♦ a subtle or covert hinting or suggestion *Syn* innuendo

**insipid** ♦ devoid of qualities that make for spirit and character *Syn* vapid, flat, jejune, banal, wishy-washy, inane *Ant* sapid; zestful

**insistent** *Syn* PRESSING, urgent, imperative, crying, importunate, exigent, instant

**insolent** *Syn* PROUD, arrogant, overbearing, supercilious, disdainful, haughty, lordly *Ant* deferential

**inspect** *Syn* SCRUTINIZE, examine, scan, audit

**inspection** *Syn* SCRUTINY, examination, scanning, audit

**inspiration** ♦ a divine or seemingly divine imparting of knowledge or power *Syn* afflatus, fury, frenzy

**inspire** *Syn* INFORM, animate, fire

**inspirit** *Syn* ENCOURAGE, hearten, embolden, cheer, nerve, steel *Ant* dispirit

**in spite of** *Syn* NOTWITHSTANDING, despite

**install** *Syn* INITIATE, induct, inaugurate, invest

**instance** *n* ♦ something that exhibits distinguishing characteristics in its category *Syn* case, illustration, example, sample, specimen

**instance** *vb Syn* MENTION, name, specify

**instant** *n* ♦ an almost imperceptible point or stretch of time *Syn* moment, minute, second, flash, jiffy, twinkling, split second

**instant** *adj Syn* PRESSING, urgent, imperative, crying, importunate, insistent, exigent

**instigate** *Syn* INCITE, abet, foment

**instill** *Syn* IMPLANT, inculcate

**instinctive 1** ♦ prompted by natural instinct or propensity *Syn* intuitive *Ant* reasoned **2** *Syn* SPONTANEOUS, impulsive, automatic, mechanical *Ant* intentional

**institute** *Syn* FOUND, establish, organize, create *Ant* abrogate

**instruct 1** *Syn* TEACH, train, educate, discipline, school **2** *Syn* COMMAND, direct, enjoin, bid, order, charge

**instrument 1** *Syn* MEAN, instrumentality, agency, medium, agent, organ, vehicle, channel **2** *Syn* IMPLEMENT, tool, appliance, utensil **3** *Syn* PAPER, document

**instrumentality** *Syn* MEAN, agent, agency, instrument, medium, organ, vehicle, channel

**insubordinate** ♦ unwilling to submit to authority *Syn* rebellious, mutinous, seditious, factious, contumacious

**insular** ♦ having the narrow and limited outlook characteristic of geographic isolation *Syn* provincial, parochial, local, small-town

**insulate** *Syn* ISOLATE, segregate, seclude, sequester

**insult** *vb Syn* OFFEND, affront, outrage *Ant* honor

**insult** *n Syn* AFFRONT, indignity

**insure** *Syn* ENSURE, assure, secure

**insurgent** *Syn* REBEL, iconoclast

**insurrection** *Syn* REBELLION, uprising, revolt, mutiny, revolution, putsch, coup

**intact** *Syn* PERFECT, whole, entire *Ant* defective

**intangible** *Syn* IMPERCEPTIBLE, impalpable, insensible, inappreciable, imponderable *Ant* tangible

**integer** *Syn* NUMBER, numeral, figure, digit

**integrate** ♦ to join together systematically *Syn* articulate, concatenate *Ant* disintegrate

**integration** ♦ the act or process of operating as a unit or whole *Syn* articulation, concatenation

**integrity 1** *Syn* UNITY, solidarity, union **2** *Syn* HONESTY, probity, honor *Ant* duplicity

**intellect** *Syn* MIND, soul, psyche, brain, intelligence, wit

**intellectual** *Syn* MENTAL, psychic, cerebral, intelligent *Ant* carnal

**intelligence 1** *Syn* MIND, brain, intellect, soul, psyche, wit **2** *Syn* NEWS, tidings, advice

**intelligent 1** *Syn* MENTAL, intellectual, cerebral, psychic **2** ◆ mentally quick or keen *Syn* clever, alert, quick-witted, bright, smart, knowing, brilliant *Ant* unintelligent

**intend** ◆ to have in mind as a purpose or goal *Syn* mean, design, propose, purpose

**intense** ◆ extreme in degree, power, or effect *Syn* vehement, fierce, exquisite, violent *Ant* subdued

**intensify** ◆ to increase markedly in degree or measure *Syn* aggravate, heighten, enhance *Ant* temper; mitigate, allay; abate

**intent** *n Syn* INTENTION, purpose, design, aim, end, object, objective, goal *Ant* accident

**intent** *adj* ◆ having one's mind or attention deeply fixed *Syn* engrossed, absorbed, rapt *Ant* distracted

**intention** ◆ what one intends to accomplish or attain *Syn* intent, purpose, design, aim, end, object, objective, goal

**intentional** *Syn* VOLUNTARY, deliberate, willful, willing *Ant* instinctive

**intercalate** *Syn* INTRODUCE, interpolate, insert, interpose, interject, insinuate

**intercede** *Syn* INTERPOSE, mediate, intervene, interfere

**interchange** *Syn* EXCHANGE, bandy

**intercourse** ◆ connection or dealing between persons or groups *Syn* commerce, traffic, dealings, communication, communion, conversation, converse, correspondence

**interdict** *Syn* FORBID, ban, inhibit, enjoin, prohibit *Ant* sanction

**interesting** ◆ holding the attention for some time *Syn* engrossing, absorbing, intriguing *Ant* boring

**interfere 1** *Syn* INTERPOSE, intervene, mediate, intercede **2** *Syn* MEDDLE, intermeddle, tamper

**interim** *Syn* BREAK, gap, interruption, interval, hiatus, lacuna

**interior** *Syn* INNER, inside, internal, inward, intestine *Ant* exterior

**interject** *Syn* INTRODUCE, interpolate, interpose, insert, intercalate, insinuate

**interlope** *Syn* INTRUDE, butt in, obtrude

**intermeddle** *Syn* MEDDLE, interfere, tamper

**interminable** *Syn* EVERLASTING, unceasing, endless

**intermission** *Syn* PAUSE, recess, respite, lull

**intermit** *Syn* DEFER, suspend, stay, postpone

**intermittent** ◆ occurring or appearing in interrupted sequence *Syn* recurrent, periodic, alternate *Ant* incessant, continual

**intern** *Syn* IMPRISON, immure, incarcerate, jail

**internal** *Syn* INNER, interior, intestine, inward, inside *Ant* external

**internuncio** *Syn* AMBASSADOR, nuncio, legate, minister, envoy, chargé d'affaires

**interpenetrate** *Syn* PERMEATE, impenetrate, penetrate, pervade, impregnate, saturate

**interpolate** *Syn* INTRODUCE, insert, intercalate, insinuate, interpose, interject

**interpose 1** *Syn* INTRODUCE, interject, insert, insinuate, interpolate, intercalate **2** ◆ to come or go between *Syn* interfere, intervene, mediate, intercede

**interpret** *Syn* EXPLAIN, elucidate, construe, expound, explicate

**interrogate** *Syn* ASK, question, catechize, quiz, examine, query, inquire

**interrupt** *Syn* ARREST, check

**interruption** *Syn* BREAK, gap, interval, interim, hiatus, lacuna

**interstice** *Syn* APERTURE, orifice

**interval** *Syn* BREAK, gap, interruption, interim, hiatus, lacuna

**intervene** *Syn* INTERPOSE, mediate, intercede, interfere

**intestine** *Syn* INNER, internal, interior, inside *Ant* foreign

**intimate** *vb Syn* SUGGEST, imply, hint, insinuate

**intimate** *adj Syn* FAMILIAR, close, confidential, chummy, thick

**intimate** *n Syn* FRIEND, confidant, acquaintance *Ant* stranger, outsider

**intimidate** ◆ to frighten into submission *Syn* cow, bulldoze, bully, browbeat

**intolerant** *Syn* ILLIBERAL, narrow-minded, narrow, bigoted, hidebound *Ant* tolerant

**intonation** *Syn* INFLECTION, accent

**intone** *Syn* SING, troll, carol, descant, warble, trill, hymn, chant

**intoxicated** *Syn* DRUNK, drunken, inebriated, tipsy, tight

**intractable** *Syn* UNRULY, ungovernable, refractory, recalcitrant, willful, headstrong *Ant* tractable

**intrepid** *Syn* BRAVE, courageous, unafraid, fearless, valiant, valorous, dauntless, undaunted, doughty, bold, audacious

**intricate** *Syn* COMPLEX, complicated, involved, knotty

**intrigue 1** *Syn* PLOT, conspiracy, machination, cabal **2** *Syn* AMOUR, liaison, affair

**intriguing** *Syn* INTERESTING, engrossing, absorbing

**intrinsic** *Syn* INHERENT, ingrained, constitutional, essential *Ant* extrinsic

**introduce 1** *Syn* ENTER, admit **2** ◆ to put among or between others *Syn* insert, insinuate, interpolate, intercalate, interpose, interject *Ant* withdraw; abstract

**introduction** ◆ something that serves as a preliminary or antecedent *Syn* prologue, prelude, preface, foreword, exordium, preamble

**introductory** *Syn* PRELIMINARY, preparatory, prefatory *Ant* closing, concluding

**intrude** ◆ to thrust or force in or upon without permission, welcome, or fitness *Syn* obtrude, interlope, butt in *Ant* stand off

**intrusive** *Syn* IMPERTINENT, officious, meddlesome, obtrusive *Ant* retiring; unintrusive

**intuition** *Syn* REASON, understanding *Ant* ratiocination

**intuitive** *Syn* INSTINCTIVE *Ant* ratiocinative

**inundation** *Syn* FLOOD, deluge, torrent, spate, cataract

**inure** *Syn* HABITUATE, accustom, addict

**invade** *Syn* TRESPASS, encroach, entrench, infringe

**invalidate** *Syn* NULLIFY, negate, annul, abrogate *Ant* validate

**invaluable** *Syn* COSTLY, priceless, precious, valuable, dear, expensive *Ant* worthless

**invasion** ◆ a hostile entrance into the territory of another *Syn* incursion, raid, inroad

**invective** *Syn* ABUSE, vituperation, obloquy, scurrility, billingsgate

**inveigle** *Syn* LURE, decoy, entice, tempt, seduce

**invent** *Syn* CONTRIVE, devise, frame, concoct

**inventory** *Syn* LIST, register, schedule, catalog, table, roll, roster

**invert** *Syn* REVERSE, transpose

**invest 1** *Syn* INITIATE, induct, install, inaugurate *Ant* divest, strip; unfrock **2** *Syn* BESIEGE, beleaguer, blockade

**investigation** *Syn* INQUIRY, probe, inquest, inquisition, research

**inveterate** ◆ so firmly established that change is almost impossible *Syn* confirmed, chronic, deep-seated, deep-rooted

**invidious** *Syn* REPUGNANT, distasteful, obnoxious, repellent, abhorrent

**invigorate** *Syn* STRENGTHEN, fortify, energize, reinforce *Ant* debilitate

**invincible** ◆ incapable of being conquered *Syn* unconquerable, indomitable, impregnable, inexpugnable, unassailable, invulnerable

**inviolable** *Syn* SACRED, inviolate, sacrosanct

**inviolate** *Syn* SACRED, sacrosanct, inviolable *Ant* violated

**invite** ◆ to request the presence or participation of *Syn* bid, solicit, court, woo

**involve 1** *Syn* ENTANGLE, enmesh **2** *Syn* INCLUDE, comprehend, embrace, imply, subsume **3** ◆ to bring a person or thing into circumstances or a situation from which extrication is difficult *Syn* implicate

**involved** *Syn* COMPLEX, intricate, complicated, knotty

**invulnerable** *Syn* INVINCIBLE, impregnable, inexpugnable, unassailable, unconquerable, indomitable *Ant* vulnerable

**inward** *Syn* INNER, interior, internal, inside, intestine *Ant* outward

**iota** *Syn* PARTICLE, jot, tittle, whit, bit, mite, smidgen, atom

**irascible** ◆ easily aroused to anger *Syn* choleric, splenetic, testy, touchy, cranky, cross

**irate** *Syn* ANGRY, wrathful, wroth, mad, indignant, acrimonious

**ire** *Syn* ANGER, rage, fury, indignation, wrath

**irenic** *Syn* PACIFIC, peaceable, peaceful, pacifist, pacifistic *Ant* acrimonious

**iridescent** *Syn* PRISMATIC, opalescent, opaline

**irk** *Syn* ANNOY, vex, bother

**irksome** ◆ tending to cause boredom or tedium *Syn* tiresome, wearisome, tedious, boring *Ant* absorbing, engrossing

**ironic** *Syn* SARCASTIC, satiric, sardonic

**irony** *Syn* WIT, satire, sarcasm, humor, repartee

**irrational** ◆ not governed or guided by reason *Syn* unreasonable *Ant* rational

**irregular** ◆ not conforming to rule, law, or custom *Syn* anomalous, unnatural *Ant* regular

**irreligious** ◆ lacking religious emotions, doctrines, or practices *Syn* unreligious, nonreligious, ungodly, godless *Ant* religious

**irritable** ◆ easily exasperated *Syn* fractious, peevish, snappish, waspish, petulant, pettish, huffy, fretful, querulous *Ant* easygoing

**irritate** ◆ to excite a feeling of anger or annoyance *Syn* exasperate, nettle, provoke, aggravate, rile, peeve

**isolate** ◆ to set apart from others *Syn* segregate, seclude, insulate, sequester

**isolation** *Syn* SOLITUDE, alienation, seclusion

**issue** *n* **1** *Syn* EFFECT, outcome, result, consequence, upshot, aftereffect, aftermath, sequel, event **2** *Syn* OFFSPRING, young, progeny, descendant, posterity

**issue** *vb Syn* SPRING, emanate, proceed, flow, derive, originate, arise, rise, stem

**item** ◆ one of the distinct parts of a whole *Syn* detail, particular

**itemized** *Syn* CIRCUMSTANTIAL, detailed, particularized, minute, particular *Ant* summarized

**iterate** *Syn* REPEAT, reiterate, ingeminate

**itinerant** ◆ traveling from place to place *Syn* peripatetic, ambulatory, ambulant, nomadic, vagrant

# J

**jabber** *Syn* CHAT, chatter, gab, patter, prate, prattle, babble, gabble, gibber

**jack** *Syn* FLAG, ensign, standard, banner, color, streamer, pennant, pendant, pennon

**jade** *Syn* TIRE, exhaust, fatigue, weary, fag, tucker *Ant* refresh

**jail** *Syn* IMPRISON, incarcerate, immure, intern

**jam** *vb Syn* PRESS, crowd, squeeze, bear, bear down

**jam** *n Syn* PREDICAMENT, plight, fix, dilemma, quandary, scrape, pickle

**jape** *Syn* JOKE, jest, quip, witticism, wisecrack, crack, gag

**jar** *Syn* IMPACT, jolt, impingement, collision, clash, shock, concussion, percussion

**jargon** *Syn* DIALECT, vernacular, patois, lingo, cant, argot, slang

**jaunt** *Syn* JOURNEY, excursion, trip, tour, voyage, cruise, expedition, pilgrimage

**jaw** *Syn* SCOLD, upbraid, rate, berate, tongue-lash, bawl, chew out, wig, rail, revile, vituperate

**jealous** *Syn* ENVIOUS

**jeer** *Syn* SCOFF, gibe, fleer, gird, sneer, flout

**jejune** *Syn* INSIPID, vapid, flat, wishy-washy, inane, banal

**jell jelly** *Syn* COAGULATE, congeal, set, curdle, clot

**jeopardize** *Syn* VENTURE, hazard, risk, chance, endanger, imperil

**jeopardy** *Syn* DANGER, peril, hazard, risk

**jeremiad** *Syn* TIRADE, diatribe, philippic

**jerk** ♦ to make a sudden sharp quick movement *Syn* snap, twitch, yank

**jest** 1 *Syn* JOKE, jape, quip, witticism, wisecrack, crack, gag 2 *Syn* FUN, sport, game, play

**jetty** *Syn* WHARF, dock, pier, quay, slip, berth, levee

**jib** *Syn* DEMUR, balk, shy, boggle, stickle, stick, strain, scruple

**jibe** *Syn* AGREE, harmonize, accord, conform, square, tally, correspond

**jiffy** *Syn* INSTANT, moment, minute, second, flash, twinkling, split second

**jittery** *Syn* IMPATIENT, jumpy, nervous, unquiet, restless, restive, uneasy, fidgety

**job** *Syn* TASK, duty, assignment, stint, chore

**jocose** *Syn* WITTY, jocular, facetious, humorous

**jocular** *Syn* WITTY, jocose, humorous, facetious

**jocund** *Syn* MERRY, blithe, jolly, jovial

**jog** *vb Syn* POKE, prod, nudge

**jog** *n Syn* POKE, prod, nudge

**join** ♦ to bring or come together into some manner of union *Syn* conjoin, combine, unite, connect, link, associate, relate *Ant* disjoin; part

**joint** ♦ a place where two or more things are united *Syn* articulation, suture

**joke** ♦ something said or done to provoke laughter *Syn* jest, jape, quip, witticism, wisecrack, crack, gag

**jollity** *Syn* MIRTH, hilarity, glee

**jolly** *adj Syn* MERRY, jovial, jocund, blithe

**jolly** *vb Syn* BANTER, chaff, kid, rag, rib, josh

**jolt** *Syn* IMPACT, jar, shock, impingement, collision, clash, concussion, percussion

**josh** *Syn* BANTER, chaff, kid, rag, rib, jolly

**jot** *Syn* PARTICLE, tittle, iota, bit, mite, smidgen, whit, atom

**journal** ♦ a publication that appears at regular intervals *Syn* periodical, newspaper, magazine, review, organ

**journey** ♦ travel or a passage from one place to another *Syn* voyage, tour, trip, jaunt, excursion, cruise, expedition, pilgrimage

**jovial** *Syn* MERRY, jolly, jocund, blithe

**joy** *Syn* PLEASURE, delight, enjoyment, delectation, fruition *Ant* sorrow; misery; abomination

**joyful** *Syn* GLAD, joyous, cheerful, happy, light-hearted *Ant* joyless

**joyous** *Syn* GLAD, joyful, happy, cheerful, light-hearted *Ant* lugubrious

**judge** *vb* 1 ♦ to decide something in dispute or controversy upon its merits and upon evidence *Syn* adjudge, adjudicate, arbitrate 2 *Syn* INFER, conclude, deduce, gather

**judge** *n* ♦ a person who impartially decides unsettled questions or controversial issues *Syn* arbiter, arbitrator, referee, umpire

**judgment** 1 *Syn* INFERENCE, conclusion, deduction 2 *Syn* SENSE, wisdom, gumption

**judicious** *Syn* WISE, sage, sapient, prudent, sensible, sane *Ant* injudicious; asinine

**jumble** *Syn* CONFUSION, disorder, chaos, disarray, clutter, snarl, muddle

**jump** *vb* ♦ to move suddenly through space by or as if by muscular action *Syn* leap, spring, bound, vault

**jump** *n* ♦ a sudden move through space *Syn* leap, spring, bound, vault

**jumpy** *Syn* IMPATIENT, jittery, nervous, restless, uneasy, fidgety, unquiet, restive *Ant* steady

**junction** ♦ the act, state, or place of meeting or uniting *Syn* confluence, concourse

**juncture** ♦ a critical or crucial time or state of affairs *Syn* pass, exigency, emergency, contingency, pinch, strait, crisis

**junk** *Syn* DISCARD, scrap, cast, shed, molt, slough

**jurisdiction** *Syn* POWER, authority, control, command, sway, dominion

**just** 1 *Syn* UPRIGHT, honorable, conscientious, scrupulous, honest 2 *Syn* FAIR, equitable, impartial, unbiased, dispassionate, uncolored, objective *Ant* unjust

**justice** ♦ awarding each what is rightly due *Syn* equity

**justify** 1 *Syn* MAINTAIN, vindicate, defend, assert 2 *Syn* EXPLAIN, account, rationalize 3 ♦ to constitute sufficient grounds *Syn* warrant

**jut** *Syn* BULGE, stick out, protrude, project, overhang, beetle

**juvenile** *Syn* YOUTHFUL, puerile, boyish, virgin, virginal, maiden *Ant* adult; senile

**juxtaposed** *Syn* ADJACENT, adjoining, contiguous, abutting, tangent, conterminous

# K

**keen** *adj* 1 *Syn* SHARP, acute *Ant* blunt 2 *Syn* EAGER, avid, agog, athirst, anxious

**keen** *vb Syn* CRY, wait, weep, whimper, blubber

**keep** *vb* 1 ♦ to notice or honor a day, occasion, or deed *Syn* observe, celebrate, solemnize, commemorate *Ant* break 2 ♦ to hold in one's possession or under one's control *Syn* keep back, keep out, retain, detain, withhold, reserve, hold back *Ant* relinquish

**keep** *n Syn* LIVING, livelihood, subsistence, sustenance, maintenance, support, bread

**keep back, keep out** *Syn* KEEP, retain, detain, withhold, reserve, hold, hold back

**keepsake** *Syn* REMEMBRANCE, remembrancer, reminder, memorial, memento, token, souvenir

**ken** *Syn* RANGE, gamut, reach, radius, compass, sweep, scope, orbit, horizon, purview

**kibitzer** *Syn* SPECTATOR, onlooker, looker-on,

bystander, observer, beholder, witness, eyewitness

**kick** *Syn* OBJECT, protest, remonstrate, expostulate

**kid** *Syn* BANTER, chaff, rag, rib, josh, jolly

**kidnap** *Syn* ABDUCT

**kidney** *Syn* TYPE, kind, sort, nature, description, character, stripe, ilk

**kill** ♦ to deprive of life *Syn* slay, murder, assassinate, dispatch, execute

**kind** *n Syn* TYPE, sort, stripe, kidney, ilk, description, nature, character

**kind** *adj* ♦ showing or having a gentle considerate nature *Syn* kindly, benign, benignant *Ant* unkind

**kindle** *Syn* LIGHT, ignite, fire *Ant* smother, stifle

**kindly** *Syn* KIND, benign, benignant *Ant* unkindly; acrid (*of temper, attitudes, comments*)

**kindred** *Syn* RELATED, cognate, allied, affiliated *Ant* alien

**kingly** ♦ of, relating to, or befitting one who occupies a throne *Syn* regal, royal, queenly, imperial, princely

**knack** *Syn* GIFT, bent, turn, faculty, aptitude, genius, talent *Ant* ineptitude

**knave** *Syn* VILLAIN, scoundrel, blackguard, rascal, rogue, scamp, rapscallion, miscreant

**knit** *Syn* WEAVE, crochet, braid, plait, tat

**knock** *vb Syn* TAP, rap, thump, thud

**knock** *n Syn* TAP, rap, thump, thud

**knotty** *Syn* COMPLEX, intricate, involved, complicated

**knowing** *Syn* INTELLIGENT, alert, bright, smart, clever, quick-witted, brilliant

**knowledge** ♦ what is or can be known by an individual or by mankind *Syn* science, learning, erudition, scholarship, information, lore *Ant* ignorance

# L

**label** *n Syn* MARK, brand, stamp, tag, ticket

**label** *vb Syn* MARK, brand, stamp, tag, ticket

**labor** *Syn* WORK, toil, travail, drudgery, grind

**labored** *Syn* FORCED, strained, farfetched

**laborer** *Syn* WORKER, working man, workman, craftsman, handicraftsman, mechanic, artisan, operative, hand, roustabout

**lack** *vb* ♦ to be without something, esp. something essential or greatly needed *Syn* want, need, require

**lack** *n* ♦ the fact or state of being wanting or deficient *Syn* want, dearth, absence, defect, privation

**lackadaisical** *Syn* LANGUID, listless, spiritless, enervated, languishing, languorous

**laconic** *Syn* CONCISE, succinct, terse, summary, pithy, compendious *Ant* verbose

**lacuna** *Syn* BREAK, gap, hiatus, interruption, interval, interim

**lade** *Syn* BURDEN, load, encumber, cumber, weigh, weight, tax, charge, saddle *Ant* unlade

**lading** *Syn* LOAD, freight, cargo, burden

**ladle** *Syn* DIP, scoop, spoon, dish, bail

**lady** *Syn* FEMALE, woman

**ladylike** *Syn* FEMALE, feminine, womanly, womanlike, womanish

**lag** *Syn* DELAY, loiter, dawdle, procrastinate

**laggard** *Syn* SLOW, dilatory, leisurely, deliberate *Ant* prompt, quick

**lambent** *Syn* BRIGHT, beaming, luminous, brilliant, radiant, lustrous, effulgent, refulgent, lucent, incandescent

**lament** *Syn* DEPLORE, bewail, bemoan *Ant* exult; rejoice

**lampoon** *Syn* LIBEL, skit, squib, pasquinade

**land** *Syn* ALIGHT, light, perch, roost

**landing field, landing strip** *Syn* AIRPORT, airdrome, airfield, airstrip, flying field

**language** 1 ♦ a body or system of words and phrases used by a large community or by a people, a nation, or a group of nations *Syn* dialect, tongue, speech, idiom 2 ♦ oral or written expression or a quality of such expression that is dependent on the variety, or arrangement, or expressiveness of words *Syn* vocabulary, phraseology, phrasing, diction, style

**languid** ♦ lacking in vim or energy *Syn* languishing, languorous, lackadaisical, listless, spiritless, enervated *Ant* vivacious; chipper

**languishing** *Syn* LANGUID, languorous, lackadaisical, listless, spiritless, enervated *Ant* thriving, flourishing; unaffected

**languor** *Syn* LETHARGY, lassitude, stupor, torpor, torpidity *Ant* alacrity

**languorous** *Syn* LANGUID, languishing, lackadaisical, listless, spiritless, enervated *Ant* vigorous; strenuous (*of times, seasons*)

**lank lanky** *Syn* LEAN, gaunt, rawboned, spare, angular, scrawny, skinny *Ant* burly

**lapse** *n* **1** *Syn* ERROR, slip, mistake, blunder, faux pas, bull, howler, boner **2** ♦ a fall back into a state or condition from which one has been raised *Syn* relapse, backsliding

**lapse** *vb* ♦ to fall from a better or higher state into a lower or poorer one *Syn* relapse, backslide

**larcener, larcenist** *Syn* THIEF, robber, burglar

**larceny** *Syn* THEFT, robbery, burglary

**large** ♦ above the average of its kind in magnitude *Syn* big, great *Ant* small

**largely** ♦ in a reasonably inclusive manner *Syn* greatly, mostly, chiefly, mainly, principally, generally

**largesse, largess** *Syn* GIFT, boon, present, gratuity, favor

**lascivious** *Syn* LICENTIOUS, lewd, libertine, lustful, libidinous, lecherous, wanton

**lassitude** *Syn* LETHARGY, languor, stupor, torpor, torpidity *Ant* vigor

**last** *vb* *Syn* CONTINUE, endure, abide, persist *Ant* fleet

**last** *adj* ♦ following all others as in time, order, or importance *Syn* latest, final, terminal, concluding, eventual, ultimate *Ant* first

**lasting** ♦ enduring so long as to seem fixed or established *Syn* permanent, perdurable, durable, stable, perpetual *Ant* fleeting

**late** **1** *Syn* TARDY, behindhand, overdue *Ant* early; punctual, prompt **2** *Syn* DEAD, departed, deceased, defunct, lifeless, inanimate **3** *Syn* MODERN, recent

**latent** ♦ not now showing signs of activity or existence *Syn* dormant, quiescent, potential, abeyant *Ant* patent

**latest** *Syn* LAST, final, terminal, concluding, eventual, ultimate *Ant* earliest

**lather** *Syn* FOAM, suds, froth, spume, scum, yeast

**laud** *Syn* PRAISE, extol, eulogize, acclaim *Ant* revile

**laughable** ♦ provoking laughter or mirth *Syn* risible, ludicrous, ridiculous, comic, comical, farcical, droll, funny

**lavish** *Syn* PROFUSE, prodigal, luxuriant, lush, exuberant *Ant* sparing

**law** **1** ♦ a principle governing action or procedure *Syn* rule, regulation, precept, statute, ordinance, canon **2** *Syn* PRINCIPLE, axiom, fundamental, theorem *Ant* chance

**lawful** ♦ being in accordance with law *Syn* legal, legitimate, licit *Ant* unlawful

**lawlessness** *Syn* ANARCHY, chaos *Ant* discipline; order

**lawsuit** *Syn* SUIT, action, cause, case

**lawyer** ♦ a person authorized to practice law in the courts or to serve clients in the capacity of legal agent or adviser *Syn* counselor, barrister, counsel, advocate, attorney, solicitor

**lax** **1** *Syn* LOOSE, relaxed, slack *Ant* rigid **2** *Syn* NEGLIGENT, remiss, neglectful *Ant* strict, stringent

**lay** *vb* *Syn* DIRECT, aim, point, level, train

**lay** *adj* *Syn* PROFANE, secular, temporal

**laze** *Syn* IDLE, loaf, lounge, loll

**lazy** ♦ not easily aroused to activity *Syn* indolent, slothful, faineant

**leading** *Syn* CHIEF, principal, main, foremost, capital *Ant* subordinate

**league** *Syn* ALLIANCE, coalition, fusion, confederacy, confederation, federation

**lean** *vb* *Syn* SLANT, slope, incline

**lean** *adj* ♦ thin because of an absence of excess flesh *Syn* spare, lank, lanky, gaunt, rawboned, angular, scrawny, skinny *Ant* fleshy

**leaning** ♦ a strong instinct or liking for something *Syn* propensity, proclivity, penchant, flair *Ant* distaste

**leap** *vb* *Syn* JUMP, spring, bound, vault

**leap** *n* *Syn* JUMP, spring, bound, vault

**learn** *Syn* DISCOVER, ascertain, determine, unearth

**learned** ♦ possessing or manifesting unusually wide and deep knowledge *Syn* scholarly, erudite

**learning** *Syn* KNOWLEDGE, erudition, scholarship, science, information, lore

**lease** *Syn* HIRE, let, charter, rent

**leave** *vb* **1** *Syn* WILL, bequeath, devise, legate **2** *Syn* RELINQUISH, resign, surrender, abandon, yield, cede, waive **3** *Syn* GO, depart, quit, withdraw, retire **4** *Syn* LET, allow, permit, suffer

**leave** *n* *Syn* PERMISSION, sufferance

**leaven** *Syn* INFUSE, imbue, inoculate, ingrain, suffuse

**leavings** *Syn* REMAINDER, remains, residue, residuum, rest, balance, remnant

**lecherous** *Syn* LICENTIOUS, libidinous, lascivious, lustful, lewd, wanton, libertine

**lecture** *Syn* SPEECH, address, oration, harangue, talk, sermon, homily

**leech** *Syn* PARASITE, sponge, sponger, sycophant, toady, lickspittle, bootlicker, hanger-on, favorite

**lees** *Syn* DEPOSIT, precipitate, sediment, dregs, grounds

**leeway** *Syn* ROOM, berth, play, elbowroom, margin, clearance

**legal** *Syn* LAWFUL, legitimate, licit *Ant* illegal

**legal tender** *Syn* MONEY, cash, currency, specie, coin, coinage

**legate** *n* *Syn* AMBASSADOR, nuncio, internuncio, chargé d'affaires, minister, envoy

**legate** *vb* *Syn* WILL, bequeath, devise, leave

**legend** **1** *Syn* MYTH, saga **2** *Syn* INSCRIPTION, caption

**legendary** *Syn* FICTITIOUS, mythical, apocryphal, fabulous

**legerity** *Syn* CELERITY, alacrity *Ant* deliberateness; sluggishness

**legion** *Syn* MULTITUDE, host, army

**legitimate** *Syn* LAWFUL, legal, licit *Ant* illegitimate; arbitrary

**leisure** *Syn* REST, relaxation, repose, ease, comfort *Ant* toil

**leisurely** *Syn* SLOW, deliberate, dilatory, laggard *Ant* hurried; abrupt

**leitmotiv** *Syn* SUBJECT, motive, motif, theme, matter, subject matter, argument, topic, text

**lengthen** *Syn* EXTEND, elongate, prolong, protract *Ant* shorten

**leniency** *Syn* FORBEARANCE, clemency, mercifulness, tolerance, indulgence

**lenient** **1** *Syn* SOFT, gentle, smooth, mild, bland, balmy *Ant* caustic **2** *Syn* FORBEARING, indulgent, merciful, clement, tolerant *Ant* stern; exacting

**leniently** *Syn* FORBEARINGLY, tolerantly, clemently, mercifully, indulgently

**lenity** *Syn* MERCY, clemency, charity, grace *Ant* severity

**lesion** *Syn* WOUND, trauma, traumatism, bruise, contusion

**lessen** *Syn* DECREASE, diminish, reduce, abate, dwindle

**let** **1** *Syn* HIRE, lease, rent, charter **2** ♦ to neither forbid nor prevent *Syn* allow, permit, suffer, leave

**lethal** *Syn* DEADLY, fatal, mortal

**lethargic** ♦ deficient in alertness or activity *Syn* sluggish, torpid, comatose *Ant* energetic, vigorous

**lethargy** ♦ physical or mental inertness *Syn* languor, lassitude, stupor, torpor, torpidity *Ant* vigor

**letter** ♦ a direct or personal written or printed message addressed to a person or organization *Syn* epistle, missive, note, message, dispatch, report, memorandum

**levee** *Syn* WHARF, dock, pier, quay, slip, berth, jetty

**level** *vb* *Syn* DIRECT, point, train, aim, lay

**level** *adj* ♦ having a surface without bends, curves, or irregularities *Syn* flat, plane, plain, even, smooth, flush

**levitate** *Syn* RISE, arise, ascend, mount, soar, tower, rocket, surge *Ant* gravitate, sink

**levity** *Syn* LIGHTNESS, light-mindedness, frivolity, flippancy, volatility, flightiness *Ant* gravity

**lewd** *Syn* LICENTIOUS, lustful, lascivious, libidinous, lecherous, wanton, libertine *Ant* chaste

**liability** *Syn* DEBT, indebtedness, obligation, debit, arrear *Ant* asset (*or plural* assets)

**liable** **1** *Syn* RESPONSIBLE, amenable, answerable, accountable **2** ♦ being by nature or through circumstances likely to experience something adverse *Syn* open, exposed, subject, prone, susceptible, sensitive *Ant* exempt, immune **3** *Syn* APT, likely

**liaison** *Syn* AMOUR, intrigue, affair

**libel** *n* ♦ a public and often satirical presentation of the faults or weaknesses, esp. of an individual *Syn* skit, squib, lampoon, pasquinade

**libel** *vb* *Syn* MALIGN, defame, slander, traduce, asperse, vilify, calumniate

**liberal** **1** ♦ giving or given freely and unstintingly *Syn* generous, bountiful, bounteous, openhanded, munificent, handsome *Ant* close **2** ♦ not bound by what is orthodox, established, or traditional *Syn* progressive, advanced, radical *Ant* authoritarian

**liberate** *Syn* FREE, release, emancipate, manumit, discharge

**libertine** *Syn* LICENTIOUS, lewd, wanton, lustful, lascivious, libidinous, lecherous *Ant* straitlaced

**liberty** *Syn* FREEDOM, license *Ant* restraint

**libidinous** *Syn* LICENTIOUS, lecherous, lustful, lascivious, lewd, wanton, libertine

**license** *n* *Syn* FREEDOM, liberty *Ant* decorum

**license** *vb* *Syn* AUTHORIZE, commission, accredit *Ant* ban

**licentious** ♦ lacking moral restraint esp. in a disregarding of sexual restraints *Syn* libertine, lewd, wanton, lustful, lascivious, libidinous, lecherous *Ant* continent

**licit** *Syn* LAWFUL, legitimate, legal *Ant* illicit

**lick** *Syn* CONQUER, beat, defeat, vanquish, subdue, subjugate, reduce, overcome, surmount, overthrow, rout

**lickspittle** *Syn* PARASITE, sycophant, toady, bootlicker, hanger-on, leech, sponge, sponger, favorite

**lie** *vb* ♦ to tell an untruth *Syn* prevaricate, equivocate, palter, fib

**lie** *n* ♦ a statement or declaration that is not true *Syn* falsehood, untruth, fib, misrepresentation, story *Ant* truth

**life** *Syn* BIOGRAPHY, memoir, autobiography, confessions

**lifeless** *Syn* DEAD, inanimate, defunct, deceased, departed, late *Ant* living

**lift** **1** ♦ to move from a lower to a higher place or position *Syn* raise, rear, elevate, hoist, heave, boost *Ant* lower **2** *Syn* STEAL, purloin, filch, pilfer, pinch, snitch, swipe, cop

**light** *vb* **1** ♦ to cause something to start burning *Syn* kindle, ignite, fire **2** *Syn* ILLUMINATE, lighten, illumine, enlighten, illustrate

**light** *adj* *Syn* EASY, simple, facile, effortless, smooth *Ant* heavy; arduous; burdensome

**light** *vb* *Syn* ALIGHT, land, perch, roost

**lighten** *vb* *Syn* ILLUMINATE, illumine, light, enlighten, illustrate *Ant* darken

**lighten** *vb Syn* RELIEVE, alleviate, mitigate, assuage, allay

**lighthearted** *Syn* GLAD, cheerful, happy, joyful, joyous *Ant* despondent

**light-mindedness** *Syn* LIGHTNESS, levity, frivolity, flippancy, volatility, flightiness

**lightness** ♦ gaiety or indifference where seriousness and attention are called for *Syn* light-mindedness, levity, frivolity, flippancy, volatility, flightiness *Ant* seriousness

**like** *vb* ♦ to feel attraction toward or take pleasure in *Syn* love, enjoy, relish, fancy, dote *Ant* dislike

**like** *adj* ♦ the same or nearly the same (as in appearance, character, or quantity) *Syn* alike, similar, analogous, comparable, akin, parallel, uniform, identical *Ant* unlike

**likely** 1 *Syn* PROBABLE, possible *Ant* unlikely 2 *Syn* APT, liable

**likeness** ♦ agreement or correspondence in details *Syn* similarity, resemblance, similitude, analogy, affinity *Ant* unlikeness

**likewise** *Syn* ALSO, too, besides, moreover, furthermore

**limb** *Syn* SHOOT, bough, branch

**limber** *Syn* SUPPLE, lithe, lithesome, lissome

**limit** *n* ♦ a material or immaterial point beyond which something does not or cannot extend *Syn* bound, confine, end, term

**limit** *vb* ♦ to set bounds for *Syn* restrict, circumscribe, confine *Ant* widen

**limn** *Syn* REPRESENT, depict, portray, delineate, picture

**limp** ♦ deficient in firmness of texture, substance, or structure *Syn* floppy, flaccid, flabby, flimsy, sleazy

**limpid** *Syn* CLEAR, transparent, translucent, lucid, pellucid, diaphanous *Ant* turbid

**line** *n* ♦ a series of things arranged in continuous or uniform order *Syn* row, rank, file, echelon, tier

**line** *vb* ♦ to arrange in a line or in lines *Syn* line up, align, range, array

**lineage** *Syn* ANCESTRY, pedigree

**line up** *Syn* LINE, align, range, array

**linger** *Syn* STAY, tarry, wait, remain, abide

**lingo** *Syn* DIALECT, vernacular, patois, jargon, cant, argot, slang

**link** *Syn* JOIN, connect, relate, associate, conjoin, combine, unite *Ant* sunder

**liquefy** ♦ to convert or to become converted to a liquid state *Syn* melt, deliquesce, fuse, thaw

**lissome** *Syn* SUPPLE, lithesome, lithe, limber

**list** *n* ♦ a series of items (as names) written down or printed as a memorandum or record *Syn* table, catalog, schedule, register, roll, roster, inventory

**list** *vb Syn* RECORD, register, enroll, catalog

**listless** *Syn* LANGUID, spiritless, languishing, languorous, lackadaisical, enervated *Ant* eager

**lithe, lithesome** *Syn* SUPPLE, lissome, limber

**little** *Syn* SMALL, diminutive, wee, tiny, minute, miniature *Ant* big

**littoral** *Syn* SHORE, coast, beach, strand, bank, foreshore

**liturgy** *Syn* FORM, ritual, rite, ceremony, ceremonial, formality

**live** *vb* 1 *Syn* BE, exist, subsist 2 *Syn* RESIDE, dwell, sojourn, lodge, stay, put up, stop

**live** *adj Syn* ACTIVE, operative, dynamic *Ant* inactive, inert; dormant; defunct

**livelihood** *Syn* LIVING, subsistence, sustenance, maintenance, support, keep, bread

**lively** ♦ keenly alive and spirited *Syn* animated, vivacious, sprightly, gay *Ant* dull

**livid** *Syn* PALE, ashen, ashy, pallid, wan

**living** *adj* ♦ having or showing life *Syn* alive, animate, animated, vital *Ant* lifeless

**living** *n* ♦ supplies or resources needed to live *Syn* livelihood, subsistence, sustenance, maintenance, support, keep, bread, bread and butter

**load** *n* ♦ something which is carried, conveyed, or transported from one place to another *Syn* burden, freight, cargo, lading

**load** *vb* 1 *Syn* BURDEN, encumber, cumber, weigh, weight, lade, tax, charge, saddle *Ant* unload 2 *Syn* ADULTERATE, weight, sophisticate, doctor

**loaf** *Syn* IDLE, lounge, loll, laze

**loath** *Syn* DISINCLINED, indisposed, averse, hesitant, reluctant *Ant* anxious

**loathe** *Syn* HATE, abominate, detest, abhor *Ant* dote on

**loathing** *Syn* ABHORRENCE, detestation, abomination, hate, hatred *Ant* tolerance

**loathsome** *Syn* OFFENSIVE, repulsive, repugnant, revolting *Ant* engaging, inviting

**local** *Syn* INSULAR, provincial, parochial, small-town *Ant* cosmopolitan

**locality** ♦ a more or less definitely circumscribed place or region *Syn* district, vicinity, neighborhood

**location** *Syn* PLACE, position, situation, site, spot, station

**locomotion** *Syn* MOTION, movement, move, stir

**locum tenens** *Syn* SUBSTITUTE, supply, alternate, understudy, pinch hitter, double, stand-in

**locution** *Syn* PHRASE, idiom, expression

**lodge** 1 *Syn* HARBOR, house, board, shelter, entertain 2 *Syn* RESIDE, live, dwell, sojourn, stay, put up, stop

**lofty** *Syn* HIGH, tall

**logical** ♦ having or showing skill in thinking or reasoning *Syn* analytical, subtle *Ant* illogical

**logistic, logistical** *Syn* STRATEGIC, tactical

**logistics** *Syn* STRATEGY, tactics

**loiter** *Syn* DELAY, dawdle, lag, procrastinate

**loll** *Syn* IDLE, loaf, lounge, laze

**lollop** 1 *Syn* SKIP, bound, hop, curvet, lope, ricochet 2 *Syn* STUMBLE, trip, blunder, lurch, flounder, lumber, galumph, bumble

**lone** 1 *Syn* ALONE, lonely, lonesome, forlorn, lorn, solitary, desolate 2 *Syn* SINGLE, sole, unique, solitary, separate, particular

**lonely** *Syn* ALONE, lonesome, lone, solitary, forlorn, lorn, desolate

**lonesome** *Syn* ALONE, lonely, lone, solitary, forlorn, lorn, desolate

**long** ♦ to have a strong desire for something *Syn* yearn, hanker, pine, hunger, thirst

**longanimity** *Syn* PATIENCE, long-suffering, forbearance, resignation

**long-suffering** *Syn* PATIENCE, resignation, forbearance

**look** *vb* 1 *Syn* SEE, watch 2 *Syn* SEEM, appear 3 *Syn* EXPECT, hope, await

**look** *n* 1 ♦ the directing of one's eyes in order to see *Syn* sight, view, glance, glimpse, peep, peek 2 *Syn* APPEARANCE, aspect, semblance

**looker-on** *Syn* SPECTATOR, onlooker, beholder, observer, witness, eyewitness, bystander, kibitzer

**loom** *Syn* APPEAR, emerge *Ant* vanish

**loose** ♦ not tightly bound, held, restrained, or stretched *Syn* relaxed, slack, lax *Ant* tight; strict

**loot** *n Syn* SPOIL, booty, plunder, swag, prize

**loot** *vb Syn* ROB, plunder, rifle, burglarize

**lop** *Syn* SHEAR, poll, clip, trim, prune, snip, crop

**lope** *Syn* SKIP, bound, hop, curvet, lollop, ricochet

**loquacious** *Syn* TALKATIVE, garrulous, voluble, glib

**loquacity, loquaciousness** *Syn* TALKATIVENESS, garrulity, volubility, glibness

**lordly** *Syn* PROUD, haughty, arrogant, overbearing, insolent, supercilious, disdainful

**lore** *Syn* KNOWLEDGE, science, learning, erudition, scholarship, information

**lorn** *Syn* ALONE, forlorn, lonely, lonesome, lone, solitary, desolate

**lot** 1 *Syn* FATE, destiny, portion, doom 2 *Syn* GROUP, cluster, bunch, parcel

**loud** ♦ marked by intensity or volume of sound *Syn* stentorian, earsplitting, hoarse, raucous, strident, stertorous *Ant* low-pitched, low

**lounge** *Syn* IDLE, loaf, loll, laze

**lout** *Syn* BOOR, churl, clown, clodhopper, bumpkin, hick, yokel, rube

**loutish** *Syn* BOORISH, churlish, clownish

**love** *n Syn* ATTACHMENT, affection *Ant* hate

**love** *vb Syn* LIKE, enjoy, dote, relish, fancy *Ant* hate

**lovely** *Syn* BEAUTIFUL, fair, comely, pretty, bonny, handsome, beauteous, pulchritudinous, good-looking *Ant* unlovely; plain

**loving** ♦ feeling or expressing love *Syn* affectionate, devoted, fond, doting *Ant* unloving

**low** *Syn* BASE, vile

**lower** *Syn* FROWN, glower, scowl, gloom

**lowly** *Syn* HUMBLE, meek, modest *Ant* pompous

**loyal** *Syn* FAITHFUL, true, constant, staunch, steadfast, resolute *Ant* disloyal

**loyalty** *Syn* FIDELITY, allegiance, fealty, devotion, piety *Ant* disloyalty

**lubricate** *Syn* OIL, grease, anoint, cream

**lucent** *Syn* BRIGHT, brilliant, radiant, luminous, lustrous, effulgent, refulgent, beaming, lambent, incandescent

**lucid** 1 *Syn* CLEAR, pellucid, transparent, translucent, diaphanous, limpid 2 *Syn* CLEAR, perspicuous *Ant* obscure, vague, dark

**luck** *Syn* CHANCE, fortune, hap, accident, hazard

**luckless** *Syn* UNLUCKY, disastrous, ill-starred, ill-fated, unfortunate, calamitous, hapless

**lucky** ♦ meeting with unforeseen success *Syn* fortunate, happy, providential *Ant* unlucky

**lucrative** *Syn* PAYING, gainful, remunerative, profitable

**ludicrous** *Syn* LAUGHABLE, risible, ridiculous, comic, comical, farcical, droll, funny

**lugubrious** *Syn* MELANCHOLY, doleful, dolorous, rueful, plaintive *Ant* joyous; facetious

**lull** *vb Syn* CALM, compose, quiet, quieten, still, soothe, settle, tranquilize *Ant* agitate

**lull** *n Syn* PAUSE, recess, respite, intermission

**lumber** *Syn* STUMBLE, trip, blunder, lurch, flounder, galumph, lollop, bumble

**luminous** *Syn* BRIGHT, brilliant, radiant, lustrous, effulgent, lucent, refulgent, beaming, lambent, incandescent

**lunacy** *Syn* INSANITY, psychosis, mania, dementia

**lunatic** *Syn* INSANE, mad, crazy, crazed, demented, deranged, maniac, non compos mentis

**lurch** *Syn* STUMBLE, trip, blunder, flounder, lumber, galumph, lollop, bumble

**lure** *n* ♦ something that leads an animal or a person into a place or situation from which escape is difficult *Syn* bait, decoy, snare, trap

**lure** *vb* ♦ to lead astray from one's true course *Syn* entice, inveigle, decoy, tempt, seduce *Ant* revolt, repel

**lurid** *Syn* GHASTLY, grisly, gruesome, macabre, grim

**lurk** ♦ to behave so as to escape attention *Syn* skulk, slink, sneak

**luscious** *Syn* DELIGHTFUL, delicious, delectable *Ant* austere; tasteless

**lush** *Syn* PROFUSE, luxuriant, lavish, prodigal, exuberant

**lust** *Syn* DESIRE, appetite, passion, urge

**luster** ♦ the quality or condition of shining by reflected light *Syn* sheen, gloss, glaze

**lustful** *Syn* LICENTIOUS, lascivious, libidinous, lecherous, wanton, lewd, libertine

**lustrous** *Syn* BRIGHT, luminous, radiant, brilliant, effulgent, refulgent, beaming, lambent, lucent, incandescent

**lusty** *Syn* VIGOROUS, energetic, strenuous, nervous *Ant* effete

**luxuriant** *Syn* PROFUSE, lush, exuberant, lavish, prodigal

**luxurious** 1 *Syn* SENSUOUS, voluptuous, sybaritic, epicurean, sensual *Ant* ascetic 2 ♦ ostentatiously rich or magnificent *Syn* sumptuous, opulent

**luxury** *Syn* AMENITY *Ant* hardship

**lying** *Syn* DISHONEST, mendacious, untruthful, deceitful *Ant* truthtelling

# M

**macabre** *Syn* GHASTLY, gruesome, grisly, grim, lurid

**macerate** *Syn* CRUSH, mash, smash, bruise, squash

**machination** *Syn* PLOT, intrigue, conspiracy, cabal

**machine** ♦ a device or system by which energy can be converted into useful work *Syn* mechanism, machinery, apparatus, engine, motor

**machinery 1** *Syn* EQUIPMENT, apparatus, paraphernalia, outfit, tackle, gear, matériel **2** *Syn* MACHINE, mechanism, apparatus, engine, motor

**mad 1** *Syn* INSANE, crazy, crazed, demented, deranged, lunatic, maniac, non compos mentis **2** *Syn* ANGRY, irate, wrathful, wroth, indignant, acrimonious

**madden** *Syn* ANGER, incense, enrage, infuriate

**maelstrom** *Syn* EDDY, whirlpool, vortex

**magazine** ♦ *Syn* JOURNAL, periodical, review, organ, newspaper

**magic** ♦ the use of means (as charms or spells) believed to have supernatural power over natural forces *Syn* sorcery, witchcraft, witchery, wizardry, alchemy, thaumaturgy

**magisterial** *Syn* DICTATORIAL, authoritarian, dogmatic, doctrinaire, oracular

**magnificent** *Syn* GRAND, imposing, stately, majestic, august, noble, grandiose *Ant* modest

**magnify** *Syn* EXALT, aggrandize *Ant* minimize, belittle

**magniloquent** *Syn* RHETORICAL, grandiloquent, aureate, flowery, euphuistic, bombastic

**magnitude** *Syn* SIZE, volume, extent, dimensions, area

**maiden 1** *Syn* UNMARRIED, single, celibate, virgin **2** *Syn* YOUTHFUL, juvenile, virgin, virginal, puerile, boyish *Ant* experienced

**maim** ♦ to injure so severely as to cause lasting damage *Syn* cripple, mutilate, batter, mangle

**main** *Syn* CHIEF, principal, leading, foremost, capital

**mainly** *Syn* LARGELY, greatly, mostly, chiefly, principally, generally

**maintain** ♦ to uphold as true, right, just, or reasonable *Syn* assert, defend, vindicate, justify

**maintenance** *Syn* LIVING, sustenance, support, livelihood, subsistence, keep, bread

**majestic** *Syn* GRAND, stately, august, noble, magnificent, imposing, grandiose

**make** ♦ to bring something into being by forming, shaping, combining, or altering materials *Syn* form, shape, fashion, fabricate, manufacture, forge

**make-believe** *Syn* PRETENSE, pretension

**maker** ♦ one who brings something into being or existence *Syn* creator, author

**makeshift** *Syn* RESOURCE, shift, expedient, resort, stopgap, substitute, surrogate

**maladroit** *Syn* AWKWARD, clumsy, gauche, inept *Ant* adroit

**malady** *Syn* DISEASE, ailment, disorder, condition, affection, complaint, distemper, syndrome

**male** ♦ of, characteristic of, or like a male, esp. of the human species *Syn* masculine, manly, manlike, mannish, manful, virile *Ant* female

**malediction** *Syn* CURSE, imprecation, anathema *Ant* benediction

**malefactor** *Syn* CRIMINAL, felon, convict, culprit, delinquent *Ant* benefactor; well-doer

**malefic, maleficent** *Syn* SINISTER, malign, baleful

**malevolence** *Syn* MALICE, ill will, malignity, malignancy, spite, despite, spleen, grudge *Ant* benevolence

**malevolent** *Syn* MALICIOUS, malignant, malign, spiteful *Ant* benevolent

**malice** ♦ the desire to see another experience pain, injury, or distress *Syn* ill will, malevolence, spite, despite, malignity, malignancy, spleen, grudge *Ant* charity

**malicious** ♦ having, showing, or indicative of intense often vicious ill will *Syn* malevolent, malignant, malign, spiteful

**malign** *adj* **1** *Syn* MALICIOUS, malignant, malevolent, spiteful *Ant* benign **2** *Syn* SINISTER, baleful, malefic, maleficent *Ant* benign

**malign** *vb* ♦ to injure by speaking ill of *Syn* traduce, asperse, vilify, calumniate, defame, slander, libel *Ant* defend

**malignancy** *Syn* MALICE, malignity, ill will, malevolence, spite, despite, spleen, grudge

**malignant** *Syn* MALICIOUS, malign, malevolent, spiteful *Ant* benignant

**malignity** *Syn* MALICE, malignancy, ill will, malevolence, spite, despite, spleen, grudge *Ant* benignity

**malinger** *Syn* DODGE, parry, sidestep, duck, shirk, fence

**malleable** *Syn* PLASTIC, pliable, pliant, ductile, adaptable *Ant* refractory

**malodorous** ♦ having an unpleasant smell *Syn* stinking, fetid, noisome, putrid, rank, rancid, fusty, musty *Ant* odorous

**maltreat** *Syn* ABUSE, mistreat, ill-treat, misuse, outrage

**mammoth** *Syn* HUGE, vast, immense, enormous, elephantine, giant, gigantic, gigantean, colossal, gargantuan, Herculean, cyclopean, titanic, Brobdingnagian

**manacle** *Syn* HAMPER, trammel, clog, fetter, shackle, hog-tie

**manage** *Syn* CONDUCT, control, direct

**mandate 1** *Syn* COMMAND, dictate, order, injunction, bidding, behest **2** ♦ an authorization to take a political action given to a representative *Syn* initiative, referendum, plebiscite

**maneuver** *Syn* TRICK, stratagem, ruse, gambit, ploy, artifice, wile, feint

**manful** *Syn* MALE, virile, mannish, manlike, manly, masculine

**mangle** *Syn* MAIM, batter, mutilate, cripple

**mania 1** *Syn* INSANITY, lunacy, psychosis, dementia *Ant* lucidity **2** ♦ a state of mind in which there is loss of control over emotional, nervous, or mental processes *Syn* delirium, frenzy, hysteria

**maniac** *Syn* INSANE, mad, crazy, crazed, demented, deranged, lunatic, non compos mentis

**manifest** *adj Syn* EVIDENT, patent, distinct, obvious, apparent, palpable, plain, clear *Ant* latent; constructive

**manifest** *vb Syn* SHOW, evidence, evince, demonstrate *Ant* suggest

**manikin** *Syn* DWARF, midget, pygmy, homunculus, runt *Ant* giant

**manipulate** *Syn* HANDLE, wield, swing, ply

**manlike** *Syn* MALE, mannish, manful, virile, manly, masculine

**manly** *Syn* MALE, manlike, manful, virile, masculine, mannish *Ant* unmanly, womanly

**manner** *Syn* METHOD, mode, way, fashion, system

**mannerism** *Syn* POSE, air, affectation

**mannish** *Syn* MALE, manlike, virile, masculine, manful, manly *Ant* womanish

**manufacture** *Syn* MAKE, fabricate, forge, form, shape, fashion

**manumit** *Syn* FREE, emancipate, enfranchise, deliver, discharge, release, liberate *Ant* enslave

**many** ♦ amounting to or being one at a large indefinite number *Syn* several, sundry, various, divers, numerous, multifarious *Ant* few

**many-sided** *Syn* VERSATILE, all-around

**map** *Syn* CHART, graph

**mar** *Syn* INJURE, damage, hurt, harm, impair, spoil

**marble** *Syn* SPOT, spatter, sprinkle, mottle, fleck, stipple, speckle, spangle, bespangle

**marbled** *Syn* SPOTTED, spattered, sprinkled, mottled, flecked, stippled, speckled, spangled, bespangled

**margin 1** *Syn* BORDER, verge, edge, rim, brim, brink **2** *Syn* ROOM, berth, play, elbowroom, leeway, clearance

**marine** ♦ of or relating to the navigation of the sea *Syn* maritime, nautical, naval

**mariner** ♦ a person engaged in sailing or handling a ship *Syn* sailor, seaman, tar, gob, bluejacket

**marital** *Syn* MATRIMONIAL, conjugal, connubial, nuptial, hymeneal

**maritime** *Syn* MARINE, nautical, naval

**mark** *n* **1** *Syn* SIGN, symptom, note, token, badge **2** *Syn* CHARACTER, symbol, sign **3** ♦ a symbol or device used for identification or indication of ownership *Syn* brand, stamp, label, tag, ticket

**mark** *vb* **1** ♦ to affix, attach, or impress something which serves for identification *Syn* brand, stamp, label, tag, ticket **2** *Syn* CHARACTERIZE, distinguish, qualify

**marriage** ♦ acts by which a man and woman become husband and wife or the state of being husband and wife *Syn* matrimony, wedlock, wedding, nuptial, espousal

**marshal** *Syn* ORDER, arrange, organize, systematize, methodize

**martial** ♦ of, relating to, or suited for war or a warrior *Syn* warlike, military

**marvel** *Syn* WONDER, prodigy, miracle, phenomenon

**masculine** *Syn* MALE, virile, manful, manly, manlike, mannish *Ant* feminine

**mash** *Syn* CRUSH, smash, bruise, squash, macerate

**mask** *Syn* DISGUISE, cloak, dissemble, camouflage

**mass** *n* **1** *Syn* BULK, volume **2** *Syn* HEAP, pile, stack, shock, cock, bank

**mass** *vb Syn* HEAP, pile, stack, shock, cock, bank

**massacre** ♦ the act or an instance of killing a number of usu. helpless or unresisting human beings under circumstances of atrocity or cruelty *Syn* slaughter, butchery, carnage, pogrom

**massive** ♦ impressively large or heavy *Syn* massy, bulky, monumental, substantial

**massy** *Syn* MASSIVE, bulky, monumental, substantial

**master** *Syn* CHIEF, chieftain, head, leader

**masterful** ♦ tending to impose one's will on others *Syn* domineering, imperious, peremptory, imperative

**masterly** *Syn* PROFICIENT, adept, skilled, skillful, expert

**match** ♦ to come up to or nearly up to the level or standard of *Syn* rival, equal, approach, touch

**material** *adj* **1** ♦ of or belonging to actuality *Syn* physical, corporeal, phenomenal, sensible, objective *Ant* immaterial **2** *Syn* RELEVANT, germane, pertinent, apposite, applicable, apropos *Ant* immaterial

**material** *n Syn* MATTER, substance, stuff

**materialize** *Syn* REALIZE, externalize, objectify, incarnate, embody, actualize, hypostatize, reify

**matériel** *Syn* EQUIPMENT, apparatus, machinery, paraphernalia, outfit, tackle, gear

**matrimonial** ♦ of, relating to, or characteristic of marriage *Syn* marital, conjugal, connubial, nuptial, hymeneal

**matrimony** *Syn* MARRIAGE, wedlock, wedding, nuptial, espousal

**matter 1** ♦ what goes into the makeup or forms the being of a thing whether physical or not *Syn* substance, material, stuff **2** *Syn* AFFAIR, business, concern, thing **3** *Syn* SUBJECT, subject matter, argument, topic, text, theme, motive, motif, leitmotiv

**matter-of-fact** *Syn* PROSAIC, prosy

**mature** *adj* ♦ having attained the normal peak of natural growth and development *Syn* matured, ripe, mellow, adult, grown-up *Ant* immature; childish

**mature** *vb* ♦ to become fully developed or ripe *Syn* develop, ripen, age

**matured** *Syn* MATURE, ripe, mellow, adult, grown-up *Ant* unmatured; premature

**maudlin** *Syn* SENTIMENTAL, mawkish, romantic, soppy, mushy, slushy

**mawkish** *Syn* SENTIMENTAL, maudlin, romantic, soppy, mushy, slushy

**maxim** *Syn* SAYING, saw, adage, proverb, motto, epigram, aphorism, apothegm

**meager** ♦ falling short of what is normal, necessary, or desirable *Syn* scanty, scant, skimpy, scrimpy, exiguous, spare, sparse *Ant* ample; copious

**mean** *adj* ♦ being below the normal standards of human decency and dignity *Syn* ignoble, abject, sordid

**mean** *vb* 1 *Syn* INTEND, design, propose, purpose 2 ♦ to convey (as an idea) to the mind *Syn* denote, signify, import

**mean** *n* 1 *Syn* AVERAGE, median, norm, par 2 ♦ one by which work is accomplished or an end effected *Syn* instrument, instrumentality, agent, agency, medium, organ, vehicle, channel 3 *pl* **means** *Syn* POSSESSIONS, resources, assets, effects, belongings

**mean** *adj* *Syn* AVERAGE, median, par *Ant* extreme

**meander** *Syn* WANDER, stray, roam, ramble, rove, range, prowl, gad, gallivant, traipse

**meaning** ♦ the idea that something conveys to the mind *Syn* sense, acceptation, signification, significance, import

**meaningful** *Syn* EXPRESSIVE, significant, pregnant, sententious, eloquent *Ant* meaningless

**measly** *Syn* PETTY, paltry, trifling, trivial, puny, picayunish, picayune

**mechanic** *Syn* WORKER, workman, workingman, artisan, operative, hand, laborer, craftsman, handicraftsman, roustabout

**mechanical** *Syn* SPONTANEOUS, automatic, instinctive, impulsive

**mechanism** *Syn* MACHINE, machinery, apparatus, engine, motor

**meddle** ♦ to interest oneself in what is not one's concern *Syn* interfere, intermeddle, tamper

**meddlesome** *Syn* IMPERTINENT, intrusive, obtrusive, officious

**median** *n* *Syn* AVERAGE, mean, norm, par

**median** *adj* *Syn* AVERAGE, mean, par

**mediate** *Syn* INTERPOSE, intercede, intervene, interfere

**medicament, medication** *Syn* REMEDY, medicine, cure, specific, physic

**medicinal** *Syn* DRUG, pharmaceutical, biologic, simple

**medicine** *Syn* REMEDY, cure, medicament, medication, specific, physic

**mediocre** *Syn* MEDIUM, middling, second-rate, moderate, average, fair, indifferent

**meditate** *Syn* PONDER, muse, ruminate

**meditative** *Syn* THOUGHTFUL, contemplative, speculative, reflective, pensive

**medium** *n* *Syn* MEAN, instrument, instrumentality, agent, agency, organ, vehicle, channel

**medium** *adj* ♦ about midway between the extremes of a scale, measurement, or evaluation *Syn* middling, mediocre, second-rate, moderate, average, fair, indifferent

**meed** *Syn* PREMIUM, guerdon, prize, award, reward, bounty, bonus

**meek** *Syn* HUMBLE, modest, lowly *Ant* arrogant

**meet** *vb* 1 ♦ to come together face-to-face or as if face-to-face *Syn* face, encounter, confront *Ant* avoid 2 *Syn* SATISFY, fulfill, answer *Ant* disappoint

**meet** *adj* *Syn* FIT, suitable, proper, appropriate, fitting, apt, happy, felicitous *Ant* unmeet

**melancholia** *Syn* SADNESS, melancholy, depression, dejection, gloom, blues, dumps

**melancholic** ♦ gloomy or depressed, esp. as a manifestation of one's temperament or state of health *Syn* melancholy, atrabilious, hypochondriac

**melancholy** *n* *Syn* SADNESS, melancholia, dejection, gloom, depression, blues, dumps *Ant* exhilaration

**melancholy** *adj* 1 *Syn* MELANCHOLIC, atrabilious, hypochondriac 2 ♦ expressing or suggesting sorrow or mourning *Syn* dolorous, doleful, lugubrious, rueful, plaintive

**melee** *Syn* BRAWL, fracas, row, broil, rumpus, scrap

**mellow** *Syn* MATURE, ripe, matured, adult, grown-up *Ant* unmellow; green

**melodramatic** *Syn* DRAMATIC, histrionic, theatrical, dramaturgic

**melody** ♦ a rhythmic succession of single tones organized as an aesthetic whole *Syn* air, tune

**melt** *Syn* LIQUEFY, deliquesce, fuse, thaw

**member** *Syn* PART, portion, piece, detail, division, section, segment, sector, fraction, fragment, parcel

**memento** *Syn* REMEMBRANCE, remembrancer, reminder, memorial, token, keepsake, souvenir

**memoir** *Syn* BIOGRAPHY, life, autobiography, confessions

**memorable** *Syn* NOTEWORTHY, notable

**memorandum** *Syn* LETTER, epistle, missive, note, message, dispatch, report

**memorial** *Syn* REMEMBRANCE, remembrancer, reminder, memento, token, keepsake, souvenir

**memory** ♦ the capacity for or the act of remembering, or the thing remembered *Syn* remembrance, recollection, reminiscence, mind, souvenir *Ant* oblivion

**menace** *Syn* THREATEN

**mend** ♦ to put into good order something that is injured, damaged, or defective *Syn* repair, patch, rebuild

**mendacious** *Syn* DISHONEST, lying, untruthful, deceitful *Ant* veracious

**menial** *Syn* SUBSERVIENT, servile, slavish, obsequious

**mental** ♦ of or relating to the mind *Syn* intellectual, psychic, intelligent, cerebral

**mention** ♦ to refer to someone or something in a clear unmistakable manner *Syn* name, instance, specify

**mephitic** *Syn* POISONOUS, toxic, venomous, virulent, pestilent, pestilential, miasmic, miasmatic, miasmal

**mercantile** *Syn* COMMERCIAL

**mercenary** ♦ serving merely for pay or sordid advantage *Syn* hireling, venal, hack

**merciful** *Syn* FORBEARING, clement, tolerant, lenient, indulgent *Ant* merciless

**mercifully** *Syn* FORBEARINGLY, tolerantly, clemently, leniently, indulgently

**mercifulness** *Syn* FORBEARANCE, clemency, tolerance, leniency, indulgence

**merciless** *Syn* GRIM, implacable, relentless, unrelenting *Ant* merciful

**mercurial** *Syn* INCONSTANT, fickle, capricious, unstable *Ant* saturnine

**mercy** ♦ a disposition to show compassion or kindness *Syn* charity, grace, clemency, lenity

**mere** ♦ being as stated with nothing more added or extra *Syn* bare, very

**meretricious** *Syn* GAUDY, tawdry, garish, flashy

**merge** *Syn* MIX, blend, fuse, coalesce, amalgamate, commingle, mingle

**merger** *Syn* CONSOLIDATION, amalgamation

**meridian** *Syn* SUMMIT, culmination, zenith, apogee, peak, pinnacle, climax, apex, acme

**merit** *n* 1 *Syn* DUE, desert 2 *Syn* EXCELLENCE, virtue, perfection *Ant* fault; defect

**merit** *vb* *Syn* DESERVE, earn, rate

**merry** ♦ showing high spirits or lightheartedness *Syn* blithe, jocund, jovial, jolly

**mesa** *Syn* MOUNTAIN, mount, peak, alp, volcano

**message** *Syn* LETTER, missive, note, epistle, dispatch, report, memorandum

**metamorphose** *Syn* TRANSFORM, transmute, convert, transmogrify, transfigure

**metamorphosis** *Syn* TRANSFORMATION, transmutation, conversion, transmogrification, transfiguration

**metaphor** *Syn* ANALOGY, simile

**metaphrase** *Syn* TRANSLATION, version, paraphrase

**meter** *Syn* RHYTHM, cadence

**method** ♦ the means taken or procedure followed in achieving an end *Syn* mode, manner, way, fashion, system

**methodical** *Syn* ORDERLY, systematic, regular *Ant* unmethodical; desultory

**methodize** *Syn* ORDER, systematize, organize, arrange, marshal

**meticulous** *Syn* CAREFUL, scrupulous, punctilious, punctual

**mettle** *Syn* COURAGE, spirit, resolution, tenacity

**mettlesome** *Syn* SPIRITED, high-spirited, spunky, fiery, peppery, gingery

**miasmic, miasmatic, miasmal** *Syn* POISONOUS, toxic, venomous, virulent, pestilent, pestilential, mephitic

**microscopic** *Syn* SMALL, minute, little, diminutive, miniature, petite, wee, tiny, teeny, weeny

**middle** *Syn* CENTER, midst, core, hub, focus, nucleus, heart

**middling** *Syn* MEDIUM, mediocre, second-rate, moderate, average, fair, indifferent

**midget** *Syn* DWARF, manikin, pygmy, homunculus, runt

**midst** *Syn* CENTER, middle, core, hub, focus, nucleus, heart

**mien** *Syn* BEARING, demeanor, deportment, port, presence

**might** *Syn* POWER, strength, energy, force, puissance

**migrant** *Syn* EMIGRANT, immigrant

**migrate** ♦ to move from one country, place, or locality to another *Syn* emigrate, immigrate

**mild** *Syn* SOFT, gentle, smooth, lenient, bland, balmy *Ant* harsh; fierce

**milieu** *Syn* BACKGROUND, environment, setting, mise-en-scène, backdrop

**militant** *Syn* AGGRESSIVE, assertive, self-assertive, pushing, pushy

**military** *Syn* MARTIAL, warlike

**mime** *Syn* ACTOR, player, performer, mummer, mimic, thespian, impersonator, trouper

**mimic** *n* *Syn* ACTOR, player, performer, mummer, mime, thespian, impersonator, trouper

**mimic** *vb* *Syn* COPY, imitate, ape, mock

**mind** *n* 1 *Syn* MEMORY, remembrance, recollection, reminiscence, souvenir 2 ♦ the element or complex of elements in an individual that feels, perceives, thinks, wills, and esp. reasons *Syn* intellect, soul, psyche, brain, intelligence, wit

**mind** *vb* 1 *Syn* REMEMBER, recollect, recall, remind, reminisce, bethink 2 *Syn* OBEY, comply 3 *Syn* TEND, attend, watch

**mingle** *Syn* MIX, commingle, blend, merge, coalesce, amalgamate, fuse

**miniature** *Syn* SMALL, minute, diminutive, little, wee, tiny, teeny, weeny

**minimize** *Syn* DECRY, depreciate, belittle, disparage, derogate, detract *Ant* magnify

**minister** *Syn* AMBASSADOR, envoy, legate, nuncio, internuncio, chargé d'affaires

**minority** *Syn* INFANCY, nonage *Ant* majority

**minstrel** *Syn* POET, bard, troubadour, versifier, rhymer, rhymester, poetaster

**minute** *n* *Syn* INSTANT, moment, second, flash, jiffy, twinkling, split second

**minute** *adj* 1 *Syn* SMALL, little, diminutive, miniature, wee, tiny, teeny, weeny 2 *Syn* CIRCUMSTANTIAL, particular, particularized, detailed, itemized

**miracle** *Syn* WONDER, marvel, prodigy, phenomenon

**miraculous** *Syn* SUPERNATURAL, supranatural, preternatural, superhuman

**mirage** *Syn* DELUSION, hallucination, illusion

**mirror** *Syn* MODEL, example, pattern, exemplar, ideal, standard, beau ideal

**mirth** ♦ a mood or temper characterized by joy

and high spirits and usu. manifested in laughter and merrymaking **Syn** glee, jollity, hilarity

**misanthropic** *Syn* CYNICAL, pessimistic **Ant** philanthropic

**miscarriage** *Syn* FAILURE, neglect, default, dereliction

**miscellaneous** ♦ consisting of diverse things or members *Syn* assorted, heterogeneous, motley, promiscuous

**mischance** *Syn* MISFORTUNE, adversity, mishap

**mischief** *Syn* INJURY, hurt, damage, harm

**mischievous** *Syn* PLAYFUL, roguish, waggish, impish, frolicsome, sportive

**miscreant** *Syn* VILLAIN, scoundrel, blackguard, knave, rascal, rogue, scamp, rapscallion

**misdoubt** *Syn* DISTRUST, mistrust, doubt, suspect

**mise-en-scène** *Syn* BACKGROUND, setting, environment, milieu, backdrop

**miserable** ♦ being in a pitiable state of distress or unhappiness (as from want or shame) *Syn* wretched **Ant** comfortable

**miserly** *Syn* STINGY, penurious, parsimonious, niggardly, tight, tightfisted, close, closefisted, cheeseparing, penny-pinching

**misery** *Syn* DISTRESS, suffering, agony, dolor, passion **Ant** felicity, blessedness

**misfortune** ♦ adverse fortune or an instance of this *Syn* mischance, adversity, mishap **Ant** happiness; prosperity

**misgiving** *Syn* APPREHENSION, foreboding, presentiment

**mishap 1** *Syn* MISFORTUNE, mischance, adversity **2** *Syn* ACCIDENT, casualty

**mislay** *Syn* MISPLACE

**mislead** *Syn* DECEIVE, delude, beguile, betray, double-cross

**misleading** ♦ having an appearance or character that leads one astray or into error *Syn* deceptive, delusive, delusory

**misplace** ♦ to put in the wrong place *Syn* mislay

**misrepresent** ♦ to give a false or misleading representation of usu. with an intent to deceive *Syn* falsify, belie, garble

**misrepresentation** *Syn* LIE, falsehood, untruth, fib, story

**missive** *Syn* LETTER, epistle, note, message, dispatch, report, memorandum

**mist** *Syn* HAZE, fog, smog

**mistake** *vb* ♦ to take one thing to be another *Syn* confuse, confound **Ant** recognize

**mistake** *n* *Syn* ERROR, slip, lapse, blunder, faux pas, bull, howler, boner

**mistreat** *Syn* ABUSE, maltreat, ill-treat, misuse, outrage

**mistrust** *n* **1** *Syn* UNCERTAINTY, suspicion, skepticism, doubt, dubiety, dubiosity **Ant** trust; assurance **2** *Syn* DISTRUST

**mistrust** *vb* *Syn* DISTRUST, doubt, suspect, misdoubt

**misuse** *Syn* ABUSE, mistreat, maltreat, ill-treat, outrage **Ant** respect

**mite** *Syn* PARTICLE, bit, smidgen, whit, atom, iota, jot, tittle

**mitigate** *Syn* RELIEVE, allay, alleviate, lighten, assuage **Ant** intensify

**mix** ♦ to combine or be combined into a more or less uniform whole *Syn* mingle, commingle, blend, merge, coalesce, amalgamate, fuse

**mixture** ♦ a product formed by the combination of two or more things *Syn* admixture, blend, compound, composite, amalgam

**moan** *n* *Syn* SIGH, groan, sob

**moan** *vb* *Syn* SIGH, groan, sob

**mob** *Syn* CROWD, throng, press, crush, rout, horde

**mobile** *Syn* MOVABLE, motive **Ant** immobile

**mock 1** *Syn* RIDICULE, taunt, deride, twit, rally **2** *Syn* COPY, imitate, mimic, ape

**mode** *n* **1** *Syn* STATE, condition, situation, posture, status **2** *Syn* METHOD, manner, way, fashion, system

**mode** *n* *Syn* FASHION, style, vogue, fad, rage, craze, dernier cri, cry

**model** ♦ someone or something set before one

for guidance or imitation *Syn* example, pattern, exemplar, ideal, standard, beau ideal, mirror

**moderate** *adj* **1** ♦ not excessive in degree, amount, or intensity *Syn* temperate **Ant** immoderate **2** *Syn* MEDIUM, middling, mediocre, second-rate, average, fair, indifferent

**moderate** *vb* ♦ to modify something so as to avoid an extreme or to keep within bounds *Syn* qualify, temper

**modern 1** ♦ having taken place, existed, or developed in times close to the present *Syn* recent, late **2** *Syn* NEW, modernistic, novel, new-fashioned, newfangled, original, fresh **Ant** antique; ancient

**modernistic** *Syn* NEW, new-fashioned, newfangled, novel, modern, original, fresh **Ant** antiquated

**modest 1** *Syn* HUMBLE, meek, lowly **Ant** ambitious **2** *Syn* SHY, bashful, diffident, coy **3** *Syn* CHASTE, decent, pure **Ant** immodest

**modification** *Syn* CHANGE, alteration, variation

**modify** *Syn* CHANGE, alter, vary

**modish** *Syn* STYLISH, fashionable, smart, chic, dashing **Ant** antiquated

**moist** *Syn* WET, damp, humid, dank

**mollify** *Syn* PACIFY, appease, placate, propitiate, conciliate **Ant** exasperate

**mollycoddle** *Syn* INDULGE, humor, pamper, spoil, baby

**molt** *Syn* DISCARD, cast, shed, slough, scrap, junk

**moment 1** *Syn* INSTANT, minute, second, flash, jiffy, twinkling, split second **2** *Syn* IMPORTANCE, consequence, significance, import, weight

**momentary** *Syn* TRANSIENT, transitory, passing, ephemeral, fugitive, fleeting, evanescent, short-lived **Ant** agelong

**momentum** *Syn* SPEED, impetus, velocity, pace, headway

**monastery** *Syn* CLOISTER, convent, nunnery, abbey, priory

**monetary** *Syn* FINANCIAL, pecuniary, fiscal

**money** ♦ something (as pieces of stamped metal or paper certificates) customarily and legally used as a medium of exchange *Syn* cash, currency, legal tender, specie, coin, coinage

**monk** *Syn* RELIGIOUS, friar, nun

**monkeyshine** *Syn* PRANK, caper, antic, dido

**monograph** *Syn* DISCOURSE, treatise, disquisition, dissertation, thesis

**monopolize** ♦ to take up completely *Syn* engross, absorb, consume

**monopoly** ♦ exclusive possession or control *Syn* corner, pool, syndicate, trust, cartel

**monotonous** *Syn* DULL, dreary, pedestrian, humdrum, stodgy

**monstrous 1** ♦ extremely impressive *Syn* prodigious, tremendous, stupendous, monumental **2** *Syn* OUTRAGEOUS, heinous, atrocious

**monument** *Syn* DOCUMENT, record, archive

**monumental 1** *Syn* MONSTROUS, prodigious, tremendous, stupendous **2** *Syn* MASSIVE, massy, bulky, substantial

**mood** ♦ a state of mind in which an emotion or set of emotions gains ascendancy *Syn* humor, temper, vein

**moor** *Syn* SECURE, anchor, rivet

**moral** ♦ conforming to a standard of what is right and good *Syn* ethical, virtuous, righteous, noble

**morale** ♦ a sense of common purpose or dedication with respect to a group *Syn* discipline, esprit de corps

**morality** *Syn* GOODNESS, virtue, rectitude

**morally** *Syn* VIRTUALLY, practically

**morbid** *Syn* UNWHOLESOME, sickly, diseased, pathological **Ant** sound

**mordant** *Syn* CAUSTIC, acrid, scathing

**moreover** *Syn* ALSO, besides, furthermore, likewise, too

**moron** *Syn* FOOL, imbecile, idiot, simpleton, natural

**morose** *Syn* SULLEN, glum, gloomy, saturnine, dour, surly, sulky, crabbed

**mortal** *Syn* DEADLY, fatal, lethal **Ant** venial (*esp. of a sin*)

**mortified** *Syn* ASHAMED, chagrined

**mostly** *Syn* LARGELY, greatly, chiefly, mainly, principally, generally

**motif 1** *Syn* FIGURE, device, design, pattern **2** *Syn* SUBJECT, matter, subject matter, argument, topic, text, theme, motive, leitmotiv

**motion** ♦ the act or an instance of moving *Syn* movement, move, locomotion, stir

**motivate** *Syn* ACTIVATE, actuate

**motive** *n* **1** ♦ a stimulus to action *Syn* spring, impulse, incentive, inducement, spur, goad **2** *Syn* SUBJECT, matter, subject matter, argument, topic, text, theme, motif, leitmotiv

**motive** *adj* *Syn* MOVABLE, mobile

**motley 1** *Syn* VARIEGATED, parti-colored, checkered, checked, pied, piebald, skewbald, dappled, freaked **2** *Syn* MISCELLANEOUS, heterogeneous, assorted, promiscuous

**motor** *Syn* MACHINE, mechanism, machinery, apparatus, engine

**motorcade** *Syn* PROCESSION, parade, cortege, cavalcade

**mottle** *Syn* SPOT, spatter, sprinkle, fleck, stipple, marble, speckle, spangle, bespangle

**mottled** *Syn* SPOTTED, spattered, sprinkled, flecked, stippled, marbled, speckled, spangled, bespangled

**motto** *Syn* SAYING, proverb, adage, saw, maxim, epigram, aphorism, apothegm

**mount** *n* *Syn* MOUNTAIN, peak, alp, volcano, mesa

**mount** *vb* **1** *Syn* RISE, ascend, soar, arise, tower, rocket, levitate, surge **Ant** drop **2** *Syn* ASCEND, climb, scale **Ant** dismount

**mountain** ♦ a relatively steep and high elevation of land *Syn* mount, peak, alp, volcano, mesa

**mountebank** *Syn* IMPOSTOR, faker, charlatan, quack

**mourn** *Syn* GRIEVE, sorrow

**movable** ♦ capable of moving or of being moved *Syn* mobile, motive **Ant** immovable; stationary

**move** *vb* **1** ♦ to set or keep in motion *Syn* actuate, drive, impel **2** ♦ to change or to cause to change from one place to another *Syn* remove, shift, transfer

**move** *n* *Syn* MOTION, movement, locomotion, stir

**movement** *Syn* MOTION, move, locomotion, stir

**moving** ♦ having the power to produce deep emotion *Syn* impressive, poignant, affecting, touching, pathetic

**muddle** *vb* *Syn* CONFUSE, addle, fuddle, befuddle **Ant** enlighten

**muddle** *n* *Syn* CONFUSION, disorder, chaos, disarray, jumble, clutter, snarl

**muddy** *Syn* TURBID, roily

**muff** *Syn* BOTCH, bungle, fumble, cobble

**mug** *Syn* FACE, countenance, visage, physiognomy, puss

**mulct** *Syn* PENALIZE, fine, amerce

**mulish** *Syn* OBSTINATE, dogged, stubborn, pertinacious, stiff-necked, pigheaded, bullheaded

**multifarious** *Syn* MANY, divers, numerous, various, several, sundry

**multiply** *Syn* INCREASE, augment, enlarge

**multitude** ♦ a very large number of individuals or things *Syn* army, host, legion

**mummer** *Syn* ACTOR, performer, mime, mimic, player, thespian, impersonator, trouper

**mummery** *Syn* GIBBERISH, hocus-pocus, abracadabra

**mundane** *Syn* EARTHLY, worldly, earthy, terrestrial, sublunary **Ant** eternal

**munificent** *Syn* LIBERAL, bountiful, bounteous, openhanded, generous, handsome

**murder** *Syn* KILL, slay, assassinate, dispatch, execute

**murky** *Syn* DARK, obscure, gloomy, dim, dusky

**muscular** ♦ strong and powerful in build or action *Syn* brawny, sinewy, athletic, burly, husky

**muse** *Syn* PONDER, meditate, ruminate

**mushy** *Syn* SENTIMENTAL, romantic, mawkish, maudlin, soppy, slushy

**muster** *Syn* SUMMON, summons, call, cite, convoke, convene

**musty** *Syn* MALODOROUS, fusty, stinking, fetid, noisome, putrid, rank, rancid

**mutable** *Syn* CHANGEABLE, changeful, variable, protean *Ant* immutable

**mutation** *Syn* CHANGE, permutation, vicissitude, alternation

**mute** *Syn* DUMB, speechless, inarticulate

**mutilate 1** *Syn* MAIM, cripple, batter, mangle **2** *Syn* STERILIZE, castrate, spay, emasculate, alter, geld

**mutinous** *Syn* INSUBORDINATE, rebellious, seditious, factious, contumacious

**mutiny** *Syn* REBELLION, revolution, uprising, revolt, insurrection, putsch, coup

**mutual** *Syn* RECIPROCAL, common

**mysterious** ♦ being beyond one's power to discover, understand, or explain *Syn* inscrutable, arcane

**mystery** ♦ something which baffles or perplexes *Syn* problem, enigma, riddle, puzzle, conundrum

**mystic** *Syn* MYSTICAL, anagogic, cabalistic

**mystical** ♦ having a spiritual meaning or reality that is neither apparent to the senses nor obvious to the intelligence *Syn* mystic, anagogic, cabalistic

**mystify** *Syn* PUZZLE, bewilder, perplex, distract, nonplus, confound, dumbfound *Ant* enlighten

**myth 1** ♦ a traditional story of ostensibly historical content whose origin has been lost *Syn* legend, saga **2** *Syn* ALLEGORY, parable, fable

**mythical** *Syn* FICTITIOUS, fabulous, legendary, apocryphal

# N

**naïve** *Syn* NATURAL, unsophisticated, artless, ingenuous, simple

**naked** *Syn* BARE, nude, bald, barren

**name** *n* ♦ the word or combination of words by which something is called and by means of which it can be distinguished or identified *Syn* designation, denomination, appellation, title, style

**name** *vb* **1** *Syn* DESIGNATE, nominate, elect, appoint **2** *Syn* MENTION, instance, specify

**nap** *Syn* SLEEP, catnap, doze, drowse, snooze, slumber

**narcotic** *Syn* ANODYNE, opiate, nepenthe

**narrate** *Syn* RELATE, rehearse, recite, recount, describe, state, report

**narrative** *Syn* STORY, tale, anecdote, yarn

**narrow, narrow-minded** *Syn* ILLIBERAL, intolerant, bigoted, hidebound *Ant* broad, broad-minded

**narrows** *Syn* STRAIT, sound, channel, passage

**nasty** *Syn* DIRTY, filthy, squalid, foul

**national** *Syn* CITIZEN, subject

**native** ♦ belonging to a particular place by birth or origin *Syn* indigenous, endemic, aboriginal, autochthonous *Ant* alien, foreign

**natural** *adj* **1** *Syn* REGULAR, normal, typical *Ant* unnatural; artificial; adventitious **2** ♦ free from pretension or calculation *Syn* simple, ingenuous, naïve, unsophisticated, artless, unaffected

**natural** *n* *Syn* FOOL, idiot, imbecile, moron, simpleton

**nature** *Syn* TYPE, kind, sort, stripe, kidney, ilk, description, character

**naughty** *Syn* BAD, evil, ill, wicked

**nauseate** *Syn* DISGUST, sicken

**nautical** *Syn* MARINE, maritime, naval

**naval** *Syn* MARINE, nautical, maritime

**near** *adj & adv* *Syn* CLOSE, nigh, nearby *Ant* far

**near** *vb* *Syn* APPROACH, approximate

**nearby** *Syn* CLOSE, near, nigh *Ant* far off

**nearly** ♦ very close to *Syn* almost, approximately, well-nigh

**neat** ♦ manifesting care and orderliness *Syn* tidy, trim, trig, snug, shipshape, spick-and-span *Ant* filthy

**neb** *Syn* BILL, beak, nib

**necessary 1** *Syn* NEEDFUL, requisite, indispensable, essential **2** *Syn* CERTAIN, inevitable

**necessitous** *Syn* POOR, indigent, needy, destitute, penniless, impecunious, poverty-stricken

**necessity** *Syn* NEED, exigency

**need** *n* ♦ a pressing lack of something essential *Syn* necessity, exigency

**need** *vb* *Syn* LACK, want, require

**needful** ♦ required for supply or relief *Syn* necessary, requisite, indispensable, essential

**needy** *Syn* POOR, indigent, destitute, penniless, impecunious, poverty-stricken, necessitous

**nefarious** *Syn* VICIOUS, iniquitous, flagitious, infamous, corrupt, degenerate, villainous

**negate** *Syn* NULLIFY, annul, abrogate, invalidate

**negative 1** *Syn* DENY, gainsay, traverse, contradict, impugn, contravene **2** *Syn* NEUTRALIZE, counteract

**neglect** *vb* ♦ to pass over without giving due attention *Syn* omit, disregard, ignore, overlook, slight, forget *Ant* cherish

**neglect** *n* **1** *Syn* FAILURE, default, miscarriage, dereliction **2** *Syn* NEGLIGENCE

**neglectful** *Syn* NEGLIGENT, lax, slack, remiss *Ant* attentive

**negligence** ♦ a failure to exercise proper or due care *Syn* neglect *Ant* attention; solicitude

**negligent** ♦ culpably careless or indicative of such carelessness *Syn* neglectful, lax, slack, remiss

**negotiate 1** *Syn* CONFER, parley, treat, commune, consult, advise **2** ♦ to bring about by mutual agreement *Syn* arrange, concert

**neighborhood** *Syn* LOCALITY, district, vicinity

**neighborly** *Syn* AMICABLE, friendly *Ant* unneighborly; ill-disposed

**neophyte** *Syn* NOVICE, novitiate, probationer, postulant, apprentice

**nepenthe** *Syn* ANODYNE, opiate, narcotic

**nerve** *n* *Syn* TEMERITY, effrontery, audacity, hardihood, cheek, gall

**nerve** *vb* *Syn* ENCOURAGE, inspirit, hearten, embolden, cheer, steel *Ant* unnerve

**nervous 1** *Syn* VIGOROUS, lusty, energetic, strenuous **2** *Syn* IMPATIENT, restless, restive, unquiet, uneasy, fidgety, jumpy, jittery *Ant* steady

**nettle** *Syn* IRRITATE, provoke, exasperate, aggravate, rile, peeve

**network** *Syn* SYSTEM, scheme, complex, organism

**neutral** ♦ lacking decisiveness or distinctiveness in character, quality, action, or effect *Syn* indifferent

**neutralize** ♦ to make inoperative or ineffective usu. by means of an opposite force, influence, or effect *Syn* counteract, negative

**new** ♦ having recently come into existence or use *Syn* novel, new-fashioned, newfangled, modern, modernistic, original, fresh *Ant* old

**newfangled** *Syn* NEW, novel, new-fashioned, modernistic, modern, original, fresh

**new-fashioned** *Syn* NEW, novel, newfangled, modernistic, modern, original, fresh

**news** ♦ a report of events or conditions not previously known *Syn* tidings, intelligence, advice

**newspaper** *Syn* JOURNAL, periodical, magazine, review, organ

**nib** *Syn* BILL, beak, neb

**nice 1** ♦ having or displaying exacting standards *Syn* dainty, fastidious, finicky, finicking, finical, particular, fussy, squeamish, persnickety, pernickety **2** *Syn* CORRECT, precise, exact, accurate, right **3** *Syn* DECOROUS, proper, seemly, decent

**niggardly** *Syn* STINGY, parsimonious, penurious, miserly, close, closefisted, tight, tightfisted, cheeseparing, penny-pinching *Ant* bountiful

**nigh** *Syn* CLOSE, near, nearby *Ant* far

**night** *Syn* NIGHTLY, nocturnal

**nightly** ♦ of, relating to, or associated with the night *Syn* nocturnal, night *Ant* daily

**nightmare** *Syn* FANCY, dream, vision, fantasy, phantasy, phantasm, daydream

**nimble** *Syn* AGILE, brisk, spry

**nip** *vb* *Syn* BLAST, blight

**nip** *n* *Syn* BLAST, blight

**nobility** *Syn* ARISTOCRACY, gentry, county, elite, society

**noble 1** *Syn* GRAND, stately, majestic, imposing, august, magnificent, grandiose *Ant* ignoble; cheap **2** *Syn* MORAL, virtuous, righteous, ethical *Ant* base (*of actions*); atrocious (*of acts, deeds*)

**nocturnal** *Syn* NIGHTLY *Ant* diurnal

**noise** *Syn* SOUND

**noiseless** *Syn* STILL, silent, quiet, stilly

**noisome** *Syn* MALODOROUS, fetid, stinking, putrid, rank, rancid, fusty, musty *Ant* balmy

**nomadic** *Syn* ITINERANT, peripatetic, ambulatory, ambulant, vagrant

**nom de guerre, nom de plume** *Syn* PSEUDONYM, alias, pen name, incognito

**nominate** *Syn* DESIGNATE, name, elect, appoint

**nominee** *Syn* CANDIDATE, aspirant, applicant

**nonage** *Syn* INFANCY, minority *Ant* age

**nonchalant** *Syn* COOL, unruffled, imperturbable, unflappable, composed, collected

**non compos mentis** *Syn* INSANE, mad, crazy, crazed, demented, deranged, lunatic, maniac

**nonconformist** *Syn* HERETIC, dissenter, sectary, sectarian, schismatic

**nonesuch** *Syn* PARAGON, apotheosis, nonpareil

**nonpareil** *Syn* PARAGON, apotheosis, nonesuch

**nonplus** *Syn* PUZZLE, bewilder, distract, confound, dumbfound, mystify, perplex

**nonreligious** *Syn* IRRELIGIOUS, unreligious, ungodly, godless

**nonsense** ♦ something said or proposed that seems senseless or absurd *Syn* twaddle, drivel, bunk, balderdash, poppycock, gobbledygook, trash, rot, bull

**nonsocial** *Syn* UNSOCIAL, asocial, antisocial

**norm** *Syn* AVERAGE, mean, median, par

**normal** *Syn* REGULAR, typical, natural *Ant* abnormal

**nosy** *Syn* CURIOUS, inquisitive, prying, snoopy

**notable** *Syn* NOTEWORTHY, memorable

**note** *vb* *Syn* SEE, remark, notice, perceive, discern, observe, contemplate, survey, view, behold, descry, espy

**note** *n* **1** *Syn* SIGN, mark, token, badge, symptom **2** *Syn* REMARK, observation, comment, commentary, obiter dictum **3** *Syn* LETTER, epistle, missive, message, dispatch, report, memorandum

**noteworthy** ♦ having some quality that attracts one's attention *Syn* notable, memorable

**notice** *Syn* SEE, remark, observe, note, perceive, discern, behold, descry, espy, view, survey, contemplate

**noticeable** ♦ attracting notice or attention *Syn* remarkable, prominent, outstanding, conspicuous, salient, signal, striking, arresting

**notify** *Syn* INFORM, apprise, advise, acquaint

**notion** *Syn* IDEA, concept, conception, thought, impression

**notoriety** *Syn* FAME, reputation, repute, éclat, celebrity, renown, honor, glory

**notwithstanding** ♦ without being prevented or obstructed by *Syn* in spite of, despite

**nourish** *Syn* FEED, pasture, graze

**nourishment** *Syn* FOOD, nutriment, sustenance, aliment, pabulum, pap

**novel** *Syn* NEW, new-fashioned, newfangled, modern, modernistic, original, fresh

**novice** ♦ one who is just entering a field in which he or she has no previous experience *Syn* novitiate, apprentice, probationer, postulant, neophyte

**novitiate** *Syn* NOVICE, apprentice, probationer, postulant, neophyte

**noxious** *Syn* PERNICIOUS, baneful, deleterious, detrimental *Ant* wholesome, sanitary

**nuance** *Syn* GRADATION, shade

**nucleus** *Syn* CENTER, middle, midst, core, hub, focus, heart

**nude** *Syn* BARE, naked, bald, barren *Ant* clothed

**nudge** *vb Syn* POKE, prod, jog

**nudge** *n Syn* POKE, prod, jog

**nugatory** *Syn* VAIN, otiose, idle, empty, hollow

**nullify** ♦ to deprive of effective or continued existence *Syn* negate, annul, abrogate, invalidate

**number** *n* 1 *Syn* SUM, quantity, whole, total, aggregate, amount 2 ♦ a character by which an arithmetical value is designated *Syn* numeral, figure, digit, integer

**number** *vb Syn* COUNT, tell, enumerate

**numeral** *Syn* NUMBER, figure, digit, integer

**numerous** *Syn* MANY, several, sundry, various, divers, multifarious

**nun** *Syn* RELIGIOUS, monk, friar

**nuncio** *Syn* AMBASSADOR, legate, internuncio, chargé d'affaires, minister, envoy

**nunnery** *Syn* CLOISTER, monastery, convent, abbey, priory

**nuptial** *adj Syn* MATRIMONIAL, conjugal, connubial, hymeneal, marital

**nuptial** *n Syn* MARRIAGE, matrimony, wedlock, wedding, espousal

**nurse** ♦ to promote the growth, development, or progress of *Syn* nurture, foster, cherish, cultivate

**nurture** *Syn* NURSE, foster, cherish, cultivate

**nutriment** *Syn* FOOD, nourishment, sustenance, aliment, pabulum, pap

# O

**obdurate** *Syn* INFLEXIBLE, inexorable, adamant, adamantine

**obedient** ♦ submissive to the will of another *Syn* docile, tractable, amenable, biddable *Ant* disobedient; contumacious

**obeisance** *Syn* HONOR, deference, homage, reverence

**obese** *Syn* FLESHY, corpulent, rotund, chubby, fat, stout, portly, plump *Ant* scrawny

**obey** ♦ to follow the wish, direction, or command of another *Syn* comply, mind *Ant* command, order

**obfuscate** *Syn* OBSCURE, dim, bedim, darken, eclipse, cloud, becloud, fog, befog

**obiter dictum** *Syn* REMARK, observation, comment, commentary, note

**object** *n* 1 *Syn* THING, article 2 *Syn* INTENTION, objective, goal, end, aim, design, purpose, intent

**object** *vb* ♦ to oppose by arguing against *Syn* protest, remonstrate, expostulate, kick *Ant* acquiesce

**objectify** *Syn* REALIZE, externalize, materialize, incarnate, embody, actualize, hypostatize, reify

**objectionable** ♦ arousing or likely to arouse objection *Syn* exceptionable, unacceptable, undesirable, unwanted, unwelcome

**objective** *adj* 1 *Syn* MATERIAL, physical, corporeal, phenomenal, sensible *Ant* subjective 2 *Syn* FAIR, impartial, unbiased, dispassionate, uncolored, just, equitable

**objective** *n Syn* INTENTION, object, end, goal, aim, design, purpose, intent

**objurgate** *Syn* EXECRATE, curse, damn, anathematize

**obligation** 1 ♦ something one is bound to do or forbear *Syn* duty 2 *Syn* DEBT, indebtedness, liability, debit, arrear

**oblige** 1 *Syn* FORCE, constrain, coerce, compel 2 ♦ to do a service or courtesy *Syn* accommodate, favor *Ant* disoblige

**obliging** *Syn* AMIABLE, good-natured, complaisant *Ant* disobliging; inconsiderate

**oblique** *Syn* CROOKED, devious

**obliterate** *Syn* ERASE, efface, cancel, expunge, blot out, delete

**oblivious** *Syn* FORGETFUL, unmindful

**obloquy** 1 *Syn* ABUSE, vituperation, invective, scurrility, billingsgate 2 *Syn* DISGRACE, dishonor, disrepute, shame, infamy, ignominy, opprobrium, odium

**obnoxious** *Syn* REPUGNANT, distasteful, invidious, abhorrent, repellent *Ant* grateful

**obscene** *Syn* COARSE, gross, vulgar, ribald *Ant* decent

**obscure** *adj* 1 *Syn* DARK, murky, gloomy, dim, dusky 2 ♦ not clearly understandable *Syn* dark, vague, enigmatic, cryptic, ambiguous, equivocal *Ant* distinct, obvious

**obscure** *vb* ♦ to make dark, dim, or indistinct *Syn* dim, bedim, darken, eclipse, cloud, becloud, fog, befog, obfuscate *Ant* illuminate, illumine

**obsequious** *Syn* SUBSERVIENT, servile, slavish, menial *Ant* contumelious

**observation** *Syn* REMARK, comment, commentary, note, obiter dictum

**observe** 1 *Syn* KEEP, celebrate, solemnize, commemorate *Ant* violate 2 *Syn* SEE, survey, view, contemplate, notice, remark, note, perceive, discern, behold, descry, espy

**observer** *Syn* SPECTATOR, beholder, looker-on, onlooker, witness, eyewitness, bystander, kibitzer

**obsolete** *Syn* OLD, antiquated, archaic, antique, ancient, venerable, antediluvian *Ant* current

**obstacle** ♦ something that seriously hampers action or progress *Syn* obstruction, impediment, bar, snag

**obstinate** ♦ fixed and unyielding in course or purpose *Syn* dogged, stubborn, pertinacious, mulish, stiff-necked, pigheaded, bullheaded *Ant* pliant, pliable

**obstreperous** *Syn* VOCIFEROUS, clamorous, blatant, strident, boisterous

**obstruct** *Syn* HINDER, impede, block, bar, dam

**obstruction** *Syn* OBSTACLE, impediment, bar, snag *Ant* assistance

**obtain** *Syn* GET, procure, secure, acquire, gain, win

**obtrude** *Syn* INTRUDE, interlope, butt in

**obtrusive** *Syn* IMPERTINENT, intrusive, meddlesome, officious *Ant* unobtrusive; shy

**obtuse** *Syn* DULL, blunt *Ant* acute

**obviate** *Syn* PREVENT, preclude, avert, ward

**obvious** *Syn* EVIDENT, manifest, patent, distinct, apparent, palpable, plain, clear *Ant* obscure; abstruse

**occasion** 1 *Syn* OPPORTUNITY, chance, break, time 2 *Syn* CAUSE, determinant, antecedent, reason

**occasional** *Syn* INFREQUENT, uncommon, scarce, rare, sporadic *Ant* customary

**occult** *Syn* RECONDITE, esoteric, abstruse

**occupation** *Syn* WORK, employment, calling, pursuit, business

**occur** *Syn* HAPPEN, chance, befall, betide, transpire

**occurrence** ♦ something that happens or takes place *Syn* event, incident, episode, circumstance

**odd** *Syn* STRANGE, queer, quaint, singular, unique, peculiar, eccentric, erratic, outlandish, curious

**odds** *Syn* ADVANTAGE, handicap, allowance, edge

**odious** *Syn* HATEFUL, abhorrent, abominable, detestable

**odium** *Syn* DISGRACE, obloquy, opprobrium, ignominy, infamy, dishonor, disrepute, shame

**odor** *Syn* SMELL, scent, aroma

**odorous** ♦ emitting and diffusing scent *Syn* fragrant, redolent, aromatic, balmy *Ant* malodorous; odorless

**offal** *Syn* REFUSE, waste, rubbish, trash, debris, garbage

**offend** ♦ to cause hurt feelings or deep resentment *Syn* outrage, affront, insult

**offense** 1 *Syn* ATTACK, offensive, aggression 2 ♦ an emotional response to a slight or indignity *Syn* resentment, umbrage, pique, dudgeon, huff 3 ♦ a transgression of law *Syn* sin, vice, crime, scandal

**offensive** *adj* 1 *Syn* ATTACKING, aggressive 2 ♦ utterly distasteful or unpleasant to the senses or sensibilities *Syn* loathsome, repulsive, repugnant, revolting

**offensive** *n Syn* ATTACK, aggression, offense

**offer** ♦ to put something before another for acceptance or consideration *Syn* proffer, tender, present, prefer

**offhand** *Syn* EXTEMPORANEOUS, extempore, extemporary, improvised, impromptu, unpremeditated

**office** *Syn* FUNCTION, duty, province

**officious** *Syn* IMPERTINENT, meddlesome, intrusive, obtrusive

**offset** *Syn* COMPENSATE, countervail, balance, counterbalance, counterpoise

**offspring** ♦ those who follow in direct parental line *Syn* young, progeny, issue, descendants, posterity

**oft** *Syn* OFTEN, frequently, oftentimes

**often** ♦ many times *Syn* frequently, oft, oftentimes

**oftentimes** *Syn* OFTEN, frequently, oft

**oil** ♦ to smear, rub over, or lubricate with oil or an oily substance *Syn* grease, lubricate, anoint, cream

**oily** *Syn* FULSOME, unctuous, oleaginous, slick, soapy

**old** 1 *Syn* AGED, elderly, superannuated *Ant* young 2 ♦ having come into existence or use in the more or less distant past *Syn* ancient, venerable, antique, antiquated, antediluvian, archaic, obsolete *Ant* new

**oleaginous** *Syn* FULSOME, oily, unctuous, slick, soapy

**oligarchy** ♦ government by, or a state governed by, the few *Syn* aristocracy, plutocracy

**omen** *Syn* FORETOKEN, augury, portent, presage, prognostic

**ominous** ♦ having a menacing or threatening aspect *Syn* portentous, fateful, inauspicious, unpropitious

**omit** *Syn* NEGLECT, disregard, ignore, overlook, slight, forget

**omnipresent** ♦ present at all places at all times *Syn* ubiquitous

**onerous** ♦ imposing great hardship or strain *Syn* burdensome, oppressive, exacting

**onlooker** *Syn* SPECTATOR, looker-on, observer, beholder, witness, eyewitness, bystander, kibitzer

**only** ♦ being one or more of which there are no others *Syn* alone

**onset** *Syn* ATTACK, assault, onslaught

**onslaught** *Syn* ATTACK, assault, onset

**onward** ♦ toward or at a point lying ahead in space or time *Syn* forward, forth

**opalescent, opaline** *Syn* PRISMATIC, iridescent

**open** 1 *Syn* LIABLE, exposed, subject, prone, susceptible, sensitive *Ant* closed 2 *Syn* FRANK, plain, candid *Ant* close, closemouthed, close-lipped; clandestine

**openhanded** *Syn* LIBERAL, bountiful, bounteous, generous, munificent, handsome *Ant* closefisted, tightfisted

**operate** *Syn* ACT, behave, work, function, react

**operative** *adj Syn* ACTIVE, dynamic, live *Ant* abeyant

**operative** *n Syn* WORKER, mechanic, artisan, hand, workman, workingman, laborer, craftsman, handicraftsman, roustabout

**opiate** *Syn* ANODYNE, narcotic, nepenthe

**opinion** ♦ a judgment one holds as true *Syn* view, belief, conviction, persuasion, sentiment

**opponent** ♦ one who expresses or manifests opposition *Syn* antagonist, adversary

**opportune** *Syn* SEASONABLE, timely, well-timed, pat *Ant* inopportune

**opportunity** ♦ a state of affairs or a combination of circumstances favorable to some end *Syn* occasion, chance, break, time

**oppose** *Syn* RESIST, contest, fight, combat, conflict, antagonize, withstand

**opposite** *n* ♦ something that is exactly opposed or contrary *Syn* contradictory, contrary, antithesis, antipode, antonym, converse, counter, reverse

**opposite** *adj* ♦ so far apart as to be or to seem irreconcilable *Syn* contradictory, contrary, antithetical, antipodal, antipodean, antonymous

**oppress** 1 *Syn* DEPRESS, weigh 2 *Syn* WRONG, persecute, aggrieve

**oppressive** *Syn* ONEROUS, burdensome, exacting

**opprobrious** *Syn* ABUSIVE, vituperative, contumelious, scurrilous

**opprobrium** *Syn* DISGRACE, obloquy, odium, ignominy, infamy, shame, dishonor, disrepute

**opt** *Syn* CHOOSE, select, elect, pick, cull, prefer, single

**optimistic** *Syn* HOPEFUL, roseate, rose-colored *Ant* pessimistic

**option** *Syn* CHOICE, alternative, preference, selection, election

**opulent** 1 *Syn* RICH, affluent, wealthy *Ant* destitute; indigent 2 *Syn* LUXURIOUS, sumptuous

**opus** *Syn* WORK, product, production, artifact

**oracular** *Syn* DICTATORIAL, doctrinaire, dogmatic, authoritarian, magisterial

**oral** *Syn* VOCAL, articulate *Ant* written

**oration** *Syn* SPEECH, address, harangue, lecture, talk, sermon, homily

**orbit** *Syn* RANGE, gamut, reach, radius, compass, sweep, scope, horizon, ken, purview

**ordain** *Syn* DICTATE, prescribe, decree, impose

**order** *n* 1 *Syn* ASSOCIATION, society, club 2 *Syn* COMMAND, injunction, bidding, behest, mandate, dictate

**order** *vb* 1 ♦ to put persons or things into their proper places in relation to each other *Syn* arrange, marshal, organize, systematize, methodize 2 *Syn* COMMAND, bid, enjoin, direct, instruct, charge

**orderly** ♦ following a set arrangement, design, or pattern *Syn* methodical, systematic, regular *Ant* disorderly; chaotic

**ordinance** *Syn* LAW, canon, precept, rule, regulation, statute

**ordinary** *Syn* COMMON, familiar, popular, vulgar *Ant* extraordinary

**organ** 1 *Syn* MEAN, medium, vehicle, channel, instrument, instrumentality, agent, agency 2 *Syn* JOURNAL, periodical, newspaper, magazine, review

**organism** *Syn* SYSTEM, scheme, network, complex

**organize** 1 *Syn* ORDER, systematize, methodize, arrange, marshal *Ant* disorganize 2 *Syn* FOUND, institute, establish, create

**oriel** *Syn* WINDOW, casement, dormer

**orifice** *Syn* APERTURE, interstice

**origin** ♦ the point at which something begins its course or its existence *Syn* source, inception, root, provenance, provenience, prime mover

**original** 1 *Syn* INITIAL, primordial 2 *Syn* NEW, fresh, novel, new-fashioned, newfangled, modern, modernistic *Ant* dependent; banal; trite

**originate** *Syn* SPRING, rise, derive, arise, flow, issue, emanate, proceed, stem

**ornament** *Syn* ADORN, decorate, embellish, beautify, deck, bedeck, garnish

**ornate** ♦ elaborately and often pretentiously decorated or designed *Syn* rococo, baroque, flamboyant, florid *Ant* chaste; austere

**orotund** *Syn* RESONANT, sonorous, ringing, resounding, vibrant

**oscillate** *Syn* SWING, sway, vibrate, fluctuate, pendulate, waver, undulate

**ostensible** *Syn* APPARENT, seeming, illusory

**ostentatious** *Syn* SHOWY, pretentious

**ostracize** *Syn* BANISH, exile, expatriate, deport, transport, extradite

**otiose** *Syn* VAIN, nugatory, idle, empty, hollow

**oust** *Syn* EJECT, expel, evict, dismiss

**out-and-out** *Syn* OUTRIGHT, unmitigated, arrant

**outcast** ♦ one that is cast out or refused acceptance by society *Syn* castaway, derelict, reprobate, pariah, untouchable

**outcome** *Syn* EFFECT, result, consequence, upshot, aftereffect, aftermath, sequel, issue, event

**outdo** *Syn* EXCEED, excel, outstrip, transcend, surpass

**outer** ♦ being or located outside something *Syn* outward, outside, external, exterior *Ant* inner

**outfit** *n Syn* EQUIPMENT, apparatus, paraphernalia, tackle, machinery, gear, matériel

**outfit** *vb Syn* FURNISH, equip, appoint, accouter, arm

**outlander** *Syn* STRANGER, foreigner, alien, outsider, immigrant, émigré

**outlandish** *Syn* STRANGE, singular, unique, peculiar, eccentric, erratic, odd, queer, quaint, curious

**outlast** *Syn* OUTLIVE, survive

**outline** *n* 1 ♦ the line that bounds and gives form to something *Syn* contour, profile, skyline, silhouette 2 *Syn* SKETCH, diagram, delineation, draft, tracing, plot, blueprint

**outline** *vb Syn* SKETCH, diagram, delineate, draft, trace, plot, blueprint

**outlive** ♦ to remain in existence longer than *Syn* outlast, survive

**outlook** *Syn* PROSPECT, anticipation, foretaste

**outrage** 1 *Syn* ABUSE, misuse, mistreat, maltreat, ill-treat 2 *Syn* OFFEND, affront, insult

**outrageous** ♦ enormously or flagrantly bad or horrible *Syn* monstrous, heinous, atrocious

**outright** ♦ being exactly what is stated *Syn* out-and-out, unmitigated, arrant

**outside** *Syn* OUTER, outward, external, exterior *Ant* inside

**outsider** *Syn* STRANGER, foreigner, alien, outlander, immigrant, émigré

**outstanding** *Syn* NOTICEABLE, prominent, conspicuous, salient, signal, striking, arresting, remarkable *Ant* commonplace

**outstrip** *Syn* EXCEED, outdo, surpass, transcend, excel

**outward** *Syn* OUTER, outside, external, exterior *Ant* inward

**outwit** *Syn* FRUSTRATE, thwart, foil, baffle, balk, circumvent

**over** *Syn* ABOVE *Ant* beneath

**overbearing** *Syn* PROUD, supercilious, disdainful, lordly, arrogant, haughty, insolent *Ant* subservient

**overcome** *Syn* CONQUER, surmount, overthrow, subjugate, rout, vanquish, defeat, beat, lick, subdue

**overdue** *Syn* TARDY, behindhand, late

**overflow** *Syn* TEEM, swarm, abound

**overhang** *Syn* BULGE, jut, stick out, protrude, project, beetle

**overlay** ♦ to lay or spread over or across *Syn* superpose, superimpose, appliqué

**overlook** *Syn* NEGLECT, slight, forget, ignore, disregard, omit

**overplus** *Syn* EXCESS, superfluity, surplus, surplusage

**overreach** *Syn* CHEAT, cozen, defraud, swindle

**overrun** *Syn* INFEST, beset

**oversight** ♦ the function or duty of watching or guarding for the sake of proper control or direction *Syn* supervision, surveillance

**overspread** *Syn* COVER, envelop, wrap, shroud, veil

**overstatement** *Syn* EXAGGERATION, hyperbole *Ant* understatement

**overthrow** 1 *Syn* OVERTURN, subvert, upset, capsize 2 *Syn* CONQUER, rout, surmount, overcome, vanquish, defeat, beat, lick, subdue, subjugate, reduce

**overture** ♦ an action taken to win the favor or approval of another person or party *Syn* approach, advance, tender, bid

**overturn** ♦ to turn from an upright or proper position *Syn* upset, capsize, overthrow, subvert

**own** 1 *Syn* HAVE, possess, hold, enjoy 2 *Syn* ACKNOWLEDGE, avow, admit, confess *Ant* disown; repudiate

# P

**pabulum** *Syn* FOOD, aliment, nutriment, nourishment, sustenance, pap

**pace** *Syn* SPEED, velocity, momentum, impetus, headway

**pacific** ♦ affording or promoting peace *Syn* peaceable, peaceful, irenic, pacifist, pacifistic *Ant* bellicose

**pacifist, pacifistic** *Syn* PACIFIC, peaceable, peaceful, irenic

**pacify** ♦ to ease the anger or disturbance of *Syn* appease, placate, mollify, propitiate, conciliate *Ant* anger

**pack** *n Syn* BUNDLE, bunch, package, packet, bale, parcel

**pack** *vb* ♦ to fill a limited space with more than is practicable or fitting *Syn* crowd, cram, stuff, ram, tamp

**package** *Syn* BUNDLE, packet, bunch, bale, parcel, pack

**packet** *Syn* BUNDLE, package, pack, bunch, bale, parcel

**pact** *Syn* CONTRACT, compact, bargain, treaty, entente, convention, cartel, concordat

**pain** 1 ♦ a bodily sensation that causes acute discomfort or suffering *Syn* ache, pang, throe, twinge, stitch 2 *pl* **pains** *Syn* EFFORT, exertion, trouble

**pair** *Syn* COUPLE, brace, yoke

**palatable** ♦ agreeable or pleasant to the taste *Syn* appetizing, savory, sapid, tasty, toothsome, flavorsome, relishing *Ant* unpalatable; distasteful

**palate** *Syn* TASTE, relish, gusto, zest

**pale** 1 ♦ deficient in color or in intensity of color *Syn* pallid, ashen, ashy, wan, livid 2 ♦ being weak and thin in substance or in vital qualities *Syn* anemic, bloodless

**pall** *Syn* SATIATE, cloy, surfeit, sate, glut, gorge

**palliate** ♦ to give a speciously fine appearance to what is base, evil, or erroneous *Syn* extenuate, gloze, gloss, whitewash, whiten

**pallid** *Syn* PALE, ashen, ashy, wan, livid

**palpable** 1 *Syn* PERCEPTIBLE, sensible, tangible,

appreciable, ponderable *Ant* insensible **2** *Syn* EVIDENT, plain, clear, apparent, manifest, patent, obvious, distinct *Ant* impalpable

**palpate** *Syn* TOUCH, feel, handle, paw

**palpitate** *Syn* PULSATE, beat, throb, pulse

**palpitation** *Syn* PULSATION, beat, throb, pulse

**palter** *Syn* LIE, prevaricate, equivocate, fib

**paltry** *Syn* PETTY, trifling, trivial, puny, measly, picayunish, picayune

**pamper** *Syn* INDULGE, humor, spoil, baby, mollycoddle *Ant* chasten

**pandect** *Syn* COMPENDIUM, syllabus, digest, survey, sketch, précis, aperçu

**pandemonium** *Syn* DIN, uproar, hullabaloo, babel, hubbub, clamor, racket

**pander** *Syn* CATER, purvey

**panegyric** *Syn* ENCOMIUM, tribute, eulogy, citation

**pang** *Syn* PAIN, ache, throe, twinge, stitch

**panic** *Syn* FEAR, terror, horror, trepidation, consternation, dismay, alarm, fright, dread

**pant** *Syn* AIM, aspire

**pap** *Syn* FOOD, aliment, pabulum, nutriment, nourishment, sustenance

**paper 1** ♦ a written or printed statement that is of value as a source of information or proof of a right, contention, or claim *Syn* instrument, document **2** *Syn* ESSAY, article, theme, composition

**par** *n Syn* AVERAGE, norm, mean, median

**par** *adj Syn* AVERAGE, mean, median

**parable** *Syn* ALLEGORY, myth, fable

**parade** *n* **1** *Syn* DISPLAY, array, pomp **2** *Syn* PROCESSION, cavalcade, cortege, motorcade

**parade** *vb Syn* SHOW, flaunt, expose, display, exhibit

**paradox** ♦ an expression or revelation of an inner or inherent contradiction *Syn* antinomy, anomaly

**paragon** ♦ a model of excellence or perfection *Syn* apotheosis, nonpareil, nonesuch

**paragraph** ♦ one of the several and individually distinct statements of a discourse or instrument, each of which deals with a particular point or item *Syn* verse, article, clause, plank, count

**parallel** *adj Syn* LIKE, alike, similar, analogous, comparable, akin, uniform, identical

**parallel** *n* **1** *Syn* COMPARISON, contrast, antithesis, collation **2** ♦ one that corresponds to or closely resembles another *Syn* counterpart, analogue, correlate

**paralyze** *Syn* DAZE, stun, bemuse, stupefy, benumb, petrify

**paramount** *Syn* DOMINANT, preponderant, preponderating, predominant, sovereign

**parapet** *Syn* BULWARK, rampart, breastwork, bastion

**paraphernalia** *Syn* EQUIPMENT, apparatus, machinery, outfit, tackle, gear, matériel

**paraphrase** *Syn* TRANSLATION, metaphrase, version

**parasite** ♦ a usu. obsequious flatterer or self-seeker *Syn* sycophant, favorite, toady, lickspittle, bootlicker, hanger-on, leech, sponge, sponger

**parboil** *Syn* BOIL, seethe, simmer, stew

**parcel** *n* **1** *Syn* PART, portion, piece, detail, member, division, section, segment, sector, fraction, fragment **2** *Syn* BUNDLE, bunch, pack, package, packet, bale **3** *Syn* GROUP, cluster, bunch, lot

**parcel** *vb Syn* APPORTION, portion, ration, prorate

**parch** *Syn* DRY, desiccate, dehydrate, bake

**pardon** *n* ♦ a remission of penalty or punishment *Syn* amnesty, absolution

**pardon** *vb Syn* EXCUSE, forgive, remit, condone *Ant* punish

**pardonable** *Syn* VENIAL

**pare** *Syn* SKIN, peel, decorticate, flay

**pariah** *Syn* OUTCAST, castaway, derelict, reprobate, untouchable

**parley** *Syn* CONFER, treat, negotiate, commune, consult, advise

**parochial** *Syn* INSULAR, provincial, local, small-town *Ant* catholic

**parody** *n Syn* CARICATURE, travesty, burlesque

**parody** *vb Syn* CARICATURE, travesty, burlesque

**paroxysm** *Syn* FIT, spasm, convulsion, attack, access, accession

**parry** *Syn* DODGE, shirk, sidestep, duck, fence, malinger

**parsimonious** *Syn* STINGY, niggardly, penurious, close, closefisted, tight, tightfisted, miserly, cheeseparing, penny-pinching *Ant* prodigal

**part** *n* ♦ something less than the whole *Syn* portion, piece, detail, member, division, section, segment, sector, fraction, fragment, parcel *Ant* whole

**part** *vb Syn* SEPARATE, divide, sever, sunder, divorce

**partake** *Syn* SHARE, participate

**partiality** *Syn* PREDILECTION, prepossession, prejudice, bias *Ant* impartiality

**participate** *Syn* SHARE, partake

**particle** ♦ a tiny or insignificant amount, part, or piece *Syn* bit, mite, smidgen, whit, atom, iota, jot, tittle

**parti-colored** *Syn* VARIEGATED, motley, checkered, checked, pied, piebald, skewbald, dappled, freaked

**particular** *adj* **1** *Syn* SINGLE, sole, separate, unique, lone, solitary *Ant* general **2** *Syn* SPECIAL, individual, specific, especial *Ant* general, universal **3** *Syn* CIRCUMSTANTIAL, particularized, detailed, itemized, minute **4** *Syn* NICE, fussy, squeamish, dainty, fastidious, finicky, finicking, finical, persnickety, pernickety

**particular** *n Syn* ITEM, detail *Ant* universal; whole; aggregate

**particularized** *Syn* CIRCUMSTANTIAL, particular, detailed, itemized, minute *Ant* generalized

**partisan** *Syn* FOLLOWER, adherent, disciple, sectary, henchman, satellite

**partner** ♦ one associated in action with another *Syn* copartner, colleague, ally, confederate *Ant* rival

**party 1** *Syn* COMPANY, band, troop, troupe **2** *Syn* COMBINATION, combine, bloc, faction, ring

**pasquinade** *Syn* LIBEL, lampoon, squib, skit

**pass** *vb* ♦ move or come to a termination or end *Syn* pass away, elapse, expire

**pass** *n Syn* WAY, passage, route, course, artery

**pass** *n Syn* JUNCTURE, exigency, emergency, contingency, pinch, strait, crisis

**passage 1** *Syn* WAY, pass, route, course, artery **2** ♦ a typically long narrow way connecting parts of a building *Syn* passageway, corridor, hall, hallway, gallery, arcade, cloister, aisle, ambulatory **3** *Syn* STRAIT, sound, channel, narrows

**passageway** *Syn* PASSAGE, corridor, hall, hallway, gallery, arcade, cloister, aisle, ambulatory

**pass away** *Syn* PASS, elapse, expire

**passing** *n Syn* DEATH, decease, demise

**passing** *adj Syn* TRANSIENT, transitory, ephemeral, momentary, fugitive, fleeting, evanescent, short-lived

**passion 1** *Syn* DISTRESS, suffering, agony, dolor, misery **2** *Syn* FEELING, emotion, affection, sentiment **3** *Syn* DESIRE, lust, appetite, urge **4** ♦ intense emotion compelling action *Syn* fervor, ardor, enthusiasm, zeal

**passionate** *Syn* IMPASSIONED, ardent, fervent, fervid, perfervid

**passive** *Syn* INACTIVE, inert, idle, supine *Ant* active

**pastoral** *Syn* RURAL, rustic, bucolic

**pasture** *Syn* FEED, graze, nourish

**pat** *Syn* SEASONABLE, timely, well-timed, opportune

**patch** *Syn* MEND, repair, rebuild

**patent** *Syn* EVIDENT, manifest, distinct, obvious, apparent, palpable, plain, clear *Ant* latent

**pathetic** *Syn* MOVING, poignant, affecting, touching, impressive *Ant* comical

**pathological** *Syn* UNWHOLESOME, morbid, sickly, diseased

**pathos** ♦ a quality that moves one to pity and sorrow *Syn* poignancy, bathos

**patience** ♦ the power or capacity to endure without complaint something difficult or disagreeable *Syn* long-suffering, longanimity, forbearance, resignation *Ant* impatience

**patois** *Syn* DIALECT, vernacular, lingo, jargon, cant, argot, slang

**patrician** *Syn* GENTLEMAN, aristocrat

**patrimony** *Syn* HERITAGE, inheritance, birthright

**patron** *Syn* SPONSOR, surety, guarantor, backer, angel *Ant* client; protégé

**patter** *Syn* CHAT, chatter, prate, gab, prattle, babble, gabble, jabber, gibber

**pattern 1** *Syn* MODEL, exemplar, example, ideal, standard, beau ideal, mirror **2** *Syn* FIGURE, design, motif, device

**paunch** *Syn* ABDOMEN, belly, stomach, gut

**pause** ♦ a temporary cessation of activity or of an activity *Syn* recess, respite, lull, intermission

**paw** *Syn* TOUCH, feel, palpate, handle

**pawn** *Syn* PLEDGE, hostage, earnest, token

**pay** *vb* ♦ to give money or its equivalent in return for something *Syn* compensate, remunerate, satisfy, reimburse, indemnify, repay, recompense

**pay** *n Syn* WAGE, wages, salary, stipend, fee, hire, emolument

**paying** ♦ yielding a profit *Syn* gainful, remunerative, lucrative, profitable

**peace** *Syn* TRUCE, cease-fire, armistice

**peaceable** *Syn* PACIFIC, peaceful, pacifist, pacifistic, irenic *Ant* contentious; acrimonious

**peaceful 1** *Syn* CALM, tranquil, serene, placid, halcyon *Ant* turbulent **2** *Syn* PACIFIC, peaceable, pacifist, pacifistic, irenic

**peak 1** *Syn* MOUNTAIN, mount, alp, volcano, mesa **2** *Syn* SUMMIT, pinnacle, climax, apex, acme, culmination, meridian, zenith, apogee

**peculiar 1** *Syn* CHARACTERISTIC, individual, distinctive **2** *Syn* STRANGE, eccentric, odd, queer, singular, unique, quaint, outlandish, curious

**pecuniary** *Syn* FINANCIAL, monetary, fiscal

**pedantic** ♦ too narrowly concerned with scholarly matters *Syn* academic, scholastic, bookish

**pedestrian** *Syn* DULL, humdrum, dreary, monotonous, stodgy

**pedigree** *Syn* ANCESTRY, lineage

**peek** *Syn* LOOK, peep, glimpse, glance, sight, view

**peel** *vb Syn* SKIN, decorticate, pare, flay

**peel** *n Syn* SKIN, bark, rind, hide, pelt

**peep** *vb Syn* CHIRP, chirrup, cheep, tweet, twitter, chitter

**peep** *n Syn* CHIRP, chirrup, cheep, tweet, twitter, chitter

**peep** *n Syn* LOOK, glance, glimpse, peek, sight, view

**peer** *Syn* GAZE, gape, stare, glare, gloat

**peerless** *Syn* SUPREME, surpassing, preeminent, superlative, transcendent, incomparable

**peeve** *Syn* IRRITATE, exasperate, nettle, provoke, aggravate, rile

**peevish** *Syn* IRRITABLE, fractious, snappish, waspish, petulant, pettish, huffy, fretful, querulous

**pejorative** *Syn* DEROGATORY, depreciatory, depreciative, disparaging, slighting

**pellucid** *Syn* CLEAR, transparent, translucent, lucid, diaphanous, limpid

**pelt** *Syn* SKIN, hide, rind, bark, peel

**pen** *Syn* ENCLOSE, envelop, fence, coop, corral, cage, wall

**penalize** ♦ to inflict a penalty on *Syn* fine, amerce, mulct

**penchant** *Syn* LEANING, propensity, proclivity, flair

**pendant** *Syn* FLAG, ensign, standard, banner, color, streamer, pennant, pennon, jack

**pendent** *Syn* SUSPENDED, pendulous

**pendulate** *Syn* SWING, sway, oscillate, vibrate, fluctuate, waver, undulate

**pendulous** *Syn* SUSPENDED, pendent

**penetrate 1** *Syn* ENTER, pierce, probe **2** *Syn* PERMEATE, pervade, impenetrate, interpenetrate, impregnate, saturate

**penetration** *Syn* DISCERNMENT, insight, acumen, discrimination, perception

**penitence** ♦ regret for sin or wrongdoing *Syn* repentance, contrition, attrition, compunction, remorse

**pen name** *Syn* PSEUDONYM, nom de plume, alias, nom de guerre, incognito

**pennant** *Syn* FLAG, ensign, standard, banner, color, streamer, pendant, pennon, jack

**penniless** *Syn* POOR, indigent, needy, destitute, impecunious, poverty-stricken, necessitous

**pennon** *Syn* FLAG, ensign, standard, banner, color, streamer, pennant, pendant, jack

**penny-pinching** *Syn* STINGY, close, closefisted, tight, tightfisted, niggardly, parsimonious, penurious, miserly, cheeseparing

**pensive** *Syn* THOUGHTFUL, reflective, speculative, contemplative, meditative

**penumbra** *Syn* SHADE, umbra, adumbration, umbrage, shadow

**penurious** *Syn* STINGY, parsimonious, niggardly, close, closefisted, tight, tightfisted, miserly, cheeseparing, penny-pinching

**penury** *Syn* POVERTY, indigence, want, destitution, privation *Ant* luxury

**peppery** *Syn* SPIRITED, fiery, gingery, high-spirited, mettlesome, spunky

**perceive** *Syn* SEE, discern, note, remark, notice, observe, contemplate, behold, descry, espy, view, survey

**percept** *Syn* SENSATION, sense-datum, sensum, image

**perceptible** ♦ apprehensible as real or existent *Syn* sensible, palpable, tangible, appreciable, ponderable *Ant* imperceptible

**perception** *Syn* DISCERNMENT, penetration, insight, acumen, discrimination

**perch** *Syn* ALIGHT, light, land, roost

**percussion** *Syn* IMPACT, concussion, clash, shock, impingement, collision, jar, jolt

**perdurable** *Syn* LASTING, durable, permanent, stable, perpetual *Ant* fleeting

**peremptory** *Syn* MASTERFUL, imperative, imperious, domineering

**perennial** *Syn* CONTINUAL, perpetual, incessant, unremitting, constant, continuous

**perfect** *adj* ♦ not lacking or faulty in any particular *Syn* whole, entire, intact *Ant* imperfect

**perfect** *vb Syn* UNFOLD, evolve, develop, elaborate

**perfection** *Syn* EXCELLENCE, virtue, merit *Ant* failing

**perfervid** *Syn* IMPASSIONED, fervid, passionate, ardent, fervent

**perfidious** *Syn* FAITHLESS, false, disloyal, traitorous, treacherous

**perforate** ♦ to pierce through so as to leave a hole *Syn* puncture, punch, prick, bore, drill

**perform** ♦ to carry out or into effect *Syn* execute, discharge, accomplish, achieve, effect, fulfill

**performer** *Syn* ACTOR, player, mummer, mime, mimic, thespian, impersonator, trouper

**perfume** *Syn* FRAGRANCE, bouquet, redolence, incense

**peril** *Syn* DANGER, jeopardy, hazard, risk

**perilous** *Syn* DANGEROUS, hazardous, risky, precarious

**perimeter** *Syn* CIRCUMFERENCE, periphery, circuit, compass

**period** ♦ a division of time *Syn* epoch, era, age, aeon

**periodic** *Syn* INTERMITTENT, recurrent, alternate

**periodical** *Syn* JOURNAL, magazine, newspaper, review, organ

**peripatetic** *Syn* ITINERANT, ambulatory, ambulant, nomadic, vagrant

**periphery** *Syn* CIRCUMFERENCE, perimeter, circuit, compass

**periphrasis** *Syn* VERBIAGE, redundancy, tautology, pleonasm, circumlocution

**perjure** ♦ to make a false swearer of oneself by violating one's oath to tell the truth *Syn* forswear

**permanent** *Syn* LASTING, perdurable, durable, stable, perpetual *Ant* temporary; ad interim (*of persons*)

**permeate** ♦ to pass or cause to pass through every part of a thing *Syn* pervade, penetrate, impenetrate, interpenetrate, impregnate, saturate

**permission** ♦ a sanctioning to act or do something that is granted by one in authority *Syn* leave, sufferance *Ant* prohibition

**permit** *Syn* LET, allow, suffer, leave *Ant* prohibit, forbid

**permutation** *Syn* CHANGE, mutation, vicissitude, alternation

**pernicious** ♦ exceedingly harmful or destructive *Syn* baneful, noxious, deleterious, detrimental *Ant* innocuous

**pernickety** *Syn* NICE, persnickety, fastidious, finicky, finicking, finical, dainty, particular, fussy, squeamish

**perpendicular** *Syn* VERTICAL, plumb *Ant* horizontal

**perpetrate** *Syn* COMMIT

**perpetual** 1 *Syn* LASTING, permanent, perdurable, durable, stable 2 *Syn* CONTINUAL, continuous, constant, incessant, unremitting, perennial *Ant* transitory, transient

**perplex** *Syn* PUZZLE, mystify, bewilder, distract, nonplus, confound, dumbfound

**perquisite** *Syn* RIGHT, prerogative, privilege, appanage, birthright

**persecute** *Syn* WRONG, oppress, aggrieve

**persevere** ♦ to continue in a given course in the face of difficulty or opposition *Syn* persist

**persiflage** *Syn* BADINAGE, raillery

**persist** 1 *Syn* PERSEVERE *Ant* desist 2 *Syn* CONTINUE, last, endure, abide *Ant* desist

**persnickety** *Syn* NICE, pernickety, fastidious, finicky, finicking, finical, dainty, particular, fussy, squeamish

**person** *Syn* ENTITY, being, creature, individual

**personality** *Syn* DISPOSITION, character, individuality, temperament, temper, complexion

**perspicacious** *Syn* SHREWD, sagacious, astute *Ant* dull

**perspicuous** *Syn* CLEAR, lucid

**persuade** *Syn* INDUCE, prevail, get *Ant* dissuade

**persuasion** 1 *Syn* OPINION, conviction, belief, view, sentiment 2 *Syn* RELIGION, denomination, sect, cult, communion, faith, creed, church

**pert** *Syn* SAUCY, arch *Ant* coy

**pertain** *Syn* BEAR, relate, appertain, belong, apply

**pertinacious** *Syn* OBSTINATE, stubborn, dogged, mulish, stiff-necked, pigheaded, bullheaded

**pertinent** *Syn* RELEVANT, germane, material, apposite, applicable, apropos *Ant* impertinent; foreign

**perturb** *Syn* DISCOMPOSE, disturb, agitate, upset, disquiet, fluster, flurry

**pervade** *Syn* PERMEATE, penetrate, impenetrate, interpenetrate, impregnate, saturate

**perverse** *Syn* CONTRARY, restive, balky, froward, wayward

**pervert** *Syn* DEBASE, deprave, corrupt, vitiate, debauch

**perverted** *Syn* DEBASED, corrupted, depraved, vitiated, debauched

**pessimistic** *Syn* CYNICAL, misanthropic *Ant* optimistic

**pester** *Syn* WORRY, plague, tease, tantalize, annoy, harass, harry

**pestilent, pestilential** *Syn* POISONOUS, venomous, virulent, toxic, mephitic, miasmic, miasmatic, miasmal

**pet** *Syn* CARESS, fondle, cosset, cuddle, dandle

**petite** *Syn* SMALL, little, diminutive, wee, tiny, teeny, weeny, minute, microscopic, miniature

**petition** *n Syn* PRAYER, suit, plea, appeal

**petition** *vb Syn* PRAY, sue, plead, appeal

**petrify** 1 *Syn* HARDEN, solidify, indurate, cake 2 *Syn* DAZE, stun, bemuse, stupefy, benumb, paralyze

**pettish** *Syn* IRRITABLE, fractious, peevish, petulant, snappish, waspish, huffy, fretful, querulous

**petty** ♦ being often contemptibly insignificant or unimportant *Syn* puny, trivial, trifling, paltry, measly, picayunish, picayune *Ant* important, momentous; gross

**petulant** *Syn* IRRITABLE, fractious, peevish, pettish, snappish, waspish, huffy, fretful, querulous

**phantasm** 1 *Syn* APPARITION, phantom, wraith, ghost, spirit, specter, shade, revenant 2 *Syn* FANCY, fantasy, phantasy, vision, dream, daydream, nightmare

**phantasy** *Syn* FANCY, fantasy, phantasm, vision, dream, daydream, nightmare

**phantom** *Syn* APPARITION, phantasm, wraith, ghost, spirit, specter, shade, revenant

**pharisaical** *Syn* HYPOCRITICAL, sanctimonious, canting

**pharisaism** *Syn* HYPOCRISY, sanctimony, cant

**pharmaceutical** *Syn* DRUG, medicinal, biologic, simple

**pharmacist** *Syn* DRUGGIST, apothecary, chemist

**phase** ♦ one of the possible ways of viewing or being presented to view *Syn* aspect, side, facet, angle

**phenomenal** 1 *Syn* MATERIAL, physical, corporeal, sensible, objective *Ant* noumenal 2 *Syn* EXCEPTIONAL, extraordinary, unusual, unwonted

**phenomenon** *Syn* WONDER, marvel, prodigy, miracle

**philanthropic** *Syn* CHARITABLE, benevolent, humane, humanitarian, eleemosynary, altruistic *Ant* misanthropic

**philanthropy** *Syn* CHARITY *Ant* misanthropy

**philippic** *Syn* TIRADE, diatribe, jeremiad

**phlegm** 1 *Syn* IMPASSIVITY, impassiveness, stolidity, apathy, stoicism 2 *Syn* EQUANIMITY, composure, sangfroid

**phlegmatic** *Syn* IMPASSIVE, stolid, apathetic, stoic

**phony** *Syn* COUNTERFEIT, spurious, bogus, fake, sham, pseudo, pinchbeck

**phrase** ♦ a group of words which, taken together, express a notion and may be used as a part of a sentence *Syn* idiom, expression, locution

**phraseology, phrasing** *Syn* LANGUAGE, vocabulary, diction, style

**physic** *Syn* REMEDY, cure, medicine, medicament, medication, specific

**physical** 1 *Syn* BODILY, corporeal, corporal, somatic 2 *Syn* MATERIAL, corporeal, phenomenal, sensible, objective

**physiognomy** *Syn* FACE, countenance, visage, mug, puss

**physique** ♦ bodily makeup or type *Syn* build, habit, constitution

**picayunish, picayune** *Syn* PETTY, trivial, trifling, puny, paltry, measly

**pick** *Syn* CHOOSE, select, elect, opt, cull, prefer, single

**picked** *Syn* SELECT, elect, exclusive

**pickle** *Syn* PREDICAMENT, plight, dilemma, quandary, scrape, fix, jam

**pictorial** *Syn* GRAPHIC, vivid, picturesque

**picture** *Syn* REPRESENT, depict, portray, delineate, limn

**picturesque** *Syn* GRAPHIC, vivid, pictorial

**piece** *Syn* PART, portion, detail, member, division, section, segment, sector, fraction, fragment, parcel

**pied, piebald** *Syn* VARIEGATED, parti-colored, motley, checkered, checked, skewbald, dappled, freaked

**pier** 1 *Syn* BUTTRESS, abutment 2 *Syn* WHARF, dock, quay, slip, berth, jetty, levee

**pierce** *Syn* ENTER, penetrate, probe

**pietistic** *Syn* DEVOUT, sanctimonious, pious, religious

**piety** *Syn* FIDELITY, devotion, allegiance, fealty, loyalty *Ant* impiety

**pigeonhole** *Syn* ASSORT, sort, classify

**pigheaded** *Syn* OBSTINATE, stubborn, mulish, stiff-necked, bullheaded, dogged, pertinacious

**pilaster** *Syn* PILLAR, column

**pile** *n* 1 *Syn* HEAP, stack, mass, bank, shock, cock 2 *Syn* BUILDING, edifice, structure

**pile** *vb Syn* HEAP, stack, mass, bank, shock, cock

**pilfer** *Syn* STEAL, filch, purloin, lift, pinch, snitch, swipe, cop

**pilgrimage** *Syn* JOURNEY, voyage, tour, trip, jaunt, excursion, cruise, expedition

**pillage** *Syn* RAVAGE, devastate, waste, sack, despoil, spoliate

**pillar** ♦ a firm upright support for a superstructure *Syn* column, pilaster

**pilot** *Syn* GUIDE, steer, lead, engineer

**pimple** *Syn* ABSCESS, boil, furuncle, carbuncle, pustule

**pinch** *vb Syn* STEAL, pilfer, filch, purloin, lift, snitch, swipe, cop

**pinch** *n Syn* JUNCTURE, pass, exigency, emergency, contingency, strait, crisis

**pinchbeck** *Syn* COUNTERFEIT, spurious, bogus, fake, sham, pseudo, phony

**pinched** *Syn* HAGGARD, cadaverous, worn, careworn, wasted

**pinch hitter** *Syn* SUBSTITUTE, supply, locum tenens, alternate, understudy, double, stand-in

**pine** *Syn* LONG, yearn, hanker, hunger, thirst

**pinnacle** *Syn* SUMMIT, peak, apex, acme, climax, culmination, meridian, zenith, apogee

**pious** *Syn* DEVOUT, religious, pietistic, sanctimonious *Ant* impious

**piquant** *Syn* PUNGENT, poignant, racy, spicy, snappy *Ant* bland

**pique** *n Syn* OFFENSE, resentment, umbrage, dudgeon, huff

**pique** *vb* 1 *Syn* PROVOKE, excite, stimulate, quicken, galvanize 2 *Syn* PRIDE, plume, preen

**pirate** ♦ a robber on the high seas *Syn* freebooter, buccaneer, privateer, corsair

**pirouette** *Syn* TURN, revolve, rotate, gyrate, circle, spin, twirl, whirl, wheel, eddy, swirl

**pitch** 1 *Syn* THROW, hurl, fling, cast, toss, sling 2 *Syn* PLUNGE, dive

**piteous** *Syn* PITIFUL, pitiable

**pith** *Syn* SUBSTANCE, purport, gist, burden, core

**pithy** *Syn* CONCISE, summary, compendious, terse, succinct, laconic

**pitiable** 1 *Syn* PITIFUL, piteous 2 *Syn* CONTEMPTIBLE, despicable, sorry, scurvy, cheap, beggarly, shabby

**pitiful** ♦ arousing or deserving pity *Syn* piteous, pitiable *Ant* cruel

**pittance** *Syn* RATION, allowance, dole

**pity** *Syn* SYMPATHY, compassion, commiseration, condolence, ruth, empathy

**pivotal** *Syn* CENTRAL, focal

**placate** *Syn* PACIFY, appease, mollify, propitiate, conciliate *Ant* enrage

**place** ♦ the portion of space occupied by or chosen for something *Syn* position, location, situation, site, spot, station

**placid** *Syn* CALM, tranquil, serene, peaceful, halcyon *Ant* choleric (*of persons*); ruffled (*of things*)

**plague** *Syn* WORRY, pester, tease, tantalize, harry, harass, annoy

**plain** 1 *Syn* LEVEL, plane, flat, even, smooth, flush *Ant* solid 2 *Syn* EVIDENT, clear, distinct, obvious, manifest, patent, apparent, palpable *Ant* abstruse 3 ♦ free from all ostentation or superficial embellishment *Syn* homely, simple, unpretentious *Ant* lovely 4 *Syn* FRANK, candid, open

**plaintive** *Syn* MELANCHOLY, dolorous, doleful, lugubrious, rueful

**plait** *Syn* WEAVE, knit, crochet, braid, tat

**plan** *n* ♦ a method devised for making or doing something or achieving an end *Syn* design, plot, scheme, project

**plan** *vb* ♦ to formulate a plan for arranging, realizing, or achieving something *Syn* design, plot, scheme, project

**plane** *Syn* LEVEL, plain, flat, even, smooth, flush *Ant* solid

**planet** *Syn* EARTH, world, globe

**plank** *Syn* PARAGRAPH, verse, article, clause, count

**plastic** ♦ susceptible of being modified in form or nature *Syn* pliable, pliant, ductile, malleable, adaptable

**platitude** *Syn* COMMONPLACE, truism, bromide, cliché

**plaudits** *Syn* APPLAUSE, acclamation, acclaim

**plausible** ♦ appearing worthy of belief *Syn* credible, believable, colorable, specious

**play** *n* 1 ♦ activity engaged in for amusement *Syn* sport, disport, frolic, rollick, romp, gambol *Ant* work 2 *Syn* FUN, jest, sport, game *Ant* earnest 3 *Syn* ROOM, berth, elbowroom, leeway, margin, clearance

**play** *vb* 1 ♦ to engage in an activity for amusement or recreation *Syn* sport, disport, frolic, rollick, romp, gambol 2 *Syn* ACT, impersonate

**player** *Syn* ACTOR, performer, mummer, mime, mimic, thespian, impersonator, trouper

**playful** ♦ given to or characterized by play, jests, or tricks *Syn* frolicsome, sportive, roguish, waggish, impish, mischievous

**plea** 1 *Syn* APOLOGY, apologia, excuse, pretext, alibi 2 *Syn* PRAYER, suit, petition, appeal

**plead** *Syn* PRAY, sue, petition, appeal

**pleasant** ♦ highly acceptable to the mind or the senses *Syn* pleasing, agreeable, grateful, gratifying, welcome *Ant* unpleasant; distasteful; harsh

**please** ♦ to give or be a source of pleasure to *Syn* gratify, delight, rejoice, gladden, tickle, regale *Ant* displease; anger; vex

**pleasing** *Syn* PLEASANT, agreeable, grateful, gratifying, welcome *Ant* displeasing; repellent

**pleasure** ♦ the agreeable emotion accompanying the expectation, acquisition, or possession of something good or greatly desired *Syn* delight, joy, delectation, enjoyment, fruition *Ant* displeasure; anger; vexation

**plebiscite** *Syn* MANDATE, initiative, referendum

**pledge** *n* ♦ something given or held as a sign of another's good faith or intentions *Syn* earnest, token, pawn, hostage

**pledge** *vb Syn* PROMISE, engage, plight, covenant, contract *Ant* abjure

**plenary** *Syn* FULL, complete, replete *Ant* limited

**plenteous** *Syn* PLENTIFUL, ample, abundant, copious

**plentiful** ♦ more than sufficient without being excessive *Syn* plenteous, ample, abundant, copious *Ant* scanty, scant

**pleonasm** *Syn* VERBIAGE, redundancy, tautology, circumlocution, periphrasis

**pliable** *Syn* PLASTIC, pliant, ductile, malleable, adaptable *Ant* obstinate

**pliant** *Syn* PLASTIC, pliable, ductile, malleable, adaptable

**plight** *vb Syn* PROMISE, engage, pledge, covenant, contract

**plight** *n Syn* PREDICAMENT, dilemma, quandary, scrape, fix, jam, pickle

**plot** *n* 1 *Syn* PLAN, design, scheme, project 2 ♦ a plan secretly devised to accomplish an evil or treacherous end *Syn* intrigue, machination, conspiracy, cabal 3 *Syn* SKETCH, outline, diagram, delineation, draft, tracing, blueprint

**plot** *vb* 1 *Syn* PLAN, design, scheme, project 2 *Syn* SKETCH, outline, diagram, delineate, draft, trace, blueprint

**ploy** *Syn* TRICK, ruse, stratagem, maneuver, gambit, artifice, wile, feint

**pluck** *Syn* FORTITUDE, grit, backbone, guts, sand

**plumb** *vb Syn* FATHOM, sound

**plumb** *adj Syn* VERTICAL, perpendicular

**plume** *Syn* PRIDE, pique, preen

**plump** *Syn* FLESHY, stout, portly, rotund, chubby, fat, corpulent, obese *Ant* cadaverous

**plunder** *vb Syn* ROB, rifle, loot, burglarize

**plunder** *n Syn* SPOIL, booty, prize, loot, swag

**plunge** ♦ to thrust or cast oneself or something into or as if into deep water *Syn* dive, pitch

**plutocracy** *Syn* OLIGARCHY, aristocracy

**ply** *Syn* HANDLE, manipulate, wield, swing

**pocket** *Syn* HOLE, hollow, cavity, void, vacuum

**poet** ♦ a writer of verse *Syn* versifier, rhymer, rhymester, poetaster, bard, minstrel, troubadour

**poetaster** *Syn* POET, versifier, rhymer, rhymester, bard, minstrel, troubadour

**pogrom** *Syn* MASSACRE, slaughter, butchery, carnage

**poignancy** *Syn* PATHOS, bathos

**poignant** 1 *Syn* PUNGENT, piquant, racy, spicy, snappy *Ant* dull 2 *Syn* MOVING, touching, pathetic, impressive, affecting

**point** *Syn* DIRECT, aim, level, train, lay

**point of view** ♦ a position from which something is considered or evaluated *Syn* viewpoint, standpoint, angle, slant

**poise** *vb Syn* STABILIZE, steady, balance, ballast, trim

**poise** *n* 1 *Syn* BALANCE, equilibrium, equipoise, tension 2 *Syn* TACT, address, savoir faire

**poison** ♦ something that harms, interferes with, or destroys the activity, progress, or welfare of something else *Syn* venom, virus, toxin, bane

**poisonous** ♦ having the properties or effects of poison *Syn* venomous, virulent, toxic, mephitic, pestilent, pestilential, miasmic, miasmatic, miasmal

**poke** *vb* ♦ to thrust something into so as to stir up, urge on, or attract attention *Syn* prod, nudge, jog

**poke** *n* ♦ a quick thrust with or as if with the hand *Syn* prod, nudge, jog

**polite** *Syn* CIVIL, courteous, courtly, gallant, chivalrous *Ant* impolite

**politic** 1 *Syn* EXPEDIENT, advisable 2 *Syn* SUAVE, diplomatic, bland, smooth, urbane

**politician** ♦ a person engaged in the art or science of government *Syn* statesman, politico

**politico** *Syn* POLITICIAN, statesman

**poll** *Syn* SHEAR, clip, trim, prune, lop, snip, crop

**pollute** *Syn* CONTAMINATE, defile, taint, attaint

**pomp** *Syn* DISPLAY, parade, array

**ponder** ♦ to consider or examine attentively or deliberately *Syn* meditate, muse, ruminate

**ponderable** *Syn* PERCEPTIBLE, appreciable, sensible, palpable, tangible

**ponderous** *Syn* HEAVY, cumbrous, cumbersome, weighty, hefty

**pool** *Syn* MONOPOLY, corner, syndicate, trust, cartel

**poor** 1 ♦ lacking money or material possessions *Syn* indigent, needy, destitute, penniless, impecunious, poverty-stricken, necessitous *Ant* rich 2 *Syn* BAD, wrong

**poppycock** *Syn* NONSENSE, twaddle, drivel, bunk, balderdash, gobbledygook, trash, rot, bull

**popular** *Syn* COMMON, ordinary, familiar, vulgar *Ant* unpopular; esoteric

**port** *n Syn* HARBOR, haven

**port** *n Syn* BEARING, presence, deportment, demeanor, mien

**portal** *Syn* DOOR, gate, doorway, gateway, postern

**portend** *Syn* FORETELL, presage, augur, prognosticate, predict, forecast, prophesy, forebode

**portent** *Syn* FORETOKEN, presage, prognostic, omen, augury

**portentous** *Syn* OMINOUS, unpropitious, inauspicious, fateful

**portion** *n* 1 *Syn* PART, piece, detail, member, division, section, segment, sector, fraction, fragment, parcel 2 *Syn* FATE, destiny, lot, doom

**portion** *vb Syn* APPORTION, parcel, ration, prorate

**portly** *Syn* FLESHY, stout, plump, rotund, chubby, fat, corpulent, obese

**portray** *Syn* REPRESENT, depict, delineate, picture, limn

**pose** *vb Syn* PROPOSE, propound

**pose** *n* 1 ♦ an adopted way of speaking or behaving *Syn* air, affectation, mannerism 2 *Syn* POSTURE, attitude

**posit** *vb Syn* PRESUPPOSE, presume, assume, postulate, premise

**posit** *n Syn* ASSUMPTION, presupposition, presumption, postulate, premise

**position** 1 ♦ a firmly held point of view or way of regarding something *Syn* stand, attitude 2 *Syn* PLACE, location, situation, site, spot, station

**positive** *Syn* SURE, certain, cocksure *Ant* doubtful

**possess** *Syn* HAVE, own, enjoy, hold

**possessions** ♦ all the items that taken together

constitute a person's or group's property or wealth *Syn* belongings, effects, means, resources, assets

**possible 1** ♦ capable of being realized *Syn* practicable, feasible **2** *Syn* PROBABLE, likely

**posterior** ♦ situated at or toward the back *Syn* rear, hind, hinder, after, back *Ant* anterior

**posterity** *Syn* OFFSPRING, young, progeny, issue, descendant *Ant* ancestry

**postern** *Syn* DOOR, gate, gateway, doorway, portal

**postpone** *Syn* DEFER, suspend, stay, intermit

**postulant** *Syn* NOVICE, novitiate, probationer, neophyte, apprentice

**postulate** *vb Syn* PRESUPPOSE, presume, assume, premise, posit

**postulate** *n Syn* ASSUMPTION, presupposition, presumption, premise, posit

**posture 1** ♦ the position or bearing of the body *Syn* attitude, pose **2** *Syn* STATE, situation, condition, mode, status

**pot** *Syn* BET, wager, stake, ante

**potent** *Syn* POWERFUL, puissant, forceful, forcible *Ant* impotent

**potential** *Syn* LATENT, dormant, quiescent, abeyant *Ant* active, actual

**pother** *Syn* STIR, flurry, fuss, ado, bustle

**pouch** *Syn* BAG, sack

**pound** *Syn* BEAT, pummel, buffet, baste, belabor, thrash

**pour** ♦ to send forth or come forth abundantly *Syn* stream, gush, sluice

**poverty** ♦ the state of one with insufficient resources *Syn* indigence, penury, want, destitution, privation *Ant* riches

**poverty-stricken** *Syn* POOR, indigent, needy, destitute, penniless, impecunious, necessitous

**power 1** ♦ the ability to exert effort *Syn* force, energy, strength, might, puissance *Ant* impotence **2** ♦ the ability of a living being to perform in a given way or a capacity for a particular kind of performance *Syn* faculty, function **3** ♦ the right to govern or rule or determine *Syn* authority, jurisdiction, control, command, sway, dominion

**powerful** ♦ having or manifesting power to effect great or striking results *Syn* potent, puissant, forceful, forcible *Ant* powerless; inefficacious

**powerless** ♦ unable to effect one's purpose, intention, or end *Syn* impotent *Ant* powerful; efficacious

**practicable** *Syn* POSSIBLE, feasible *Ant* impracticable

**practically** *Syn* VIRTUALLY, morally

**practice** *vb* ♦ to perform or cause one to perform an act or series of acts repeatedly in order to master or strengthen a skill or ability *Syn* exercise, drill

**practice** *n* **1** *Syn* HABIT, habitude, usage, custom, use, wont **2** ♦ repeated activity or exertion in order to develop or improve a strength or skill *Syn* exercise, drill *Ant* theory; precept

**praise** ♦ to express approval of or esteem for *Syn* laud, acclaim, extol, eulogize *Ant* blame

**prank** ♦ a playful, often a mischievous, act or trick *Syn* caper, antic, monkeyshine, dido

**prate** *Syn* CHAT, chatter, gab, patter, prattle, babble, gabble, jabber, gibber

**prattle** *Syn* CHAT, chatter, patter, prate, gab, babble, gabble, jabber, gibber

**pray** ♦ to request or make a request for in a humble, beseeching manner *Syn* plead, petition, appeal, sue

**prayer** ♦ an earnest and usu. a formal request for something *Syn* suit, plea, petition, appeal

**preamble** *Syn* INTRODUCTION, prologue, prelude, preface, foreword, exordium

**precarious** *Syn* DANGEROUS, hazardous, perilous, risky

**precedence** *Syn* PRIORITY

**precedent** *Syn* PRECEDING, antecedent, foregoing, previous, prior, former, anterior

**preceding** ♦ being before, esp. in time or in arrangement *Syn* antecedent, precedent, foregoing, previous, prior, former, anterior *Ant* following

**precept** *Syn* LAW, rule, canon, regulation, statute, ordinance *Ant* practice; counsel

**precious** *Syn* COSTLY, expensive, dear, valuable, invaluable, priceless

**precipitate** *vb Syn* SPEED, accelerate, quicken, hasten, hurry

**precipitate** *n Syn* DEPOSIT, sediment, dregs, lees, grounds

**precipitate** *adj* ♦ showing undue haste or unexpectedness *Syn* headlong, abrupt, impetuous, hasty, sudden *Ant* deliberate

**precipitous** *Syn* STEEP, abrupt, sheer

**précis** *Syn* COMPENDIUM, sketch, aperçu, survey, syllabus, digest, pandect

**precise** *Syn* CORRECT, exact, accurate, nice, right *Ant* loose

**preciseness** *Syn* PRECISION

**precision** ♦ the quality or character of what is precise *Syn* preciseness

**preclude** *Syn* PREVENT, obviate, avert, ward

**precocious** *Syn* PREMATURE, untimely, forward, advanced *Ant* backward

**precursor** *Syn* FORERUNNER, harbinger, herald

**predicament** ♦ a difficult, perplexing, or trying situation *Syn* dilemma, quandary, plight, scrape, fix, jam, pickle

**predicate** *Syn* ASSERT, affirm, declare, profess, aver, protest, avouch, avow, warrant

**predict** *Syn* FORETELL, forecast, prophesy, prognosticate, augur, presage, portend, forebode

**predilection** ♦ an attitude of mind that predisposes one to favor something *Syn* partiality, prepossession, prejudice, bias *Ant* aversion

**predispose** *Syn* INCLINE, dispose, bias

**predominant** *Syn* DOMINANT, paramount, preponderant, preponderating, sovereign

**preeminent** *Syn* SUPREME, surpassing, transcendent, superlative, peerless, incomparable

**preempt** *Syn* ARROGATE, usurp, appropriate, confiscate

**preen** *Syn* PRIDE, plume, pique

**preface** *Syn* INTRODUCTION, prologue, prelude, foreword, exordium, preamble

**prefatory** *Syn* PRELIMINARY, introductory, preparatory

**prefer 1** *Syn* CHOOSE, select, elect, opt, pick, cull, single **2** *Syn* OFFER, proffer, tender, present

**preferable** *Syn* BETTER, superior

**preference** *Syn* CHOICE, selection, election, option, alternative

**preferment** *Syn* ADVANCEMENT, promotion, elevation

**pregnant** *Syn* EXPRESSIVE, meaningful, significant, eloquent, sententious

**prejudice** *Syn* PREDILECTION, bias, partiality, prepossession

**preliminary** ♦ serving to make ready the way for something that follows *Syn* introductory, preparatory, prefatory

**prelude** *Syn* INTRODUCTION, prologue, preface, foreword, exordium, preamble

**premature** ♦ unduly early in coming, happening, or developing *Syn* untimely, forward, advanced, precocious *Ant* matured

**premeditated** *Syn* DELIBERATE, considered, advised, designed, studied *Ant* unpremeditated; casual, accidental

**premise** *n Syn* ASSUMPTION, postulate, posit, presupposition, presumption

**premise** *vb Syn* PRESUPPOSE, postulate, posit, presume, assume

**premium** ♦ something that is offered or given for some service or attainment *Syn* prize, award, reward, meed, guerdon, bounty, bonus

**preoccupied** *Syn* ABSTRACTED, absent, absentminded, distraught

**preparatory** *Syn* PRELIMINARY, introductory, prefatory

**prepare** ♦ to make ready beforehand usu. for

some purpose, use, or activity *Syn* fit, qualify, condition, ready

**preponderant, preponderating** *Syn* DOMINANT, predominant, paramount, sovereign

**prepossession** *Syn* PREDILECTION, partiality, prejudice, bias

**preposterous** *Syn* FOOLISH, absurd, silly

**prerequisite** *Syn* REQUIREMENT, requisite

**prerogative** *Syn* RIGHT, privilege, perquisite, appanage, birthright

**presage** *n Syn* FORETOKEN, prognostic, omen, augury, portent

**presage** *vb Syn* FORETELL, augur, portend, forebode, prognosticate, predict, forecast, prophesy

**prescribe 1** *Syn* DICTATE, ordain, decree, impose **2** ♦ to fix arbitrarily or authoritatively for the sake of order or of a clear understanding *Syn* assign, define

**prescription** *Syn* RECEIPT, recipe

**presence** *Syn* BEARING, deportment, demeanor, mien, port

**present** *n Syn* GIFT, gratuity, favor, boon, largesse

**present** *vb* **1** *Syn* GIVE, bestow, confer, donate, afford **2** *Syn* OFFER, tender, proffer, prefer

**presentiment** *Syn* APPREHENSION, misgiving, foreboding

**presently** ♦ without undue time lapse *Syn* shortly, soon, directly

**preserve** *Syn* SAVE, conserve

**press** *n Syn* CROWD, throng, crush, mob, rout, horde

**press** *vb* ♦ to act upon through steady pushing or thrusting force exerted in contact *Syn* bear, bear down, squeeze, crowd, jam

**pressing** ♦ demanding or claiming esp. immediate attention *Syn* urgent, imperative, crying, importunate, insistent, exigent, instant

**pressure** *Syn* STRESS, strain, tension

**prestige** *Syn* INFLUENCE, authority, weight, credit

**presume** *Syn* PRESUPPOSE, postulate, premise, posit, assume

**presumption** *Syn* ASSUMPTION, presupposition, postulate, premise, posit

**presumptuous** *Syn* CONFIDENT, assured, sanguine, sure

**presuppose** ♦ to take something for granted or as true or existent esp. as a basis for action or reasoning *Syn* presume, assume, postulate, premise, posit

**presupposition** *Syn* ASSUMPTION, presumption, postulate, premise, posit

**pretend** *Syn* ASSUME, affect, simulate, feign, counterfeit, sham

**pretense 1** *Syn* CLAIM, pretension, title **2** ♦ the offering of something false as real or true *Syn* pretension, make-believe

**pretension 1** *Syn* CLAIM, title, pretense **2** *Syn* PRETENSE, make-believe **3** *Syn* AMBITION, aspiration

**pretentious 1** *Syn* SHOWY, ostentatious *Ant* unpretentious **2** *Syn* AMBITIOUS, utopian

**preternatural** *Syn* SUPERNATURAL, supranatural, miraculous, superhuman

**pretext** *Syn* APOLOGY, excuse, plea, alibi, apologia

**pretty** *Syn* BEAUTIFUL, bonny, comely, fair, lovely, handsome, good-looking, beauteous, pulchritudinous

**prevail** *Syn* INDUCE, persuade, get

**prevailing** ♦ general (as in circulation, acceptance, or use) in a given place or at a given time *Syn* prevalent, rife, current

**prevalent** *Syn* PREVAILING, rife, current

**prevaricate** *Syn* LIE, equivocate, palter, fib

**prevent 1** ♦ to deal with beforehand *Syn* anticipate, forestall **2** ♦ to stop from advancing or occurring *Syn* preclude, obviate, avert, ward *Ant* permit

**previous** *Syn* PRECEDING, foregoing, prior, antecedent, precedent, former, anterior *Ant* subsequent; consequent

**prey** *Syn* VICTIM, quarry

**price** ♦ the quantity of one thing that is exchanged

or demanded in barter or sale for another **Syn** charge, cost, expense

**priceless** *Syn* COSTLY, invaluable, precious, expensive, dear, valuable

**prick 1** *Syn* PERFORATE, punch, puncture, bore, drill **2** *Syn* URGE, egg, exhort, goad, spur, prod, sic

**pride** *n* ♦ an attitude of inordinate self-esteem or superiority *Syn* vanity, vainglory **Ant** humility; shame

**pride** *vb* ♦ to congratulate oneself because of something one is, has, or has done or achieved *Syn* plume, pique, preen

**priggish 1** *Syn* COMPLACENT, smug, self-complacent, self-satisfied **2** *Syn* PRIM, prissy, prudish, puritanical, straitlaced, stuffy

**prim** ♦ excessively concerned with what one regards as proper or right *Syn* priggish, prissy, prudish, puritanical, straitlaced, stuffy

**primal** *Syn* PRIMARY, primordial, primitive, pristine, primeval, prime

**primary** ♦ first in some respect (as order, character, or importance) *Syn* primal, primordial, primitive, pristine, primeval, prime

**prime** *Syn* PRIMARY, primal, primordial, primitive, pristine, primeval

**prime mover** *Syn* ORIGIN, source, provenance, provenience, inception, root

**primeval** *Syn* PRIMARY, pristine, primitive, primordial, primal, prime

**primitive 1** *Syn* PRIMARY, primal, primordial, pristine, primeval, prime **2** *Syn* ELEMENTAL, basic, elementary, essential, fundamental, underlying

**primordial 1** *Syn* PRIMARY, primeval, pristine, primitive, primal, prime **2** *Syn* INITIAL, original

**princely** *Syn* KINGLY, regal, royal, queenly, imperial

**principal** *Syn* CHIEF, main, leading, foremost, capital

**principally** *Syn* LARGELY, mainly, chiefly, mostly, greatly, generally

**principle** ♦ a comprehensive and fundamental rule, doctrine, or assumption *Syn* axiom, fundamental, law, theorem

**print** *Syn* IMPRESSION, impress, imprint, stamp

**printing** *Syn* EDITION, impression, reprinting, reissue

**prior** *Syn* PRECEDING, previous, foregoing, precedent, anterior, former, antecedent

**priority** ♦ the act, the fact, or the right of preceding another *Syn* precedence

**priory** *Syn* CLOISTER, monastery, nunnery, convent, abbey

**prismatic** ♦ marked by or displaying a variety of colors *Syn* iridescent, opalescent, opaline

**prisoner** ♦ one who is deprived of liberty and kept under involuntary restraint *Syn* captive

**prissy** *Syn* PRIM, priggish, prudish, puritanical, straitlaced, stuffy

**pristine** *Syn* PRIMARY, primeval, primordial, primitive, primal, prime

**privateer** *Syn* PIRATE, freebooter, buccaneer, corsair

**privation 1** *Syn* LACK, want, dearth, absence, defect **2** *Syn* POVERTY, want, destitution, indigence, penury

**privilege** *Syn* RIGHT, prerogative, birthright, perquisite, appanage

**prize** *n Syn* PREMIUM, award, reward, meed, guerdon, bounty, bonus **Ant** forfeit

**prize** *vb Syn* APPRECIATE, value, treasure, cherish

**prize** *n Syn* SPOIL, booty, plunder, loot, swag

**probable** ♦ almost sure to be or to become true or real *Syn* possible, likely **Ant** certain; improbable

**probationer** *Syn* NOVICE, novitiate, apprentice, postulant, neophyte

**probe** *n Syn* INQUIRY, investigation, inquisition, inquest, research

**probe** *vb Syn* ENTER, pierce, penetrate

**probity** *Syn* HONESTY, honor, integrity

**problem** *Syn* MYSTERY, enigma, fiddle, puzzle, conundrum **Ant** solution

**problematic** *Syn* DOUBTFUL, dubious, questionable

**procedure** *Syn* PROCESS, proceeding

**proceed** *Syn* SPRING, issue, emanate, stem, flow, derive, arise, rise, originate

**proceeding** *Syn* PROCESS, procedure

**process** ♦ the series of actions, operations, or motions involved in the accomplishment of an end *Syn* procedure, proceeding

**procession** ♦ a body (as of persons and vehicles) moving along in a usu. ceremonial order *Syn* parade, cortege, cavalcade, motorcade

**proclaim** *Syn* DECLARE, announce, publish, advertise, promulgate, broadcast

**proclamation** *Syn* DECLARATION, announcement, publication, advertisement, promulgation, broadcasting

**proclivity** *Syn* LEANING, propensity, penchant, flair

**procrastinate** *Syn* DELAY, lag, dawdle, loiter **Ant** hasten, hurry

**procreate** *Syn* GENERATE, engender, beget, get, sire, breed, propagate, reproduce

**procure** *Syn* GET, obtain, secure, acquire, gain, win

**prod** *vb* **1** *Syn* POKE, nudge, jog **2** *Syn* URGE, egg, exhort, goad, spur, prick, sic

**prod** *n Syn* POKE, nudge, jog

**prodigal** *adj Syn* PROFUSE, lavish, exuberant, luxuriant, lush **Ant** parsimonious; frugal

**prodigal** *n Syn* SPENDTHRIFT, profligate, waster, wastrel

**prodigious** *Syn* MONSTROUS, tremendous, stupendous, monumental

**prodigy** *Syn* WONDER, marvel, miracle, phenomenon

**produce** *vb Syn* BEAR, yield, turn out

**produce** *n Syn* PRODUCT, production

**product 1** *Syn* WORK, production, opus, artifact **2** ♦ something produced by physical labor or intellectual effort *Syn* production, produce

**production 1** *Syn* WORK, product, opus, artifact **2** *Syn* PRODUCT, produce

**profanation** ♦ a violation or a misuse of something normally held sacred *Syn* desecration, sacrilege, blasphemy

**profane 1** ♦ not concerned with religion or religious purposes *Syn* secular, lay, temporal **Ant** sacred **2** *Syn* IMPIOUS, blasphemous, sacrilegious

**profanity** *Syn* BLASPHEMY, cursing, swearing

**profess** *Syn* ASSERT, declare, affirm, aver, protest, avouch, avow, predicate, warrant

**profession** *Syn* TRADE, art, handicraft, craft

**proffer** *Syn* OFFER, tender, present, prefer

**proficient** ♦ having great knowledge and experience in a trade or profession *Syn* adept, skilled, skillful, expert, masterly

**profile** *Syn* OUTLINE, contour, silhouette, skyline

**profit** *n Syn* USE, service, advantage, account, avail

**profit** *vb Syn* BENEFIT, avail

**profitable 1** *Syn* BENEFICIAL, advantageous **Ant** unprofitable **2** *Syn* PAYING, gainful, remunerative, lucrative

**profligate** *adj Syn* ABANDONED, dissolute, reprobate

**profligate** *n Syn* SPENDTHRIFT, prodigal, wastrel, waster

**profound** *Syn* DEEP, abysmal **Ant** shallow

**profuse** ♦ giving or given out in great abundance *Syn* lavish, prodigal, luxuriant, lush, exuberant **Ant** spare, scanty, scant

**progenitor** *Syn* ANCESTOR, forefather, forebear **Ant** progeny

**progeny** *Syn* OFFSPRING, young, issue, descendant, posterity **Ant** progenitor

**prognostic** *Syn* FORETOKEN, presage, omen, augury, portent

**prognosticate** *Syn* FORETELL, predict, forecast, prophesy, augur, presage, portend, forebode

**program** ♦ a formulated plan listing things to be done or to take place esp. in chronological order *Syn* schedule, timetable, agenda

**progress** *n* **1** *Syn* ADVANCE **2** ♦ a movement forward (as in time or space) *Syn* progression

**progress** *vb Syn* ADVANCE **Ant** retrogress

**progression 1** *Syn* SUCCESSION, series, sequence, chain, train, string **2** *Syn* PROGRESS

**progressive** *Syn* LIBERAL, advanced, radical **Ant** reactionary

**prohibit** *Syn* FORBID, inhibit, enjoin, interdict, ban **Ant** permit

**project** *n Syn* PLAN, scheme, design, plot

**project** *vb* **1** *Syn* PLAN, scheme, design, plot **2** *Syn* BULGE, jut, stick out, protrude, overhang, beetle

**projection** ♦ an extension beyond the normal line or surface *Syn* protrusion, protuberance, bulge

**prolific** *Syn* FERTILE, fruitful, fecund **Ant** barren, unfruitful

**prolificacy** *Syn* FERTILITY, fruitfulness, fecundity **Ant** barrenness, unfruitfulness

**prolix** *Syn* WORDY, verbose, diffuse, redundant

**prologue** *Syn* INTRODUCTION, prelude, preface, foreword, exordium, preamble

**prolong** *Syn* EXTEND, protract, lengthen, elongate **Ant** curtail

**prominent** *Syn* NOTICEABLE, remarkable, conspicuous, salient, outstanding, signal, striking, arresting

**promiscuous** *Syn* MISCELLANEOUS, heterogeneous, motley

**promise** ♦ to give one's word to do, bring about, or provide *Syn* engage, pledge, plight, covenant, contract

**promote** *Syn* ADVANCE, forward, further **Ant** impede

**promotion 1** *Syn* ADVANCEMENT, preferment, elevation **Ant** demotion **2** *Syn* PUBLICITY, ballyhoo, propaganda

**prompt** *Syn* QUICK, ready, apt

**promulgate** *Syn* DECLARE, proclaim, announce, publish, advertise, broadcast

**promulgation** *Syn* DECLARATION, proclamation, announcement, publication, advertisement, broadcasting

**prone 1** *Syn* LIABLE, subject, exposed, open, susceptible, sensitive **2** ♦ lying down *Syn* supine, prostrate, recumbent, couchant, dormant **Ant** erect

**pronounce** *Syn* ARTICULATE, enunciate

**proof 1** *Syn* REASON, ground, argument **2** ♦ something that serves as evidence compelling the acceptance of a truth or fact *Syn* demonstration, test, trial **Ant** disproof

**prop** *Syn* SUPPORT, sustain, bolster, buttress, brace

**propaganda** *Syn* PUBLICITY, ballyhoo, promotion

**propagate** *Syn* GENERATE, engender, breed, beget, procreate, sire, reproduce **2** *Syn* SPREAD, circulate, disseminate, diffuse, radiate

**propel** *Syn* PUSH, shove, thrust

**propensity** *Syn* LEANING, proclivity, penchant, flair **Ant** antipathy

**proper 1** *Syn* FIT, meet, appropriate, fitting, apt, happy, felicitous, suitable **Ant** improper **2** *Syn* DECOROUS, seemly, decent, nice

**property** *Syn* QUALITY, character, attribute, accident

**prophecy** *Syn* REVELATION, vision, apocalypse

**prophesy** *Syn* FORETELL, predict, forecast, prognosticate, augur, presage, portend, forebode

**propinquity** *Syn* PROXIMITY

**propitiate** *Syn* PACIFY, appease, placate, mollify, conciliate

**propitious** *Syn* FAVORABLE, auspicious, benign **Ant** unpropitious; adverse

**proportion** *Syn* SYMMETRY, balance, harmony

**proportional** ♦ corresponding in size, degree, or intensity *Syn* proportionate, commensurate, commensurable

**proportionate** *Syn* PROPORTIONAL, commensurate, commensurable **Ant** disproportionate

**proposal** ♦ something put forward, offered, or otherwise stated for consideration *Syn* proposition

**propose 1** *Syn* INTEND, purpose, mean, design **2** ♦ to set before the mind for consideration *Syn* propound, pose

**proposition** *Syn* PROPOSAL

**propound** *Syn* PROPOSE, pose

**propriety** *Syn* DECORUM, decency, etiquette, dignity

**prorate** *Syn* APPORTION, portion, parcel, ration

**prosaic** ♦ having a plain, practical, everyday character or quality *Syn* prosy, matter-of-fact

**proscribe** *Syn* SENTENCE, condemn, damn, doom
**proselyte** *Syn* CONVERT
**prospect** ♦ an advance realization of something to come *Syn* outlook, anticipation, foretaste
**prosper** *Syn* SUCCEED, thrive, flourish
**prostrate** *Syn* PRONE, supine, recumbent, couchant, dormant
**prosy** *Syn* PROSAIC, matter-of-fact
**protean** *Syn* CHANGEABLE, changeful, variable, mutable
**protect** *Syn* DEFEND, shield, guard, safeguard
**protest 1** *Syn* ASSERT, avouch, avow, profess, affirm, aver, declare, predicate, warrant **2** *Syn* OBJECT, remonstrate, expostulate, kick *Ant* agree
**protract** *Syn* EXTEND, prolong, lengthen, elongate *Ant* curtail
**protrude** *Syn* BULGE, jut, stick out, project, overhang, beetle
**protrusion** *Syn* PROJECTION, protuberance, bulge
**protuberance** *Syn* PROJECTION, protrusion, bulge
**protuberate** *Syn* BULGE, jut, stick out, protrude, project, overhang, beetle
**proud 1** ♦ showing scorn for inferiors *Syn* arrogant, haughty, lordly, insolent, overbearing, supercilious, disdainful *Ant* humble; ashamed **2** ♦ having or exhibiting undue or excessive pride esp. in one's appearance or achievements *Syn* vain, vainglorious *Ant* ashamed; humble
**prove 1** ♦ to establish a point by appropriate objective means *Syn* try, test, demonstrate *Ant* disprove **2** *Syn* INDICATE, betoken, attest, bespeak, argue
**provenance, provenience** *Syn* ORIGIN, source, inception, root, prime mover
**provender** *Syn* FOOD, fodder, forage, feed, victuals, viands, provisions, comestibles
**proverb** *Syn* SAYING, maxim, adage, motto, saw, epigram, aphorism, apothegm
**provide** ♦ to give or acquire and make available something wanted or needed *Syn* supply, furnish
**providence** *Syn* PRUDENCE, foresight, forethought, discretion *Ant* improvidence
**provident** *Syn* PRUDENT, foresighted, forethoughtful, discreet *Ant* improvident
**providential** *Syn* LUCKY, fortunate, happy
**providing** *Syn* IF
**province 1** *Syn* FIELD, domain, sphere, territory, bailiwick **2** *Syn* FUNCTION, office, duty
**provincial** *Syn* INSULAR, parochial, local, small-town *Ant* catholic
**provision 1** *Syn* CONDITION, stipulation, terms, proviso, reservation, strings **2** *pl* **provisions** *Syn* FOOD, feed, victuals, viands, comestibles, provender, fodder, forage
**provisional 1** ♦ not final or definitive *Syn* tentative *Ant* definitive **2** *Syn* TEMPORARY, ad interim, acting
**proviso** *Syn* CONDITION, stipulation, terms, provision, reservation, strings
**provoke 1** ♦ to arouse as if pricking *Syn* excite, stimulate, pique, quicken, galvanize **2** *Syn* IRRITATE, exasperate, nettle, aggravate, rile, peeve *Ant* gratify
**prowess** *Syn* HEROISM, valor, gallantry

**prowl** *Syn* WANDER, stray, roam, ramble, rove, range, gad, gallivant, traipse, meander
**proximity** ♦ the quality or state of being near *Syn* propinquity *Ant* distance
**proxy** *Syn* AGENT, deputy, attorney, factor
**prudence** ♦ good sense or shrewdness in the management of affairs *Syn* providence, foresight, forethought, discretion
**prudent 1** *Syn* WISE, judicious, sensible, sane, sage, sapient **2** ♦ making provision for the future *Syn* provident, foresighted, forethoughtful, discreet
**prudish** *Syn* PRIM, priggish, prissy, puritanical, straitlaced, stuffy
**prune** *Syn* SHEAR, trim, lop, poll, clip, snip, crop
**prying** *Syn* CURIOUS, inquisitive, snoopy, nosy
**pseudo** *Syn* COUNTERFEIT, spurious, bogus, fake, sham, pinchbeck, phony
**pseudonym** ♦ a fictitious or assumed name *Syn* alias, nom de guerre, pen name, nom de plume, incognito
**psyche** *Syn* MIND, intellect, soul, brain, intelligence, wit
**psychic** *Syn* MENTAL, intellectual, intelligent, cerebral
**psychosis** *Syn* INSANITY, lunacy, mania, dementia
**puberty, pubescence** *Syn* YOUTH, adolescence
**public** *Syn* FOLLOWING, clientele, audience
**publication** *Syn* DECLARATION, announcement, advertisement, proclamation, promulgation, broadcasting
**publicity** ♦ an act or device designed to attract public interest and to mold public opinion *Syn* ballyhoo, promotion, propaganda
**publish** *Syn* DECLARE, announce, advertise, proclaim, promulgate, broadcast
**puerile** *Syn* YOUTHFUL, juvenile, boyish, virgin, virginal, maiden *Ant* adult
**puff** *Syn* CRITICISM, critique, review, blurb
**pugnacious** *Syn* BELLIGERENT, combative, bellicose, quarrelsome, contentious *Ant* pacific
**puissance** *Syn* POWER, might, strength, force, energy
**puissant** *Syn* POWERFUL, potent, forceful, forcible *Ant* impuissant
**pulchritudinous** *Syn* BEAUTIFUL, beauteous, good-looking, comely, bonny, pretty, handsome, fair, lovely
**pull** ♦ to cause to move toward or after an applied force *Syn* draw, drag, haul, hale, tug, tow
**pulsate** ♦ to course or move with or as if with rhythmic strokes *Syn* pulse, beat, throb, palpitate
**pulsation** ♦ a rhythmical movement or one single step in recurring rhythmic steps *Syn* pulse, beat, throb, palpitation
**pulse** *n* *Syn* PULSATION, beat, throb, palpitation
**pulse** *vb* *Syn* PULSATE, beat, throb, palpitate
**pummel** *Syn* BEAT, pound, buffet, baste, belabor, thrash
**punch** *vb* **1** *Syn* STRIKE, hit, smite, slug, slog, swat, clout, slap, box, cuff **2** *Syn* PERFORATE, puncture, prick, bore, drill
**punch** *n* *Syn* VIGOR, vim, spirit, dash, esprit, verve, élan, drive

**punctilious** *Syn* CAREFUL, punctual, meticulous, scrupulous
**punctual** *Syn* CAREFUL, punctilious, meticulous, scrupulous
**puncture** *Syn* PERFORATE, punch, prick, bore, drill
**pungent** ♦ sharp and stimulating to the mind or the senses *Syn* piquant, poignant, racy, spicy, snappy *Ant* bland
**punish** ♦ to inflict a penalty on in requital for wrongdoing *Syn* chastise, castigate, chasten, discipline, correct *Ant* excuse; pardon
**puny** *Syn* PETTY, trivial, trifling, paltry, measly, picayunish, picayune
**purblind** *Syn* BLIND, sightless
**purchase** *Syn* BUY
**pure 1** ♦ containing nothing that does not properly belong *Syn* absolute, simple, sheer *Ant* contaminated, polluted; adulterated; applied (*of science*) **2** *Syn* CHASTE, modest, decent *Ant* impure; immoral
**purge** *Syn* RID, clear, unburden, disabuse
**puritanical** *Syn* PRIM, priggish, prissy, prudish, straitlaced, stuffy
**purloin** *Syn* STEAL, pilfer, filch, lift, pinch, snitch, swipe, cop
**purport** *Syn* SUBSTANCE, gist, burden, core, pith
**purported** *Syn* SUPPOSED, supposititious, suppositious, reputed, putative, conjectural, hypothetical
**purpose** *n* *Syn* INTENTION, intent, design, aim, end, object, objective, goal
**purpose** *vb* *Syn* INTEND, propose, design, mean
**pursue** *Syn* FOLLOW, chase, trail, tag, tail
**pursuit** *Syn* WORK, calling, occupation, employment, business
**purvey** *Syn* CATER, pander
**purview** *Syn* RANGE, gamut, reach, radius, compass, sweep, scope, orbit, horizon, ken
**push** ♦ to press against with force so as to cause to move ahead or aside *Syn* shove, thrust, propel
**pushing, pushy** *Syn* AGGRESSIVE, militant, assertive, self-assertive
**puss** *Syn* FACE, countenance, visage, physiognomy, mug
**pustule** *Syn* ABSCESS, boil, furuncle, carbuncle, pimple
**putative** *Syn* SUPPOSED, supposititious, suppositious, reputed, purported, conjectural, hypothetical
**putrefy** *Syn* DECAY, rot, decompose, spoil, disintegrate, crumble
**putrid** *Syn* MALODOROUS, fetid, noisome, stinking, rank, rancid, fusty, musty
**putsch** *Syn* REBELLION, revolution, uprising, revolt, insurrection, mutiny, coup
**put up** *Syn* RESIDE, live, dwell, sojourn, lodge, stay, stop
**puzzle** *vb* ♦ to baffle and disturb mentally *Syn* perplex, mystify, bewilder, distract, nonplus, confound, dumbfound
**puzzle** *n* *Syn* MYSTERY, problem, enigma, riddle, conundrum
**pygmy** *Syn* DWARF, midget, manikin, homunculus, runt

# Q

**quack** *Syn* IMPOSTOR, faker, mountebank, charlatan
**quail** *Syn* RECOIL, shrink, flinch, wince, blench
**quaint** *Syn* STRANGE, odd, queer, outlandish, curious, peculiar, eccentric, erratic, singular, unique
**quake** *Syn* SHAKE, tremble, totter, quiver, shiver, shudder, quaver, wobble, teeter, shimmy, dither
**qualified** *Syn* ABLE, competent, capable *Ant* unqualified
**qualify 1** *Syn* MODERATE, temper **2** *Syn* CHARAC-

TERIZE, distinguish, mark **3** *Syn* PREPARE, fit, condition, ready
**quality 1** ♦ an intelligible feature by which a thing may be identified *Syn* property, character, attribute, accident **2** ♦ a usu. high level of merit or superiority *Syn* stature, caliber
**qualm** ♦ a misgiving about what one is doing or is going to do *Syn* scruple, compunction, demur
**quandary** *Syn* PREDICAMENT, dilemma, plight, scrape, fix, jam, pickle

**quantity** *Syn* SUM, amount, aggregate, total, whole, number
**quarrel** *n* ♦ a usu. verbal dispute marked by anger or discord *Syn* wrangle, altercation, squabble, bickering, spat, tiff
**quarrel** *vb* *Syn* wrangle, altercate, squabble, bicker, spat, tiff
**quarrelsome** *Syn* BELLIGERENT, pugnacious, combative, bellicose, contentious
**quarry** *Syn* VICTIM, prey

**quash 1** *Syn* ANNUL, abrogate, void, vacate **2** *Syn* CRUSH, quell, extinguish, suppress, quench

**quaver** *Syn* SHAKE, tremble, shudder, quake, totter, quiver, shiver, wobble, teeter, shimmy, dither

**quay** *Syn* WHARF, dock, pier, slip, berth, jetty, levee

**queenly** *Syn* KINGLY, regal, royal, imperial, princely

**queer** *Syn* STRANGE, odd, erratic, eccentric, peculiar, quaint, outlandish, curious

**quell** *Syn* CRUSH, extinguish, suppress, quench, quash *Ant* foment

**quench** *Syn* CRUSH, quell, extinguish, suppress, quash

**querulous** *Syn* IRRITABLE, fretful, petulant, pettish, huffy, peevish, fractious, snappish, waspish

**query** *Syn* ASK, question, interrogate, inquire, examine, quiz, catechize

**quest** *Syn* ADVENTURE, enterprise

**question** *Syn* ASK, interrogate, query, inquire, examine, quiz, catechize *Ant* answer

**questionable** *Syn* DOUBTFUL, dubious, problematic *Ant* authoritative; unquestioned

**quick 1** *Syn* FAST, fleet, swift, rapid, speedy, expeditious, hasty **2** ♦ able to respond without delay or hesitation or indicative of such ability *Syn* prompt, ready, apt *Ant* sluggish

**quicken 1** ♦ to make alive or lively *Syn* animate, enliven, vivify *Ant* deaden **2** *Syn* PROVOKE, excite, stimulate, pique, galvanize *Ant* arrest **3** *Syn* SPEED, hasten, hurry, accelerate, precipitate *Ant* slacken

**quick-witted** *Syn* INTELLIGENT, clever, bright, smart, alert, knowing, brilliant

**quiescent** *Syn* LATENT, dormant, potential, abeyant

**quiet** *adj* *Syn* STILL, silent, noiseless, stilly *Ant* unquiet

**quiet, quieten** *vb* *Syn* CALM, compose, still, lull, soothe, settle, tranquilize *Ant* disquiet; arouse, rouse

**quip** *Syn* JOKE, jest, jape, witticism, wisecrack, crack, gag

**quit 1** *Syn* BEHAVE, acquit, comport, deport, demean, conduct **2** *Syn* GO, leave, depart, withdraw, retire **3** *Syn* STOP, cease, discontinue, desist

**quiver** *Syn* SHAKE, shiver, shudder, quaver, totter, tremble, quake, wobble, teeter, shimmy, dither

**quixotic** *Syn* IMAGINARY, chimerical, fantastic, visionary, fanciful

**quiz** *Syn* ASK, question, interrogate, examine, catechize, query, inquire

**quote** ♦ to speak or write again something already said or written by another *Syn* cite, repeat

**quotidian** *Syn* DAILY, diurnal, circadian

# R

**rabid** *Syn* FURIOUS, frantic, frenzied, wild, frenetic, delirious

**race** *Syn* VARIETY, subspecies, breed, cultivar, strain, clone, stock

**rack** *Syn* AFFLICT, torment, torture, try

**racket** *Syn* DIN, uproar, pandemonium, hullabaloo, babel, hubbub, clamor

**racking** *Syn* EXCRUCIATING, agonizing

**racy** *Syn* PUNGENT, piquant, poignant, spicy, snappy

**radiant** *Syn* BRIGHT, brilliant, luminous, lustrous, effulgent, refulgent, beaming, lambent, lucent, incandescent

**radiate** *Syn* SPREAD, circulate, disseminate, diffuse, propagate

**radical 1** *Syn* FUNDAMENTAL, basic, basal, underlying *Ant* superficial **2** *Syn* LIBERAL, advanced, progressive

**radius** *Syn* RANGE, gamut, reach, compass, sweep, scope, orbit, horizon, ken, purview

**rag** *Syn* BANTER, chaff, kid, rib, josh, jolly

**rage 1** *Syn* ANGER, ire, fury, indignation, wrath **2** *Syn* FASHION, style, mode, vogue, craze, cry, dernier cri, fad

**raid** *Syn* INVASION, incursion, inroad

**rail** *Syn* SCOLD, revile, vituperate, rate, berate, upbraid, tongue-lash, jaw, bawl, chew out, wig

**raillery** *Syn* BADINAGE, persiflage

**raiment** *Syn* CLOTHES, apparel, attire, clothing, dress

**raise 1** *Syn* LIFT, elevate, hoist, heave, rear, boost **2** *Syn* BUILD, construct, erect, frame, rear *Ant* raze

**rally** *vb* *Syn* STIR, rouse, arouse, awaken, waken

**rally** *vb* *Syn* RIDICULE, deride, mock, taunt, twit

**ram** *Syn* PACK, crowd, cram, stuff, tamp

**ramble** *Syn* WANDER, stray, roam, rove, range, prowl, gad, gallivant, traipse, meander

**rampant** *Syn* RANK

**rampart** *Syn* BULWARK, breastwork, parapet, bastion

**rancid** *Syn* MALODOROUS, stinking, fetid, rank, noisome, putrid, fusty, musty

**rancor** *Syn* ENMITY, antagonism, animosity, animus, antipathy, hostility

**random** ♦ determined by accident rather than by design *Syn* haphazard, chance, chancy, casual, desultory, hit-or-miss, happy-go-lucky

**range** *n* **1** *Syn* HABITAT, biotope, station **2** ♦ the extent that lies within the powers of something to cover or control *Syn* gamut, reach, radius, compass, sweep, scope, orbit, horizon, ken, purview

**range** *vb* **1** *Syn* LINE, line up, align, array **2** *Syn* WANDER, rove, ramble, roam, stray, prowl, gad, gallivant, traipse, meander

**rank** *adj* **1** ♦ growing or increasing at an immoderate rate *Syn* rampant **2** *Syn* MALODOROUS, fusty, musty, rancid, stinking, fetid, noisome, putrid *Ant* balmy **3** *Syn* FLAGRANT, glaring, gross

**rank** *n* *Syn* LINE, row, file, echelon, tier

**rank** *vb* *Syn* CLASS, grade, rate, graduate, gradate

**ransack** *Syn* SEEK, search, hunt, rummage, scour, comb, ferret out

**ransom** *Syn* RESCUE, deliver, redeem, reclaim, save

**rant** *Syn* BOMBAST, fustian, rodomontade, rhapsody

**rap** *n* *Syn* TAP, knock, thump, thud

**rap** *vb* *Syn* TAP, knock, thump, thud

**rapacious** *Syn* VORACIOUS, ravening, ravenous, gluttonous

**rapacity** *Syn* CUPIDITY, greed, avarice

**rapid** *Syn* FAST, swift, fleet, quick, speedy, hasty, expeditious *Ant* deliberate; leisurely

**rapscallion** *Syn* VILLAIN, scoundrel, blackguard, knave, rascal, rogue, scamp, miscreant

**rapt** *Syn* INTENT, absorbed, engrossed

**rapture** *Syn* ECSTASY, transport

**rare 1** *Syn* THIN, tenuous, slight, slender, slim **2** *Syn* CHOICE, delicate, dainty, exquisite, elegant, recherché **3** *Syn* INFREQUENT, scarce, uncommon, occasional, sporadic

**rarefy** *Syn* THIN, attenuate, extenuate, dilute

**rascal** *Syn* VILLAIN, scoundrel, blackguard, knave, rogue, scamp, rapscallion, miscreant

**rash** *Syn* ADVENTUROUS, daring, daredevil, reckless, foolhardy, venturesome *Ant* calculating

**rasp** *Syn* SCRAPE, scratch, grate, grind

**rate** *vb* *Syn* SCOLD, berate, upbraid, tongue-lash, jaw, bawl, chew out, wig, rail, revile, vituperate

**rate** *vb* **1** *Syn* ESTIMATE, value, evaluate, appraise, assess, assay **2** *Syn* CLASS, grade, rank, graduate, gradate

**ratify** ♦ to make something legally valid or operative usu. by formal approval or sanctioning *Syn* confirm

**ratiocination** *Syn* INFERENCE *Ant* intuition

**ratiocinative** *Syn* INFERENTIAL *Ant* intuitive

**ration** *n* ♦ an amount allotted or made available esp. from a limited supply *Syn* allowance, dole, pittance

**ration** *vb* *Syn* APPORTION, portion, prorate, parcel

**rational** ♦ relating to, based on, or agreeable to reason *Syn* reasonable *Ant* irrational; animal (*of nature*); demented (*of state of mind*); absurd (*of actions, behavior*)

**rationalize** *Syn* EXPLAIN, account, justify

**rattle** *Syn* EMBARRASS, faze, discomfit, disconcert, abash

**raucous** *Syn* LOUD, stentorian, earsplitting, hoarse, strident, stertorous

**ravage** ♦ to lay waste by plundering or destroying *Syn* devastate, waste, sack, pillage, despoil, spoliate

**ravening** *Syn* VORACIOUS, rapacious, ravenous, gluttonous

**ravenous** *Syn* VORACIOUS, ravening, rapacious, gluttonous

**ravish** *Syn* TRANSPORT, enrapture, entrance

**raw** *Syn* RUDE, crude, callow, green, rough, uncouth

**rawboned** *Syn* LEAN, gaunt, angular, lank, lanky, spare, scrawny, skinny

**ray** ♦ a shaft of light *Syn* beam

**raze** *Syn* DESTROY, demolish

**reach** *vb* ♦ to arrive at a point by effort or work *Syn* gain, compass, achieve, attain

**reach** *n* *Syn* RANGE, gamut, radius, compass, sweep, scope, orbit, horizon, ken, purview

**react** *Syn* ACT, operate, work, function, behave

**readiness** ♦ the power of doing something without evidence of effort *Syn* ease, facility, dexterity

**ready** *adj* *Syn* QUICK, prompt, apt

**ready** *vb* *Syn* PREPARE, fit, qualify, condition

**real** ♦ corresponding to known facts *Syn* actual, true *Ant* unreal; apparent; imaginary

**realize 1** ♦ to bring into concrete existence something that has existed as an abstraction or a conception or a possibility *Syn* actualize, embody, incarnate, materialize, externalize, objectify, hypostatize, reify **2** *Syn* THINK, conceive, imagine, fancy, envisage, envision

**reap** ♦ to do the work of collecting ripened crops *Syn* glean, gather, garner, harvest

**rear** *vb* **1** *Syn* BUILD, construct, erect, frame, raise **2** *Syn* LIFT, raise, elevate, hoist, heave, boost

**rear** *adj* *Syn* POSTERIOR, after, back, hind, hinder *Ant* front

**reason** *n* **1** ♦ a point or points that support something open to question *Syn* ground, argument, proof **2** *Syn* CAUSE, determinant, antecedent, occasion **3** ♦ the power of the mind by which man attains truth or knowledge *Syn* understanding, intuition

**reason** *vb* *Syn* THINK, reflect, deliberate, speculate, cogitate

**reasonable** *Syn* RATIONAL *Ant* unreasonable

**rebate** *Syn* DEDUCTION, abatement, discount

**rebel** ♦ one who rises up against constituted authority or the established order *Syn* insurgent, iconoclast

**rebellion** ♦ an outbreak against authority *Syn* revolution, uprising, revolt, insurrection, mutiny, putsch, coup

**rebellious** *Syn* INSUBORDINATE, mutinous, seditious, factious, contumacious *Ant* acquiescent; resigned; submissive

**rebound** ♦ to spring back to an original position or shape *Syn* reverberate, recoil, resile, repercuss

**rebuild** *Syn* MEND, repair, patch

**rebuke** *Syn* REPROVE, reprimand, admonish, reproach, chide

**rebut** *Syn* DISPROVE, refute, confute, controvert

**recalcitrant** *Syn* UNRULY, refractory, intractable, headstrong, willful, ungovernable *Ant* amenable

**recall 1** *Syn* REMEMBER, recollect, remind, reminisce, bethink, mind **2** *Syn* REVOKE, reverse, repeal, rescind

**recant** *Syn* ABJURE, retract, renounce, forswear

**recede** ♦ to move backward *Syn* retreat, retrograde, retract, back *Ant* proceed; advance

**receipt** ♦ a formula or set of directions for the compounding of ingredients esp. in cookery and medicine *Syn* recipe, prescription

**receive** ♦ to bring and accept into one's possession, one's presence, a group, or the mind *Syn* accept, admit, take

**recent** *Syn* MODERN, late

**recess** *Syn* PAUSE, respite, lull, intermission

**recherché** *Syn* CHOICE, elegant, exquisite, delicate, dainty, rare *Ant* banal

**recipe** *Syn* RECEIPT, prescription

**reciprocal 1** ♦ shared, felt, or shown by both sides concerned *Syn* mutual, common **2** ♦ like, equivalent, or similarly related to each other (as in kind, quality, or value) *Syn* corresponding, correlative, complementary, complemental, convertible

**reciprocate** ♦ to give back usu. in kind or in quantity *Syn* retaliate, requite, return

**recite** *Syn* RELATE, rehearse, recount, narrate, describe, state, report

**reckless** *Syn* ADVENTUROUS, daring, daredevil, rash, foolhardy, venturesome *Ant* calculating

**reckon 1** *Syn* CALCULATE, compute, estimate **2** *Syn* CONSIDER, regard, account, deem **3** *Syn* RELY, count, bank, trust, depend

**reclaim** *Syn* RESCUE, save, ransom, redeem, deliver *Ant* abandon

**recluse** ♦ a person who leads a secluded or solitary life *Syn* hermit, eremite, anchorite, cenobite

**recognition** ♦ a learning process that relates a perception of something new to knowledge already possessed *Syn* identification, assimilation, apperception

**recognize** *Syn* ACKNOWLEDGE

**recoil 1** ♦ to draw back in fear or distaste *Syn* shrink, flinch, wince, blench, quail *Ant* confront; defy **2** *Syn* REBOUND, reverberate, resile, repercuss

**recollect** *Syn* REMEMBER, recall, remind, reminisce, bethink, mind

**recollection** *Syn* MEMORY, remembrance, reminiscence, mind, souvenir

**recommend** *Syn* COMMEND, compliment, applaud

**recommendation** *Syn* CREDENTIAL, testimonial, character, reference

**recompense** *Syn* PAY, reimburse, indemnify, repay, satisfy, remunerate, compensate

**reconcile** *Syn* ADAPT, conform, accommodate, adjust

**recondite** ♦ beyond the reach of the average intelligence *Syn* abstruse, occult, esoteric

**record** *vb* ♦ to set down in writing usu. for the purpose of written evidence or official record of *Syn* register, list, enroll, catalog

**record** *n Syn* DOCUMENT, monument, archive

**recount** *Syn* RELATE, recite, rehearse, narrate, describe, state, report

**recoup** *Syn* RECOVER, recruit, retrieve, regain

**recover 1** ♦ to get back again *Syn* regain, retrieve, recoup, recruit **2** *Syn* IMPROVE, recuperate, convalesce, gain

**recreant** *Syn* RENEGADE, apostate, turncoat, backslider

**recreate** *Syn* AMUSE, divert, entertain

**recreation** *Syn* AMUSEMENT, diversion, entertainment

**recrudesce** *Syn* RETURN, revert, recur

**recrudescence** *Syn* RETURN, reversion, recurrence

**recruit** *Syn* RECOVER, regain, retrieve, recoup

**rectify** *Syn* CORRECT, emend, amend, reform, revise, remedy, redress

**rectitude** *Syn* GOODNESS, virtue, morality

**recumbent** *Syn* PRONE, supine, prostrate, couchant, dormant *Ant* upright, erect

**recuperate** *Syn* IMPROVE, recover, convalesce, gain

**recur** *Syn* RETURN, revert, recrudesce

**recurrence** *Syn* RETURN, reversion, recrudescence

**recurrent** *Syn* INTERMITTENT, periodic, alternate

**redact** *Syn* EDIT, compile, revise, rewrite, adapt

**redeem** *Syn* RESCUE, deliver, ransom, save, reclaim

**redolence** *Syn* FRAGRANCE, perfume, incense, bouquet

**redolent** *Syn* ODOROUS, aromatic, balmy, fragrant

**redress** *vb Syn* CORRECT, emend, remedy, amend, rectify, reform, revise

**redress** *n Syn* REPARATION, amends, restitution, indemnity

**reduce 1** *Syn* DECREASE, lessen, diminish, abate, dwindle **2** *Syn* CONQUER, vanquish, defeat, subjugate, beat, overcome, lick, subdue, surmount, overthrow, rout **3** *Syn* DEGRADE, demote, declass, disrate

**redundancy** *Syn* VERBIAGE, tautology, pleonasm, circumlocution, periphrasis

**redundant** *Syn* WORDY, verbose, prolix, diffuse *Ant* concise

**reef** *Syn* SHOAL, bank, bar

**reel** ♦ to move uncertainly or uncontrollably or unsteadily (as from weakness or intoxication) *Syn* whirl, stagger, totter

**refer 1** *Syn* ASCRIBE, assign, credit, accredit, attribute, impute, charge **2** *Syn* RESORT, apply, go, turn **3** ♦ to call or direct attention to something *Syn* allude, advert

**referee** *Syn* JUDGE, umpire, arbiter, arbitrator

**reference** *Syn* CREDENTIAL, testimonial, recommendation, character

**referendum** *Syn* MANDATE, initiative, plebiscite

**refinement** *Syn* CULTURE, cultivation, breeding *Ant* vulgarity

**reflect** *Syn* THINK, cogitate, reason, speculate, deliberate

**reflection** *Syn* ANIMADVERSION, stricture, aspersion

**reflective** *Syn* THOUGHTFUL, contemplative, meditative, pensive, speculative

**reform** *Syn* CORRECT, rectify, emend, amend, remedy, redress, revise

**refractory** *Syn* UNRULY, recalcitrant, intractable, ungovernable, headstrong, willful *Ant* malleable; amenable

**refrain** ♦ to hold oneself back from doing or indulging in *Syn* abstain, forbear

**refresh** *Syn* RENEW, restore, rejuvenate, renovate, refurbish *Ant* jade, addle

**refuge** *Syn* SHELTER, asylum, sanctuary, cover, retreat

**refulgent** *Syn* BRIGHT, effulgent, luminous, radiant, lustrous, brilliant, beaming, lambent, lucent, incandescent

**refurbish** *Syn* RENEW, renovate, refresh, restore, rejuvenate

**refuse** *vb Syn* DECLINE, reject, repudiate, spurn

**refuse** *n* ♦ matter that is regarded as worthless and fit only for throwing away *Syn* waste, rubbish, trash, debris, garbage, offal

**refute** *Syn* DISPROVE, confute, rebut, controvert

**regain** *Syn* RECOVER, recruit, recoup, retrieve

**regal** *Syn* KINGLY, royal, queenly, imperial, princely

**regale** *Syn* PLEASE, tickle, gratify, delight, rejoice, gladden *Ant* vex

**regard** *n* ♦ a feeling of deferential approval and liking *Syn* respect, esteem, admiration *Ant* despite

**regard** *vb* **1** ♦ to recognize the worth of a person or thing *Syn* respect, esteem, admire *Ant* despise **2** *Syn* CONSIDER, account, reckon, deem

**regarding** *Syn* ABOUT, concerning, respecting

**region** *Syn* AREA, tract, zone, belt

**register** *n Syn* LIST, table, catalog, schedule, roll, roster, inventory

**register** *vb Syn* RECORD, list, enroll, catalog

**regressive** *Syn* BACKWARD, retrogressive, retrograde *Ant* progressive

**regret** *Syn* SORROW, grief, heartache, heartbreak, anguish, woe

**regular 1** ♦ being of the sort or kind that is expected as usual, ordinary, or average *Syn* normal, typical, natural *Ant* irregular **2** *Syn* ORDERLY, methodical, systematic, regular *Ant* irregular

**regulate** *Syn* ADJUST, fix

**regulation** *Syn* LAW, rule, precept, statute, ordinance, canon

**regurgitate** *Syn* BELCH, burp, vomit, disgorge, spew, throw up

**rehearse** *Syn* RELATE, narrate, describe, recite, recount, state, report

**reify** *Syn* REALIZE, actualize, embody, incarnate, materialize, externalize, objectify, hypostatize

**reimburse** *Syn* PAY, indemnify, repay, recompense, compensate, remunerate, satisfy

**reinforce** *Syn* STRENGTHEN, invigorate, fortify, energize

**reissue** *Syn* EDITION, impression, reprinting, printing

**reiterate** *Syn* REPEAT, iterate, ingeminate

**reject** *Syn* DECLINE, repudiate, spurn, refuse *Ant* accept; choose, select

**rejoice** *Syn* PLEASE, delight, gladden, gratify, tickle, regale *Ant* grieve; aggrieve; bewail

**rejoin** *Syn* ANSWER, respond, reply, retort

**rejoinder** *Syn* ANSWER, response, reply, retort

**rejuvenate** *Syn* RENEW, restore, refresh, renovate, refurbish

**relapse** *n Syn* LAPSE, backsliding

**relapse** *vb Syn* LAPSE, backslide

**relate 1** ♦ to tell orally or in writing the details or circumstances of a situation *Syn* rehearse, recite, recount, narrate, describe, state, report **2** *Syn* JOIN, associate, link, connect, conjoin, combine, unite **3** *Syn* BEAR, pertain, appertain, belong, apply

**related** ♦ connected by or as if by family ties *Syn* cognate, kindred, allied, affiliated

**relative** *Syn* DEPENDENT, contingent, conditional *Ant* absolute

**relaxation** *Syn* REST, repose, leisure, ease, comfort

**relaxed** *Syn* LOOSE, slack, lax *Ant* stiff

**release** *Syn* FREE, liberate, emancipate, manumit, discharge, *Ant* detain; check; oblige

**relegate** *Syn* COMMIT, entrust, confide, consign

**relent** *Syn* YIELD, submit, capitulate, succumb, defer, bow, cave

**relentless** *Syn* GRIM, unrelenting, merciless, implacable

**relevant** ♦ relating to or bearing upon the matter in hand *Syn* germane, material, pertinent, apposite, applicable, apropos *Ant* extraneous

**reliable** ♦ having qualities that merit confidence or trust *Syn* dependable, trustworthy, trusty, tried *Ant* dubious

**reliance** *Syn* TRUST, confidence, dependence, faith

**relieve** ♦ to make something more tolerable or less grievous *Syn* alleviate, lighten, assuage, mitigate, allay *Ant* intensify; embarrass; alarm

**religion** ♦ a system of religious belief or the body of persons who accept such a system *Syn* denomination, sect, cult, communion, faith, creed, persuasion, church

**religious** *adj* **1** *Syn* DEVOUT, pious, pietistic, sanctimonious *Ant* irreligious **2** *Syn* HOLY, spiritual, sacred, divine, blessed *Ant* secular; profane

**religious** *n* ♦ a member of a religious order usu. bound by monastic vows of poverty, chastity, and obedience *Syn* monk, friar, nun

**relinquish** ♦ to give up completely *Syn* yield, leave, resign, surrender, cede, abandon, waive *Ant* keep

**relish** *n* **1** *Syn* TASTE, savor, tang, flavor, smack **2** *Syn* TASTE, palate, gusto, zest

**relish** *vb Syn* LIKE, fancy, dote, enjoy, love

**relishing** *Syn* PALATABLE, appetizing, savory, sapid, tasty, toothsome, flavorsome

**reluctant** *Syn* DISINCLINED, indisposed, hesitant, loath, averse

**rely on, rely upon** ♦ to have or place full confidence *Syn* trust, depend, count, reckon, bank

**remain** *Syn* STAY, wait, abide, tarry, linger *Ant* depart

**remainder** ♦ a remaining or left-over group, part, or trace *Syn* residue, residuum, remains, leavings, rest, balance, remnant

**remains** *Syn* REMAINDER, leavings, residue, residuum, rest, balance, remnant

**remark** *vb* 1 *Syn* SEE, notice, note, observe, perceive, discern, behold, descry, espy, view, survey, contemplate 2 ♦ to make observations and pass judgment thereon *Syn* comment, commentate, animadvert

**remark** *n* ♦ an expression of opinion or judgment *Syn* observation, comment, commentary, note, obiter dictum

**remarkable** *Syn* NOTICEABLE, prominent, outstanding, conspicuous, salient, signal, striking, arresting

**remedial** *Syn* CURATIVE, restorative, sanative, corrective

**remedy** *n* ♦ something prescribed or used for the treatment of disease *Syn* cure, medicine, medicament, medication, specific, physic

**remedy** *vb* 1 *Syn* CURE, heal 2 *Syn* CORRECT, rectify, emend, amend, redress, reform, revise

**remember** ♦ to bring an image or idea from the past into the mind *Syn* recollect, recall, remind, reminisce, bethink, mind *Ant* forget

**remembrance** 1 *Syn* MEMORY, recollection, reminiscence, mind, souvenir *Ant* forgetfulness 2 ♦ something that serves to keep a person or thing in mind *Syn* remembrancer, reminder, memorial, memento, token, keepsake, souvenir

**remembrancer** *Syn* REMEMBRANCE, reminder, memorial, memento, token, keepsake, souvenir

**remind** *Syn* REMEMBER, recollect, recall, reminisce, bethink, mind

**reminder** *Syn* REMEMBRANCE, remembrancer, memorial, memento, token, keepsake, souvenir

**reminisce** *Syn* REMEMBER, recollect, recall, remind, bethink, mind

**reminiscence** *Syn* MEMORY, remembrance, recollection, mind, souvenir

**remiss** *Syn* NEGLIGENT, lax, slack, neglectful *Ant* scrupulous

**remit** 1 *Syn* EXCUSE, pardon, forgive, condone 2 *Syn* SEND, forward, transmit, route, ship, dispatch

**remnant** *Syn* REMAINDER, residue, residuum, remains, leavings, rest, balance

**remonstrate** *Syn* OBJECT, expostulate, protest, kick

**remorse** *Syn* PENITENCE, repentance, contrition, attrition, compunction

**remote** *Syn* DISTANT, far, faraway, far-off, removed *Ant* close

**remove** *Syn* MOVE, shift, transfer

**removed** *Syn* DISTANT, remote, far-off, faraway, far

**remunerate** *Syn* PAY, compensate, satisfy, reimburse, indemnify, repay, recompense

**remunerative** *Syn* PAYING, gainful, lucrative, profitable

**rend** *Syn* TEAR, split, cleave, rive, rip

**rendezvous** *Syn* ENGAGEMENT, tryst, appointment, assignation, date

**renegade** ♦ a person who forsakes his or her faith, party, cause, or allegiance and aligns with another *Syn* apostate, turncoat, recreant, backslider *Ant* adherent

**renew** ♦ to make like new *Syn* restore, refresh, renovate, refurbish, rejuvenate

**renounce** 1 *Syn* ABDICATE, resign *Ant* arrogate; covet 2 *Syn* ABJURE, forswear, recant, retract *Ant* confess; claim

**renovate** *Syn* RENEW, refurbish, rejuvenate, restore, refresh

**renown** *Syn* FAME, honor, glory, celebrity, reputation, repute, notoriety, éclat

**renowned** *Syn* FAMOUS, famed, celebrated, eminent, illustrious

**rent** *vb* *Syn* HIRE, let, lease, charter

**rent** *n* *Syn* BREACH, break, split, schism, rupture, rift

**renunciation** ♦ voluntary surrender or putting aside of something desired or desirable *Syn* abnegation, self-abnegation, self-denial

**repair** *Syn* MEND, patch, rebuild

**reparation** ♦ a return for something lost or suffered, usu. through the fault of another *Syn* redress, amends, restitution, indemnity

**repartee** *Syn* WIT, humor, irony, sarcasm, satire

**repay** *Syn* PAY, compensate, remunerate, recompense, satisfy, reimburse, indemnify

**repeal** *Syn* REVOKE, reverse, rescind, recall

**repeat** 1 ♦ to say or do again *Syn* iterate, reiterate, ingeminate 2 *Syn* QUOTE, cite

**repellent** *Syn* REPUGNANT, abhorrent, distasteful, obnoxious, invidious *Ant* attractive; pleasing

**repentance** *Syn* PENITENCE, contrition, attrition, remorse, compunction

**repercuss** *Syn* REBOUND, reverberate, recoil, resile

**replace** ♦ to put out of a usual or proper place or into the place of another *Syn* displace, supplant, supersede

**replete** *Syn* FULL, complete, plenary

**replica** *Syn* REPRODUCTION, facsimile, duplicate, copy, carbon copy, transcript

**reply** *vb* *Syn* ANSWER, respond, rejoin, retort

**reply** *n* *Syn* ANSWER, response, rejoinder, retort

**report** *n* 1 ♦ common talk or an instance of it that spreads rapidly *Syn* rumor, gossip, hearsay 2 *Syn* ACCOUNT, story, chronicle, version 3 *Syn* LETTER, dispatch, message, note, epistle, missive, memorandum

**report** *vb* *Syn* RELATE, narrate, describe, state, recite, recount, rehearse

**repose** *Syn* REST, relaxation, leisure, ease, comfort

**reprehend** *Syn* CRITICIZE, censure, reprobate, condemn, denounce, blame

**represent** ♦ to present an image or lifelike imitation of (as in art) *Syn* depict, portray, delineate, picture, limn

**representative** *Syn* DELEGATE, deputy

**repress** *Syn* SUPPRESS

**reprimand** *Syn* REPROVE, rebuke, reproach, admonish, chide

**reprinting** *Syn* EDITION, impression, printing, reissue

**reprisal** *Syn* RETALIATION, retribution, revenge, vengeance

**reproach** *Syn* REPROVE, chide, admonish, rebuke, reprimand

**reprobate** *vb* *Syn* CRITICIZE, censure, reprehend, blame, condemn, denounce

**reprobate** *adj* *Syn* ABANDONED, profligate, dissolute *Ant* elect (*in theology*)

**reprobate** *n* *Syn* OUTCAST, castaway, derelict, pariah, untouchable

**reproduce** *Syn* GENERATE, propagate, engender, breed, beget, get, sire, procreate

**reproduction** ♦ a thing made to closely resemble another *Syn* duplicate, copy, carbon copy, facsimile, replica, transcript

**reprove** ♦ to criticize adversely *Syn* rebuke, reprimand, admonish, reproach, chide

**repudiate** 1 *Syn* DECLINE, spurn, reject, refuse *Ant* adopt 2 *Syn* DISCLAIM, disavow, disown, disallow *Ant* own

**repugnant** 1 ♦ so alien or unlikable as to arouse antagonism and aversion *Syn* repellent, abhorrent, distasteful, obnoxious, invidious *Ant* congenial 2 *Syn* OFFENSIVE, repulsive, revolting, loathsome

**repulsive** *Syn* OFFENSIVE, repugnant, revolting, loathsome *Ant* alluring, captivating

**reputation** *Syn* FAME, repute, renown, honor, glory, celebrity, éclat, notoriety

**repute** *Syn* FAME, reputation, renown, celebrity, notoriety, éclat, honor, glory *Ant* disrepute

**reputed** *Syn* SUPPOSED, supposititious, suppositious, putative, purported, conjectural, hypothetical

**request** *Syn* ASK, solicit

**require** 1 *Syn* DEMAND, exact, claim 2 *Syn* LACK, want, need

**requirement** ♦ something essential to the existence or occurrence of something else *Syn* requisite, prerequisite

**requisite** *adj* *Syn* NEEDFUL, necessary, indispensable, essential

**requisite** *n* *Syn* REQUIREMENT, prerequisite

**requite** *Syn* RECIPROCATE, retaliate, return

**rescind** *Syn* REVOKE, reverse, repeal, recall

**rescue** ♦ to set free from confinement or danger *Syn* deliver, redeem, ransom, reclaim, save

**research** *Syn* INQUIRY, investigation, inquisition, inquest, probe

**resemblance** *Syn* LIKENESS, similarity, similitude, analogy, affinity *Ant* difference; distinction

**resentment** *Syn* OFFENSE, umbrage, pique, dudgeon, huff

**reservation** *Syn* CONDITION, stipulation, terms, provision, proviso, strings

**reserve** *Syn* KEEP, keep back, keep out, hold, hold back, retain, withhold, detain

**reserved** *Syn* SILENT, reticent, uncommunicative, taciturn, secretive, close, close-lipped, closemouthed, tight-lipped *Ant* affable; expansive; blatant

**reside** ♦ to have as one's habitation or domicile *Syn* live, dwell, sojourn, lodge, stay, put up, stop

**residence** *Syn* HABITATION, dwelling, abode, domicile, home, house

**resident** *Syn* INHABITANT, denizen, citizen

**residue, residuum** *Syn* REMAINDER, remains, leavings, rest, balance, remnant

**resign** 1 *Syn* RELINQUISH, yield, surrender, leave, abandon, cede, waive 2 *Syn* ABDICATE, renounce

**resignation** 1 *Syn* COMPLIANCE, acquiescence 2 *Syn* PATIENCE, long-suffering, longanimity, forbearance

**resigned** *Syn* COMPLIANT, acquiescent *Ant* rebellious

**resile** *Syn* REBOUND, recoil, reverberate, repercuss

**resilient** 1 *Syn* ELASTIC, springy, flexible, supple 2 *Syn* ELASTIC, expansive, buoyant, volatile, effervescent *Ant* flaccid

**resist** ♦ to stand firm against a person or influence *Syn* withstand, contest, oppose, fight, combat, conflict, antagonize *Ant* submit; abide

**resolute** *Syn* FAITHFUL, steadfast, staunch, true, loyal

**resolution** 1 *Syn* ANALYSIS, dissection, breakdown 2 *Syn* COURAGE, mettle, spirit, tenacity

**resolve** 1 *Syn* ANALYZE, dissect, break down *Ant* blend 2 *Syn* DECIDE, determine, settle, rule 3 *Syn* SOLVE, unfold, unravel, decipher

**resolved** *Syn* decided, decisive, determined

**resonant** ♦ marked by conspicuously full and rich sounds or tones (as of speech or music) *Syn* sonorous, ringing, resounding, vibrant, orotund

**resort** *n* *Syn* RESOURCE, expedient, shift, makeshift, stopgap, substitute, surrogate

**resort** *vb* ♦ to betake oneself or to have recourse when in need of help or relief *Syn* refer, apply, go, turn

**resounding** *Syn* RESONANT, sonorous, ringing, vibrant, orotund

**resource** 1 *pl* **resources** *Syn* POSSESSIONS, assets, belongings, effects, means 2 ♦ something one turns to in the absence of the usual means or source of supply *Syn* resort, expedient, shift, makeshift, stopgap, substitute, surrogate

**respect** *n* *Syn* REGARD, esteem, admiration *Ant* contempt

**respect** *vb* *Syn* REGARD, esteem, admire *Ant* abuse; misuse

**respecting** *Syn* ABOUT, concerning, regarding

**respectively** *Syn* EACH, apiece, severally, individually

**respite** *Syn* PAUSE, recess, lull, intermission

**resplendent** *Syn* SPLENDID, gorgeous, glorious, sublime, superb

**respond** *Syn* ANSWER, reply, rejoin, retort

**response** *Syn* ANSWER, reply, rejoinder, retort

**responsible** ♦ subject to being held to account *Syn* answerable, accountable, amenable, liable

**responsive** **1** *Syn* SENTIENT, sensitive, impressible, impressionable, susceptible *Ant* impassive **2** *Syn* TENDER, sympathetic, warm, warmhearted, compassionate

**rest** *n* ♦ freedom from toil or strain *Syn* repose, relaxation, leisure, ease, comfort

**rest** *vb* *Syn* BASE, found, ground, bottom, stay

**rest** *n* *Syn* REMAINDER, residue, residuum, remains, leavings, balance, remnant

**restful** *Syn* COMFORTABLE, cozy, snug, easy

**restitution** *Syn* REPARATION, amends, redress, indemnity

**restive** **1** *Syn* CONTRARY, perverse, balky, froward, wayward **2** *Syn* IMPATIENT, restless, nervous, unquiet, uneasy, fidgety, jumpy, jittery

**restless** *Syn* IMPATIENT, restive, nervous, unquiet, uneasy, fidgety, jumpy, jittery

**restorative** *Syn* CURATIVE, remedial, corrective, sanative

**restore** **1** *Syn* RENEW, refresh, rejuvenate, renovate, refurbish **2** ♦ to help or cause to regain signs of life and vigor *Syn* revive, revivify, resuscitate

**restrain** ♦ to hold back from or control in doing something *Syn* curb, check, bridle, inhibit *Ant* impel; incite; activate; abandon (*oneself*)

**restraint** *Syn* FORCE, constraint, compulsion, coercion, duress, violence *Ant* incitement; liberty

**restrict** *Syn* LIMIT, circumscribe, confine

**result** *Syn* EFFECT, consequence, upshot, aftereffect, aftermath, sequel, issue, outcome, event

**resuscitate** *Syn* RESTORE, revive, revivify

**retain** *Syn* KEEP, keep back, keep out, detain, withhold, reserve, hold, hold back

**retaliate** *Syn* RECIPROCATE, requite, return

**retaliation** ♦ the act of inflicting or the intent to inflict injury in return for injury *Syn* reprisal, revenge, vengeance, retribution

**retard** *Syn* DELAY, slow, slacken, detain *Ant* accelerate; advance, further

**reticent** *Syn* SILENT, reserved, uncommunicative, taciturn, secretive, close, close-lipped, closemouthed, tight-lipped *Ant* frank

**retire** *Syn* GO, withdraw, leave, depart, quit

**retort** *vb* *Syn* ANSWER, rejoin, reply, respond

**retort** *n* *Syn* ANSWER, rejoinder, reply, response

**retract** **1** *Syn* RECEDE, retrograde, back, retreat *Ant* protract **2** *Syn* ABJURE, recant, renounce, forswear

**retreat** *n* *Syn* SHELTER, cover, refuge, asylum, sanctuary

**retreat** *vb* *Syn* RECEDE, retrograde, back, retract

**retrench** *Syn* SHORTEN, curtail, abridge, abbreviate

**retribution** *Syn* RETALIATION, reprisal, vengeance, revenge

**retrieve** *Syn* RECOVER, regain, recoup, recruit *Ant* lose

**retrograde** *adj* *Syn* BACKWARD, retrogressive, regressive

**retrograde** *vb* *Syn* RECEDE, retreat, back, retract

**retrogressive** *Syn* BACKWARD, regressive, retrograde *Ant* progressive

**return** *vb* **1** ♦ to go or come back (as to a person, place, or condition) *Syn* revert, recur, recrudesce **2** *Syn* RECIPROCATE, retaliate, requite

**return** *n* ♦ the act of coming back to or from a place or condition *Syn* reversion, recurrence, recrudescence

**reveal** ♦ to make known what has been or should be concealed *Syn* discover, disclose, divulge, tell, betray *Ant* conceal

**revelation** ♦ disclosure or something disclosed by or as if by divine or preternatural means *Syn* vision, apocalypse, prophecy *Ant* adumbration

**revenant** *Syn* APPARITION, phantasm, phantom, wraith, ghost, spirit, specter, shade

**revenge** *vb* *Syn* AVENGE

**revenge** *n* *Syn* RETALIATION, vengeance, retribution, reprisal

**revengeful** *Syn* VINDICTIVE, vengeful

**reverberate** *Syn* REBOUND, repercuss, recoil, resile

**revere** ♦ to honor and admire profoundly and respectfully *Syn* reverence, venerate, worship, adore *Ant* flout

**reverence** *n* **1** *Syn* HONOR, homage, deference, obeisance **2** ♦ a feeling of worshipful respect *Syn* veneration, worship, adoration **3** ♦ the emotion inspired by what arouses one's deep respect or veneration *Syn* awe, fear

**reverence** *vb* *Syn* REVERE, venerate, worship, adore

**reverse** *vb* **1** ♦ to change to the opposite position *Syn* transpose, invert **2** *Syn* REVOKE, repeal, rescind, recall

**reverse** *n* *Syn* OPPOSITE, contradictory, contrary, antithesis, antipode, antonym, converse, counter

**reversion** **1** *Syn* RETURN, recurrence, recrudescence **2** ♦ a return to an ancestral type or condition or an instance of such return *Syn* atavism, throwback

**reversionary** ♦ relating to a return to an ancestral type *Syn* atavistic

**revert** *Syn* RETURN, recur, recrudesce

**review** **1** *Syn* CRITICISM, critique, blurb, puff **2** *Syn* JOURNAL, periodical, magazine, organ, newspaper

**revile** *Syn* SCOLD, vituperate, rail, berate, rate, upbraid, tongue-lash, jaw, bawl, chew out, wig *Ant* laud

**revise** **1** *Syn* CORRECT, rectify, emend, remedy, redress, amend, reform **2** *Syn* EDIT, compile, redact, rewrite, adapt

**revive** *Syn* RESTORE, revivify, resuscitate

**revivify** *Syn* RESTORE, revive, resuscitate

**revoke** ♦ to annul by recalling or taking back *Syn* reverse, repeal, rescind, recall

**revolt** *Syn* REBELLION, revolution, uprising, insurrection, mutiny, putsch, coup

**revolting** *Syn* OFFENSIVE, loathsome, repulsive, repugnant

**revolution** *Syn* REBELLION, uprising, revolt, insurrection, mutiny, putsch, coup

**revolve** *Syn* TURN, rotate, gyrate, circle, spin, twirl, whirl, wheel, eddy, swirl, pirouette

**reward** *Syn* PREMIUM, prize, award, meed, guerdon, bounty, bonus

**rewrite** *Syn* EDIT, compile, revise, redact, adapt

**rhapsody** *Syn* BOMBAST, rant, fustian, rodomontade

**rhetorical** ♦ emphasizing style often at the expense of thought *Syn* grandiloquent, magniloquent, aureate, flowery, euphuistic, bombastic

**rhymer, rhymester** *Syn* POET, versifier, poetaster, bard, minstrel, troubadour

**rhythm** ♦ the regular rise and fall in intensity of sounds that is associated chiefly with poetry and music *Syn* meter, cadence

**rib** *Syn* BANTER, chaff, kid, rag, josh, jolly

**ribald** *Syn* COARSE, obscene, gross, vulgar

**ribbon** *Syn* STRIP, fillet, band, stripe

**rich** ♦ having goods, property, and money in abundance *Syn* wealthy, affluent, opulent *Ant* poor

**ricochet** *Syn* SKIP, bound, hop, curvet, lope, lollop

**rid** ♦ to set a person or thing free of something that encumbers *Syn* clear, unburden, disabuse, purge

**riddle** *Syn* MYSTERY, puzzle, conundrum, enigma, problem

**ride** *vb* **1** ♦ to travel by automobile or other conveyance *Syn* drive **2** *Syn* BAIT, badger, heckle, hector, chivy, hound

**ride** *n* ♦ a usu. short trip in a vehicle or by other conveyance *Syn* drive

**ridicule** ♦ to make an object of laughter of *Syn* deride, mock, taunt, twit, rally

**ridiculous** *Syn* LAUGHABLE, risible, ludicrous, droll, funny, comic, comical, farcical

**rife** *Syn* PREVAILING, prevalent, current

**rifle** *Syn* ROB, plunder, loot, burglarize

**rift** *Syn* BREACH, break, split, schism, rent, rupture

**right** *adj* **1** *Syn* GOOD *Ant* wrong **2** *Syn* CORRECT, accurate, exact, precise, nice *Ant* wrong

**right** *n* ♦ something to which one has a just claim *Syn* prerogative, privilege, perquisite, appanage, birthright

**righteous** *Syn* MORAL, virtuous, noble, ethical *Ant* iniquitous

**rightful** *Syn* DUE, condign

**rigid** **1** *Syn* STIFF, inflexible, tense, stark, wooden *Ant* elastic **2** ♦ extremely severe or stern *Syn* rigorous, strict, stringent *Ant* lax

**rigor** *Syn* DIFFICULTY, hardship, vicissitude *Ant* amenity

**rigorous** *Syn* RIGID, strict, stringent

**rile** *Syn* IRRITATE, exasperate, nettle, provoke, aggravate, peeve

**rim** *Syn* BORDER, brim, brink, margin, verge, edge

**rind** *Syn* SKIN, bark, peel, hide, pelt

**ring** *n* *Syn* COMBINATION, combine, party, bloc, faction

**ring** *vb* *Syn* SURROUND, environ, encircle, circle, encompass, compass, hem, gird, girdle

**ringing** *Syn* RESONANT, sonorous, resounding, vibrant, orotund

**rip** *Syn* TEAR, rend, split, cleave, rive

**ripe** *Syn* MATURE, matured, mellow, adult, grown-up *Ant* green; unripe

**ripen** *Syn* MATURE, develop, age

**rise** *vb* **1** *Syn* SPRING, arise, originate, derive, flow, issue, emanate, proceed, stem *Ant* abate **2** ♦ to move or come up from a lower to a higher level *Syn* arise, ascend, mount, soar, tower, rocket, levitate, surge *Ant* decline; set (*as the sun*)

**rise** *n* *Syn* BEGINNING, genesis, initiation *Ant* fall

**risible** *Syn* LAUGHABLE, droll, funny, ludicrous, ridiculous, comic, comical, farcical

**risk** *n* *Syn* DANGER, hazard, peril, jeopardy

**risk** *vb* *Syn* VENTURE, hazard, chance, jeopardize, endanger, imperil

**risky** *Syn* DANGEROUS, precarious, hazardous, perilous

**rite, ritual** *Syn* FORM, liturgy, ceremonial, ceremony, formality

**rival** **1** ♦ to strive to equal or surpass *Syn* compete, vie, emulate **2** *Syn* MATCH, equal, approach, touch

**rive** *Syn* TEAR, cleave, split, rend, rip

**rivet** *Syn* SECURE, anchor, moor

**roam** *Syn* WANDER, stray, ramble, rove, range, prowl, gad, gallivant, traipse, meander

**roar** *vb* ♦ to make a very loud and often a continuous or protracted noise *Syn* bellow, bluster, bawl, vociferate, clamor, howl, ululate

**roar** *n* ♦ a very loud and often a continuous noise *Syn* bellow, bluster, bawl, vociferation, ululation

**rob** ♦ to take possessions unlawfully *Syn* plunder, rifle, loot, burglarize

**robber** *Syn* THIEF, burglar, larcener, larcenist

**robbery** *Syn* THEFT, larceny, burglary

**robe** *Syn* CLOTHE, attire, dress, apparel, array

**robust** *Syn* HEALTHY, sound, wholesome, hale, well *Ant* frail, feeble

**rock** *Syn* SHAKE, agitate, convulse

**rocket** *Syn* RISE, arise, ascend, mount, soar, tower, levitate, surge

**rococo** *Syn* ORNATE, baroque, flamboyant, florid

**rodomontade** *Syn* BOMBAST, rhapsody, rant, fustian

**rogue** *Syn* VILLAIN, scoundrel, blackguard, knave, rascal, scamp, rapscallion, miscreant

**roguish** *Syn* PLAYFUL, frolicsome, sportive, waggish, impish, mischievous

**roily** *Syn* TURBID, muddy

**roll** *Syn* LIST, table, catalog, schedule, register, roster, inventory

**rollick** *vb* *Syn* PLAY, frolic, disport, sport, romp, gambol

**rollick** *n* *Syn* PLAY, frolic, disport, sport, romp, gambol

**romantic** *Syn* SENTIMENTAL, mawkish, maudlin, soppy, mushy, slushy

**romp** *n Syn* PLAY, frolic, rollick, gambol, disport, sport

**romp** *vb Syn* PLAY, frolic, rollick, gambol, disport, sport

**room 1** ♦ space in a building enclosed or set apart by a partition *Syn* chamber, apartment **2** ♦ enough space or range for free movement *Syn* berth, play, elbowroom, leeway, margin, clearance

**roost** *Syn* ALIGHT, perch, light, land

**root** *n Syn* ORIGIN, source, inception, provenance, provenience, prime mover

**root** *vb Syn* APPLAUD, cheer

**roseate** *Syn* HOPEFUL, optimistic, rose-colored

**rose-colored** *Syn* HOPEFUL, optimistic, roseate

**roster** *Syn* LIST, table, catalog, schedule, register, roll, inventory

**rot** *vb Syn* DECAY, decompose, putrefy, spoil, disintegrate, crumble

**rot** *n Syn* NONSENSE, twaddle, drivel, bunk, balderdash, poppycock, gobbledygook, trash, bull

**rotate 1** *Syn* TURN, revolve, gyrate, circle, spin, twirl, whirl, wheel, eddy, swirl, pirouette **2** ♦ to succeed or cause to succeed each other in turn *Syn* alternate

**rotter** *Syn* CAD, bounder

**rotund** *Syn* FLESHY, plump, chubby, portly, stout, fat, corpulent, obese *Ant* angular

**rough 1** ♦ not smooth or even *Syn* harsh, uneven, rugged, scabrous *Ant* smooth **2** *Syn* RUDE, crude, uncouth, raw, callow, green *Ant* gentle

**roundabout** *Syn* INDIRECT, circuitous

**rouse** *Syn* STIR, arouse, awaken, rally, waken

**roustabout** *Syn* WORKER, workman, workingman, laborer, mechanic, artisan, operative, hand, craftsman, handicraftsman

**rout** *n Syn* CROWD, throng, press, crush, mob, horde

**rout** *vb Syn* CONQUER, vanquish, defeat, subdue, subjugate, reduce, overcome, surmount, overthrow, beat, lick

**route** *n Syn* WAY, course, passage, pass, artery

**route** *vb Syn* SEND, forward, transmit, remit, ship, dispatch

**rove** *Syn* WANDER, stray, roam, ramble, range, prowl, gad, gallivant, traipse, meander

**row** *n Syn* LINE, rank, file, echelon, tier

**row** *n Syn* BRAWL, broil, fracas, melee, rumpus, scrap

**royal** *Syn* KINGLY, regal, queenly, imperial, princely

**rubbish** *Syn* REFUSE, waste, trash, debris, garbage, offal

**rube** *Syn* BOOR, bumpkin, hick, yokel, clodhopper, clown, lout, churl

**rude 1** ♦ lacking in social refinement *Syn* rough, crude, raw, callow, green, uncouth **2** ♦ offensive in manner or action *Syn* ill-mannered, impolite, discourteous, uncivil, ungracious *Ant* civil; urbane

**rudimentary** *Syn* ELEMENTARY, basal, beginning, elemental

**rueful** *Syn* MELANCHOLY, dolorous, doleful, lugubrious, plaintive

**rugged** *Syn* ROUGH, scabrous, harsh, uneven *Ant* fragile

**ruin** *n* ♦ the bringing about of or the results of disaster *Syn* havoc, devastation, destruction

**ruin** *vb* ♦ to subject to forces that are destructive of soundness, worth, or usefulness *Syn* wreck, dilapidate

**rule** *n Syn* LAW, regulation, precept, statute, ordinance, canon

**rule** *vb* **1** *Syn* GOVERN **2** *Syn* DECIDE, determine, settle, resolve

**rule out** *Syn* EXCLUDE, eliminate, debar, shut out, suspend, disbar, blackball

**ruminate** *Syn* PONDER, muse, meditate

**rummage** *Syn* SEEK, comb, ransack, search, hunt, scour, ferret out

**rumor** *Syn* REPORT, gossip, hearsay

**rumpus** *Syn* BRAWL, broil, fracas, melee, row, scrap

**runt** *Syn* DWARF, pygmy, midget, manikin, homunculus

**rupture** *Syn* BREACH, break, split, schism, rent, rift

**rural** ♦ relating to or characteristic of the country *Syn* rustic, pastoral, bucolic

**ruse** *Syn* TRICK, stratagem, maneuver, gambit, ploy, artifice, wile, feint

**rush** ♦ to move or cause to move quickly, impetuously, and often heedlessly *Syn* dash, tear, shoot, charge

**rustic** *Syn* RURAL, pastoral, bucolic

**ruth** *Syn* SYMPATHY, commiseration, compassion, pity, condolence, empathy

# S

**sack** *n Syn* BAG, pouch

**sack** *vb Syn* DISMISS, discharge, cashier, drop, fire, bounce

**sack** *vb Syn* RAVAGE, pillage, despoil, spoliate, devastate, waste

**sacred 1** *Syn* HOLY, divine, blessed, spiritual, religious *Ant* profane **2** ♦ protected (as by law, custom, or human respect) against abuse *Syn* sacrosanct, inviolate, inviolable

**sacrifice** *Syn* FORGO, abnegate, forbear, eschew

**sacrilege** *Syn* PROFANATION, desecration, blasphemy

**sacrilegious** *Syn* IMPIOUS, blasphemous, profane

**sacrosanct** *Syn* SACRED, inviolate, inviolable

**saddle** *Syn* BURDEN, encumber, cumber, weigh, weight, load, lade, tax, charge

**sadness** ♦ the quality, state, or instance of being unhappy or low in spirits *Syn* depression, melancholy, melancholia, dejection, gloom, blues, dumps *Ant* gladness

**safe** ♦ affording security from threat of danger, harm, or loss *Syn* secure *Ant* dangerous

**safeguard** *Syn* DEFEND, guard, shield, protect

**sag** *Syn* DROOP, wilt, flag

**saga** *Syn* MYTH, legend

**sagacious** *Syn* SHREWD, perspicacious, astute

**sage** *Syn* WISE, sapient, judicious, prudent, sensible, sane

**sail** *Syn* FLY, float, skim, scud, shoot, dart

**sailor** *Syn* MARINER, seaman, tar, gob, bluejacket

**salary** *Syn* WAGE, wages, stipend, pay, hire, emolument, fee

**salient** *Syn* NOTICEABLE, conspicuous, outstanding, signal, striking, arresting, prominent, remarkable

**salubrious** *Syn* HEALTHFUL, healthy, wholesome, salutary, hygienic, sanitary

**salutary** *Syn* HEALTHFUL, wholesome, healthy, salubrious, hygienic, sanitary *Ant* deleterious; evil

**salutation** *Syn* GREETING, salute

**salute** *vb Syn* ADDRESS, greet, hail, accost

**salute** *n Syn* GREETING, salutation

**same** ♦ not different or not differing from one

another *Syn* selfsame, very, identical, identic, equivalent, equal, tantamount *Ant* different

**sample** *Syn* INSTANCE, specimen, example, case, illustration

**sanative** *Syn* CURATIVE, remedial, restorative, corrective

**sanctimonious 1** *Syn* DEVOUT, pietistic, religious, pious **2** *Syn* HYPOCRITICAL, pharisaical, canting

**sanctimony** *Syn* HYPOCRISY, pharisaism, cant

**sanction** *Syn* APPROVE, endorse, accredit, certify *Ant* interdict

**sanctity** *Syn* HOLINESS

**sanctuary** *Syn* SHELTER, refuge, asylum, cover, retreat

**sand** *Syn* FORTITUDE, grit, backbone, pluck, guts

**sane** *Syn* WISE, judicious, prudent, sensible, sage, sapient *Ant* insane

**sangfroid** *Syn* EQUANIMITY, phlegm, composure

**sanguinary** *Syn* BLOODY, sanguine, sanguineous, gory

**sanguine 1** *also* **sanguineous** *Syn* BLOODY, sanguinary, gory *Ant* bloodless **2** *Syn* CONFIDENT, assured, sure, presumptuous *Ant* afraid

**sanitary** *Syn* HEALTHFUL, hygienic, salutary, salubrious, healthy, wholesome *Ant* noxious

**sanitize** *Syn* STERILIZE, disinfect, fumigate

**sap** *Syn* WEAKEN, undermine, enfeeble, debilitate, cripple, disable

**sapid** *Syn* PALATABLE, appetizing, savory, tasty, toothsome, flavorsome, relishing *Ant* insipid

**sapient** *Syn* WISE, sage, judicious, prudent, sensible, sane

**sarcasm** *Syn* WIT, satire, irony, humor, repartee

**sarcastic** ♦ marked by bitterness and a power or will to cut or sting *Syn* satiric, ironic, sardonic

**sardonic** *Syn* SARCASTIC, ironic, satiric

**sate** *Syn* SATIATE, surfeit, cloy, pall, glut, gorge

**satellite** *Syn* FOLLOWER, adherent, henchman, partisan, disciple, sectary

**satiate** ♦ to fill to repletion *Syn* sate, surfeit, cloy, pall, glut, gorge

**satiny** *Syn* SLEEK, silky, silken, velvety, glossy, slick

**satire** *Syn* WIT, irony, humor, sarcasm, repartee

**satiric** *Syn* SARCASTIC, ironic, sardonic

**satisfied** ♦ showing or expressing satisfaction from the fulfillment of one's desires *Syn* content, contented

**satisfy 1** ♦ to appease desires or longings *Syn* content *Ant* tantalize **2** *Syn* PAY, recompense, compensate, remunerate, repay, reimburse, indemnify **3** ♦ to measure up to a set of criteria or requirements *Syn* fulfill, meet, answer

**saturate 1** *Syn* SOAK, steep, impregnate, drench, sop, waterlog **2** *Syn* PERMEATE, impregnate, impenetrate, interpenetrate, penetrate, pervade

**saturnine** *Syn* SULLEN, dour, gloomy, glum, morose, surly, sulky, crabbed *Ant* genial; mercurial

**saucy** ♦ flippant and bold in manner or attitude *Syn* pert, arch

**saunter** ♦ to walk slowly in an idle or aimless manner *Syn* stroll, amble

**savage 1** *Syn* FIERCE, ferocious, barbarous, inhuman, cruel, fell, truculent **2** *Syn* BARBARIAN, barbaric, barbarous

**save 1** *Syn* RESCUE, deliver, redeem, ransom, reclaim *Ant* lose; waste; damn (*in theology*) **2** ♦ to keep secure or maintain intact from injury, decay, or loss *Syn* preserve, conserve *Ant* spend; consume

**savoir faire** *Syn* TACT, poise, address

**savor** *Syn* TASTE, flavor, tang, relish, smack

**savory** *Syn* PALATABLE, appetizing, sapid, tasty, toothsome, flavorsome, relishing *Ant* bland; acrid

**saw** *Syn* SAYING, adage, proverb, maxim, motto, epigram, aphorism, apothegm

**say** ♦ to express in words *Syn* utter, tell, state

**saying** ♦ an often repeated statement that usu. is brief and expresses a common observation or general truth *Syn* saw, adage, proverb, maxim, motto, epigram, aphorism, apothegm

**scabrous** *Syn* ROUGH, harsh, uneven, rugged *Ant* glabrous; smooth

**scale** *Syn* ASCEND, climb, mount

**scamp** *Syn* VILLAIN, scoundrel, blackguard, knave, rascal, rogue, rapscallion, miscreant

**scamper** *Syn* SCUTTLE, scurry, skedaddle, sprint

**scan** *Syn* SCRUTINIZE, examine, inspect, audit

**scandal 1** *Syn* OFFENSE, sin, vice, crime **2** *Syn* DETRACTION, calumny, slander, backbiting

**scanning** *Syn* SCRUTINY, examination, inspection, audit

**scant, scanty** *Syn* MEAGER, skimpy, scrimpy, exiguous, spare, sparse *Ant* plentiful; profuse

**scarce** *Syn* INFREQUENT, rare, uncommon, occasional, sporadic *Ant* abundant

**scare** *Syn* FRIGHTEN, alarm, fright, terrify, terrorize, startle, affray, affright *Ant* entice

**scathing** *Syn* CAUSTIC, mordant, acrid *Ant* scorching, searing, burning; fierce, ferocious, truculent, savage; incisive, biting, cutting, trenchant

**scatter 1** ♦ to cause to separate or break up *Syn* disperse, dissipate, dispel **2** *Syn* STREW, straw, broadcast, sow

**scent** *Syn* SMELL, odor, aroma

**schedule 1** *Syn* LIST, table, catalog, register, roll, roster, inventory **2** *Syn* PROGRAM, timetable, agenda

**scheme** *n* **1** *Syn* PLAN, design, plot, project **2** *Syn* SYSTEM, network, complex, organism

**scheme** *vb Syn* PLAN, design, plot, project

**schism** *Syn* BREACH, split, rupture, break, rent, rift

**schismatic** *Syn* HERETIC, sectarian, dissenter, nonconformist

**scholarly** *Syn* LEARNED, erudite

**scholarship** *Syn* KNOWLEDGE, learning, erudition, science, information, lore

**scholastic** *Syn* PEDANTIC, academic, bookish

**school** *Syn* TEACH, discipline, train, instruct, educate

**science** *Syn* KNOWLEDGE, learning, erudition, scholarship, information, lore

**scintillate** *Syn* FLASH, gleam, glance, glint, sparkle, glitter, glisten, coruscate, twinkle

**scoff** ♦ to show one's contempt in derision or mockery *Syn* jeer, gibe, fleer, gird, sneer, flout

**scold** *n Syn* VIRAGO, shrew, vixen, termagant, amazon

**scold** *vb* ♦ to reproach angrily and abusively *Syn* upbraid, rate, berate, tongue-lash, jaw, bawl, chew out, wig, rail, revile, vituperate

**scoop** *Syn* DIP, bail, ladle, spoon, dish

**scope** *Syn* RANGE, gamut, reach, radius, compass, sweep, orbit, horizon, ken, purview

**scorch** *Syn* BURN, char, sear, singe

**scorn** *n Syn* DISDAIN, contempt, despite

**scorn** *vb Syn* DESPISE, disdain, scout, contemn

**scoundrel** *Syn* VILLAIN, blackguard, knave, rascal, rogue, scamp, rapscallion, miscreant

**scour** *Syn* SEEK, search, hunt, ransack, rummage, comb, ferret out

**scout** *Syn* DESPISE, scorn, contemn, disdain

**scowl** *Syn* FROWN, glower, lower, gloom

**scrap** *vb Syn* DISCARD, junk, cast, shed, molt, slough

**scrap** *n Syn* BRAWL, broil, fracas, melee, row, rumpus

**scrape** *vb* ♦ to rub or slide against something that is harsh, rough, or sharp *Syn* scratch, grate, rasp, grind

**scrape** *n Syn* PREDICAMENT, dilemma, quandary, plight, fix, jam, pickle

**scratch** *Syn* SCRAPE, grate, rasp, grind

**scrawny** *Syn* LEAN, skinny, lank, lanky, spare, gaunt, rawboned, angular *Ant* brawny; fleshy; obese

**scream** *vb Syn* SHOUT, shriek, screech, yell, squeal, holler, whoop

**scream** *n Syn* SHOUT, shriek, screech, yell, squeal, holler, whoop

**screech** *vb Syn* SHOUT, scream, shriek, yell, squeal, holler, whoop

**screech** *n Syn* SHOUT, scream, shriek, yell, squeal, holler, whoop

**screen** *Syn* HIDE, conceal, secrete, cache, bury, ensconce

**scrimpy** *Syn* MEAGER, scanty, scant, skimpy, exiguous, spare, sparse

**scruple** *n Syn* QUALM, demur, compunction

**scruple** *vb Syn* DEMUR, balk, jib, shy, boggle, stickle, stick, strain

**scrupulous 1** *Syn* CAREFUL, meticulous, punctilious, punctual *Ant* remiss **2** *Syn* UPRIGHT, conscientious, honest, just, honorable *Ant* unscrupulous

**scrutinize** ♦ to look at or over *Syn* scan, inspect, examine, audit

**scrutiny** ♦ a close study, inquiry, or visual inspection *Syn* examination, scanning, inspection, audit

**scud** *Syn* FLY, skim, shoot, sail, dart, float

**scuffle** *Syn* WRESTLE, tussle, grapple

**sculpture, sculpt, sculp** *Syn* CARVE, chisel, engrave, incise, etch

**scum** *Syn* FOAM, froth, spume, lather, suds, yeast

**scurrility** *Syn* ABUSE, billingsgate, invective, vituperation, obloquy

**scurrilous** *Syn* ABUSIVE, opprobrious, vituperative, contumelious

**scurry** *Syn* SCUTTLE, scamper, skedaddle, sprint

**scurvy** *Syn* CONTEMPTIBLE, despicable, pitiable, sorry, cheap, beggarly, shabby

**scuttle** ♦ to move with or as if with short brisk steps *Syn* scurry, scamper, skedaddle, sprint

**seaman** *Syn* MARINER, sailor, tar, gob, bluejacket

**sear** *Syn* BURN, scorch, char, singe

**search** *Syn* SEEK, scour, hunt, comb, ransack, rummage, ferret out

**season** *Syn* HARDEN, acclimatize, acclimate

**seasonable** ♦ done or occurring at a good, suitable, or proper time *Syn* timely, well-timed, opportune, pat *Ant* unseasonable

**seclude** *Syn* ISOLATE, segregate, insulate, sequester

**seclusion** *Syn* SOLITUDE, isolation, alienation

**second** *Syn* INSTANT, moment, minute, flash, jiffy, twinkling, split second

**secondary** *Syn* SUBORDINATE, dependent, subject, tributary, collateral *Ant* primary

**second-rate** *Syn* MEDIUM, mediocre, middling, moderate, average, fair, indifferent

**secret** ♦ done without attracting observation *Syn* covert, stealthy, furtive, clandestine, surreptitious, underhand, underhanded

**secrete** *Syn* HIDE, conceal, screen, cache, bury, ensconce

**secretive** *Syn* SILENT, close, close-lipped, close-mouthed, tight-lipped, uncommunicative, taciturn, reticent, reserved

**sect** *Syn* RELIGION, denomination, cult, communion, faith, creed, persuasion, church

**sectary 1** *Syn* FOLLOWER, adherent, disciple, partisan, henchman, satellite **2** *also* **sectarian** *Syn* HERETIC, schismatic, dissenter, nonconformist

**section** *Syn* PART, sector, segment, division, portion, piece, detail, member, fraction, fragment, parcel

**sector** *Syn* PART, segment, section, division, portion, piece, detail, member, fraction, fragment, parcel

**secular** *Syn* PROFANE, temporal, lay *Ant* religious; sacred; regular

**secure** *adj Syn* SAFE *Ant* precarious, dangerous

**secure** *vb* **1** ♦ to fasten or fix firmly *Syn* anchor, moor, rivet **2** *Syn* ENSURE, insure, assure **3** *Syn* GET, procure, obtain, acquire, gain, win

**security** *Syn* GUARANTEE, surety, guaranty, bond, bail

**sedate** *Syn* SERIOUS, grave, staid, earnest, sober, solemn, somber *Ant* flighty

**sediment** *Syn* DEPOSIT, precipitate, dregs, lees, grounds

**sedition** ♦ an offense against a ruling authority to which one owes allegiance *Syn* treason

**seditious** *Syn* INSUBORDINATE, mutinous, rebellious, factious, contumacious

**seduce** *Syn* LURE, tempt, entice, inveigle, decoy

**sedulous** *Syn* BUSY, assiduous, diligent, industrious

**see 1** ♦ to take cognizance of by physical or mental vision *Syn* behold, descry, espy, view, survey, contemplate, observe, notice, remark, note, perceive, discern **2** ♦ to perceive something by means of the eyes *Syn* look, watch

**seedy** *Syn* SHABBY, dilapidated, dingy, faded, threadbare

**seek** ♦ to look for *Syn* search, scour, hunt, comb, ferret out, ransack, rummage

**seem** ♦ to give the impression of being without necessarily being so in fact *Syn* look, appear

**seeming** *Syn* APPARENT, illusory, ostensible

**seemly** *Syn* DECOROUS, proper, nice, decent *Ant* unseemly

**seethe** *Syn* BOIL, simmer, parboil, stew

**segment** *Syn* PART, section, sector, division, portion, piece, detail, member, fraction, fragment, parcel

**segregate** *Syn* ISOLATE, seclude, insulate, sequester

**seize** *Syn* TAKE, grasp, clutch, snatch, grab

**select** *adj* ♦ chosen from a number or group by fitness, superiority, or preference *Syn* elect, picked, exclusive *Ant* indiscriminate

**select** *vb Syn* CHOOSE, elect, prefer, opt, pick, cull, single *Ant* reject

**selection** *Syn* CHOICE, preference, election, option, alternative *Ant* rejection

**self-abnegation** *Syn* RENUNCIATION, abnegation, self-denial

**self-assertive** *Syn* AGGRESSIVE, assertive, pushing, pushy, militant

**self-assurance** *Syn* CONFIDENCE, assurance, self-confidence, aplomb, self-possession

**self-complacent** *Syn* COMPLACENT, self-satisfied, smug, priggish

**self-confidence** *Syn* CONFIDENCE, assurance, self-assurance, self-possession, aplomb

**self-denial** *Syn* RENUNCIATION, self-abnegation, abnegation

**self-esteem** *Syn* CONCEIT, self-love, egotism, egoism, amour propre *Ant* self-distrust

**self-love** *Syn* CONCEIT, self-esteem, egotism, egoism, amour propre *Ant* self-forgetfulness

**self-possession** *Syn* CONFIDENCE, self-confidence, assurance, self-assurance, aplomb

**selfsame** *Syn* SAME, very, identical, identic, equivalent, equal, tantamount *Ant* diverse

**self-satisfied** *Syn* COMPLACENT, self-complacent, smug, priggish

**semblance** *Syn* APPEARANCE, look, aspect

**sempiternal** *Syn* INFINITE, eternal, boundless, illimitable, uncircumscribed

**send** ♦ to cause to go or to be taken from one place, person or condition to another *Syn* dispatch, forward, transmit, remit, route, ship

**senescence** *Syn* AGE, senility, dotage *Ant* adolescence

**senility** *Syn* AGE, dotage, senescence

**sensation 1** ♦ awareness (as of heat or pain) due to stimulation of a sense organ *Syn* percept, sense-datum, sensum, image **2** ♦ the power to respond or an act of responding to stimuli *Syn* sense, feeling, sensibility

**sense 1** *Syn* SENSATION, feeling, sensibility **2** ♦ the ability to reach intelligent conclusions *Syn* common sense, good sense, horse sense, gumption, judgment, wisdom **3** *Syn* MEANING, acceptation, signification, significance, import

**sense-datum** *Syn* SENSATION, sensum, percept, image

**sensibility** *Syn* SENSATION, feeling, sense

**sensible 1** *Syn* MATERIAL, physical, corporeal, phenomenal, objective *Ant* intelligible **2** *Syn* PERCEPTIBLE, palpable, tangible, appreciable, ponderable *Ant* insensible **3** *Syn* AWARE, conscious, cognizant, alive, awake *Ant* insensible (of *or* to) **4** *Syn* WISE, prudent, sane, judicious, sage, sapient *Ant* absurd, foolish; fatuous, asinine

**sensitive 1** *Syn* LIABLE, susceptible, subject, exposed, open, prone *Ant* insensitive **2** *Syn* SENTIENT, impressible, impressionable, responsive, susceptible

**sensual 1** *Syn* CARNAL, fleshly, animal **2** *Syn* SENSUOUS, luxurious, voluptuous, sybaritic, epicurean

**sensum** *Syn* SENSATION, sense-datum, percept, image

**sensuous** ♦ relating to or providing pleasure through gratification of the senses *Syn* sensual, luxurious, voluptuous, sybaritic, epicurean

**sentence** ♦ to decree the fate or punishment of one adjudged guilty, unworthy, or unfit *Syn* condemn, damn, doom, proscribe

**sententious** *Syn* EXPRESSIVE, pregnant, meaningful, significant, eloquent

**sentient** ♦ readily affected by external stimuli *Syn* sensitive, impressible, impressionable, responsive, susceptible

**sentiment 1** *Syn* FEELING, emotion, affection, passion **2** *Syn* OPINION, view, belief, conviction, persuasion

**sentimental** ♦ unduly or affectedly emotional *Syn* romantic, mawkish, maudlin, soppy, mushy, slushy

**separate** *vb* ♦ to become or cause to become disunited or disjoined *Syn* part, divide, sever, sunder, divorce *Ant* combine

**separate** *adj* **1** *Syn* DISTINCT, several, discrete **2** *Syn* SINGLE, solitary, particular, unique, sole, lone

**sequel** *Syn* EFFECT, outcome, issue, result, consequence, upshot, aftereffect, aftermath, event

**sequence** *Syn* SUCCESSION, series, progression, chain, train, string

**sequent, sequential** *Syn* CONSECUTIVE, successive, serial

**sequester** *Syn* ISOLATE, segregate, seclude, insulate

**serene** *Syn* CALM, tranquil, peaceful, placid, halcyon

**serial** *Syn* CONSECUTIVE, successive, sequent, sequential

**series** *Syn* SUCCESSION, progression, sequence, chain, train, string

**serious** ♦ not light or frivolous (as in disposition, appearance, or manner) *Syn* grave, solemn, somber, sedate, staid, sober, earnest *Ant* light, flippant

**sermon** *Syn* SPEECH, homily, address, oration, harangue, talk, lecture

**serpentine** *Syn* WINDING, sinuous, tortuous, flexuous

**service** *Syn* USE, advantage, profit, account, avail

**servile** *Syn* SUBSERVIENT, menial, slavish, obsequious *Ant* authoritative

**servitude** ♦ the state of subjection to a master *Syn* slavery, bondage

**set** *vb* **1** ♦ to position (something) in a specified place *Syn* settle, fix, establish **2** *Syn* COAGULATE, congeal, curdle, clot, jelly, jell

**set** *n* ♦ a group of persons associated by common interest *Syn* circle, coterie, clique

**setting** *Syn* BACKGROUND, environment, milieu, mise-en-scène, backdrop

**settle 1** *Syn* SET, fix, establish *Ant* unsettle **2** *Syn* CALM, compose, quiet, quieten, still, lull, soothe, tranquilize *Ant* unsettle **3** *Syn* DECIDE, determine, rule, resolve

**sever** *Syn* SEPARATE, sunder, part, divide, divorce

**several 1** *Syn* DISTINCT, separate, discrete **2** *Syn* MANY, sundry, various, divers, numerous, multifarious

**severally** *Syn* EACH, individually, respectively, apiece

**severe** ♦ given to or marked by strict discipline and firm restraint *Syn* stern, austere, ascetic *Ant* tolerant; tender

**shabby 1** ♦ being ill-kept and showing signs of wear and tear *Syn* dilapidated, dingy, faded, seedy, threadbare **2** *Syn* CONTEMPTIBLE, despicable, pitiable, sorry, scurvy, cheap, beggarly

**shackle** *Syn* HAMPER, fetter, clog, trammel, manacle, hog-tie

**shade 1** ♦ comparative darkness or obscurity due to interception of light rays *Syn* shadow, umbrage, umbra, penumbra, adumbration **2** *Syn* APPARITION, ghost, spirit, specter, phantasm, phantom, wraith, revenant **3** *Syn* BLIND, shutter **4** *Syn*

COLOR, tint, hue, tinge, tone **5** *Syn* GRADATION, nuance **6** *Syn* TOUCH, suggestion, suspicion, soupçon, tinge, smack, spice, dash, vein, strain, tincture, streak

**shadow** *n* *Syn* SHADE, umbrage, umbra, penumbra, adumbration

**shadow** *vb* *Syn* SUGGEST, adumbrate

**shake 1** ♦ to exhibit vibratory, wavering, or oscillating movement often as an evidence of instability *Syn* tremble, quake, totter, quiver, shiver, shudder, quaver, wobble, teeter, shimmy, dither **2** ♦ to move up and down or to and fro with some violence *Syn* agitate, rock, convulse **3** *Syn* SWING, wave, flourish, brandish, thrash

**shallow** *Syn* SUPERFICIAL, cursory, uncritical

**sham** *n* *Syn* IMPOSTURE, cheat, fake, humbug, fraud, deceit, deception, counterfeit

**sham** *vb* *Syn* ASSUME, feign, simulate, counterfeit, pretend, affect

**sham** *n* *Syn* COUNTERFEIT, spurious, bogus, fake, pseudo, pinchbeck, phony

**shame** *Syn* DISGRACE, dishonor, disrepute, infamy, ignominy, opprobrium, obloquy, odium *Ant* glory; pride

**shameless** ♦ characterized by or exhibiting boldness and a lack of shame *Syn* brazen, barefaced, brash, impudent

**shape** *vb* *Syn* MAKE, form, fashion, fabricate, manufacture, forge

**shape** *n* *Syn* FORM, figure, conformation, configuration

**shapeless** *Syn* FORMLESS, unformed *Ant* shapely

**share** ♦ to have, get, or use in common with another or others *Syn* participate, partake

**sharp** ♦ having or showing alert competence and clear understanding *Syn* keen, acute *Ant* dull; blunt

**shatter** *Syn* BREAK, shiver, crack, burst, bust, snap

**shave** *Syn* BRUSH, graze, glance, skim

**shear** ♦ to cut or cut off with or as if with shears *Syn* poll, clip, trim, prune, lop, snip, crop

**shed** *Syn* DISCARD, cast, molt, slough, scrap, junk

**sheen** *Syn* LUSTER, gloss, glaze

**sheer** *adj* **1** *Syn* PURE, simple, absolute **2** *Syn* STEEP, precipitous, abrupt

**sheer** *vb* *Syn* TURN, divert, deflect, avert

**shelter** *n* ♦ something that covers or affords protection *Syn* cover, retreat, refuge, asylum, sanctuary

**shelter** *vb* *Syn* HARBOR, lodge, house, entertain, board

**shibboleth** *Syn* CATCHWORD, byword, slogan

**shield** *Syn* DEFEND, protect, guard, safeguard

**shift** *vb* *Syn* MOVE, remove, transfer

**shift** *n* **1** *Syn* RESOURCE, makeshift, expedient, resort, stopgap, substitute, surrogate **2** *Syn* SPELL, tour, trick, turn, stint, bout, go

**shimmy** *Syn* SHAKE, tremble, quake, totter, quiver, shiver, shudder, quaver, wobble, teeter, dither

**ship** *n* *Syn* BOAT, vessel, craft

**ship** *vb* *Syn* SEND, forward, transmit, remit, route, dispatch

**shipshape** *Syn* NEAT, tidy, trim, trig, snug, spick-and-span

**shirk** *Syn* DODGE, parry, sidestep, duck, fence, malinger

**shiver** *vb* *Syn* BREAK, shatter, crack, burst, bust, snap

**shiver** *vb* *Syn* SHAKE, quiver, shudder, quaver, tremble, quake, totter, wobble, teeter, shimmy, dither

**shoal** ♦ a shallow place in a body of water *Syn* bank, reef, bar

**shock** *n* *Syn* HEAP, cock, stack, pile, mass, bank

**shock** *vb* *Syn* HEAP, cock, stack, pile, mass, bank

**shock** *n* *Syn* IMPACT, collision, clash, concussion, impingement, percussion, jar, jolt

**shocking** *Syn* FEARFUL, appalling, awful, dreadful, frightful, terrible, terrific, horrible, horrific

**shoot** *vb* **1** *Syn* FLY, dart, float, skim, scud, sail **2** *Syn* RUSH, dash, tear, charge

**shoot** *n* ♦ a branch or a part of a plant that is an

outgrowth from a main stem *Syn* branch, bough, limb

**shopworn** *Syn* TRITE, hackneyed, stereotyped, threadbare

**shore** ♦ land bordering a usu. large body of water *Syn* coast, beach, strand, bank, littoral, foreshore

**short 1** *Syn* BRIEF *Ant* long **2** *Syn* FRAGILE, crisp, brittle, friable, frangible

**shortcoming** *Syn* IMPERFECTION, deficiency, fault

**shorten** ♦ to reduce in extent *Syn* curtail, abbreviate, abridge, retrench *Ant* lengthen, elongate; extend

**short-lived** *Syn* TRANSIENT, transitory, passing, ephemeral, momentary, fugitive, fleeting, evanescent *Ant* agelong

**shortly** *Syn* PRESENTLY, soon, directly

**shout** *vb* ♦ to utter a sudden loud cry (as to attract attention) *Syn* yell, shriek, scream, screech, squeal, holler, whoop

**shout** *n* ♦ a sudden loud cry *Syn* yell, shriek, scream, screech, squeal, holler, whoop

**shove** *Syn* PUSH, thrust, propel

**show** *vb* **1** ♦ to reveal outwardly or make apparent *Syn* manifest, evidence, evince, demonstrate **2** ♦ to present so as to invite notice or attention *Syn* exhibit, display, expose, parade, flaunt *Ant* disguise

**show** *n* *Syn* EXHIBITION, exhibit, exposition, fair

**showy** ♦ given to excess outward display *Syn* pretentious, ostentatious

**shrew** *Syn* VIRAGO, scold, vixen, termagant, amazon

**shrewd** ♦ acute in perception and sound in judgment *Syn* sagacious, perspicacious, astute

**shriek** *vb* *Syn* SHOUT, yell, scream, screech, squeal, holler, whoop

**shriek** *n* *Syn* SHOUT, yell, scream, screech, squeal, holler, whoop

**shrink 1** *Syn* CONTRACT, constrict, compress, condense, deflate *Ant* swell **2** *Syn* RECOIL, flinch, quail, blench, wince

**shrivel** *Syn* WITHER, wizen

**shroud** *Syn* COVER, overspread, envelop, wrap, veil

**shudder** *Syn* SHAKE, shiver, quiver, quaver, tremble, quake, totter, wobble, teeter, shimmy, dither

**shun** *Syn* ESCAPE, avoid, evade, elude, eschew *Ant* habituate

**shut** *Syn* CLOSE

**shut out** *Syn* EXCLUDE, eliminate, debar, rule out, blackball, disbar

**shutter** *Syn* BLIND, shade

**shy** *adj* ♦ not inclined to be forward *Syn* bashful, diffident, modest, coy *Ant* obtrusive

**shy** *vb* *Syn* DEMUR, balk, boggle, scruple, jib, stickle, stick, strain

**sic** *Syn* URGE, egg, exhort, goad, spur, prod, prick

**sicken** *Syn* DISGUST, nauseate

**sickly** *Syn* UNWHOLESOME, morbid, diseased, pathological *Ant* robust

**side** *Syn* PHASE, aspect, facet, angle

**sidereal** *Syn* STARRY, stellar, astral

**sidestep** *Syn* DODGE, parry, shirk, duck, fence, malinger

**siege** *Syn* BLOCKADE

**sigh** *vb* ♦ to let out a deep audible breath (as in weariness or sorrow) *Syn* sob, moan, groan

**sigh** *n* ♦ a usu. inarticulate sound indicating mental or physical pain or distress *Syn* groan, moan, sob

**sight** *Syn* LOOK, view, glance, glimpse, peep, peek

**sightless** *Syn* BLIND, purblind

**sign 1** ♦ a discernible indication of what is not itself directly perceptible *Syn* mark, token, badge, note, symptom **2** ♦ a motion, action, gesture, or word by which a command, thought, or wish is expressed *Syn* signal **3** *Syn* CHARACTER, symbol, mark

**signal** *n* *Syn* SIGN

**signal** *adj* *Syn* NOTICEABLE, salient, striking, arresting, outstanding, prominent, remarkable, conspicuous

**significance 1** *Syn* MEANING, signification, import, sense, acceptation **2** *Syn* IMPORTANCE, import, consequence, moment, weight
**significant** *Syn* EXPRESSIVE, meaningful, pregnant, eloquent, sententious
**signification** *Syn* MEANING, significance, import, sense, acceptation
**signify** *Syn* MEAN, import, denote
**silent 1** ♦ showing restraint in speaking *Syn* uncommunicative, taciturn, reticent, reserved, secretive, close, close-lipped, closemouthed, tight-lipped *Ant* talkative **2** *Syn* STILL, stilly, quiet, noiseless
**silhouette** *Syn* OUTLINE, contour, profile, skyline
**silken, silky** *Syn* SLEEK, slick, glossy, velvety, satiny
**silly 1** *Syn* SIMPLE, foolish, fatuous, asinine **2** *Syn* FOOLISH, absurd, preposterous
**similar** *Syn* LIKE, alike, analogous, comparable, akin, parallel, uniform, identical *Ant* dissimilar
**similarity** *Syn* LIKENESS, resemblance, similitude, analogy, affinity *Ant* dissimilarity
**simile** *Syn* ANALOGY, metaphor
**similitude** *Syn* LIKENESS, similarity, resemblance, analogy, affinity *Ant* dissimilitude, dissimilarity
**simmer** *Syn* BOIL, seethe, parboil, stew
**simper** *vb Syn* SMILE, smirk, grin
**simper** *n Syn* SMILE, smirk, grin
**simple** *adj* **1** *Syn* PURE, absolute, sheer *Ant* compound; complex **2** *Syn* EASY, facile, light, effortless, smooth *Ant* complicated; difficult **3** *Syn* PLAIN, homely, unpretentious **4** *Syn* NATURAL, ingenuous, naïve, unsophisticated, artless **5** ♦ actually or apparently deficient in intelligence *Syn* foolish, silly, fatuous, asinine *Ant* wise
**simple** *n Syn* DRUG, medicinal, pharmaceutical, biologic
**simpleton** *Syn* FOOL, moron, imbecile, idiot, natural
**simulate** *Syn* ASSUME, feign, counterfeit, sham, pretend, affect
**simultaneous** *Syn* CONTEMPORARY, synchronous, coincident, contemporaneous, coeval, coetaneous, concomitant, concurrent
**sin** *Syn* OFFENSE, vice, crime, scandal
**since** *Syn* BECAUSE, for, as, inasmuch as
**sincere** ♦ genuine in feeling *Syn* wholehearted, whole-souled, heartfelt, hearty, unfeigned *Ant* insincere
**sinewy** *Syn* MUSCULAR, athletic, husky, brawny, burly
**sing** ♦ to produce musical tones by or as if by means of the voice *Syn* troll, carol, descant, warble, trill, hymn, chant, intone
**singe** *Syn* BURN, sear, scorch, char
**single** *adj* **1** *Syn* UNMARRIED, celibate, virgin, maiden **2** ♦ one as distinguished from two or more or all others *Syn* sole, unique, lone, solitary, separate, particular *Ant* accompanied; supported; conjugal
**single** *vb Syn* CHOOSE, prefer, select, elect, opt, pick, cull
**singular** *Syn* STRANGE, unique, peculiar, eccentric, erratic, odd, queer, quaint, outlandish, curious
**sinister** ♦ seriously threatening evil or disaster *Syn* baleful, malign, malefic, maleficent
**sink** *Syn* FALL, drop, slump, subside
**sinuous** *Syn* WINDING, flexuous, serpentine, tortuous
**sire** *Syn* GENERATE, beget, get, procreate, engender, breed, propagate, reproduce
**site** *Syn* PLACE, position, location, situation, spot, station
**situation 1** *Syn* PLACE, position, location, site, spot, station **2** *Syn* STATE, condition, mode, posture, status
**size** ♦ the amount of measurable space or area occupied by a thing *Syn* dimensions, area, extent, magnitude, volume
**skedaddle** *Syn* SCUTTLE, scurry, scamper, sprint
**skeleton** *Syn* STRUCTURE, anatomy, framework

**skepticism** *Syn* UNCERTAINTY, doubt, dubiety, mistrust
**sketch** *n* **1** ♦ a rough drawing representing the chief features of an object or scene *Syn* outline, diagram, delineation, draft, tracing, plot, blueprint **2** *Syn* COMPENDIUM, précis, aperçu, syllabus, digest, pandect, survey
**sketch** *vb* ♦ to make a sketch, rough draft, or outline of *Syn* outline, diagram, delineate, draft, trace, plot, blueprint
**skewbald** *Syn* VARIEGATED, parti-colored, motley, checkered, checked, pied, piebald, dappled, freaked
**skid** *Syn* SLIDE, slip, glide, glissade, slither, coast, toboggan
**skill** *Syn* ART, cunning, craft, artifice
**skilled** *Syn* PROFICIENT, skillful, adept, expert, masterly *Ant* unskilled
**skillful** *Syn* PROFICIENT, adept, expert, skilled, masterly *Ant* unskillful
**skim 1** *Syn* FLY, float, dart, scud, shoot, sail **2** *Syn* BRUSH, graze, glance, shave
**skimpy** *Syn* MEAGER, scrimpy, exiguous, scanty, scant, spare, sparse
**skin** *n* ♦ an outer or surface layer esp. the outer limiting layer of an animal body *Syn* hide, pelt, rind, bark, peel
**skin** *vb* ♦ to remove the surface, skin, or thin outer covering of *Syn* decorticate, peel, pare, flay
**skinny** *Syn* LEAN, scrawny, rawboned, angular, gaunt, lank, lanky, spare *Ant* fleshy
**skip** ♦ to move or advance with successive springs or leaps *Syn* bound, hop, curvet, lope, lollop, ricochet
**skirmish** *Syn* ENCOUNTER, brush
**skit** *Syn* LIBEL, squib, lampoon, pasquinade
**skulk** *Syn* LURK, couch, slink, sneak
**skyline** *Syn* OUTLINE, profile, contour, silhouette
**slack 1** *Syn* NEGLIGENT, lax, remiss, neglectful **2** *Syn* LOOSE, relaxed, lax
**slacken** *Syn* DELAY, retard, slow, detain *Ant* quicken
**slander** *n Syn* DETRACTION, calumny, backbiting, scandal
**slander** *vb Syn* MALIGN, defame, libel, calumniate, traduce, asperse, vilify
**slang** *Syn* DIALECT, vernacular, patois, lingo, jargon, cant, argot
**slant** *vb* ♦ to set or be set at an angle *Syn* slope, incline, lean
**slant** *n Syn* POINT OF VIEW, viewpoint, standpoint, angle
**slap** *Syn* STRIKE, hit, smite, punch, slug, slog, swat, clout, cuff, box
**slash** *Syn* CUT, slit, hew, chop, carve
**slatternly** ♦ being habitually untidy and very dirty esp. in dress or appearance *Syn* dowdy, frowzy, blowsy
**slaughter** *Syn* MASSACRE, butchery, carnage, pogrom
**slavery** *Syn* SERVITUDE, bondage
**slavish** *Syn* SUBSERVIENT, servile, menial, obsequious
**slay** *Syn* KILL, murder, assassinate, dispatch, execute
**sleazy** *Syn* LIMP, flimsy, floppy, flaccid, flabby
**sleek** ♦ having a smooth bright surface or appearance *Syn* slick, glossy, velvety, silken, silky, satiny
**sleep** ♦ to take rest by a suspension of consciousness *Syn* slumber, drowse, doze, nap, catnap, snooze
**sleepy** ♦ affected by or inducing of a desire to sleep *Syn* drowsy, somnolent, slumberous
**slender** *Syn* THIN, slim, slight, tenuous, rare
**slick 1** *Syn* SLEEK, glossy, velvety, silken, satiny, silky **2** *Syn* FULSOME, oily, unctuous, oleaginous, soapy
**slide** ♦ to go or progress with a smooth continuous motion *Syn* slip, glide, skid, glissade, slither, coast, toboggan
**slight** *adj Syn* THIN, tenuous, rare, slender, slim

**slight** *vb Syn* NEGLECT, ignore, overlook, disregard, omit, forget
**slighting** *Syn* DEROGATORY, depreciatory, depreciative, disparaging, pejorative
**slim** *Syn* THIN, slender, slight, tenuous, rare *Ant* chubby
**sling** *vb Syn* THROW, hurl, fling, pitch, toss, cast
**sling** *vb Syn* HANG, suspend, dangle
**slink** *Syn* LURK, skulk, sneak
**slip** *vb Syn* SLIDE, glide, skid, glissade, slither, coast, toboggan
**slip** *n* **1** *Syn* WHARF, dock, pier, quay, berth, jetty, levee **2** *Syn* ERROR, lapse, mistake, blunder, faux pas, bull, howler, boner
**slipshod** ♦ negligent of or marked by lack of neatness and order esp. in appearance or dress *Syn* slovenly, unkempt, disheveled, sloppy
**slit** *Syn* CUT, slash, hew, chop, carve
**slither** *Syn* SLIDE, slip, glide, skid, glissade, coast, toboggan
**slog** *Syn* STRIKE, hit, smite, punch, slug, swat, clout, slap, cuff, box
**slogan** *Syn* CATCHWORD, byword, shibboleth
**slope** *Syn* SLANT, incline, lean
**sloppy** *Syn* SLIPSHOD, slovenly, unkempt, disheveled
**slothful** *Syn* LAZY, indolent, faineant *Ant* industrious
**slough** *Syn* DISCARD, cast, shed, molt, scrap, junk
**slovenly** *Syn* SLIPSHOD, unkempt, disheveled, sloppy
**slow** *adj* **1** *Syn* STUPID, dull, dense, crass, dumb **2** ♦ moving, flowing, or proceeding at less than the usual, desirable, or required speed *Syn* dilatory, laggard, deliberate, leisurely *Ant* fast
**slow** *vb Syn* DELAY, slacken, retard, detain *Ant* speed
**slug** *Syn* STRIKE, hit, smite, punch, slog, swat, clout, slap, cuff, box
**sluggish** *Syn* LETHARGIC, torpid, comatose *Ant* brisk; expeditious; quick
**sluice** *Syn* POUR, stream, gush
**slumber** *Syn* SLEEP, drowse, doze, nap, catnap, snooze
**slumberous** *Syn* SLEEPY, drowsy, somnolent
**slump** *Syn* FALL, drop, sink, subside
**slushy** *Syn* SENTIMENTAL, mushy, romantic, mawkish, maudlin, soppy
**sly** ♦ attaining or seeking to attain one's ends by devious means *Syn* cunning, crafty, tricky, foxy, insidious, wily, guileful, artful
**smack 1** *Syn* TASTE, flavor, savor, tang, relish **2** *Syn* TOUCH, suggestion, suspicion, soupçon, tincture, tinge, shade, spice, dash, vein, strain, streak
**small** ♦ noticeably below average in size *Syn* little, diminutive, petite, wee, tiny, teeny, weeny, minute, microscopic, miniature *Ant* large
**small-town** *Syn* INSULAR, provincial, parochial, local *Ant* cosmopolitan
**smart 1** *Syn* INTELLIGENT, bright, knowing, quick-witted, clever, alert *Ant* dull (*of mind*) **2** *Syn* STYLISH, modish, fashionable, chic, dashing *Ant* dowdy, frowzy, blowsy
**smash** *Syn* CRUSH, mash, bruise, squash, macerate
**smell** ♦ the quality that makes a thing perceptible to the olfactory sense *Syn* scent, odor, aroma
**smidgen** *Syn* PARTICLE, bit, mite, whit, atom, iota, jot, tittle
**smile** *vb* ♦ to have, produce, or exhibit a smile *Syn* grin, simper, smirk *Ant* frown
**smile** *n* ♦ a facial expression in which the lips curve slightly upward esp. in expression of pleasure or amusement *Syn* simper, smirk, grin *Ant* frown
**smirch** *Syn* SOIL, dirty, sully, tarnish, foul, befoul, besmirch, grime, begrime
**smirk** *vb Syn* SMILE, simper, grin
**smirk** *n Syn* SMILE, simper, grin
**smite** *Syn* STRIKE, hit, punch, slug, slog, swat, clout, slap, cuff, box
**smog** *Syn* HAZE, fog, mist

**smooth 1** *Syn* LEVEL, even, plane, plain, flat, flush *Ant* rough **2** *Syn* EASY, effortless, light, simple, facile *Ant* labored **3** *Syn* SUAVE, bland, diplomatic, politic, urbane *Ant* bluff **4** *Syn* SOFT, bland, mild, gentle, lenient, balmy
**smother** *Syn* SUFFOCATE, asphyxiate, stifle, choke, strangle, throttle
**smug** *Syn* COMPLACENT, self-complacent, self-satisfied, priggish
**smuggled** ♦ imported or exported secretly and in violation of the law *Syn* bootleg, contraband
**snag** *Syn* OBSTACLE, obstruction, impediment, bar
**snap 1** *Syn* JERK, twitch, yank **2** *Syn* BREAK, crack, burst, bust, shatter, shiver
**snappish** *Syn* IRRITABLE, fractious, peevish, waspish, petulant, pettish, huffy, fretful, querulous
**snappy** *Syn* PUNGENT, piquant, poignant, racy, spicy
**snare** *n* *Syn* LURE, trap, bait, decoy
**snare** *vb* *Syn* CATCH, ensnare, trap, entrap, bag, capture
**snarl** *n* *Syn* CONFUSION, disorder, chaos, disarray, jumble, clutter, muddle
**snarl** *vb* *Syn* BARK, bay, howl, growl, yelp, yap
**snatch** *Syn* TAKE, grasp, grab, clutch, seize
**sneak** *Syn* LURK, slink, skulk
**sneer** *Syn* SCOFF, jeer, gird, flout, gibe, fleer
**snip** *Syn* SHEAR, poll, clip, trim, prune, lop, crop
**snitch** *Syn* STEAL, pilfer, filch, purloin, lift, pinch, swipe, cop
**snoopy** *Syn* CURIOUS, inquisitive, prying, nosy
**snooze** *Syn* SLEEP, slumber, drowse, doze, nap, catnap
**snug 1** *Syn* NEAT, trim, trig, shipshape, tidy, spick-and-span **2** *Syn* COMFORTABLE, cozy, easy, restful
**so** *Syn* THEREFORE, hence, consequently, then, accordingly
**soak** *vb* ♦ to permeate or be permeated with a liquid *Syn* saturate, drench, steep, impregnate, sop, waterlog
**soak** *n* *Syn* DRUNKARD, inebriate, alcoholic, dipsomaniac, sot, toper, tosspot, tippler
**soapy** *Syn* FULSOME, slick, oily, unctuous, oleaginous
**soar** *Syn* RISE, arise, ascend, mount, tower, rocket, levitate, surge
**sob** *vb* *Syn* SIGH, moan, groan
**sob** *n* *Syn* SIGH, moan, groan
**sober 1** ♦ having or exhibiting self-control and avoiding extremes of behavior *Syn* temperate, continent, unimpassioned *Ant* drunk; excited **2** *Syn* SERIOUS, grave, sedate, staid, solemn, somber, earnest *Ant* gay
**sobriety** *Syn* TEMPERANCE, abstinence, abstemiousness, continence *Ant* drunkenness; excitement
**sociable** *Syn* GRACIOUS, cordial, affable, genial *Ant* unsociable
**social** ♦ inclined to seek or enjoy the company of others *Syn* gregarious, cooperative, convivial, companionable, hospitable *Ant* unsocial, antisocial, asocial
**society 1** *Syn* ARISTOCRACY, elite, nobility, gentry, county **2** *Syn* ASSOCIATION, order, club
**soft** ♦ free from all harshness, roughness, or intensity *Syn* bland, mild, gentle, smooth, lenient, balmy *Ant* hard; stern
**soil** ♦ to make or become unclean *Syn* dirty, sully, tarnish, foul, befoul, smirch, besmirch, grime, begrime
**sojourn** *Syn* RESIDE, lodge, stay, put up, stop, live, dwell
**solace** *Syn* COMFORT, console
**sole** *Syn* SINGLE, unique, solitary, lone, separate, particular
**solecism** *Syn* BARBARISM, corruption, impropriety, vulgarism, vernacular
**solemn 1** *Syn* CEREMONIAL, ceremonious, formal, conventional **2** *Syn* SERIOUS, grave, somber, sedate, earnest, staid, sober
**solemnize** *Syn* KEEP, celebrate, observe, commemorate

**solicit 1** *Syn* ASK, request **2** *Syn* INVITE, bid, court, woo
**solicitor** *Syn* LAWYER, attorney, counselor, barrister, counsel, advocate
**solicitous** *Syn* WORRIED, concerned, anxious *Ant* unmindful; negligent
**solicitude** *Syn* CARE, concern, anxiety, worry *Ant* negligence; unmindfulness
**solid** *Syn* FIRM, hard *Ant* fluid, liquid
**solidarity** *Syn* UNITY, union, integrity
**solidify** *Syn* HARDEN, indurate, petrify, cake
**solitary 1** *Syn* ALONE, lonely, lonesome, lone, forlorn, lorn, desolate **2** *Syn* SINGLE, sole, unique, lone, separate, particular
**solitude** ♦ the state of one who is alone *Syn* isolation, alienation, seclusion
**solve** ♦ to find an explanation or solution for something obscure, mysterious, or incomprehensible *Syn* resolve, unfold, unravel, decipher
**somatic** *Syn* BODILY, physical, corporeal, corporal
**somber** *Syn* SERIOUS, grave, solemn, sedate, staid, sober, earnest *Ant* garish
**somnolent** *Syn* SLEEPY, drowsy, slumberous
**sonorous** *Syn* RESONANT, ringing, resounding, vibrant, orotund
**soon 1** *Syn* PRESENTLY, shortly, directly **2** *Syn* EARLY, beforehand, betimes
**soothe** *Syn* CALM, compose, quiet, quieten, still, lull, settle, tranquilize *Ant* annoy; excite
**sop** *Syn* SOAK, saturate, drench, steep, impregnate, waterlog
**sophism** *Syn* FALLACY, sophistry, casuistry
**sophistical** *Syn* FALLACIOUS, casuistical *Ant* valid
**sophisticate** *Syn* ADULTERATE, load, weight, doctor
**sophisticated** ♦ experienced in the ways of the world *Syn* worldly-wise, worldly, blasé, disillusioned *Ant* unsophisticated
**sophistry** *Syn* FALLACY, sophism, casuistry
**soppy** *Syn* SENTIMENTAL, romantic, mawkish, maudlin, mushy, slushy
**sorcery** *Syn* MAGIC, witchcraft, witchery, wizardry, alchemy, thaumaturgy
**sordid** *Syn* MEAN, ignoble, abject
**sorrow** *n* ♦ distress of mind *Syn* grief, heartache, heartbreak, anguish, woe, regret *Ant* joy
**sorrow** *vb* *Syn* GRIEVE, mourn
**sorry** *Syn* CONTEMPTIBLE, pitiable, despicable, scurvy, cheap, beggarly, shabby
**sort** *n* *Syn* TYPE, kind, stripe, kidney, ilk, description, nature, character
**sort** *vb* *Syn* ASSORT, classify, pigeonhole
**sot** *Syn* DRUNKARD, inebriate, alcoholic, dipsomaniac, soak, toper, tosspot, tippler
**soul 1** *Syn* MIND, intellect, psyche, brain, intelligence, wit **2** ♦ the immortal part of a human being believed to have permanent individual existence *Syn* spirit *Ant* body
**sound** *adj* **1** *Syn* HEALTHY, wholesome, robust, hale, well **2** *Syn* VALID, cogent, convincing, compelling, telling *Ant* fallacious
**sound** *n* ♦ a sensation or effect produced by stimulation of the auditory receptors *Syn* noise *Ant* silence
**sound** *n* *Syn* STRAIT, channel, passage, narrows
**sound** *vb* *Syn* FATHOM, plumb
**soupçon** *Syn* TOUCH, suspicion, suggestion, tincture, tinge, shade, smack, spice, dash, vein, strain, streak
**sour** ♦ having a taste devoid of sweetness *Syn* acid, acidulous, tart, dry
**source** *Syn* ORIGIN, root, inception, provenance, provenience, prime mover *Ant* termination; outcome
**souse** *Syn* DIP, immerse, submerge, duck, dunk
**souvenir 1** *Syn* REMEMBRANCE, remembrancer, reminder, memorial, memento, token, keepsake **2** *Syn* MEMORY, remembrance, recollection, reminiscence, mind
**sovereign 1** *Syn* DOMINANT, predominant, paramount, preponderant, preponderating **2** *Syn* FREE, independent, autonomous, autarchic, autarkic

**sovereignty** *Syn* FREEDOM, independence, autonomy, autarky, autarchy
**sow** *Syn* STREW, straw, scatter, broadcast
**spacious** ♦ larger in extent or capacity than the average *Syn* commodious, capacious, ample
**spade** *Syn* DIG, delve, grub, excavate
**spangle** *Syn* SPOT, spatter, sprinkle, mottle, fleck, stipple, marble, speckle, bespangle
**spangled** *Syn* SPOTTED, spattered, sprinkled, mottled, flecked, stippled, marbled, speckled, bespangled
**spare 1** *Syn* SUPERFLUOUS, extra, surplus, supernumerary **2** *Syn* LEAN, lank, lanky, skinny, scrawny, gaunt, rawboned, angular *Ant* corpulent **3** *Syn* MEAGER, exiguous, sparse, scanty, scant, skimpy, scrimpy *Ant* profuse
**sparing** ♦ careful in the use of one's money or resources *Syn* frugal, thrifty, economical *Ant* lavish
**sparkle** *Syn* FLASH, gleam, glance, glint, glitter, glisten, scintillate, coruscate, twinkle
**sparse** *Syn* MEAGER, spare, exiguous, scanty, scant, skimpy, scrimpy *Ant* dense
**spasm** *Syn* FIT, paroxysm, convulsion, attack, access, accession
**spasmodic** *Syn* FITFUL, convulsive
**spat** *n* *Syn* QUARREL, bickering, squabble, wrangle, altercation, tiff
**spat** *vb* *Syn* QUARREL, bicker, squabble, wrangle, altercate, tiff
**spate** *Syn* FLOOD, deluge, inundation, torrent, cataract
**spatter** *Syn* SPOT, sprinkle, mottle, fleck, stipple, marble, speckle, spangle, bespangle
**spattered** *Syn* SPOTTED, sprinkled, mottled, flecked, stippled, marbled, speckled, spangled, bespangled
**spay** *Syn* STERILIZE, castrate, emasculate, alter, mutilate, geld
**speak** ♦ to articulate words so as to express thoughts *Syn* talk, converse
**special** ♦ of or relating to one thing or class *Syn* especial, specific, particular, individual
**specie** *Syn* MONEY, cash, currency, legal tender, coin, coinage
**specific** *adj* **1** *Syn* SPECIAL, especial, particular, individual *Ant* generic **2** *Syn* EXPLICIT, definite, express, categorical *Ant* vague
**specific** *n* *Syn* REMEDY, cure, medicine, medicament, medication, physic
**specify** *Syn* MENTION, name, instance
**specimen** *Syn* INSTANCE, example, sample, illustration, case
**specious** *Syn* PLAUSIBLE, believable, colorable, credible
**speckle** *Syn* SPOT, spatter, sprinkle, mottle, fleck, stipple, marble, spangle, bespangle
**speckled** *Syn* SPOTTED, spattered, sprinkled, mottled, flecked, stippled, marbled, spangled, bespangled
**spectator** ♦ one who looks on or watches *Syn* observer, beholder, looker-on, onlooker, witness, eyewitness, bystander, kibitzer
**specter** *Syn* APPARITION, spirit, ghost, phantasm, phantom, wraith, shade, revenant
**speculate** *Syn* THINK, reason, reflect, cogitate, deliberate
**speculative 1** *Syn* THOUGHTFUL, contemplative, meditative, reflective, pensive **2** *Syn* THEORETICAL, academic
**speech 1** *Syn* LANGUAGE, tongue, dialect, idiom **2** ♦ a usu. formal discourse delivered to an audience *Syn* address, oration, harangue, lecture, talk, sermon, homily
**speechless** *Syn* DUMB, mute, inarticulate
**speed** *n* **1** *Syn* HASTE, hurry, expedition, dispatch **2** ♦ rate of motion, performance, or action *Syn* velocity, momentum, impetus, pace, headway
**speed** *vb* ♦ to go or make go fast or faster *Syn* accelerate, quicken, hasten, hurry, precipitate
**speedy** *Syn* FAST, expeditious, quick, swift, fleet, rapid, hasty *Ant* dilatory

**spell** ♦ a limited period or amount of activity *Syn* shift, tour, trick, turn, stint, bout, go

**spend** ♦ to use up or pay out *Syn* expend, disburse *Ant* save

**spendthrift** ♦ a person who spends foolishly and wastefully *Syn* prodigal, profligate, waster, wastrel

**spew** *Syn* BELCH, burp, vomit, disgorge, regurgitate, throw up

**sphere** *Syn* FIELD, domain, province, territory, bailiwick

**spice** *Syn* TOUCH, suggestion, suspicion, soupçon, tincture, tinge, shade, smack, dash, vein, strain, streak

**spick-and-span** *Syn* NEAT, tidy, trim, trig, snug, shipshape *Ant* filthy

**spicy** *Syn* PUNGENT, piquant, poignant, racy, snappy

**spin** *Syn* TURN, revolve, rotate, gyrate, circle, twirl, whirl, wheel, eddy, swirl, pirouette

**spine** ♦ the articulated column of bones that is the central and axial feature of a vertebrate skeleton *Syn* backbone, back, vertebrae, chine

**spirit** 1 *Syn* SOUL 2 *Syn* APPARITION, ghost, phantasm, phantom, wraith, specter, shade, revenant 3 *Syn* COURAGE, mettle, resolution, tenacity 4 *Syn* VIGOR, vim, dash, esprit, verve, punch, élan, drive

**spirited** ♦ full of energy, animation, or courage *Syn* high-spirited, mettlesome, spunky, fiery, peppery, gingery *Ant* spiritless

**spiritless** *Syn* LANGUID, languishing, languorous, listless, enervated, lackadaisical *Ant* spirited

**spiritual** 1 *Syn* IMMATERIAL, incorporeal *Ant* physical 2 *Syn* HOLY, sacred, divine, religious, blessed *Ant* physical; carnal; material; temporal

**spite** *Syn* MALICE, despite, malignity, malignancy, spleen, grudge, ill will, malevolence

**spiteful** *Syn* MALICIOUS, malignant, malevolent, malign

**spleen** *Syn* MALICE, malignity, malignancy, grudge, spite, despite, malevolence, ill will

**splendid** ♦ extraordinarily or transcendently impressive *Syn* resplendent, gorgeous, glorious, sublime, superb

**splenetic** *Syn* IRASCIBLE, choleric, testy, touchy, cranky, cross

**split** *vb Syn* TEAR, rend, cleave, rive, rip

**split** *n Syn* BREACH, break, schism, rent, rupture, rift

**split second** *Syn* INSTANT, moment, second, minute, flash, jiffy, twinkling

**spoil** *n* ♦ something taken from another by force or craft *Syn* plunder, booty, prize, loot, swag

**spoil** *vb* 1 *Syn* INJURE, harm, hurt, damage, impair, mar 2 *Syn* INDULGE, pamper, humor, baby, mollycoddle 3 *Syn* DECAY, decompose, rot, putrefy, disintegrate, crumble

**spoliate** *Syn* RAVAGE, despoil, devastate, waste, sack, pillage

**sponge, sponger** *Syn* PARASITE, sycophant, favorite, toady, lickspittle, bootlicker, hanger-on, leech

**sponsor** ♦ one who assumes responsibility for some other person or thing *Syn* patron, surety, guarantor, backer, angel

**spontaneity** *Syn* UNCONSTRAINT, abandon

**spontaneous** ♦ acting or activated without deliberation *Syn* impulsive, instinctive, automatic, mechanical

**spoon** *Syn* DIP, ladle, dish, bail, scoop

**sporadic** *Syn* INFREQUENT, occasional, rare, scarce, uncommon

**sport** *vb Syn* PLAY, disport, frolic, rollick, romp, gambol

**sport** *n* 1 *Syn* PLAY, disport, frolic, rollick, romp, gambol 2 *Syn* FUN, jest, game, play 3 *pl* **sports** *Syn* ATHLETICS, games

**sportive** *Syn* PLAYFUL, frolicsome, roguish, waggish, impish, mischievous

**spot** *n Syn* PLACE, position, location, situation, site, station

**spot** *vb* ♦ to mark or become marked with or as if

with spots or sometimes streaks *Syn* spatter, sprinkle, mottle, fleck, stipple, marble, speckle, spangle, bespangle

**spotted** ♦ marked with spots or streaks *Syn* spattered, sprinkled, mottled, flecked, stippled, marbled, speckled, spangled, bespangled

**sprain** *n Syn* STRAIN

**sprain** *vb Syn* STRAIN

**spread** *vb* ♦ to extend or cause to extend over an area or space *Syn* circulate, disseminate, diffuse, propagate, radiate

**spread** *n Syn* EXPANSE, amplitude, stretch

**sprightly** *Syn* LIVELY, animated, vivacious, gay

**spring** *vb* 1 ♦ to come up or out of something into existence *Syn* arise, rise, originate, derive, flow, issue, emanate, proceed, stem 2 *Syn* JUMP, leap, bound, vault

**spring** *n* 1 *Syn* MOTIVE, impulse, incentive, inducement, spur, goad 2 *Syn* JUMP, leap, bound, vault

**springy** *Syn* ELASTIC, resilient, flexible, supple

**sprinkle** *Syn* SPOT, spatter, mottle, fleck, stipple, marble, speckle, spangle, bespangle

**sprinkled** *Syn* SPOTTED, spattered, mottled, flecked, stippled, marbled, speckled, spangled, bespangled

**sprint** *Syn* SCUTTLE, scurry, scamper, skedaddle

**spry** *Syn* AGILE, brisk, nimble *Ant* doddering

**spume** *Syn* FOAM, froth, scum, lather, suds, yeast

**spunky** *Syn* SPIRITED, high-spirited, mettlesome, fiery, peppery, gingery

**spur** *n Syn* MOTIVE, goad, spring, impulse, incentive, inducement

**spur** *vb Syn* URGE, egg, exhort, goad, prod, prick, sic *Ant* curb

**spurious** *Syn* COUNTERFEIT, bogus, fake, sham, pseudo, pinchbeck, phony *Ant* genuine

**spurn** *Syn* DECLINE, reject, repudiate, refuse *Ant* crave; embrace

**squabble** *n Syn* QUARREL, wrangle, altercation, bickering, spat, tiff

**squabble** *vb Syn* QUARREL, wrangle, altercate, bicker, spat, tiff

**squalid** *Syn* DIRTY, nasty, filthy, foul

**squander** *Syn* WASTE, dissipate, fritter, consume

**square** *Syn* AGREE, conform, accord, harmonize, correspond, tally, jibe

**squash** *Syn* CRUSH, mash, smash, bruise, macerate

**squat** *Syn* STOCKY, thickset, thick, chunky, stubby, dumpy *Ant* lanky

**squeal** *vb Syn* SHOUT, yell, shriek, scream, screech, holler, whoop

**squeal** *n Syn* SHOUT, yell, shriek, scream, screech, holler, whoop

**squeamish** *Syn* NICE, finicky, finicking, finical, particular, fussy, persnickety, pernickety, fastidious, dainty

**squeeze** *Syn* PRESS, bear, bear down, crowd, jam

**squib** *Syn* LIBEL, skit, lampoon, pasquinade

**squirm** *Syn* WRITHE, agonize

**stabilize** ♦ to make or become stable, steadfast, or firm *Syn* steady, poise, balance, ballast, trim

**stable** *Syn* LASTING, durable, perdurable, permanent, perpetual *Ant* unstable; changeable

**stack** *n Syn* HEAP, pile, mass, bank, shock, cock

**stack** *vb Syn* HEAP, pile, mass, bank, shock, cock

**stagger** *Syn* REEL, whirl, totter

**staid** *Syn* SERIOUS, sedate, grave, somber, sober, earnest *Ant* jaunty

**stain** *Syn* STIGMA, blot, brand

**stake** *Syn* BET, wager, pot, ante

**stalemate** *Syn* DRAW, tie, deadlock, standoff

**stalwart** *Syn* STRONG, stout, sturdy, tough, tenacious

**stammer** ♦ to make involuntary stops and repetitions in speaking *Syn* stutter

**stamp** *vb Syn* MARK, brand, label, tag, ticket

**stamp** *n* 1 *Syn* IMPRESSION, impress, imprint, print 2 *Syn* MARK, brand, label, tag, ticket

**stand** *vb Syn* BEAR, tolerate, brook, suffer, endure, abide

**stand** *n Syn* POSITION, attitude

**standard** 1 *Syn* FLAG, ensign, banner, color,

streamer, pennant, pendant, pennon, jack 2 ♦ a means of determining what a thing should be *Syn* criterion, gauge, yardstick, touchstone 3 *Syn* MODEL, ideal, beau ideal, pattern, exemplar, example, mirror

**stand-in** *Syn* SUBSTITUTE, supply, understudy, double, locum tenens, alternate, pinch hitter

**standoff** *Syn* DRAW, tie, stalemate, deadlock

**standpoint** *Syn* POINT OF VIEW, viewpoint, angle, slant

**stare** *Syn* GAZE, gape, glare, peer, gloat

**stark** *Syn* STIFF, rigid, inflexible, tense, wooden

**starry** ♦ of, relating to, or suggestive of a star or group of stars *Syn* stellar, astral, sidereal

**start** *Syn* BEGIN, commence, initiate, inaugurate

**startle** *Syn* FRIGHTEN, scare, alarm, terrify, terrorize, fright, affray, affright

**state** *n* ♦ the way in which one manifests existence or the circumstances under which one exists or by which one is given distinctive character *Syn* condition, mode, situation, posture, status

**state** *vb* 1 *Syn* SAY, utter, tell 2 *Syn* RELATE, report, rehearse, recite, recount, narrate, describe

**stately** *Syn* GRAND, magnificent, imposing, majestic, august, noble, grandiose

**statesman** *Syn* POLITICIAN, politico

**station** 1 *Syn* PLACE, position, location, situation, site, spot 2 *Syn* HABITAT, biotope, range

**stature** *Syn* QUALITY, caliber

**status** *Syn* STATE, situation, posture, condition, mode

**statute** *Syn* LAW, ordinance, regulation, rule, precept, canon

**staunch** *Syn* FAITHFUL, loyal, true, constant, steadfast, resolute

**stay** *vb* 1 ♦ to continue to be in one place for a noticeable time *Syn* remain, wait, abide, tarry, linger 2 *Syn* RESIDE, sojourn, lodge, put up, stop, live, dwell 3 *Syn* DEFER, postpone, suspend, intermit

**stay** *vb Syn* BASE, found, ground, bottom, rest

**steadfast** *Syn* FAITHFUL, staunch, resolute, constant, true, loyal *Ant* capricious

**steady** *adj* ♦ not varying throughout a course or extent *Syn* uniform, even, equable, constant *Ant* unsteady; nervous, jumpy

**steady** *vb Syn* STABILIZE, poise, balance, ballast, trim

**steal** ♦ to take from another without right or without detection *Syn* pilfer, filch, purloin, lift, pinch, snitch, swipe, cop

**stealthy** *Syn* SECRET, covert, furtive, clandestine, surreptitious, underhand, underhanded

**steel** *Syn* ENCOURAGE, inspirit, hearten, embolden, cheer, nerve

**steep** *adj* ♦ having an incline approaching the perpendicular *Syn* abrupt, precipitous, sheer

**steep** *vb Syn* SOAK, saturate, impregnate, drench, sop, waterlog

**steer** *Syn* GUIDE, lead, pilot, engineer

**stellar** *Syn* STARRY, sidereal, astral

**stem** *Syn* SPRING, proceed, issue, emanate, derive, flow, originate, arise, rise

**stentorian** *Syn* LOUD, earsplitting, hoarse, raucous, strident, stertorous

**stereotyped** *Syn* TRITE, hackneyed, threadbare, shopworn *Ant* changeful

**sterile** ♦ not able to bear fruit, crops, or offspring *Syn* barren, impotent, unfruitful, infertile *Ant* fertile; exuberant

**sterilize** 1 ♦ to make incapable of producing offspring *Syn* castrate, spay, emasculate, alter, mutilate, geld *Ant* fertilize 2 ♦ to free from living microorganisms *Syn* disinfect, sanitize, fumigate

**stern** *Syn* SEVERE, austere, ascetic *Ant* soft; lenient

**stertorous** *Syn* LOUD, stentorian, earsplitting, hoarse, raucous, strident

**stew** *Syn* BOIL, seethe, simmer, parboil

**stick** 1 ♦ to become or cause to become closely and firmly attached *Syn* adhere, cohere, cling, cleave 2 *Syn* DEMUR, stickle, balk, shy, boggle, scruple, jib, strain

**stickle** *Syn* DEMUR, balk, shy, boggle, jib, scruple, stick, strain

**stick out** *Syn* BULGE, jut, protrude, project, overhang, beetle

**stiff** ♦ difficult to bend *Syn* rigid, inflexible, tense, stark, wooden *Ant* relaxed; supple

**stiff-necked** *Syn* OBSTINATE, stubborn, mulish, dogged, pertinacious, pigheaded, bullheaded

**stifle** *Syn* SUFFOCATE, asphyxiate, smother, choke, strangle, throttle

**stigma** ♦ a mark of shame or discredit *Syn* brand, blot, stain

**still** *adj* ♦ making no stir or noise *Syn* stilly, quiet, silent, noiseless *Ant* stirring; noisy

**still** *vb* *Syn* CALM, compose, quiet, quieten, lull, soothe, settle, tranquilize *Ant* agitate

**stilly** *Syn* STILL, quiet, silent, noiseless

**stimulant** *Syn* STIMULUS, excitant, incitement, impetus *Ant* anesthetic; anodyne

**stimulate** *Syn* PROVOKE, excite, quicken, pique, galvanize *Ant* unnerve; deaden

**stimulus** ♦ something that rouses or incites to activity *Syn* stimulant, excitant, incitement, impetus

**stingy** ♦ being unwilling or showing unwillingness to share with others *Syn* close, closefisted, tight, tightfisted, niggardly, parsimonious, penurious, miserly, cheeseparing, penny-pinching *Ant* generous

**stinking** *Syn* MALODOROUS, fetid, noisome, putrid, rank, rancid, fusty, musty

**stint** 1 *Syn* TASK, duty, assignment, job, chore 2 *Syn* SPELL, bout, shift, tour, trick, turn, go

**stipend** *Syn* WAGE, wages, salary, fee, emolument, pay, hire

**stipple** *Syn* SPOT, spatter, sprinkle, mottle, fleck, marble, speckle, spangle, bespangle

**stippled** *Syn* SPOTTED, spattered, sprinkled, mottled, flecked, marbled, speckled, spangled, bespangled

**stipulation** *Syn* CONDITION, terms, provision, proviso, reservation, strings

**stir** *vb* ♦ to cause to shift from quiescence or torpor into activity *Syn* rouse, arouse, awaken, waken, rally

**stir** *n* 1 *Syn* MOTION, movement, move, locomotion 2 ♦ signs of excited activity, hurry, or commotion *Syn* bustle, flurry, pother, fuss, ado *Ant* tranquillity

**stitch** *Syn* PAIN, twinge, ache, pang, throe

**stock** *Syn* VARIETY, subspecies, race, breed, cultivar, strain, clone

**stocky** ♦ compact, sturdy, and relatively thick in build *Syn* thickset, thick, chunky, stubby, squat, dumpy

**stodgy** *Syn* DULL, humdrum, dreary, monotonous, pedestrian

**stoic** *Syn* IMPASSIVE, phlegmatic, apathetic, stolid

**stoicism** *Syn* IMPASSIVITY, impassiveness, phlegm, apathy, stolidity

**stolid** *Syn* IMPASSIVE, phlegmatic, apathetic *Ant* adroit

**stolidity** *Syn* IMPASSIVITY, impassiveness, phlegm, apathy, stoicism

**stomach** *Syn* ABDOMEN, belly, paunch, gut

**stoop** ♦ to descend from one's real or pretended level of dignity *Syn* condescend, deign

**stop** 1 ♦ to suspend or cause to suspend activity *Syn* cease, quit, discontinue, desist 2 *Syn* RESIDE, stay, put up, lodge, sojourn, live, dwell

**stopgap** *Syn* RESOURCE, makeshift, shift, expedient, resort, substitute, surrogate

**storm** *Syn* ATTACK, bombard, assault, assail

**story** 1 *Syn* ACCOUNT, report, chronicle, version 2 ♦ a recital of happenings less elaborate than a novel *Syn* narrative, tale, anecdote, yarn 3 *Syn* LIE, falsehood, untruth, fib, misrepresentation

**stout** 1 *Syn* STRONG, sturdy, stalwart, tough, tenacious 2 *Syn* FLESHY, fat, portly, corpulent, obese, plump, rotund, chubby *Ant* cadaverous

**straightforward** ♦ free from all that is dishonest

or secretive *Syn* forthright, aboveboard *Ant* devious; indirect

**strain** *n* 1 *Syn* VARIETY, subspecies, race, breed, cultivar, clone, stock 2 *Syn* TOUCH, streak, vein, suggestion, suspicion, soupçon, tincture, tinge, shade, smack, spice, dash

**strain** *vb* 1 ♦ to injure (as a body part) by overuse or misuse *Syn* sprain 2 *Syn* DEMUR, scruple, balk, jib, shy, boggle, stickle, stick

**strain** *n* 1 *Syn* STRESS, pressure, tension 2 ♦ an injury to a part of the body from undue stretching *Syn* sprain

**strained** *Syn* FORCED, labored, farfetched

**strait** 1 ♦ a comparatively narrow stretch of water connecting two larger bodies of water *Syn* sound, channel, passage, narrows 2 *Syn* JUNCTURE, pass, exigency, pinch, emergency, contingency, crisis

**straitlaced** *Syn* PRIM, priggish, prissy, prudish, puritanical, stuffy *Ant* libertine

**strand** *Syn* SHORE, coast, beach, bank, littoral, foreshore

**strange** ♦ departing from what is ordinary, usual, and to be expected *Syn* singular, unique, peculiar, eccentric, erratic, odd, queer, quaint, outlandish, curious *Ant* familiar

**stranger** ♦ a nonresident or an unknown person in a community *Syn* foreigner, alien, outlander, outsider, immigrant, émigré

**strangle** *Syn* SUFFOCATE, asphyxiate, stifle, smother, choke, throttle

**stratagem** *Syn* TRICK, ruse, maneuver, gambit, ploy, artifice, wile, feint

**strategic** ♦ of, relating to, or marked by strategy *Syn* tactical, logistic

**strategy** ♦ the art of devising or employing plans toward a usu. military goal *Syn* tactics, logistics

**straw** *Syn* STREW, scatter, sow, broadcast

**stray** *Syn* WANDER, roam, ramble, rove, range, prowl, gad, gallivant, traipse, meander

**streak** *Syn* TOUCH, strain, vein, suggestion, suspicion, soupçon, tincture, tinge, shade, smack, spice, dash

**stream** *n* *Syn* FLOW, current, flood, tide, flux

**stream** *vb* *Syn* POUR, gush, sluice

**streamer** *Syn* FLAG, pennant, pendant, pennon, banner, ensign, standard, color

**strength** *Syn* POWER, force, might, energy, puissance

**strengthen** ♦ to make strong or stronger *Syn* invigorate, fortify, energize, reinforce *Ant* weaken

**strenuous** *Syn* VIGOROUS, energetic, lusty, nervous

**stress** 1 ♦ the action or effect of force exerted within or upon a thing *Syn* strain, pressure, tension 2 *Syn* EMPHASIS, accent, accentuation

**stretch** *Syn* EXPANSE, amplitude, spread

**strew** ♦ to throw loosely or at intervals *Syn* straw, scatter, sow, broadcast

**strict** *Syn* RIGID, stringent, rigorous *Ant* lax; loose; lenient, indulgent

**stricture** *Syn* ANIMADVERSION, aspersion, reflection *Ant* commendation

**strident** 1 *Syn* LOUD, stentorian, earsplitting, hoarse, raucous, stertorous 2 *Syn* VOCIFEROUS, blatant, clamorous, boisterous, obstreperous

**strife** *Syn* DISCORD, conflict, contention, dissension, difference, variance *Ant* peace; accord

**strike** 1 ♦ to deliver (a blow) in a strong, vigorous manner *Syn* hit, smite, punch, slug, slog, swat, clout, slap, cuff, box 2 *Syn* AFFECT, impress, touch, influence, sway

**striking** *Syn* NOTICEABLE, arresting, signal, salient, conspicuous, outstanding, remarkable, prominent

**string** 1 *Syn* SUCCESSION, progression, series, sequence, chain, train 2 *pl* **strings** *Syn* CONDITION, stipulation, terms, provision, proviso, reservation

**stringent** *Syn* RIGID, strict, rigorous

**strip** *vb* ♦ to remove what clothes, furnishes, or invests a person or thing *Syn* divest, denude, bare, dismantle *Ant* furnish; invest

**strip** *n* ♦ long narrow piece or area *Syn* stripe, band, ribbon, fillet

**stripe** 1 *Syn* STRIP, band, ribbon, fillet 2 *Syn* TYPE, character, description, nature, kind, sort, kidney, ilk

**strive** *Syn* ATTEMPT, struggle, endeavor, essay, try

**striving** *Syn* ATTEMPT, struggle, endeavor, essay, try

**stroll** *Syn* SAUNTER, amble

**strong** ♦ showing power to resist or to endure *Syn* stout, sturdy, stalwart, tough, tenacious *Ant* weak

**stronghold** *Syn* FORT, citadel, fortress, fastness

**structure** 1 *Syn* BUILDING, edifice, pile 2 ♦ something made up of interdependent parts in a definite pattern of organization *Syn* anatomy, framework, skeleton

**struggle** *vb* *Syn* ATTEMPT, strive, endeavor, essay, try

**struggle** *n* *Syn* ATTEMPT, striving, endeavor, essay, try

**strut** ♦ to walk with an air of pomposity or affected dignity *Syn* swagger, bristle, bridle

**stubborn** *Syn* OBSTINATE, dogged, pertinacious, mulish, stiff-necked, pigheaded, bullheaded

**stubby** *Syn* STOCKY, thickset, thick, chunky, squat, dumpy

**studied** *Syn* DELIBERATE, considered, advised, premeditated, designed

**study** *n* *Syn* ATTENTION, concentration, application

**study** *vb* *Syn* CONSIDER, contemplate, weigh, excogitate

**stuff** *n* *Syn* MATTER, substance, material

**stuff** *vb* *Syn* PACK, crowd, cram, ram, tamp

**stuffy** *Syn* PRIM, priggish, prissy, prudish, puritanical, straitlaced

**stumble** ♦ to move so clumsily or unsteadily as to fall or nearly fall *Syn* trip, blunder, lurch, flounder, lumber, galumph, lollop, bumble

**stun** *Syn* DAZE, bemuse, stupefy, benumb, paralyze, petrify

**stupefy** *Syn* DAZE, stun, bemuse, benumb, paralyze, petrify

**stupendous** *Syn* MONSTROUS, tremendous, prodigious, monumental

**stupid** ♦ lacking in power to absorb ideas or impressions *Syn* slow, dull, dense, crass, dumb *Ant* intelligent

**stupor** *Syn* LETHARGY, torpor, torpidity, lassitude, languor

**sturdy** *Syn* STRONG, stout, stalwart, tough, tenacious *Ant* decrepit

**stutter** *Syn* STAMMER

**stygian** *Syn* INFERNAL, chthonic, chthonian, Hadean, Tartarean, hellish

**style** 1 *Syn* LANGUAGE, diction, phraseology, phrasing, vocabulary 2 *Syn* FASHION, mode, vogue, fad, rage, craze, dernier cri, cry 3 *Syn* NAME, designation, title, denomination, appellation

**stylish** ♦ conforming to current fashion *Syn* fashionable, modish, smart, chic, dashing

**suave** ♦ pleasantly tactful and well-mannered *Syn* urbane, diplomatic, bland, smooth, politic *Ant* bluff

**subdue** *Syn* CONQUER, subjugate, reduce, overcome, surmount, overthrow, rout, vanquish, defeat, beat, lick *Ant* awaken, waken

**subdued** *Syn* TAME, submissive *Ant* intense; barbaric (*of taste*); bizarre (*of effects*); effervescent (*of character and temperament*)

**subject** *n* 1 *Syn* CITIZEN, national *Ant* sovereign 2 ♦ the basic idea or the principal object of attention in a discourse or artistic composition *Syn* matter, subject matter, argument, topic, text, theme, motive, motif, leitmotiv

**subject** *adj* 1 *Syn* SUBORDINATE, dependent, secondary, tributary, collateral *Ant* sovereign, dominant 2 *Syn* LIABLE, open, exposed, prone, susceptible, sensitive *Ant* exempt

**subject matter** *Syn* SUBJECT, matter, argument, topic, text, theme, motive, motif, leitmotiv

**subjoin** *Syn* ADD, append, annex, superadd

**subjugate** *Syn* CONQUER, subdue, reduce, overcome, surmount, overthrow, rout, vanquish, defeat, beat, lick

**sublime** *Syn* SPLENDID, glorious, superb, resplendent, gorgeous

**sublunary** *Syn* EARTHLY, terrestrial, earthy, mundane, worldly

**submerge** *Syn* DIP, immerse, duck, souse, dunk

**submission** *Syn* SURRENDER, capitulation *Ant* resistance

**submissive** *Syn* TAME, subdued *Ant* rebellious

**submit** *Syn* YIELD, capitulate, succumb, relent, defer, bow, cave *Ant* resist, withstand

**subordinate** *adj* ♦ placed in or occupying a lower class, rank, or status *Syn* secondary, dependent, subject, tributary, collateral *Ant* chief, leading; dominant

**subordinate** *n Syn* INFERIOR, underling *Ant* chief

**subscribe** *Syn* ASSENT, agree, acquiesce, consent, accede *Ant* boggle

**subservient 1** *Syn* AUXILIARY, subsidiary, contributory, ancillary, adjuvant, accessory **2** ♦ showing or characterized by extreme compliance or abject obedience *Syn* servile, slavish, menial, obsequious *Ant* domineering; overbearing

**subside 1** *Syn* FALL, drop, sink, slump **2** *Syn* ABATE, wane, ebb

**subsidiary** *Syn* AUXILIARY, contributory, subservient, ancillary, adjuvant, accessory

**subsidy** *Syn* APPROPRIATION, grant, subvention

**subsist** *Syn* BE, exist, live

**subsistence** *Syn* LIVING, livelihood, sustenance, maintenance, support, keep, bread, bread and butter

**subspecies** *Syn* VARIETY, race, breed, cultivar, strain, clone, stock

**substance 1** ♦ the inner significance or central meaning of something written or said *Syn* purport, gist, burden, core, pith **2** *Syn* MATTER, material, stuff

**substantial** *Syn* MASSIVE, massy, bulky, monumental *Ant* airy, ethereal

**substantiate** *Syn* CONFIRM, verify, corroborate, authenticate, validate

**substitute 1** *Syn* RESOURCE, surrogate, resort, expedient, shift, makeshift, stopgap **2** ♦ a person who takes the place of or acts instead of another *Syn* supply, locum tenens, alternate, understudy, double, stand-in, pinch hitter

**subsume** *Syn* INCLUDE, comprehend, embrace, involve, imply

**subtle** *Syn* LOGICAL, analytical *Ant* dense; blunt

**subtract** *Syn* DEDUCT *Ant* add

**subvention** *Syn* APPROPRIATION, grant, subsidy

**subvert** *Syn* OVERTURN, overthrow, capsize, upset *Ant* uphold, sustain

**succeed 1** *Syn* FOLLOW, ensue, supervene *Ant* precede **2** ♦ to attain or be attaining a desired end *Syn* prosper, thrive, flourish *Ant* fail; attempt

**succession** ♦ a number of things that follow each other in some order *Syn* progression, series, sequence, chain, train, string

**successive** *Syn* CONSECUTIVE, sequent, sequential, serial

**succinct** *Syn* CONCISE, terse, laconic, summary, pithy, compendious *Ant* discursive

**succumb** *Syn* YIELD, submit, capitulate, relent, defer, bow, cave

**sudden** *Syn* PRECIPITATE, hasty, headlong, abrupt, impetuous

**suds** *Syn* FOAM, froth, spume, lather, scum, yeast

**sue** *Syn* PRAY, plead, petition

**suffer 1** *Syn* BEAR, endure, abide, tolerate, stand, brook **2** *Syn* EXPERIENCE, undergo, sustain **3** *Syn* LET, permit, allow, leave

**sufferance** *Syn* PERMISSION, leave

**suffering** *Syn* DISTRESS, misery, agony, dolor, passion

**sufficient** ♦ being what is necessary or desirable *Syn* enough, adequate, competent

**suffocate** ♦ to stop the respiration of *Syn* asphyxiate, stifle, smother, choke, strangle, throttle

**suffrage** ♦ the right, privilege, or power of expressing one's choice or wish (as in an election or in the determination of policy) *Syn* franchise, vote, ballot

**suffuse** *Syn* INFUSE, imbue, ingrain, inoculate, leaven

**suggest 1** ♦ to convey an idea indirectly *Syn* imply, hint, intimate, insinuate *Ant* express **2** ♦ to call to mind by thought, through close connection, or by association *Syn* adumbrate, shadow *Ant* manifest

**suggestion** *Syn* TOUCH, suspicion, soupçon, tincture, tinge, shade, smack, spice, dash, vein, strain, streak

**suit 1** *Syn* PRAYER, plea, petition, appeal **2** ♦ a legal proceeding instituted for the sake of demanding justice or enforcing a right *Syn* lawsuit, action, cause, case

**suitable** *Syn* FIT, meet, proper, appropriate, fitting, apt, happy, felicitous *Ant* unsuitable; unbecoming

**sulky** *Syn* SULLEN, surly, morose, glum, crabbed, saturnine, dour, gloomy

**sullen** ♦ showing a forbidding or disagreeable mood *Syn* glum, morose, surly, sulky, crabbed, saturnine, dour, gloomy

**sully** *Syn* SOIL, dirty, tarnish, foul, befoul, smirch, besmirch, grime, begrime

**sum** *n* ♦ the result of simple addition of all the numbers or particulars in a given group *Syn* amount, number, aggregate, total, whole, quantity

**sum** *vb Syn* ADD, total, tot, cast, figure, foot

**summary** *Syn* CONCISE, pithy, compendious, terse, succinct, laconic *Ant* circumstantial

**summative** *Syn* CUMULATIVE, accumulative, additive

**summit** ♦ the highest point attained or attainable *Syn* peak, pinnacle, climax, apex, acme, culmination, meridian, zenith, apogee

**summon, summons** ♦ to demand or request the presence or service of *Syn* call, cite, convoke, convene, muster

**sumptuous** *Syn* LUXURIOUS, opulent

**sunder** *Syn* SEPARATE, sever, divide, part, divorce *Ant* link

**sundry** *Syn* MANY, several, various, divers, numerous, multifarious

**superadd** *Syn* ADD, annex, append, subjoin

**superannuated** *Syn* AGED, old, elderly

**superb** *Syn* SPLENDID, resplendent, glorious, gorgeous, sublime

**supercilious** *Syn* PROUD, disdainful, overbearing, arrogant, haughty, lordly, insolent

**supererogatory** ♦ given or done without compulsion, need, or warrant *Syn* gratuitous, uncalled-for, wanton

**superficial** ♦ lacking in depth or solidity *Syn* shallow, cursory, uncritical *Ant* radical

**superfluity** *Syn* EXCESS, surplus, surplusage, overplus

**superfluous** ♦ exceeding what is needed or necessary *Syn* surplus, supernumerary, extra, spare

**superhuman** *Syn* SUPERNATURAL, preternatural, miraculous, supranatural

**superimpose** *Syn* OVERLAY, superpose, appliqué

**superior** *Syn* BETTER, preferable *Ant* inferior

**superlative** *Syn* SUPREME, transcendent, surpassing, peerless, incomparable, preeminent

**supernatural** ♦ of or relating to an order of existence beyond the visible observable universe *Syn* supranatural, preternatural, miraculous, superhuman

**supernumerary** *Syn* SUPERFLUOUS, surplus, extra, spare

**superpose** *Syn* OVERLAY, superimpose, appliqué

**supersede** *Syn* REPLACE, displace, supplant

**supervene** *Syn* FOLLOW, succeed, ensue

**supervision** *Syn* OVERSIGHT, surveillance

**supine 1** *Syn* PRONE, prostrate, recumbent, couchant, dormant **2** *Syn* INACTIVE, inert, passive, idle

**supplant** *Syn* REPLACE, displace, supersede

**supple 1** *Syn* ELASTIC, flexible, resilient, springy *Ant* stiff **2** ♦ able to bend or twist with ease and grace *Syn* limber, lithe, lithesome, lissome

**supplement** *n* **1** *Syn* COMPLEMENT **2** *Syn* APPENDIX, addendum, addenda

**supplement** *vb Syn* COMPLEMENT

**supplicate** *Syn* BEG, implore, beseech, entreat, importune, adjure

**supply** *vb Syn* PROVIDE, furnish

**supply** *n Syn* SUBSTITUTE, locum tenens, alternate, understudy, pinch hitter, double, stand-in

**supply** *adj Syn* TEMPORARY, provisional, ad interim, acting

**support** *vb* **1** ♦ to hold up in position by serving as a foundation or base for *Syn* sustain, prop, bolster, buttress, brace **2** ♦ to favor actively one that meets opposition *Syn* uphold, advocate, back, champion

**support** *n Syn* LIVING, maintenance, sustenance, livelihood, subsistence, keep, bread *Ant* adversary, antagonist

**supposed** ♦ accepted or advanced as true or real on the basis of less than conclusive evidence *Syn* supposititious, suppositious, reputed, putative, purported, conjectural, hypothetical *Ant* certain

**supposititious, suppositious** *Syn* SUPPOSED, reputed, putative, purported, conjectural, hypothetical

**suppress 1** *Syn* CRUSH, quell, extinguish, quench, quash **2** ♦ to hold back more or less forcefully someone or something that seeks an outlet *Syn* repress

**supranatural** *Syn* SUPERNATURAL, miraculous, preternatural, superhuman

**supremacy** ♦ the position of being first (as in rank, power, or influence) *Syn* ascendancy

**supreme** ♦ developed to the utmost and not exceeded by any other in degree, quality, or intensity *Syn* superlative, transcendent, surpassing, preeminent, peerless, incomparable

**sure 1** *Syn* CONFIDENT, assured, sanguine, presumptuous **2** ♦ having no doubt or uncertainty *Syn* certain, positive, cocksure *Ant* unsure

**surety 1** *Syn* GUARANTEE, security, bond, guaranty, bail **2** *Syn* SPONSOR, guarantor, backer, patron, angel

**surfeit** *Syn* SATIATE, sate, cloy, pall, glut, gorge *Ant* whet

**surge** *Syn* RISE, arise, ascend, mount, soar, tower, rocket, levitate

**surly** *Syn* SULLEN, morose, glum, crabbed, sulky, saturnine, dour, gloomy *Ant* amiable

**surmise** *vb Syn* CONJECTURE, guess

**surmise** *n Syn* CONJECTURE, guess

**surmount** *Syn* CONQUER, overcome, overthrow, rout, vanquish, defeat, subdue, subjugate, reduce, beat, lick

**surpass** *Syn* EXCEED, transcend, excel, outdo, outstrip

**surpassing** *Syn* SUPREME, transcendent, superlative, preeminent, peerless, incomparable

**surplus** *n Syn* EXCESS, superfluity, surplusage, overplus *Ant* deficiency

**surplus** *adj Syn* SUPERFLUOUS, supernumerary, extra, spare

**surplusage** *Syn* EXCESS, surplus, superfluity, overplus

**surprise 1** ♦ to attack unawares *Syn* waylay, ambush **2** ♦ to impress forcibly through unexpectedness *Syn* astonish, astound, amaze, flabbergast

**surrender** *vb Syn* RELINQUISH, abandon, resign, yield, cede, waive

**surrender** *n* ♦ the yielding of one's person, forces, or possessions to another *Syn* submission, capitulation

**surreptitious** *Syn* SECRET, underhand, underhanded, covert, stealthy, furtive, clandestine

**surrogate** *Syn* RESOURCE, substitute, shift, makeshift, expedient, resort, stopgap

**surround** ♦ to close in or as if in a ring about something *Syn* environ, encircle, circle, encompass, compass, hem, gird, girdle, ring
**surveillance** *Syn* OVERSIGHT, supervision
**survey** *vb Syn* SEE, view, espy, descry, behold, observe, notice, remark, note, perceive, discern
**survey** *n Syn* COMPENDIUM, syllabus, digest, pandect, sketch, précis, aperçu
**survive** *Syn* OUTLIVE, outlast
**susceptible 1** *Syn* LIABLE, sensitive, subject, exposed, prone, open *Ant* immune **2** *Syn* SENTIENT, sensitive, impressible, impressionable, responsive
**suspect** *Syn* DISTRUST, mistrust, doubt, misdoubt
**suspend 1** *Syn* EXCLUDE, disbar, shut out, eliminate, debar, blackball, rule out **2** *Syn* DEFER, stay, intermit, postpone **3** *Syn* HANG, sling, dangle
**suspended** ♦ hanging from or remaining in place as if hanging from a support *Syn* pendent, pendulous
**suspicion 1** *Syn* UNCERTAINTY, mistrust, doubt, dubiety, dubiosity, skepticism **2** *Syn* TOUCH, suggestion, soupçon, tincture, tinge, shade, smack, spice, dash, vein, strain, streak
**sustain 1** *Syn* SUPPORT, prop, bolster, buttress, brace *Ant* subvert **2** *Syn* EXPERIENCE, undergo, suffer
**sustenance 1** *Syn* FOOD, nourishment, nutriment, aliment, pabulum, pap **2** *Syn* LIVING, maintenance, support, livelihood, subsistence, keep, bread
**suture** *Syn* JOINT, articulation
**swag** *Syn* SPOIL, plunder, loot, booty, prize
**swagger** *Syn* STRUT, bristle, bridle
**swallow** *Syn* EAT, ingest, devour, consume
**swarm** *Syn* TEEM, abound, overflow

**swat** *Syn* STRIKE, hit, smite, punch, slug, slog, clout, slap, cuff, box
**sway** *vb* **1** *Syn* SWING, oscillate, fluctuate, pendulate, vibrate, waver, undulate **2** *Syn* AFFECT, influence, impress, strike, touch
**sway** *n Syn* POWER, dominion, control, command, authority
**swearing** *Syn* BLASPHEMY, profanity, cursing
**sweep** *Syn* RANGE, gamut, reach, radius, compass, scope, orbit, horizon, ken, purview
**sweeping** *Syn* INDISCRIMINATE, wholesale
**sweet** ♦ distinctly pleasing or charming *Syn* engaging, winning, winsome, dulcet *Ant* sour; bitter
**swell** *Syn* EXPAND, amplify, distend, inflate, dilate *Ant* shrink
**swerve** ♦ to turn aside from a straight course *Syn* veer, deviate, depart, digress, diverge
**swift** *Syn* FAST, rapid, fleet, quick, speedy, hasty, expeditious
**swimming** *Syn* GIDDY, dizzy, vertiginous, dazzled
**swindle** *Syn* CHEAT, overreach, cozen, defraud
**swing 1** ♦ to wield or cause to move to and fro or up and down *Syn* wave, flourish, brandish, shake, thrash **2** ♦ to move from one direction to its opposite *Syn* sway, oscillate, vibrate, fluctuate, pendulate, waver, undulate **3** *Syn* HANDLE, wield, manipulate, ply
**swipe** *Syn* STEAL, pilfer, filch, purloin, lift, pinch, snitch, cop
**swirl** *Syn* TURN, circle, spin, twirl, whirl, wheel, eddy, revolve, rotate, gyrate, pirouette
**sybaritic** *Syn* SENSUOUS, sensual, luxurious, voluptuous, epicurean
**sycophant** *Syn* PARASITE, favorite, toady, lickspittle, bootlicker, hanger-on, leech, sponge, sponger

**syllabus** *Syn* COMPENDIUM, digest, pandect, survey, sketch, précis, aperçu
**symbol 1** ♦ something concrete that represents or suggests another thing that cannot in itself be pictured *Syn* emblem, attribute, type **2** *Syn* CHARACTER, sign, mark
**symbolism** *Syn* ALLEGORY
**symmetry** ♦ beauty of form or arrangement arising from balanced proportions *Syn* proportion, balance, harmony
**sympathetic 1** *Syn* CONSONANT, congenial, congruous, compatible, consistent **2** *Syn* TENDER, compassionate, warm, warmhearted, responsive *Ant* unsympathetic
**sympathy 1** *Syn* ATTRACTION, affinity *Ant* antipathy **2** ♦ the act or capacity for sharing in the interests and esp. in the painful experiences of another *Syn* pity, compassion, commiseration, condolence, ruth, empathy
**symptom** *Syn* SIGN, mark, token, badge
**synchronous** *Syn* CONTEMPORARY, coeval, coetaneous, contemporaneous, simultaneous, coincident, concomitant, concurrent
**syndicate** *Syn* MONOPOLY, corner, pool, trust, cartel
**syndrome** *Syn* DISEASE, disorder, condition, affection, ailment, malady, complaint, distemper
**synopsis** *Syn* ABRIDGMENT, brief, conspectus, epitome, abstract
**synthetic** *Syn* ARTIFICIAL, ersatz, factitious
**system 1** ♦ an organized integrated whole made up of diverse but interrelated and interdependent parts *Syn* scheme, network, complex, organism *Ant* chaos **2** *Syn* METHOD, mode, manner, way, fashion
**systematic** *Syn* ORDERLY, methodical, regular
**systematize** *Syn* ORDER, organize, methodize, arrange, marshal

# T

**table** *Syn* LIST, catalog, schedule, register, roll, roster, inventory
**taciturn** *Syn* SILENT, uncommunicative, reserved, reticent, secretive, close, close-lipped, closemouthed, tight-lipped *Ant* garrulous; clamorous (*esp. of crowds*); convivial
**tackle** *Syn* EQUIPMENT, apparatus, machinery, paraphernalia, outfit, gear, matériel
**tact** ♦ skill and grace in dealing with others *Syn* address, poise, savoir faire *Ant* awkwardness
**tactical** *Syn* STRATEGIC, logistic
**tactics** *Syn* STRATEGY, logistics
**tag** *n Syn* MARK, brand, stamp, label, ticket
**tag** *vb* **1** *Syn* MARK, brand, stamp, label, ticket **2** *Syn* FOLLOW, pursue, chase, trail, tail
**tail** *Syn* FOLLOW, pursue, chase, trail, tag
**taint** *Syn* CONTAMINATE, pollute, defile
**take 1** ♦ to get hold of by or as if by catching up with the hand *Syn* seize, grasp, clutch, snatch, grab **2** *Syn* RECEIVE, accept, admit **3** *Syn* BRING, fetch
**tale** *Syn* STORY, narrative, anecdote, yarn
**talent** *Syn* GIFT, genius, faculty, aptitude, knack, bent, turn
**talisman** *Syn* FETISH, charm, amulet
**talk** *vb Syn* SPEAK, converse
**talk** *n Syn* SPEECH, address, oration, harangue, lecture, sermon, homily
**talkative** ♦ given to talk or talking *Syn* loquacious, garrulous, voluble, glib *Ant* silent
**talkativeness** ♦ the inclination to talk or to talking *Syn* loquacity, loquaciousness, garrulity, garrulousness, volubility, glibness *Ant* silence
**tall** *Syn* HIGH, lofty *Ant* short
**tally** *Syn* AGREE, square, accord, harmonize, correspond, conform, jibe
**tame** ♦ made docile and tractable *Syn* subdued, submissive *Ant* fierce

**tamp** *Syn* PACK, crowd, cram, stuff, ram
**tamper** *Syn* MEDDLE, interfere, intermeddle
**tang** *Syn* TASTE, flavor, savor, relish, smack
**tangent** *Syn* ADJACENT, abutting, adjoining, contiguous, conterminous, juxtaposed
**tangible** *Syn* PERCEPTIBLE, sensible, palpable, appreciable, ponderable *Ant* intangible
**tantalize** *Syn* WORRY, tease, harass, harry, annoy, plague, pester *Ant* satisfy
**tantamount** *Syn* SAME, selfsame, very, identical, identic, equivalent, equal
**tap** *vb* ♦ to strike or hit audibly *Syn* knock, rap, thump, thud
**tap** *n* ♦ a light usu. audible blow or the sound made by such a blow *Syn* rap, knock, thump, thud
**tar** *Syn* MARINER, sailor, seaman, gob, bluejacket
**tardy** ♦ not arriving, occurring, or done at the set, due, or expected time *Syn* late, behindhand, overdue *Ant* prompt
**tarnish** *Syn* SOIL, dirty, sully, foul, befoul, smirch, besmirch, grime, begrime *Ant* polish
**tarry** *Syn* STAY, remain, wait, abide, linger
**tart** *Syn* SOUR, acid, acidulous, dry
**Tartarean** *Syn* INFERNAL, chthonian, chthonic, Hadean, stygian, hellish
**task** ♦ a piece of work to be done *Syn* duty, assignment, job, stint, chore
**taste 1** ♦ the property of a substance which makes it perceptible to the gustatory sense *Syn* flavor, savor, tang, relish, smack **2** ♦ a liking for or enjoyment of something because of the pleasure it gives *Syn* palate, relish, gusto, zest *Ant* antipathy
**tasty** *Syn* PALATABLE, savory, sapid, appetizing, toothsome, flavorsome, relishing *Ant* bland
**tat** *Syn* WEAVE, knit, crochet, braid, plait
**tattle** *Syn* GOSSIP, blab

**taunt** *Syn* RIDICULE, mock, deride, twit, rally
**taut** *Syn* TIGHT, tense
**tautology** *Syn* VERBIAGE, redundancy, pleonasm, circumlocution, periphrasis
**tawdry** *Syn* GAUDY, garish, flashy, meretricious
**tax** *Syn* BURDEN, encumber, cumber, weigh, weight, load, lade, charge, saddle
**teach** ♦ to cause to acquire knowledge or skill *Syn* instruct, educate, train, discipline, school
**tear** ♦ to separate forcibly *Syn* rip, rend, split, cleave, rive **2** *Syn* RUSH, dash, shoot, charge
**tease** *Syn* WORRY, tantalize, pester, plague, harass, harry, annoy
**tedious** *Syn* IRKSOME, tiresome, wearisome, boring *Ant* exciting
**tedium** ♦ a state of dissatisfaction and weariness *Syn* boredom, ennui, doldrums
**teem** ♦ to be present in large quantity *Syn* abound, swarm, overflow
**teeny** *Syn* SMALL, tiny, little, diminutive, petite, wee, weeny, minute, microscopic, miniature
**teeter** *Syn* SHAKE, tremble, quake, totter, quiver, shiver, shudder, quaver, wobble, shimmy, dither
**tell 1** *Syn* COUNT, enumerate, number **2** *Syn* SAY, utter, state **3** *Syn* REVEAL, divulge, discover, disclose, betray
**telling** *Syn* VALID, compelling, convincing, cogent, sound
**temerity** ♦ conspicuous or flagrant boldness *Syn* audacity, hardihood, effrontery, nerve, cheek, gall *Ant* caution
**temper** *vb Syn* MODERATE, qualify *Ant* intensify
**temper** *n* **1** *Syn* MOOD, humor, vein **2** *Syn* DISPOSITION, temperament, complexion, character, personality, individuality
**temperament** *Syn* DISPOSITION, temper, complexion, character, personality, individuality
**temperance** ♦ self-restraint in the gratification of

appetites or passions **Syn** sobriety, abstinence, abstemiousness, continence

**temperate 1 Syn** MODERATE **Ant** intemperate; inordinate **2 Syn** SOBER, continent, unimpassioned

**temporal Syn** PROFANE, secular, lay **Ant** spiritual

**temporary** ♦ lasting, continuing, or serving for a limited time **Syn** provisional, ad interim, acting, **Ant** permanent

**tempt Syn** LURE, entice, inveigle, decoy, seduce

**tenacious Syn** STRONG, tough, stout, sturdy, stalwart

**tenacity Syn** COURAGE, resolution, spirit, mettle

**tend** ♦ to supervise or take charge of **Syn** attend, mind, watch

**tendency** ♦ movement in a particular direction **Syn** trend, drift, tenor

**tender** *adj* ♦ showing or expressing interest in another **Syn** compassionate, sympathetic, warm, warmhearted, responsive **Ant** callous; severe

**tender** *vb* **Syn** OFFER, proffer, present, prefer

**tender** *n* **Syn** OVERTURE, approach, advance, bid

**tenet Syn** DOCTRINE, dogma

**tenor Syn** TENDENCY, drift, trend

**tense 1 Syn** TIGHT, taut **Ant** slack **2 Syn** STIFF, rigid, inflexible, stark, wooden **Ant** expansive

**tension 1 Syn** STRESS, strain, pressure **2 Syn** BALANCE, equilibrium, equipoise, poise

**tentative Syn** PROVISIONAL **Ant** definitive

**tenuous Syn** THIN, rare, slender, slim, slight **Ant** dense

**tergiversation Syn** AMBIGUITY, equivocation, double entendre

**term 1 Syn** LIMIT, end, confine, bound **2 Syn** WORD, vocable **3** *pl* **terms Syn** CONDITION, stipulation, provision, proviso, reservation, strings

**termagant Syn** VIRAGO, scold, shrew, vixen, amazon

**terminal Syn** LAST, final, concluding, latest, eventual, ultimate **Ant** initial

**terminate Syn** CLOSE, end, conclude, finish, complete

**termination Syn** END, ending, terminus **Ant** inception; source

**terminus Syn** END, termination, ending **Ant** starting point

**terrestrial Syn** EARTHLY, earthy, mundane, worldly, sublunary **Ant** celestial

**terrible Syn** FEARFUL, terrific, frightful, dreadful, awful, horrible, horrific, shocking, appalling

**terrific Syn** FEARFUL, terrible, frightful, dreadful, horrible, horrific, awful, shocking, appalling

**terrify Syn** FRIGHTEN, fright, scare, alarm, terrorize, startle

**territory Syn** FIELD, domain, province, sphere, bailiwick

**terror Syn** FEAR, panic, consternation, dread, fright, alarm, dismay, horror, trepidation

**terrorize Syn** FRIGHTEN, terrify, fright, alarm, scare, startle, affray, affright

**terse Syn** CONCISE, succinct, laconic, summary, pithy, compendious

**test** *n* **Syn** PROOF, trial, demonstration

**test** *vb* **Syn** PROVE, try, demonstrate

**testimonial Syn** CREDENTIAL, recommendation, character, reference

**testy Syn** IRASCIBLE, choleric, splenetic, touchy, cranky, cross

**text Syn** SUBJECT, topic, argument, theme, matter, subject matter, motive, motif, leitmotiv

**thankful Syn** GRATEFUL **Ant** thankless

**thaumaturgy Syn** MAGIC, sorcery, witchcraft, witchery, wizardry, alchemy

**thaw Syn** LIQUEFY, melt, deliquesce, fuse **Ant** freeze

**theatrical Syn** DRAMATIC, dramaturgic, melodramatic, histrionic

**theft** ♦ an unlawful taking of property esp. personal property stolen from its rightful owner **Syn** larceny, robbery, burglary

**theme 1 Syn** SUBJECT, text, topic, argument, matter, subject matter, motive, motif, leitmotiv **2 Syn** ESSAY, composition, paper, article

**then Syn** THEREFORE, hence, consequently, accordingly, so

**theorem Syn** PRINCIPLE, axiom, fundamental, law

**theoretical** ♦ concerned principally with abstractions and theories **Syn** speculative, academic

**therefore** ♦ for this or that reason **Syn** hence, consequently, then, accordingly, so

**thesis Syn** DISCOURSE, dissertation, treatise, monograph, disquisition

**thespian Syn** ACTOR, player, impersonator, trouper, performer, mummer, mime, mimic

**thick 1 Syn** STOCKY, thick, thickset, chunky, stubby, squat, dumpy **Ant** thin **2 Syn** CLOSE, compact, dense **3 Syn** FAMILIAR, close, confidential, chummy, intimate

**thickset Syn** STOCKY, thick, chunky, stubby, squat, dumpy

**thief** ♦ one that steals esp. stealthily or secretly **Syn** robber, burglar, larcener, larcenist

**thin** *adj* ♦ not thick, broad, abundant, or dense **Syn** slender, slim, slight, tenuous, rare **Ant** thick

**thin** *vb* ♦ to make thin or thinner or less dense **Syn** attenuate, extenuate, dilute, rarefy **Ant** thicken

**thing 1 Syn** AFFAIR, matter, concern, business **2** ♦ whatever is apprehended as having actual, distinct, and demonstrable existence **Syn** object, article

**think 1** ♦ to form an idea of **Syn** conceive, imagine, fancy, realize, envisage, envision **2** ♦ to use one's powers of conception, judgment, or inference **Syn** cogitate, reflect, reason, speculate, deliberate

**thirst Syn** LONG, hunger, pine, yearn, hanker

**though** ♦ in spite of the fact that **Syn** although, albeit

**thought Syn** IDEA, concept, conception, notion, impression

**thoughtful 1** ♦ characterized by or exhibiting the power to think **Syn** reflective, speculative, contemplative, meditative, pensive **2** ♦ mindful of others **Syn** considerate, attentive **Ant** thoughtless

**thoughtless Syn** CARELESS, heedless, inadvertent **Ant** thoughtful

**thrash 1 Syn** BEAT, pound, pummel, buffet, baste, belabor **2 Syn** SWING, flourish, brandish, shake, wave

**threadbare 1 Syn** SHABBY, dilapidated, dingy, faded, seedy **2 Syn** TRITE, shopworn, hackneyed, stereotyped

**threaten** ♦ to announce or forecast impending danger or evil **Syn** menace

**thrifty Syn** SPARING, economical, frugal **Ant** wasteful

**thrill** ♦ to fill with emotions that stir or excite or to be so excited **Syn** electrify, enthuse

**thrive Syn** SUCCEED, prosper, flourish **Ant** languish

**throb** *vb* **Syn** PULSATE, beat, pulse, palpitate

**throb** *n* **Syn** PULSATION, beat, pulse, palpitation

**throe Syn** PAIN, ache, pang, twinge, stitch

**throng Syn** CROWD, press, crush, mob, rout, horde

**throttle Syn** SUFFOCATE, asphyxiate, stifle, smother, choke, strangle

**through Syn** BY, with

**throw** ♦ to cause to move swiftly through space by a propulsive movement or a propelling force **Syn** cast, fling, hurl, pitch, toss, sling

**throwback Syn** REVERSION, atavism

**throw up Syn** BELCH, burp, vomit, disgorge, regurgitate, spew

**thrust Syn** PUSH, shove, propel

**thud** *vb* **Syn** TAP, thump, knock, rap

**thud** *n* **Syn** TAP, thump, knock, rap

**thump** *vb* **Syn** TAP, thud, knock, rap

**thump** *n* **Syn** TAP, thud, knock, rap

**thwart Syn** FRUSTRATE, foil, baffle, balk, circumvent, outwit

**ticket** *n* **Syn** MARK, brand, stamp, label, tag

**ticket** *vb* **Syn** MARK, brand, stamp, label, tag

**tickle Syn** PLEASE, regale, gratify, delight, rejoice, gladden

**tide Syn** FLOW, flood, stream, current, flux

**tidings Syn** NEWS, intelligence, advice

**tidy Syn** NEAT, trim, trig, snug, shipshape, spick-and-span **Ant** untidy

**tie** *n* **1 Syn** BOND, band **2 Syn** DRAW, stalemate, deadlock, standoff

**tie** *vb* ♦ to make fast and secure **Syn** bind **Ant** untie

**tier Syn** LINE, row, rank, file, echelon

**tiff** *n* **Syn** QUARREL, bickering, spat, squabble, wrangle, altercation

**tiff** *vb* **Syn** QUARREL, spat, bicker, squabble, wrangle, altercate

**tight 1** ♦ fitting, drawn, or stretched so that there is no slackness or looseness **Syn** taut, tense **Ant** loose **2** *also* **tightfisted Syn** STINGY, close, close-fisted, niggardly, parsimonious, penurious, miserly, cheeseparing, penny-pinching **3 Syn** DRUNK, tipsy, intoxicated, drunken, inebriated

**tight-lipped Syn** SILENT, uncommunicative, taciturn, close, close-lipped, closemouthed, reticent, reserved, secretive

**time Syn** OPPORTUNITY, occasion, chance, break

**timely Syn** SEASONABLE, well-timed, opportune, pat **Ant** untimely

**timetable Syn** PROGRAM, schedule, agenda

**timid** ♦ marked by or exhibiting a lack of boldness, courage, or determination **Syn** timorous

**timorous Syn** TIMID **Ant** assured

**tincture Syn** TOUCH, suggestion, tinge, suspicion, soupçon, shade, smack, spice, dash, vein, strain, streak

**tinge 1 Syn** COLOR, tint, shade, hue, tone **2 Syn** TOUCH, tincture, suggestion, shade, suspicion, soupçon, smack, spice, dash, vein, strain, streak

**tint Syn** COLOR, hue, shade, tinge, tone

**tiny Syn** SMALL, minute, miniature, diminutive, wee, little, teeny, weeny

**tippler Syn** DRUNKARD, inebriate, alcoholic, dipsomaniac, sot, soak, toper, tosspot

**tipsy Syn** DRUNK, intoxicated, inebriated, drunken, tight

**tirade** ♦ a violent, often long-winded, and usu. denunciatory speech or writing **Syn** diatribe, jeremiad, philippic **Ant** eulogy

**tire** ♦ to make or become unable or unwilling to continue (as from a loss of physical strength or endurance) **Syn** weary, fatigue, exhaust, jade, fag, tucker

**tireless Syn** INDEFATIGABLE, weariless, untiring, unwearying, unwearied, unflagging

**tiresome Syn** IRKSOME, wearisome, tedious, boring

**titanic Syn** HUGE, vast, immense, enormous, elephantine, mammoth, giant, gigantic, gigantean, colossal, gargantuan, Herculean, cyclopean, Brobdingnagian

**title 1 Syn** CLAIM, pretension, pretense **2 Syn** NAME, designation, denomination, appellation, style

**tittle Syn** PARTICLE, bit, mite, smidgen, whit, atom, iota, jot

**toady** *n* **Syn** PARASITE, sycophant, favorite, lickspittle, bootlicker, hanger-on, leech, sponge, sponger

**toady** *vb* **Syn** FAWN, truckle, cringe, cower

**toboggan Syn** SLIDE, coast, slip, glide, skid, glissade, slither

**tocsin Syn** ALARM, alert

**toil Syn** WORK, labor, travail, drudgery, grind **Ant** leisure

**token 1 Syn** SIGN, mark, symptom, badge, note **2 Syn** PLEDGE, pawn, hostage **3 Syn** REMEMBRANCE, remembrancer, reminder, memorial, memento, keepsake, souvenir

**tolerance Syn** FORBEARANCE, leniency, indulgence, clemency, mercifulness **Ant** intolerance; loathing

**tolerant Syn** FORBEARING, lenient, indulgent, clement, merciful **Ant** intolerant; severe

**tolerantly Syn** FORBEARINGLY, clemently, mercifully, leniently, indulgently

**tolerate Syn** BEAR, endure, abide, suffer, stand, brook

**tone Syn** COLOR, hue, shade, tint, tinge

**tongue** *Syn* LANGUAGE, dialect, speech, idiom

**tongue-lash** *Syn* SCOLD, upbraid, rate, berate, jaw, bawl, chew out, wig, rail, revile, vituperate

**too** *Syn* ALSO, likewise, besides, moreover, furthermore

**tool** *Syn* IMPLEMENT, instrument, appliance, utensil

**toothsome** *Syn* PALATABLE, appetizing, savory, sapid, tasty, flavorsome, relishing

**toper** *Syn* DRUNKARD, inebriate, alcoholic, dipsomaniac, sot, soak, tosspot, tippler

**topic** *Syn* SUBJECT, matter, subject matter, argument, text, theme, motive, motif, leitmotiv

**torment** *Syn* AFFLICT, torture, rack, try

**tornado** ♦ a violent whirling wind accompanied by a funnel-shaped cloud *Syn* cyclone, twister

**torpid** *Syn* LETHARGIC, sluggish, comatose *Ant* agile

**torpidity** *Syn* LETHARGY, torpor, stupor, languor, lassitude

**torpor** *Syn* LETHARGY, torpidity, stupor, languor, lassitude *Ant* animation

**torrent** *Syn* FLOOD, deluge, inundation, spate, cataract

**tortuous** *Syn* WINDING, sinuous, serpentine, flexuous

**torture** *Syn* AFFLICT, rack, torment, try

**toss** *Syn* THROW, pitch, sling, cast, fling, hurl

**tosspot** *Syn* DRUNKARD, inebriate, alcoholic, dipsomaniac, sot, soak, toper, tippler

**tot** *Syn* ADD, total, sum, cast, figure, foot

**total** *adj Syn* WHOLE, entire, all, gross

**total** *n Syn* SUM, aggregate, whole, amount, number, quantity

**total** *vb Syn* ADD, tot, sum, figure, cast, foot

**totter** 1 *Syn* SHAKE, tremble, quake, quaver, quiver, shiver, shudder, wobble, teeter, shimmy, dither 2 *Syn* REEL, stagger, whirl

**touch** *vb* 1 ♦ to probe with a sensitive part of the body (as a finger) so as to get or produce a sensation often in the course of examining or exploring *Syn* feel, palpate, handle, paw 2 *Syn* AFFECT, influence, impress, strike, sway 3 *Syn* MATCH, approach, rival, equal

**touch** *n* 1 *Syn* CONTACT 2 ♦ a very small amount or perceptible trace of something added *Syn* suggestion, suspicion, soupçon, tincture, tinge, shade, smack, spice, dash, vein, strain, streak

**touching** *Syn* MOVING, affecting, impressive, poignant, pathetic

**touchstone** *Syn* STANDARD, criterion, gauge, yardstick

**touchy** *Syn* IRASCIBLE, choleric, splenetic, testy, cranky, cross *Ant* imperturbable

**tough** *Syn* STRONG, tenacious, stout, sturdy, stalwart *Ant* fragile

**tour** 1 *Syn* SPELL, shift, trick, turn, stint, bout, go 2 *Syn* JOURNEY, voyage, trip, cruise, expedition, jaunt, excursion, pilgrimage

**tow** *Syn* PULL, tug, haul, hale, draw, drag

**tower** *Syn* RISE, mount, ascend, soar, rocket, arise, levitate, surge

**toxic** *Syn* POISONOUS, venomous, virulent, mephitic, pestilent, pestilential, miasmic, miasmatic, miasmal

**toxin** *Syn* POISON, venom, virus, bane

**toy** *Syn* TRIFLE, dally, flirt, coquet

**trace** *n* ♦ a perceptible sign made by something that has passed *Syn* vestige, track

**trace** *vb Syn* SKETCH, outline, diagram, delineate, draft, plot, blueprint

**tracing** *Syn* SKETCH, outline, diagram, delineation, draft, plot, blueprint

**track** *Syn* TRACE, vestige

**tract** *Syn* AREA, region, zone, belt

**tractable** *Syn* OBEDIENT, amenable, biddable, docile *Ant* intractable; unruly

**trade** 1 ♦ a pursuit followed as an occupation or means of livelihood and requiring technical knowledge and skill *Syn* craft, handicraft, art, profession 2 *Syn* BUSINESS, commerce, industry, traffic

**traduce** *Syn* MALIGN, asperse, vilify, calumniate, defame, slander, libel

**traffic** 1 *Syn* BUSINESS, commerce, trade, industry 2 *Syn* INTERCOURSE, commerce, dealings, communication, communion, conversation, converse, correspondence

**trail** *Syn* FOLLOW, pursue, chase, tag, tail

**train** *n Syn* SUCCESSION, progression, series, sequence, chain, string

**train** *vb* 1 *Syn* TEACH, discipline, school, instruct, educate 2 *Syn* DIRECT, aim, point, level, lay

**traipse** *Syn* WANDER, stray, roam, ramble, rove, range, prowl, gad, gallivant, meander

**trait** *Syn* CHARACTERISTIC, feature

**traitorous** *Syn* FAITHLESS, treacherous, perfidious, false, disloyal

**trammel** *Syn* HAMPER, fetter, shackle, clog, manacle, hog-tie

**tramp** *Syn* VAGABOND, vagrant, hobo, truant, bum

**tranquil** *Syn* CALM, serene, placid, peaceful, halcyon *Ant* troubled

**tranquilize** *Syn* CALM, compose, quiet, quieten, still, lull, soothe, settle *Ant* agitate

**transcend** *Syn* EXCEED, surpass, excel, outdo, outstrip

**transcendent** 1 *Syn* SUPREME, surpassing, superlative, peerless, preeminent, incomparable 2 *Syn* ABSTRACT, transcendental, ideal

**transcendental** *Syn* ABSTRACT, transcendent, ideal

**transcript** *Syn* REPRODUCTION, copy, carbon copy, duplicate, facsimile, replica

**transfer** 1 *Syn* MOVE, remove, shift 2 ♦ to shift title or possession from one owner to another *Syn* convey, alienate, deed

**transfiguration** *Syn* TRANSFORMATION, metamorphosis, transmutation, conversion, transmogrification

**transfigure** *Syn* TRANSFORM, metamorphose, transmute, convert, transmogrify

**transform** ♦ to change a thing into a different thing *Syn* metamorphose, transmute, convert, transmogrify, transfigure

**transformation** ♦ change of one thing into another different thing *Syn* metamorphosis, transmutation, conversion, transmogrification, transfiguration

**transgression** *Syn* BREACH, trespass, violation, infraction, infringement, contravention

**transient** ♦ lasting or staying only a short time *Syn* transitory, passing, ephemeral, momentary, fugitive, fleeting, evanescent, short-lived *Ant* perpetual

**transitory** *Syn* TRANSIENT, passing, ephemeral, momentary, fugitive, fleeting, evanescent, short-lived *Ant* everlasting; perpetual

**translation** ♦ a restating often in a simpler language of something previously stated or written *Syn* version, paraphrase, metaphrase

**translucent** *Syn* CLEAR, lucid, pellucid, diaphanous, limpid, transparent

**transmit** 1 *Syn* SEND, forward, remit, route, ship, dispatch 2 *Syn* CARRY, bear, convey, transport

**transmogrification** *Syn* TRANSFORMATION, metamorphosis, transmutation, conversion, transfiguration

**transmogrify** *Syn* TRANSFORM, metamorphose, transmute, convert, transfigure

**transmutation** *Syn* TRANSFORMATION, metamorphosis, conversion, transmogrification, transfiguration

**transmute** *Syn* TRANSFORM, metamorphose, convert, transmogrify, transfigure

**transparent** *Syn* CLEAR, lucid, pellucid, diaphanous, translucent, limpid *Ant* opaque

**transpire** *Syn* HAPPEN, occur, chance, befall, betide

**transport** *vb* 1 *Syn* CARRY, bear, convey, transmit 2 ♦ to carry away by strong and usu. pleasurable emotion *Syn* ravish, enrapture, entrance 3 *Syn* BANISH, deport, exile, expatriate, ostracize, extradite

**transport** *n Syn* ECSTASY, rapture

**transpose** *Syn* REVERSE, invert

**trap** *n Syn* LURE, bait, decoy, snare

**trap** *vb Syn* CATCH, entrap, snare, ensnare, bag, capture

**trash** 1 *Syn* REFUSE, waste, rubbish, debris, garbage, offal 2 *Syn* NONSENSE, twaddle, drivel, bunk, balderdash, poppycock, gobbledygook, rot, bull

**trauma, traumatism** *Syn* WOUND, lesion, bruise, contusion

**travail** *Syn* WORK, labor, toil, drudgery, grind

**traverse** *Syn* DENY, gainsay, contradict, negative, impugn, contravene *Ant* allege

**travesty** *n Syn* CARICATURE, parody, burlesque

**travesty** *vb Syn* CARICATURE, parody, burlesque

**treacherous** *Syn* FAITHLESS, perfidious, traitorous, false, disloyal

**treason** *Syn* SEDITION *Ant* allegiance

**treasure** *Syn* APPRECIATE, prize, value, cherish

**treat** 1 *Syn* CONFER, parley, negotiate, commune, consult, advise 2 ♦ to have to do with or behave toward (a person or thing) in a specified manner *Syn* deal, handle

**treatise** *Syn* DISCOURSE, disquisition, dissertation, thesis, monograph

**treaty** *Syn* CONTRACT, bargain, compact, pact, entente, convention, cartel, concordat

**tremble** *Syn* SHAKE, quake, quiver, shiver, shudder, quaver, totter, wobble, teeter, shimmy, dither

**tremendous** *Syn* MONSTROUS, stupendous, monumental, prodigious

**trenchant** *Syn* INCISIVE, clear-cut, cutting, biting, crisp

**trend** *Syn* TENDENCY, drift, tenor

**trepidation** *Syn* FEAR, horror, terror, panic, consternation, dread, fright, alarm, dismay

**trespass** *n Syn* BREACH, transgression, violation, infraction, infringement, contravention

**trespass** *vb* ♦ to make inroads upon the property, territory, or rights of another *Syn* encroach, entrench, infringe, invade

**trial** 1 *Syn* PROOF, test, demonstration 2 ♦ the state or fact of being tested (as by suffering) *Syn* tribulation, affliction, visitation, cross

**tribulation** *Syn* TRIAL, affliction, visitation, cross *Ant* consolation

**tributary** *Syn* SUBORDINATE, secondary, dependent, subject, collateral

**tribute** *Syn* ENCOMIUM, eulogy, panegyric, citation

**trick** *n* 1 ♦ an indirect means to gain an end *Syn* ruse, stratagem, maneuver, gambit, ploy, artifice, wile, feint 2 *Syn* SPELL, turn, tour, shift, stint, bout, go

**trick** *vb Syn* DUPE, gull, befool, hoax, hoodwink, bamboozle

**trickery** *Syn* DECEPTION, double-dealing, chicanery, chicane, fraud

**tricky** *Syn* SLY, crafty, foxy, insidious, cunning, wily, guileful, artful

**tried** *Syn* RELIABLE, dependable, trustworthy, trusty

**trifle** ♦ to deal with or act toward without serious purpose *Syn* toy, dally, flirt, coquet

**trifling** *Syn* PETTY, trivial, puny, paltry, measly, picayunish, picayune

**trig** *Syn* NEAT, trim, tidy, spick-and-span, snug, shipshape

**trill** *Syn* SING, troll, carol, descant, warble, hymn, chant, intone

**trim** *vb* 1 *Syn* SHEAR, poll, clip, prune, lop, snip, crop 2 *Syn* STABILIZE, steady, poise, balance, ballast

**trim** *adj Syn* NEAT, tidy, trig, snug, shipshape, spick-and-span *Ant* frowzy

**trip** *vb Syn* STUMBLE, blunder, lurch, flounder, lumber, galumph, lollop, bumble

**trip** *n Syn* JOURNEY, voyage, tour, excursion, cruise, expedition, jaunt, pilgrimage

**trite** ♦ lacking the freshness that evokes attention or interest *Syn* hackneyed, stereotyped, threadbare, shopworn *Ant* original; fresh

**triumph** *Syn* VICTORY, conquest

**trivial** *Syn* PETTY, trifling, puny, paltry, measly, picayunish, picayune *Ant* weighty; momentous

**troll** *Syn* SING, carol, descant, warble, trill, hymn, chant, intone

**troop** *Syn* COMPANY, band, troupe, party

**troubadour** *Syn* POET, versifier, rhymer, rhymester; poetaster, bard, minstrel

**trouble** *vb* 1 ♦ to cause to be uneasy or upset *Syn* distress, ail 2 *Syn* INCONVENIENCE, incommode, discommode

**trouble** *n* *Syn* EFFORT, exertion, pains

**troupe** *Syn* COMPANY, troop, band, party

**trouper** *Syn* ACTOR, player, performer, mummer, mime, mimic, thespian, impersonator

**truant** *Syn* VAGABOND, vagrant, tramp, hobo, bum

**truce** ♦ a suspension of or an agreement for suspending hostilities *Syn* cease-fire, armistice, peace

**truckle** *Syn* FAWN, toady, cringe, cower

**truculent** *Syn* FIERCE, ferocious, barbarous, savage, inhuman, cruel, fell

**true** 1 *Syn* FAITHFUL, loyal, constant, staunch, steadfast, resolute *Ant* false; fickle 2 *Syn* REAL, actual *Ant* false

**truism** *Syn* COMMONPLACE, platitude, bromide, cliche

**trust** *n* 1 ♦ assured reliance on the character, ability, strength, or truth of someone or something *Syn* confidence, reliance, dependence, faith *Ant* mistrust 2 *Syn* MONOPOLY, corner, pool, syndicate, cartel

**trust** *vb* *Syn* RELY, depend, count, reckon, bank

**trustworthy** *Syn* RELIABLE, dependable, trusty, tried *Ant* deceitful; dubious

**trusty** *Syn* RELIABLE, trustworthy, tried, dependable

**truth** ♦ the quality or state of keeping close to fact and avoiding distortion or misrepresentation *Syn* veracity, verity, verisimilitude *Ant* untruth; lie, falsehood

**try** *vb* 1 *Syn* PROVE, test, demonstrate 2 *Syn* AFFLICT, torment, torture, rack 3 *Syn* ATTEMPT, endeavor, essay, strive, struggle

**try** *n* *Syn* ATTEMPT, endeavor, essay, striving, struggle

**tryst** *Syn* ENGAGEMENT, rendezvous, assignation, appointment, date

**tucker** *Syn* TIRE, fatigue, exhaust, jade, fag, weary

**tug** *Syn* PULL, tow, hale, haul, drag, draw

**tumid** *Syn* INFLATED, flatulent, turgid

**tumult** *Syn* COMMOTION, agitation, turmoil, turbulence, confusion, convulsion, upheaval

**tune** *n* *Syn* MELODY, air

**tune** *vb* *Syn* HARMONIZE, attune

**turbid** ♦ not clear or translucent but clouded with or as if with sediment *Syn* muddy, roily *Ant* clear; limpid

**turbulence** *Syn* COMMOTION, agitation, tumult, turmoil, confusion, convulsion, upheaval

**turgid** *Syn* INFLATED, tumid, flatulent

**turmoil** *Syn* COMMOTION, agitation, tumult, turbulence, confusion, convulsion, upheaval

**turn** *vb* 1 ♦ to move or cause to move in a curved or circular path on or as if on an axis *Syn* revolve, rotate, gyrate, circle, spin, twirl, whirl, wheel, eddy, swirl, pirouette 2 ♦ to change or cause to change course or direction *Syn* divert, deflect, avert, sheer 3 *Syn* RESORT, refer, apply, go 4 *Syn* DEPEND, hinge, hang

**turn** *n* 1 *Syn* SPELL, trick, tour, shift, stint, bout, go 2 *Syn* GIFT, bent, faculty, aptitude, genius, talent, knack

**turncoat** *Syn* RENEGADE, apostate, recreant, backslider

**turn out** *Syn* BEAR, produce, yield

**tussle** *Syn* WRESTLE, grapple, scuffle

**twaddle** *Syn* NONSENSE, drivel, bunk, balderdash, poppycock, gobbledygook, trash, rot, bull

**tweet** *n* *Syn* CHIRP, chirrup, cheep, peep, twitter, chitter

**tweet** *vb* *Syn* CHIRP, chirrup, cheep, peep, twitter, chitter

**twine** *Syn* WIND, coil, curl, twist, wreathe, entwine

**twinge** *Syn* PAIN, ache, pang, throe, stitch

**twinkle** *Syn* FLASH, gleam, glance, glint, sparkle, glitter, glisten, scintillate, coruscate

**twinkling** *Syn* INSTANT, moment, minute, second, flash, jiffy, split second

**twirl** *Syn* TURN, revolve, rotate, gyrate, circle, spin, whirl, wheel, eddy, swirl, pirouette

**twist** 1 *Syn* WIND, coil, curl, twine, wreathe, entwine 2 *Syn* CURVE, bend

**twister** *Syn* TORNADO, cyclone

**twit** *Syn* RIDICULE, deride, mock, taunt, rally

**twitch** *Syn* JERK, snap, yank

**twitter** *vb* *Syn* CHIRP, chirrup, cheep, peep, tweet, chitter

**twitter** *n* *Syn* CHIRP, chirrup, cheep, peep, tweet, chitter

**type** 1 *Syn* SYMBOL, emblem, attribute *Ant* antitype 2 ♦ a number of individuals thought of as a group because of a common quality or qualities *Syn* kind, sort, stripe, kidney, ilk, description, nature, character

**typhoon** *Syn* HURRICANE, tropical storm

**typical** *Syn* REGULAR, natural, normal *Ant* atypical; distinctive

**tyrannical, tyrannous** *Syn* ABSOLUTE, despotic, arbitrary, autocratic

**tyro** *Syn* AMATEUR, dilettante, dabbler

# U

**ubiquitous** *Syn* OMNIPRESENT

**ugly** ♦ unpleasing to the sight *Syn* hideous, ill-favored, unsightly *Ant* beautiful

**ultimate** 1 *Syn* LAST, latest, final, terminal, concluding, eventual 2 ♦ being so fundamental as to represent the extreme limit of actual or possible knowledge *Syn* absolute, categorical

**ululate** *Syn* ROAR, bellow, bluster, bawl, vociferate, clamor, howl

**ululation** *Syn* ROAR, bellow, bluster, bawl, vociferation

**umbra** *Syn* SHADE, penumbra, shadow, umbrage, adumbration

**umbrage** 1 *Syn* SHADE, shadow, umbra, penumbra, adumbration 2 *Syn* OFFENSE, resentment, pique, dudgeon, huff

**umpire** *Syn* JUDGE, referee, arbiter, arbitrator

**unacceptable** *Syn* OBJECTIONABLE, undesirable, unwanted, unwelcome

**unaffected** *Syn* NATURAL, artless, simple, ingenuous, naïve, unsophisticated

**unafraid** *Syn* BRAVE, fearless, dauntless, undaunted, bold, intrepid, audacious, courageous, valiant, valorous, doughty *Ant* afraid

**unassailable** *Syn* INVINCIBLE, impregnable, inexpugnable, invulnerable, unconquerable, indomitable

**unavoidable** *Syn* INEVITABLE, ineluctable, inescapable, unescapable

**unbecoming** *Syn* INDECOROUS, improper, unseemly, indecent, indelicate

**unbelief** ♦ the attitude or state of mind of one who does not believe *Syn* disbelief, incredulity *Ant* belief

**unbeliever** *Syn* ATHEIST, freethinker, agnostic, infidel, deist

**unbiased** *Syn* FAIR, impartial, dispassionate, just, equitable, uncolored, objective *Ant* biased

**unburden** *Syn* RID, clear, disabuse, purge *Ant* burden

**uncalled-for** *Syn* SUPEREROGATORY, gratuitous, wanton

**uncanny** *Syn* WEIRD, eerie

**unceasing** *Syn* EVERLASTING, endless, interminable

**uncertainty** ♦ lack of sureness about someone or something *Syn* doubt, dubiety, dubiosity, skepticism, suspicion, mistrust *Ant* certainty

**uncircumscribed** *Syn* INFINITE, boundless, illimitable, sempiternal, eternal *Ant* circumscribed

**uncivil** *Syn* RUDE, ill-mannered, impolite, discourteous, ungracious *Ant* civil

**uncolored** 1 *Syn* COLORLESS, achromatic 2 *Syn* FAIR, dispassionate, impartial, objective, unbiased, just, equitable

**uncommon** *Syn* INFREQUENT, scarce, rare, occasional, sporadic *Ant* common

**uncommunicative** *Syn* SILENT, taciturn, reticent, reserved, secretive, close, close-lipped, close-mouthed, tight-lipped *Ant* communicative

**unconcerned** *Syn* INDIFFERENT, incurious, aloof, detached, uninterested, disinterested *Ant* concerned

**uncongenial** *Syn* INCONSONANT, unsympathetic, incompatible, inconsistent, incongruous, discordant, discrepant *Ant* congenial

**unconquerable** *Syn* INVINCIBLE, indomitable, impregnable, inexpugnable, unassailable, invulnerable *Ant* conquerable

**unconstraint** ♦ freedom from constraint or pressure *Syn* abandon, spontaneity

**uncouth** *Syn* RUDE, rough, crude, raw, callow, green

**uncritical** *Syn* SUPERFICIAL, shallow, cursory *Ant* critical

**unctuous** *Syn* FULSOME, oily, oleaginous, slick, soapy *Ant* brusque

**undaunted** *Syn* BRAVE, courageous, unafraid, fearless, intrepid, valiant, valorous, dauntless, doughty, bold, audacious *Ant* afraid

**under** *Syn* BELOW, beneath, underneath

**undergo** *Syn* EXPERIENCE, sustain, suffer

**underhand, underhanded** *Syn* SECRET, covert, stealthy, furtive, clandestine, surreptitious *Ant* aboveboard

**underling** *Syn* INFERIOR, subordinate *Ant* leader, master

**underlying** 1 *Syn* FUNDAMENTAL, basic, basal, radical 2 *Syn* ELEMENTAL, basic, elementary, essential, fundamental, primitive

**undermine** *Syn* WEAKEN, enfeeble, debilitate, sap, cripple, disable *Ant* reinforce

**underneath** *Syn* BELOW, under, beneath

**understand** ♦ to have a clear or complete idea of *Syn* comprehend, appreciate

**understanding** 1 *Syn* REASON, intuition 2 *Syn* AGREEMENT, accord

**understudy** *Syn* SUBSTITUTE, supply, locum tenens, alternate, pinch hitter, double, stand-in

**undesirable** *Syn* OBJECTIONABLE, unacceptable, unwanted, unwelcome

**undulate** *Syn* SWING, waver, sway, oscillate, vibrate, fluctuate, pendulate

**undying** *Syn* IMMORTAL, deathless, unfading

**unearth** *Syn* DISCOVER, ascertain, determine, learn

**uneasy** *Syn* IMPATIENT, nervous, unquiet, restless, restive, fidgety, jumpy, jittery

**uneducated** *Syn* IGNORANT, illiterate, unlettered, untaught, untutored, unlearned *Ant* educated

**unerring** *Syn* INFALLIBLE, inerrable, inerrant

**unescapable** *Syn* INEVITABLE, ineluctable, inescapable, unavoidable

**uneven** *Syn* ROUGH, harsh, rugged, scabrous *Ant* even

**unfading** *Syn* IMMORTAL, deathless, undying

**unfeigned** *Syn* SINCERE, wholehearted, whole-souled, heartfelt, hearty

**unfit** ♦ not adapted or appropriate to a particular end or purpose *Syn* unsuitable, improper, inappropriate, unfitting, inapt, unhappy, infelicitous *Ant* fit

**unfitting** *Syn* UNFIT, inappropriate, improper, unsuitable, inapt, unhappy, infelicitous *Ant* fitting

**unflagging** *Syn* INDEFATIGABLE, unwearied, unwearying, tireless, untiring, weariless

**unflappable** *Syn* COOL, composed, collected, unruffled, imperturbable, nonchalant

**unfold 1** ♦ to disclose by degrees to the sight or understanding *Syn* evolve, develop, elaborate, perfect **2** *Syn* SOLVE, resolve, unravel, decipher

**unformed** *Syn* FORMLESS, shapeless *Ant* formed

**unfortunate** *Syn* UNLUCKY, disastrous, ill-starred, ill-fated, calamitous, luckless, hapless *Ant* fortunate

**unfounded** *Syn* BASELESS, groundless, unwarranted

**unfruitful** *Syn* STERILE, barren, infertile, impotent *Ant* fruitful, prolific

**ungodly** *Syn* IRRELIGIOUS, godless, unreligious, nonreligious

**ungovernable** *Syn* UNRULY, intractable, refractory, recalcitrant, willful, headstrong *Ant* governable; docile

**ungracious** *Syn* RUDE, ill-mannered, impolite, discourteous, uncivil *Ant* gracious

**unhappy** *Syn* UNFIT, infelicitous, inapt, unsuitable, improper, inappropriate, unfitting *Ant* happy

**uniform 1** *Syn* LIKE, alike, similar, analogous, comparable, akin, parallel, identical *Ant* various **2** *Syn* STEADY, constant, even, equable *Ant* multiform

**unify** *Syn* COMPACT, consolidate, concentrate

**unimpassioned** *Syn* SOBER, temperate, continent *Ant* impassioned

**uninterested** *Syn* INDIFFERENT, unconcerned, incurious, aloof, detached, disinterested

**union** *Syn* UNITY, solidarity, integrity

**unique 1** *Syn* SINGLE, sole, lone, solitary, separate, particular **2** *Syn* STRANGE, singular, peculiar, eccentric, erratic, odd, queer, quaint, outlandish, curious

**unite 1** *Syn* JOIN, conjoin, combine, connect, link, associate, relate *Ant* divide; alienate **2** ♦ to join forces or act in concert *Syn* combine, conjoin, cooperate, concur *Ant* part

**unity** ♦ the character of a thing that is a whole composed of many parts *Syn* solidarity, integrity, union

**universal 1** ♦ present or significant throughout the world *Syn* cosmic, ecumenical, catholic, cosmopolitan **2** ♦ of, belonging, or relating to all or the whole *Syn* general, generic, common *Ant* particular

**unkempt** *Syn* SLIPSHOD, slovenly, sloppy, disheveled

**unlawful** ♦ contrary to or prohibited by the law *Syn* illegal, illegitimate, illicit *Ant* lawful

**unlearned** *Syn* IGNORANT, illiterate, unlettered, uneducated, untaught, untutored

**unlettered** *Syn* IGNORANT, illiterate, uneducated, untaught, untutored, unlearned

**unlikeness** *Syn* DISSIMILARITY, difference, divergence, divergency, distinction *Ant* likeness

**unlucky** ♦ involving or suffering misfortune that results from chance *Syn* disastrous, ill-starred, ill-fated, unfortunate, calamitous, luckless, hapless *Ant* lucky

**unman** *Syn* UNNERVE, emasculate, enervate

**unmarried** ♦ being without a spouse *Syn* single, celibate, virgin, maiden

**unmatured** *Syn* IMMATURE, unripe, unmellow *Ant* matured

**unmellow** *Syn* IMMATURE, unmatured, unripe *Ant* mellow, mellowed

**unmindful** *Syn* FORGETFUL, oblivious *Ant* mindful; solicitous

**unmitigated** *Syn* OUTRIGHT, out-and-out, arrant

**unnatural** *Syn* IRREGULAR, anomalous *Ant* natural

**unnerve** ♦ to deprive of strength or vigor and the capacity for effective action *Syn* enervate, unman, emasculate

**unoffending** *Syn* HARMLESS, innocuous, innocent, inoffensive

**unpremeditated** *Syn* EXTEMPORANEOUS, extempore, extemporary, improvised, impromptu, offhand *Ant* premeditated

**unpretentious** *Syn* PLAIN, homely, simple

**unpropitious** *Syn* OMINOUS, portentous, fateful, inauspicious *Ant* propitious

**unqualified** *Syn* INCAPABLE, incompetent *Ant* qualified

**unquiet** *Syn* IMPATIENT, nervous, restless, restive, uneasy, fidgety, jumpy, jittery *Ant* quiet

**unravel** *Syn* SOLVE, resolve, unfold, decipher

**unreasonable** *Syn* IRRATIONAL *Ant* reasonable

**unrelenting** *Syn* GRIM, implacable, relentless, merciless *Ant* forbearing

**unreligious** *Syn* IRRELIGIOUS, ungodly, godless, nonreligious

**unremitting** *Syn* CONTINUAL, constant, incessant, continuous, perpetual, perennial

**unripe** *Syn* IMMATURE, unmatured, unmellow *Ant* ripe

**unruffled** *Syn* COOL, imperturbable, unflappable, nonchalant, composed, collected *Ant* ruffled; excited

**unruly** ♦ not submissive to government or control *Syn* ungovernable, intractable, refractory, recalcitrant, willful, headstrong *Ant* tractable, docile

**unseemly** *Syn* INDECOROUS, improper, unbecoming, indecent, indelicate *Ant* seemly

**unsettle** *Syn* DISORDER, derange, disarrange, disorganize, disturb *Ant* settle

**unsightly** *Syn* UGLY, hideous, illfavored

**unsocial** ♦ disliking or avoiding the company of others *Syn* asocial, antisocial, nonsocial *Ant* social

**unsophisticated** *Syn* NATURAL, simple, ingenuous, naïve, artless *Ant* sophisticated

**unspeakable** *Syn* UNUTTERABLE, inexpressible, ineffable, indescribable, indefinable

**unstable** *Syn* INCONSTANT, fickle, capricious, mercurial *Ant* stable

**unsuitable** *Syn* UNFIT, improper, inappropriate, unfitting, inapt, unhappy, infelicitous *Ant* suitable

**unsympathetic 1** *Syn* INCONSONANT, uncongenial, discordant, incongruous, incompatible, inconsistent, discrepant *Ant* sympathetic **2** *Syn* ANTIPATHETIC *Ant* sympathetic

**untangle** *Syn* EXTRICATE, disentangle, disencumber, disembarrass

**untaught** *Syn* IGNORANT, illiterate, unlettered, uneducated, untutored, unlearned *Ant* taught

**untimely** *Syn* PREMATURE, forward, advanced, precocious *Ant* timely

**untiring** *Syn* INDEFATIGABLE, tireless, weariless, unwearying, unwearied, unflagging

**untouchable** *Syn* OUTCAST, castaway, derelict, reprobate, pariah

**untruth** *Syn* LIE, falsehood, fib, misrepresentation, story *Ant* truth

**untruthful** *Syn* DISHONEST, lying, mendacious, deceitful *Ant* truthful

**untutored** *Syn* IGNORANT, illiterate, unlettered, uneducated, untaught, unlearned *Ant* tutored

**unusual** *Syn* exceptional, extraordinary, phenomenal, unwonted

**unutterable** ♦ not capable of being put into words *Syn* inexpressible, unspeakable, ineffable, indescribable, indefinable

**unwanted** *Syn* OBJECTIONABLE, unacceptable, undesirable, unwelcome

**unwarranted** *Syn* BASELESS, groundless, unfounded *Ant* warranted

**unwearied** *Syn* INDEFATIGABLE, tireless, weariless, untiring, unwearying, unflagging

**unwearying** *Syn* INDEFATIGABLE, tireless, weariless, untiring, unwearied, unflagging

**unwelcome** *Syn* OBJECTIONABLE, unacceptable, undesirable, unwanted

**unwholesome** ♦ detrimental to physical, mental, or moral well-being *Syn* morbid, sickly, diseased, pathological *Ant* wholesome

**unwonted** *Syn* EXCEPTIONAL, extraordinary, phenomenal, unusual

**upbraid** *Syn* SCOLD, rate, berate, tongue-lash, revile, vituperate, jaw, bawl, chew out, wig, rail

**upheaval** *Syn* COMMOTION, agitation, tumult, turmoil, turbulence, confusion, convulsion

**uphold** *Syn* SUPPORT, advocate, back, champion *Ant* contravene; subvert

**upright** ♦ having or showing a strict regard for what is morally right *Syn* honest, just, conscientious, scrupulous, honorable

**uprising** *Syn* REBELLION, revolution, revolt, insurrection, mutiny, putsch, coup

**uproar** *Syn* DIN, pandemonium, hullabaloo, babel, hubbub, clamor, racket

**uproot** *Syn* EXTERMINATE, eradicate, deracinate, extirpate, wipe *Ant* establish; inseminate

**upset 1** *Syn* OVERTURN, capsize, overthrow, subvert **2** *Syn* DISCOMPOSE, agitate, perturb, disturb, disquiet, fluster, flurry

**upshot** *Syn* EFFECT, outcome, issue, result, consequence, aftereffect, aftermath, event, sequel

**urbane** *Syn* SUAVE, smooth, diplomatic, bland, politic *Ant* rude; clownish, bucolic

**urge** *vb* ♦ to press or impel to action, effort, or speed *Syn* egg, exhort, goad, spur, prod, prick, sic

**urge** *n Syn* DESIRE, lust, passion, appetite

**urgent** *Syn* PRESSING, imperative, crying, importunate, insistent, exigent, instant

**usage 1** *Syn* HABIT, practice, custom, use, habitude, wont **2** *Syn* FORM, convention, convenance

**use** *n* **1** ♦ a useful or valuable end, result, or purpose *Syn* service, advantage, profit, account, avail **2** ♦ a capacity for serving an end or purpose *Syn* usefulness, utility **3** *Syn* HABIT, wont, practice, usage, custom, habitude

**use** *vb* ♦ to put into service esp. to attain an end *Syn* employ, utilize, apply, avail

**usefulness** *Syn* USE, utility

**usual** ♦ familiar through frequent or regular repetition *Syn* customary, habitual, wonted, accustomed

**usurp** *Syn* ARROGATE, preempt, appropriate, confiscate *Ant* abdicate

**utensil** *Syn* IMPLEMENT, tool, instrument, appliance

**utility** *Syn* USE, usefulness

**utilize** *Syn* USE, employ, apply, avail

**utopian** *Syn* AMBITIOUS, pretentious

**utter 1** *Syn* SAY, tell, state **2** *Syn* EXPRESS, vent, voice, broach, air, ventilate

# V

**vacant** *Syn* EMPTY, blank, vacuous

**vacate** *Syn* ANNUL, abrogate, void, quash

**vacillate** *Syn* HESITATE, waver, falter

**vacuous** *Syn* EMPTY, vacant, blank, void

**vacuum** *Syn* HOLE, void, cavity, hollow, pocket

**vagabond** ♦ a person who wanders at will or as a habit *Syn* vagrant, truant, tramp, bum, hobo

**vagary** *Syn* CAPRICE, freak, fancy, whim, whimsy, conceit, crotchet

**vagrant** *n Syn* VAGABOND, truant, tramp, hobo, bum

**vagrant** *adj Syn* ITINERANT, peripatetic, ambulatory, ambulant, nomadic

**vague** *Syn* OBSCURE, dark, enigmatic, cryptic, ambiguous, equivocal *Ant* definite; specific; lucid

**vain 1** ♦ being without worth or significance *Syn*

nugatory, otiose, idle, empty, hollow **2 Syn** FU-TILE, fruitless, bootless, abortive **3 Syn** PROUD, vainglorious

**vainglorious Syn** PROUD, vain

**vainglory Syn** PRIDE, vanity

**valiant Syn** BRAVE, courageous, unafraid, fearless, intrepid, valorous, dauntless, undaunted, doughty, bold, audacious **Ant** timid; dastardly

**valid** ♦ having such force as to compel serious attention and usu. acceptance **Syn** sound, cogent, convincing, compelling, telling **Ant** fallacious, sophistical

**validate Syn** CONFIRM, authenticate, substantiate, verify, corroborate **Ant** invalidate

**valor Syn** HEROISM, prowess, gallantry

**valorous Syn** BRAVE, courageous, unafraid, fearless, intrepid, valiant, dauntless, undaunted, doughty, bold, audacious

**valuable Syn** COSTLY, precious, invaluable, priceless, expensive, dear

**value** *n* **Syn** WORTH

**value** *vb* **1 Syn** ESTIMATE, appraise, evaluate, rate, assess, assay **2 Syn** APPRECIATE, prize, treasure, cherish

**vanish** ♦ to pass from view or out of existence **Syn** evanesce, evaporate, disappear, fade **Ant** appear; loom

**vanity Syn** PRIDE, vainglory

**vanquish Syn** CONQUER, defeat, beat, lick, subdue, subjugate, reduce, overcome, surmount, overthrow, rout

**vanquisher Syn** VICTOR, conqueror, winner, champion

**vapid Syn** INSIPID, flat, jejune, banal, wishy-washy, inane

**variable Syn** CHANGEABLE, protean, changeful, mutable **Ant** constant; equable

**variance Syn** DISCORD, contention, dissension, difference, strife, conflict

**variation Syn** CHANGE, alteration, modification

**variegated** ♦ having a pattern involving different colors or shades of color **Syn** parti-colored, motley, checkered, checked, pied, piebald, skewbald, dappled, freaked

**variety 1** ♦ the quality or state of being composed of different parts, elements, or individuals **Syn** diversity **2** ♦ a group of related plants or animals narrower in scope than a species **Syn** subspecies, race, breed, cultivar, strain, clone, stock

**various 1 Syn** DIFFERENT, diverse, divergent, disparate **Ant** uniform; cognate **2 Syn** MANY, several, sundry, divers, numerous, multifarious

**vary 1 Syn** CHANGE, alter, modify **2 Syn** DIFFER, disagree, dissent

**vast Syn** HUGE, immense, enormous, elephantine, mammoth, giant, gigantic, gigantean, colossal, gargantuan, Herculean, cyclopean, titanic, Brobdingnagian

**vault** *vb* **Syn** JUMP, leap, spring, bound

**vault** *n* **Syn** JUMP, leap, spring, bound

**vaunt Syn** BOAST, brag, crow, gasconade

**veer Syn** SWERVE, deviate, depart, digress, diverge

**vehement Syn** INTENSE, fierce, exquisite, violent

**vehicle Syn** MEAN, instrument, instrumentality, agent, agency, medium, organ, channel

**veil Syn** COVER, overspread, envelop, wrap, shroud

**vein 1 Syn** MOOD, humor, temper **2 Syn** TOUCH, strain, streak, suggestion, suspicion, soupçon, tincture, tinge, shade, smack, spice, dash

**velocity Syn** SPEED, momentum, impetus, pace, headway

**velvety Syn** SLEEK, silken, silky, satiny, glossy, slick

**venal Syn** MERCENARY, hireling, hack

**venerable Syn** OLD, ancient, antique, antiquated, archaic, obsolete, antediluvian

**venerate Syn** REVERE, reverence, worship, adore

**veneration Syn** REVERENCE, worship, adoration

**vengeance Syn** RETALIATION, revenge, retribution, reprisal

**vengeful Syn** VINDICTIVE, revengeful

**venial** ♦ not warranting punishment or the imposition of a penalty **Syn** pardonable **Ant** heinous; mortal

**venom Syn** POISON, toxin, virus, bane

**venomous Syn** POISONOUS, virulent, toxic, mephitic, pestilent, pestilential, miasmic, miasmatic, miasmal

**vent Syn** EXPRESS, utter, voice, broach, air, ventilate **Ant** bridle

**ventilate Syn** EXPRESS, vent, air, utter, voice, broach

**venture** ♦ to expose to risk or loss **Syn** hazard, risk, chance, jeopardize, endanger, imperil

**venturesome Syn** ADVENTUROUS, daring, daredevil, rash, reckless, foolhardy

**veracity Syn** TRUTH, verity, verisimilitude

**verbiage** ♦ an excess of words usu. of little or obscure content **Syn** redundancy, tautology, pleonasm, circumlocution, periphrasis

**verbose Syn** WORDY, prolix, diffuse, redundant **Ant** laconic

**verge Syn** BORDER, edge, rim, brim, brink, margin

**verify Syn** CONFIRM, corroborate, substantiate, authenticate, validate

**verisimilitude Syn** TRUTH, veracity, verity

**veritable Syn** AUTHENTIC, genuine, bona fide **Ant** factitious

**verity Syn** TRUTH, veracity, verisimilitude

**vernacular 1 Syn** DIALECT, patois, lingo, jargon, cant, argot, slang **2 Syn** BARBARISM, corruption, impropriety, solecism, vulgarism

**versatile** ♦ having a wide range of skills or abilities or many different uses **Syn** many-sided, all-around

**verse Syn** PARAGRAPH, article, clause, plank, count

**versed Syn** CONVERSANT

**versifier Syn** POET, rhymer, rhymester, poetaster, bard, minstrel, troubadour

**version 1 Syn** TRANSLATION, paraphrase, metaphrase **2 Syn** ACCOUNT, report, story, chronicle

**vertebrae Syn** SPINE, backbone, back, chine

**vertical** ♦ being at right angles to a base line **Syn** perpendicular, plumb **Ant** horizontal

**vertiginous Syn** GIDDY, dizzy, swimming, dazzled

**verve Syn** VIGOR, vim, spirit, dash, esprit, punch, élan, drive

**very 1 Syn** SAME, selfsame, identical, identic, equivalent, equal, tantamount **2 Syn** MERE, bare

**vessel Syn** BOAT, ship, craft

**vestige Syn** TRACE, track

**vex Syn** ANNOY, irk, bother **Ant** please, regale

**viands Syn** FOOD, provisions, comestibles, feed, victuals, provender, fodder, forage

**vibrant Syn** RESONANT, sonorous, ringing, resounding, orotund

**vibrate Syn** SWING, sway, oscillate, fluctuate, pendulate, waver, undulate

**vice 1 Syn** FAULT, failing, frailty, foible **2 Syn** OFFENSE, sin, crime, scandal **Ant** virtue

**vicinity Syn** LOCALITY, neighborhood, district

**vicious** ♦ highly reprehensible or offensive in character, nature, or conduct **Syn** villainous, iniquitous, nefarious, flagitious, infamous, corrupt, degenerate **Ant** virtuous

**vicissitude 1 Syn** CHANGE, alteration, mutation, permutation **2 Syn** DIFFICULTY, hardship, rigor

**victim** ♦ one killed or injured for the ends of the one who kills or injures **Syn** prey, quarry

**victor** ♦ one that defeats an enemy or opponent **Syn** winner, conqueror, champion, vanquisher

**victory** ♦ a successful outcome in a contest or struggle **Syn** conquest, triumph **Ant** defeat

**victuals Syn** FOOD, feed, viands, provisions, comestibles, provender, fodder, forage

**vie Syn** RIVAL, compete, emulate

**view** *n* **1 Syn** LOOK, sight, glance, glimpse, peep, peek **2 Syn** OPINION, belief, conviction, persuasion, sentiment

**view** *vb* **Syn** SEE, survey, contemplate, observe, note, remark, notice, perceive, discern, behold, descry, espy

**viewpoint Syn** POINT OF VIEW, standpoint, angle, slant

**vigilant Syn** WATCHFUL, alert, wide-awake

**vigor** ♦ a quality of force, forcefulness, or energy **Syn** vim, spirit, dash, esprit, verve, punch, élan, drive

**vigorous** ♦ having or showing great vitality and force **Syn** energetic, strenuous, lusty, nervous **Ant** languorous; lethargic

**vile Syn** BASE, low

**vilify Syn** MALIGN, traduce, asperse, calumniate, defame, slander, libel **Ant** eulogize

**villain** ♦ a low, mean, reprehensible person utterly lacking in principles **Syn** scoundrel, blackguard, knave, rascal, rogue, scamp, rapscallion, miscreant

**villainous Syn** VICIOUS, iniquitous, nefarious, flagitious, infamous, corrupt, degenerate

**vim Syn** VIGOR, spirit, dash, esprit, verve, punch, élan, drive

**vindicate 1 Syn** MAINTAIN, justify, defend, assert **2 Syn** EXCULPATE, exonerate, absolve, acquit **Ant** calumniate

**vindictive** ♦ showing or motivated by a desire for vengeance **Syn** revengeful, vengeful

**violation Syn** BREACH, infraction, transgression, trespass, infringement, contravention

**violence Syn** FORCE, compulsion, coercion, duress, constraint, restraint

**violent Syn** INTENSE, vehement, fierce, exquisite

**virago** ♦ a loud, overbearing, ill-tempered woman **Syn** amazon, termagant, scold, shrew, vixen

**virgin Syn** UNMARRIED, single, celibate, maiden

**virginal Syn** YOUTHFUL, maiden, boyish, juvenile, puerile

**virile Syn** MALE, manful, manly, masculine, manlike, mannish **Ant** effeminate; impotent

**virtual Syn** IMPLICIT, constructive **Ant** actual

**virtually** ♦ not absolutely or actually, yet so nearly so that the difference is negligible **Syn** practically, morally

**virtue 1 Syn** GOODNESS, morality, rectitude **Ant** vice **2 Syn** EXCELLENCE, merit, perfection

**virtuoso Syn** EXPERT, adept, artist, artiste, wizard

**virtuous Syn** MORAL, ethical, righteous, noble **Ant** vicious

**virulent Syn** POISONOUS, venomous, toxic, mephitic, pestilent, pestilential, miasmic, miasmatic, miasmal

**visage Syn** FACE, countenance, physiognomy, mug, puss

**vision 1 Syn** REVELATION, prophecy, apocalypse **2 Syn** FANCY, fantasy, phantasy, phantasm, dream, daydream, nightmare

**visionary Syn** IMAGINARY, fanciful, fantastic, chimerical, quixotic

**visit** ♦ a usu. brief stay with another as an act of friendship or courtesy **Syn** visitation, call

**visitant Syn** VISITOR, guest, caller

**visitation 1 Syn** VISIT, call **2 Syn** TRIAL, tribulation, affliction, cross

**visitor** ♦ one who visits another **Syn** visitant, guest, caller

**vital 1 Syn** LIVING, alive, animate, animated **2 Syn** ESSENTIAL, fundamental, cardinal

**vitalize** ♦ to arouse to activity, animation, or life **Syn** energize, activate **Ant** atrophy

**vitiate Syn** DEBASE, deprave, corrupt, pervert, debauch

**vitiated Syn** DEBASED, depraved, corrupted, debauched, perverted

**vituperate Syn** SCOLD, revile, berate, rate, upbraid, tongue-lash, jaw, bawl, chew out, wig, rail

**vituperation Syn** ABUSE, invective, obloquy, scurrility, billingsgate **Ant** acclaim, praise

**vituperative Syn** ABUSIVE, opprobrious, contumelious, scurrilous

**vivacious Syn** LIVELY, animated, gay, sprightly **Ant** languid

**vivid Syn** GRAPHIC, picturesque, pictorial

**vivify Syn** QUICKEN, animate, enliven

**vixen Syn** VIRAGO, shrew, scold, termagant, amazon

**vocable Syn** WORD, term

**vocabulary** *Syn* LANGUAGE, phraseology, diction, phrasing, style

**vocal 1** ♦ uttered by the voice or having to do with such utterance *Syn* articulate, oral **2** ♦ being able to express oneself clearly or easily *Syn* articulate, fluent, eloquent, voluble, glib

**vociferate** *Syn* ROAR, bellow, bluster, bawl, clamor, howl, ululate

**vociferation** *Syn* ROAR, bellow, bluster, bawl, ululation

**vociferous** ♦ so loud or insistent as to compel attention *Syn* clamorous, blatant, strident, boisterous, obstreperous

**vogue** *Syn* FASHION, mode, style, fad, rage, craze, dernier cri, cry

**voice** *Syn* EXPRESS, utter, vent, broach, air, ventilate

**void** *adj* **1** *Syn* EMPTY, vacant, blank, vacuous **2** *Syn* DEVOID, destitute

**void** *n* *Syn* HOLE, vacuum, hollow, cavity, pocket

**void** *vb* *Syn* ANNUL, vacate, abrogate, quash

**volatile** *Syn* ELASTIC, effervescent, buoyant, expansive, resilient

**volatility** *Syn* LIGHTNESS, light-mindedness, levity, frivolity, flippancy, flightiness

**volcano** *Syn* MOUNTAIN, mount, peak, alp, mesa

**volition** *Syn* WILL, conation

**volubility** *Syn* TALKATIVENESS, glibness, garrulity, loquacity

**voluble 1** *Syn* VOCAL, fluent, glib, eloquent, articulate *Ant* stuttering, stammering **2** *Syn* TALKATIVE, glib, garrulous, loquacious *Ant* curt

**volume 1** *Syn* SIZE, magnitude, extent, dimensions, area **2** *Syn* BULK, mass

**voluntary** ♦ done or brought about of one's own will *Syn* intentional, deliberate, willful, willing *Ant* involuntary; instinctive

**voluptuous** *Syn* SENSUOUS, luxurious, sybaritic, epicurean, sensual *Ant* ascetic

**vomit** *Syn* BELCH, burp, disgorge, regurgitate, spew, throw up

**voracious** ♦ excessively greedy *Syn* gluttonous, ravenous, ravening, rapacious

**vortex** *Syn* EDDY, whirlpool, maelstrom

**votary** *Syn* ADDICT, devotee, habitué

**vote** *Syn* SUFFRAGE, franchise, ballot

**vouch** *Syn* CERTIFY, attest, witness

**vouchsafe** *Syn* GRANT, accord, concede, award

**voyage** *Syn* JOURNEY, tour, trip, excursion, cruise, expedition, jaunt, pilgrimage

**vulgar 1** *Syn* COMMON, ordinary, familiar, popular **2** *Syn* COARSE, gross, obscene, ribald

**vulgarism** *Syn* BARBARISM, corruption, impropriety, solecism, vernacular

# W

**wage, wages** ♦ the price paid a person for his or her labor or services *Syn* salary, stipend, fee, pay, hire, emolument

**wager** *Syn* BET, stake, pot, ante

**waggish** *Syn* PLAYFUL, sportive, frolicsome, impish, mischievous, roguish

**wail** *Syn* CRY, weep, whimper, blubber, keen

**wait** *Syn* STAY, remain, abide, tarry, linger

**waive** *Syn* RELINQUISH, cede, yield, resign, abandon, surrender, leave

**waken** *Syn* STIR, awaken, arouse, rouse, rally *Ant* subdue

**wall** *Syn* ENCLOSE, envelop, fence, pen, coop, corral, cage

**wallow** ♦ to move clumsily and in a debased or pitable condition *Syn* welter, grovel

**wan** *Syn* PALE, pallid, ashen, ashy, livid

**wander** ♦ to move about from place to place more or less aimlessly and without a plan *Syn* stray, roam, ramble, rove, range, prowl, gad, gallivant, traipse, meander

**wane** *Syn* ABATE, subside, ebb *Ant* wax

**want** *vb* **1** *Syn* LACK, need, require **2** *Syn* DESIRE, wish, crave, covet

**want** *n* **1** *Syn* LACK, dearth, absence, defect, privation **2** *Syn* POVERTY, destitution, indigence, privation, penury

**wanton 1** *Syn* LICENTIOUS, libertine, lewd, lustful, lascivious, libidinous, lecherous *Ant* chaste **2** *Syn* SUPEREROGATORY, uncalled-for, gratuitous

**war** *Syn* CONTEND, battle, fight

**warble** *Syn* SING, troll, carol, descant, trill, hymn, chant, intone

**ward** *Syn* PREVENT, avert, preclude, obviate *Ant* conduce to

**wariness** *Syn* CAUTION, chariness, circumspection, calculation *Ant* foolhardiness; brashness

**warlike** *Syn* MARTIAL, military

**warm** *Syn* TENDER, warmhearted, sympathetic, compassionate, responsive *Ant* cool; austere

**warmhearted** *Syn* TENDER, warm, sympathetic, compassionate, responsive *Ant* coldhearted

**warn** ♦ to let one know of approaching danger or risk *Syn* forewarn, caution

**warp** *Syn* DEFORM, distort, contort

**warrant 1** *Syn* ASSERT, declare, profess, affirm, aver, protest, avouch, avow, predicate **2** *Syn* JUSTIFY

**wary** *Syn* CAUTIOUS, chary, circumspect, calculating *Ant* foolhardy; brash

**waspish** *Syn* IRRITABLE, snappish, fractious, peevish, petulant, pettish, huffy, fretful, querulous

**waste** *n* **1** ♦ an area of the earth unsuitable for cultivation or general habitation *Syn* desert, badlands, wilderness **2** *Syn* REFUSE, rubbish, trash, debris, garbage, offal

**waste** *vb* **1** *Syn* RAVAGE, devastate, sack, pillage, despoil, spoliate *Ant* conserve, save **2** ♦ to spend or expend freely and usu. foolishly or futilely *Syn* squander, dissipate, fritter, consume *Ant* save; conserve

**wasted** *Syn* HAGGARD, pinched, cadaverous, worn, careworn

**waster** *Syn* SPENDTHRIFT, profligate, prodigal, wastrel

**wastrel** *Syn* SPENDTHRIFT, profligate, prodigal, waster

**watch 1** *Syn* TEND, mind, attend **2** *Syn* SEE, look

**watchful** ♦ on the lookout esp. for danger or for opportunities *Syn* vigilant, wide-awake, alert

**waterlog** *Syn* SOAK, drench, saturate, steep, impregnate, sop

**wave** *Syn* SWING, flourish, brandish, shake, thrash

**waver 1** *Syn* SWING, fluctuate, oscillate, pendulate, vibrate, sway, undulate **2** *Syn* HESITATE, falter, vacillate

**way 1** ♦ a track or path traversed in going from one place to another *Syn* route, course, passage, pass, artery **2** *Syn* METHOD, mode, manner, fashion, system

**waylay** *Syn* SURPRISE, ambush

**wayward** *Syn* CONTRARY, perverse, froward, restive, balky

**weak** ♦ lacking physical, mental, or moral strength *Syn* feeble, frail, fragile, infirm, decrepit *Ant* strong

**weaken** ♦ to lose or cause to lose strength, vigor, or energy *Syn* enfeeble, debilitate, undermine, sap, cripple, disable *Ant* strengthen

**wealthy** *Syn* RICH, affluent, opulent *Ant* indigent

**wean** *Syn* ESTRANGE, alienate, disaffect *Ant* addict

**weariless** *Syn* INDEFATIGABLE, unwearying, unwearied, tireless, untiring, unflagging

**wearisome** *Syn* IRKSOME, tiresome, tedious, boring

**weary** *Syn* TIRE, fatigue, exhaust, jade, fag, tucker

**weave** ♦ to make a textile or to form an article by interlacing threads or strands of material *Syn* knit, crochet, braid, plait, tat

**wedding** *Syn* MARRIAGE, matrimony, nuptial, espousal, wedlock

**wedlock** *Syn* MARRIAGE, matrimony, nuptial, espousal, wedding

**wee** *Syn* SMALL, diminutive, tiny, teeny, weeny, little, minute, microscopic, miniature, petite

**weeny** *Syn* SMALL, tiny, teeny, wee, diminutive, minute, microscopic, miniature, little

**weep** *Syn* CRY, wail, keen, whimper, blubber

**weigh 1** *Syn* CONSIDER, study, contemplate, excogitate **2** *Syn* BURDEN, encumber, cumber, weight, load, lade, tax, charge, saddle **3** *Syn* DEPRESS, oppress

**weight** *n* **1** *Syn* IMPORTANCE, significance, moment, consequence, import **2** *Syn* INFLUENCE, authority, prestige, credit

**weight** *vb* **1** *Syn* ADULTERATE, load, sophisticate **2** *Syn* BURDEN, encumber, cumber, weigh, load, lade, tax, charge, saddle

**weighty** *Syn* HEAVY, ponderous, cumbrous, cumbersome, hefty

**weird** ♦ fearfully and mysteriously strange or fantastic *Syn* eerie, uncanny

**welcome** *Syn* PLEASANT, pleasing, agreeable, grateful, gratifying *Ant* unwelcome

**well** *Syn* HEALTHY, sound, wholesome, robust, hale *Ant* unwell, ill

**well-nigh** *Syn* NEARLY, almost, approximately

**well-timed** *Syn* SEASONABLE, timely, opportune, pat

**welter** *Syn* WALLOW, grovel

**wet** ♦ covered or more or less soaked with liquid *Syn* damp, dank, moist, humid *Ant* dry

**wharf** ♦ a structure used by boats and ships for taking on or landing cargo or passengers *Syn* dock, pier, quay, slip, berth, jetty, levee

**wheedle** *Syn* COAX, blandish, cajole

**wheel** *Syn* TURN, revolve, rotate, gyrate, circle, spin, twirl, whirl, swirl, pirouette, eddy

**while** ♦ to pass time, esp. leisure time, without boredom or in pleasant ways *Syn* wile, beguile, fleet

**whim** *Syn* CAPRICE, freak, fancy, whimsy, conceit, vagary, crotchet

**whimper** *Syn* CRY, weep, blubber, wail, keen

**whimsy** *Syn* CAPRICE, freak, fancy, whim, conceit, vagary, crotchet

**whirl 1** *Syn* TURN, twirl, spin, wheel, swirl, revolve, rotate, gyrate, circle, pirouette, eddy **2** *Syn* REEL, stagger, totter

**whirlpool** *Syn* EDDY, maelstrom, vortex

**whirlwind** ♦ a rotating windstorm of limited extent *Syn* whirly

**whirly** *Syn* WHIRLWIND

**whit** *Syn* PARTICLE, mite, jot, iota, bit, smidgen, tittle, atom

**whiten 1** ♦ to change from an original color to white or almost to white *Syn* blanch, bleach, decolorize, etiolate *Ant* blacken **2** *Syn* PALLIATE, whitewash, gloze, gloss, extenuate

**whitewash** *Syn* PALLIATE, whiten, gloze, gloss, extenuate

**whole** *adj* **1** *Syn* PERFECT, entire, intact **2** ♦ having every constituent element or individual *Syn* entire, total, all, gross *Ant* partial

**whole** *n* *Syn* SUM, total, aggregate, amount, number, quantity *Ant* part; constituent; particular

**wholehearted** *Syn* SINCERE, whole-souled, heartfelt, hearty, unfeigned

**wholesale** *Syn* INDISCRIMINATE, sweeping

**wholesome 1** *Syn* HEALTHFUL, healthy, salubrious, salutary, hygienic, sanitary *Ant* noxious **2** *Syn* HEALTHY, sound, robust, hale, well

**whole-souled** *Syn* SINCERE, wholehearted, heartfelt, hearty, unfeigned

**whoop** *vb Syn* SHOUT, yell, shriek, scream, screech, squeal, holler

**whoop** *n Syn* SHOUT, yell, shriek, scream, screech, squeal, holler

**wicked** *Syn* BAD, evil, ill, naughty

**wide** *Syn* BROAD, deep *Ant* strait

**wide-awake** *Syn* WATCHFUL, vigilant, alert

**wield** *Syn* HANDLE, swing, manipulate, ply

**wig** *Syn* SCOLD, tongue-lash, jaw, bawl, chew out, berate, upbraid, rate, rail, revile, vituperate

**wild** *Syn* FURIOUS, frantic, frenzied, frenetic, delirious, rabid

**wilderness** *Syn* WASTE, desert, badlands

**wile** *n Syn* TRICK, artifice, feint, ruse, maneuver, stratagem, gambit, ploy

**wile** *vb Syn* WHILE, beguile, fleet

**will** *n* ♦ the power or act of making or effecting a choice or decision *Syn* volition, conation

**will** *vb* ♦ to give to another by will *Syn* bequeath, devise, leave, legate

**willful** 1 *Syn* VOLUNTARY, deliberate, intentional, willing 2 *Syn* UNRULY, headstrong, intractable, refractory, recalcitrant, ungovernable *Ant* biddable

**willing** *Syn* VOLUNTARY, intentional, deliberate, willful *Ant* unwilling

**wilt** *Syn* DROOP, flag, sag

**wily** *Syn* SLY, cunning, crafty, tricky, foxy, insidious, guileful, artful

**win** *Syn* GET, gain, acquire, obtain, procure, secure *Ant* lose

**wince** *Syn* RECOIL, flinch, shrink, blench, quail

**wind** ♦ to follow a circular, spiral, or writhing course *Syn* coil, curl, twist, twine, wreathe, entwine

**winding** ♦ curving repeatedly first one way and then another *Syn* sinuous, serpentine, tortuous, flexuous *Ant* straight

**window** ♦ an opening in the wall of a building that is usu. covered with glass and serves to admit light and air *Syn* casement, oriel

**wing** *Syn* ANNEX, ell, extension

**wink** ♦ to close and open one's eyelids quickly *Syn* blink

**winner** *Syn* VICTOR, conqueror, champion, vanquisher *Ant* loser

**winning** *Syn* SWEET, engaging, winsome, dulcet

**winsome** *Syn* SWEET, engaging, winning, dulcet

**wipe** *Syn* EXTERMINATE, extirpate, eradicate, uproot, deracinate

**wisdom** *Syn* SENSE, judgment, gumption *Ant* folly; injudiciousness

**wise** ♦ exercising or involving sound judgment *Syn* sage, sapient, judicious, prudent, sensible, sane *Ant* simple

**wisecrack** *Syn* JOKE, crack, gag, jest, jape, quip, witticism

**wish** *Syn* DESIRE, want, crave, covet

**wishy-washy** *Syn* INSIPID, vapid, flat, jejune, banal, inane

**wit** 1 *Syn* MIND, intelligence, brain, intellect, soul, psyche 2 ♦ a mode of expression intended to arouse amusement *Syn* humor, irony, sarcasm, satire, repartee

**witchcraft** *Syn* MAGIC, wizardry, witchery, sorcery, alchemy, thaumaturgy

**witchery** *Syn* MAGIC, sorcery, witchcraft, wizardry, alchemy, thaumaturgy

**with** *Syn* BY, through

**withdraw** *Syn* GO, leave, depart, quit, retire

**wither** ♦ to lose freshness and substance by or as if by loss of natural moisture *Syn* shrivel, wizen

**withhold** *Syn* KEEP, detain, keep back, keep out, retain, hold, hold back, reserve

**withstand** *Syn* RESIST, contest, oppose, fight, combat, conflict, antagonize

**witness** *n Syn* SPECTATOR, observer, beholder, looker-on, onlooker, eyewitness, bystander, kibitzer

**witness** *vb Syn* CERTIFY, attest, vouch

**witticism** *Syn* JOKE, jest, jape, quip, wisecrack, crack, gag

**witty** ♦ provoking or intended to provoke laughter *Syn* humorous, facetious, jocular, jocose

**wizard** *Syn* EXPERT, adept, artist, artiste, virtuoso

**wizardry** *Syn* MAGIC, witchcraft, witchery, sorcery, alchemy, thaumaturgy

**wizen** *Syn* WITHER, shrivel

**wobble** *Syn* SHAKE, teeter, totter, shimmy, quiver, shiver, shudder, quaver, quake, tremble, dither

**woe** *Syn* SORROW, grief, anguish, heartache, heartbreak, regret

**woebegone** *Syn* DOWNCAST, disconsolate, dispirited, dejected, depressed

**woman** *Syn* FEMALE, lady

**womanish** *Syn* FEMALE, womanlike, womanly, ladylike, feminine *Ant* mannish

**womanlike** *Syn* FEMALE, womanly, womanish, ladylike, feminine

**womanly** *Syn* FEMALE, womanlike, ladylike, womanish, feminine *Ant* unwomanly, manly

**wonder** 1 ♦ something that causes astonishment or admiration *Syn* marvel, prodigy, miracle, phenomenon 2 ♦ the complex emotion aroused by the incomprehensible and esp. the awe-inspiring *Syn* wonderment, amazement, admiration

**wonderment** *Syn* WONDER, amazement, admiration

**wont** *Syn* HABIT, habitude, practice, usage, custom, use

**wonted** *Syn* USUAL, accustomed, customary, habitual

**woo** *Syn* INVITE, court, solicit, bid

**wooden** *Syn* STIFF, rigid, inflexible, tense, stark

**word** ♦ a pronounceable sound or combination of sounds that expresses and symbolizes an idea *Syn* vocable, term

**wordy** ♦ using or marked by the use of more words than are necessary to express the thought *Syn* verbose, prolix, diffuse, redundant

**work** *n* 1 ♦ strenuous activity that involves difficulty and effort and usually affords no pleasure *Syn* labor, travail, toil, drudgery, grind *Ant* play 2 ♦ a sustained activity that affords one a livelihood *Syn* employment, occupation, calling, pursuit, business 3 ♦ something brought into being by the exertion of effort and the exercise of skill *Syn* product, production, opus, artifact

**work** *vb Syn* ACT, operate, function, behave, react

**worker** ♦ one who earns his living by labor, esp. by manual labor *Syn* workman, workingman, laborer, craftsman, handicraftsman, mechanic, artisan, hand, operative, roustabout *Ant* idler

**workingman** *Syn* WORKER, workman, laborer, craftsman, handicraftsman, mechanic, artisan, operative, hand, roustabout

**workman** *Syn* WORKER, workingman, laborer, craftsman, handicraftsman, mechanic, artisan, operative, hand, roustabout

**world** *Syn* EARTH, globe, planet

**worldly** 1 *Syn* EARTHLY, mundane, terrestrial, earthy, sublunary 2 *Syn* SOPHISTICATED, worldly-wise, blasé, disillusioned

**worldly-wise** *Syn* SOPHISTICATED, worldly, blasé, disillusioned

**worn** *Syn* HAGGARD, careworn, pinched, wasted, cadaverous

**worried** ♦ distressed or troubled usu. about something anticipated *Syn* anxious, concerned, careful, solicitous

**worry** *vb* ♦ to disturb one or destroy one's peace of mind by repeated or persistent tormenting attacks *Syn* annoy, harass, harry, plague, pester, tease, tantalize

**worry** *n Syn* CARE, anxiety, concern, solicitude

**worship** *n Syn* REVERENCE, adoration, veneration

**worship** *vb* 1 *Syn* REVERE, adore, venerate, reverence 2 *Syn* ADORE, idolize

**worth** ♦ equivalence in good qualities expressed or implied *Syn* value

**wound** ♦ an injury to the body *Syn* trauma, traumatism, lesion, bruise, contusion

**wraith** *Syn* APPARITION, phantasm, phantom, ghost, spirit, specter, shade, revenant

**wrangle** *vb Syn* QUARREL, altercate, squabble, bicker, spat, tiff

**wrangle** *n Syn* QUARREL, altercation, squabble, bickering, spat, tiff

**wrap** *Syn* COVER, overspread, envelop, shroud, veil

**wrath** *Syn* ANGER, rage, indignation, ire, fury

**wrathful** *Syn* ANGRY, irate, indignant, mad, wroth, acrimonious

**wreathe** *Syn* WIND, coil, curl, twist, twine, entwine

**wreck** *Syn* RUIN, dilapidate

**wrench** ♦ to turn or twist forcibly *Syn* wrest, wring

**wrest** *Syn* WRENCH, wring

**wrestle** ♦ to struggle with an opponent at close quarters *Syn* tussle, grapple, scuffle

**wretched** *Syn* MISERABLE

**wring** *Syn* WRENCH, wrest

**writhe** ♦ to twist or turn in physical or mental distress *Syn* agonize, squirm

**wrong** *n Syn* INJUSTICE, injury, grievance

**wrong** *adj* 1 *Syn* FALSE *Ant* right 2 *Syn* BAD, poor

**wrong** *vb* ♦ to inflict injury without just cause or in an outrageous manner *Syn* oppress, persecute, aggrieve

**wroth** *Syn* ANGRY, irate, indignant, wrathful, acrimonious, mad

# Y

**yank** *Syn* JERK, snap, twitch

**yap** *Syn* BARK, bay, howl, growl, snarl, yelp

**yardstick** *Syn* STANDARD, criterion, gauge, touchstone

**yarn** *Syn* STORY, tale, narrative, anecdote

**yearn** *Syn* LONG, pine, hanker, hunger, thirst

**yeast** *Syn* FOAM, froth, spume, scum, lather, suds

**yell** *vb Syn* SHOUT, shriek, scream, screech, squeal, holler, whoop

**yell** *n Syn* SHOUT, shriek, scream, screech, squeal, holler, whoop

**yelp** *Syn* BARK, bay, howl, growl, snarl, yap

**yield** 1 *Syn* BEAR, produce, turn out 2 *Syn* RELINQUISH, surrender, cede, abandon, leave, resign, waive 3 ♦ to give way before a force that one cannot further resist *Syn* submit, capitulate, succumb, relent, defer, bow, cave

**yoke** *Syn* COUPLE, pair, brace

**yokel** *Syn* BOOR, bumpkin, hick, rube, clodhopper, clown, lout, churl

**young** *Syn* OFFSPRING, progeny, issue, descendant, posterity

**youth** ♦ the period in life when one passes from childhood to maturity *Syn* adolescence, puberty, pubescence *Ant* age

**youthful** ♦ relating to or characteristic of one who is between childhood and adulthood *Syn* juvenile, puerile, boyish, virgin, virginal, maiden *Ant* aged

# Z

**zeal** *Syn* PASSION, enthusiasm, fervor, ardor *Ant* apathy

**zealot** *Syn* ENTHUSIAST, fanatic, bigot

**zenith** *Syn* SUMMIT, apogee, culmination, meridian, peak, pinnacle, climax, apex, acme *Ant* nadir

**zest** *Syn* TASTE, relish, gusto, palate

**zone** *Syn* AREA, belt, tract, region